Leaving Home

Diethelm Knauf, Barry Moreno (eds.)

Leaving Home
Migration Yesterday and Today

Edition Temmen

The Deutsche Nationalbibliothek lists this publication in the Deutsche Nationalbibliografie; detailed bibliographical data are available on the Internet at http://dnb.d-nb.de

In Memoriam
Christiane Harzig

First edition 2010

© EDITION TEMMEN – Hohenlohestr. 21 – 28209 Bremen
Tel. +49–421–34843-0 – Fax +49–421–348094
info@edition-temmen.de – www.edition-temmen.de

Produced by: EDITION TEMMEN
ISBN 978–3–8378–4007-0

Contents

"Over The Rhine", Cincinnati's German neighborhood with all the distinctive features of German culture: Beer gardens, theaters, churches and a flourishing German press. Photo ca. 1905

Japanese print from 1856 entitled "Oranda fune nu" (depiction of a Dutch ship); above left, presumably the portrait of a Dutchman

Jan Lucassen & Leo Lucassen

The World We Lost. European Migrations 1500–1830*

The bulk of the contributions in this book are devoted to permanent transatlantic European long-distance migrations from 1830 onwards. This unprecedented long-distance mobility, however, did not start from scratch (Moch 2003; Lucassen and Lucassen 1997). It is therefore important to concentrate on its immediate predecessors. Not that Europeans were the only emigrants in pre-modern times, nor that they were necessarily the most important ones – although their impact on the Americas can hardly be underestimated. On the contrary: as it is now well known that simultaneous with the transatlantic population movements to the Americas and the other white settler colonies similar movements took place to southern and northern Asia, the pre-1830 world also witnessed major migrations originating outside Europe (Hoerder 2002; Manning 2005).

Concentrating here on European mobility and the part played in it by the crossing of the Atlantic Ocean before the surge from the 1840s onwards, our overview will cover the period 1500–1830. Not only will we discuss the importance of transatlantic migrations in comparison with other permanent long-distance movements, we will also call attention to migrations over shorter distances as well as to temporary migrations. This three-tiered approach will enable us to offer a balanced overview of various sorts of mobility in pre-modern Europe. Within each type of migration a number of themes will be dealt with systematically. First, the motives for migrating: were these mainly economic or mainly ideological or is it a mix of the two?

Second, was it forced or free migration or something in between (Eltis 2002b)? Third, who were the migrants: men, women, children, or whole families? Fourth, and finally, what happened to the migrants once they settled?

Transatlantic Migrations in the Western Hemisphere

Many of the laboring poor who wanted to try their luck overseas in the 17th and 18th centuries did not have the means to take such a step. One of the more common ways to overcome this problem was to enter a contract in which the costs for the transatlantic crossing was traded off for a fixed period of (forced) labor in the New World, known as indentured labor. Some legal systems, in particular in England, allowed for the practice of indentured labor or indentured servitude where individuals voluntarily contracted to serve for a term in exchange for compensation. This compensation could not only consist of freedom dues like a plot of land, but especially of transportation costs. This solution was practized on a large scale in the emigration of the poor from the British Isles and later from the German lands to the English colonies in the Americas between the beginning of the 17th and the beginning of the 19th century (Steinfeld 1991; Wokeck 1999).

It took place in three slightly different forms. In classic indentured servitude immigrants, while still in Europe, signed multiyear labor agreements, called indentures, in exchange for a passage to America. They were exported to the Americas by those who held their indentures, often merchants and ship-owners who, upon arrival, sold their indentured laborers for cash to employers. Some emigrants, however, only signed an indenture agreement on their arrival. A third form, the redemption system, developed in the 18th century and was mainly used in the German servant trade. A redemptioner negotiated directly with an employer who came on board in the North American port of arrival. The deal involved the payment of the passage debt by the future employer in return for an indenture in which the immigrant committed himseld or herself to serve the buyer for some multiyear period (Steinfeld 1991: 6; Bailyn 1987: 166–167). To the dismay of many observers, the sales and distribution of convicts (for seven years) and of indentured servants (often for five years) at American ports took place simultaneously and resem-

Indentured servitude contract, Middlesex County, Massachusetts, 1683/84

*   We thank the editors of the Enzyklopädie der Neuzeit for letting us use the entries we wrote on migration and Leslie Page Moch for her comments on an earlier version.

bled very much the public sale of slaves (Bailyn 1987: 324–325).

The contracts of the indentured servants in the French colonies in the Americas (called "engagés"), which amounted to 35,000, differed from the British custom. These engagés entered into a contract of three years' service with a salary and often a free passage back to France (Choquette 1997), whereas the English contracts took the form of assisted one-way emigration (Canny 1994: 275). The difference between the English colonies in the West Indies and North America and the other colonies is directly related to the unfree aspects of English labor law before the reforms in the 19th century.

The total number of indentured servants from Europe to the Americas, including the Caribbean, is estimated at about half a million. Among European states differences were considerable: virtually none from the Iberian Peninsula to about two thirds of all English migrants, at least in the 17th century.

The Dutch, French and German models were closer to the English than to the Iberian model. As the table shows, the indentured system for Europeans reached its peak in the second half of the 17th century, after which it declined close to zero in 1820. Among the less than 100,000 German immigrants in North America, redemptioners became important in the second half of the 18th century (Fertig 1994: 216–217). After 1820, Asians (Indians and Chinese) replaced the Europeans. Apart from the numerous indentured migrants and slaves, many others left Europe to cross the oceans as free persons, often economically motivated and with the aim of settling permanently at destination.

How the Europeans fared outside Europe was to a large extent determined by climatological and biological conditions. Contacts between Europeans and inhabitants of other parts of the world often led to the decimation of the latter, as on the Caribbean islands and in North and South America, where as a result "empty spaces" became available for European colonists. But alien climates could also be fatal for Europeans, as is shown by the hundred of thousands of soldiers who died in the tropics. This explains why less than 100,000 French emigrants were able to establish a vigorous Francophone colony in North America, from whom millions descend, while a million people who were transported by the Dutch V.O.C. to the Dutch Indies barely left a demographic trace (Lucassen 2004). Equally different were the demographic effects of the English emigration before 1776. Those who went to the Caribbean islands disappeared, whereas those who settled in North America established a world empire and a world language.

European expansion had already started in the High Middle Ages with the crusades to the Middle east and the founding of crusader states in the Near east and a few centuries later with the Portuguese and Spanish conquests in north-west Africa and the Atlantic islands. It took, however, until 1492 for larger numbers to leave the continent. From 1500 onwards we can distinguish two economic aims with respect to emigration: mainly agricultural-industrial colonization (in America and Siberia) and mainly merchant strongholds, especially in Africa and Asia. Apart from the already mentioned climatological and epidemical conditions, this distinction is also explained by the existence of powerful states in Asia, like the Moghuls in India, the Ming and

Growing tobacco was extremely labor-intensive. Therefore the early indentured laborers were brought as farm workers to Virginia. Indentured servitude was of such significance that in 1618 the colony offered a so-called headright of 50 acres of land (about 17 hectares) per indentured laborer in order to entice plantation owners to recruit more indentured laborers from England

Qing (from 1644) dynasties in China and Tokugawa Japan. Russian expansion across the Ural ridge after 1581 for a long time resembled the expansion in Canada. In both cases fur was the core merchandise. Fur hunters and merchants were soon accompanied and followed by emigrants, in Siberia mainly poor farmers, fleeing the "second feudalization' and military obligations. Such "Kossacks" could be acknowledged by the Tsars as free subjects in exchange for military help against the enemies of the empire. It took until the 19th century before a more extensive settlement of Siberia was achieved, both by free and forced migrants (Treadgold 1957; Hoerder 2002).

Portuguese and more importantly the Spanish emigration to South and middle America numbered approximately one million people, half of all Europeans who arrived before 1650. As the majority were men, this led to an extensive mixed Indian-European population, to whom can be added the descendants of Europeans and imported African slaves. The stream of emigrants from Britain to North America was much smaller, even when we include 100,000 Scots and an equal number of Irish. Even the 70,000 Germans to North America and small numbers of Dutch, Swedes, and the French emigrants already mentioned cannot alter the conclusion that before the modern era European emigration to the Americas was dominated by people from the Iberian Peninsula.

Table 1: Share of slaves, indentured servants, prisoners and convicts, and free persons carried to the Americas, 1492–1880
Source: Eltis 2002a: 67

	Slaves	Servants	Convicts	Free Persons
Before 1550	25%	0%	1%	73%
1580–1640	61%	5%	1%	34%
1640–1700	61%	17%	2%	20%
1700–1760	79%	4%	2%	15%
1760–1820	85%	2%	1%	13%
Total number	8,700,000	500,000	130,000	2,000,000

From Europe to Asia

The economic activities of the Europeans in America varied greatly, but by far the greatest success were the slave plantations (sugar, cotton, coffee) and the silver and gold mines, which mushroomed all over the globe. Early Modern emigration to Asia – and the numerically insignificant emigration to Africa – was characterized by rather small merchant colonies on the coast, apart from a few larger settlements like Goa (Portuguese), Batavia/Jakarta, Ceylon and South Africa (Dutch), and Madras and Bombay (English). Apart from the voyages by Tasman and Roggeveen Oceania was barely discovered, until Cook undertook his voyages in the years 1768–1780.

While the Spaniards and Portuguese dominated emigration to the Americas in the Early Modern period, the Dutch were the prime movers in Asia. At the beginning of the 17th century the VOC took over the ruling position from the Portuguese. From the Cape of Good Hope in the south-west up to Decima-Nagasaki in the north they were the most powerful European trading nation, that not only made money with the trade between Asia and Europe, but also and foremost through

the inter-Asian trade (Vink 2003). It was only during the second half of the 18th century that they were temporarily eclipsed by the French, before the English took over. The human cost of this European expansion in Asia was tremendous and predominantly caused by disease. Although the sea passage in itself was quite dangerous – only 80 to 85 % of the persons who boarded ship in the Netherlands arrived in Asia alive – the first days off the ship were even more dangerous. Between 1725 and 1786 a quarter of those who debarked died soon thereafter in Batavia's hospital, similar to the English in Bengal (Lucassen 2004).

No wonder that the VOC was always hungry for fresh personnel and transported as many people to Asia as all the east India companies together: about a million, of whom not even a third returned; and no wonder that the poor from all over Europe were welcome in Amsterdam. Thus, hundreds of thousands of Germans tried their luck, never to see Europe again.

Although the trade in goods was central to the Europeans in Asia, the Indian companies (the Dutch VOC 1602–1795, the English 1600–1658, the French 1664–1769 and the smaller ones from Denmark, Sweden and

Coat of arms of the Dutch East India Company

Oostende) also depended on the labor of free and unfree Asians. Slaves from Africa, northeast India and parts of Indonesia, Chinese sailors, soldiers and workers, as well as many others were part of the European expansionist system, and at the end of the 16th century the first Asian sailors could be seen in European port cities.

Map of North and South America published by Wilhelm Blaeu around 1630

Colonization in the East and in the West[1]

When we turn our attention to those migrants who remained in Europe but nevertheless traveled considerable distances, it is first of all the numerous colonizations, especially in the east, which attract our attention. The first important colonization migration in medieval Europe took place east of the River Elbe between the 9th and 13th centuries, an area which until then was not yet populated by peasants. The same was true for the peat moors along the Dutch coast, where migrants settled from the 11th century onwards. These areas were attractive because the settlers,

---

1 This paragraph is based on Hellie 2002; Hoerder 2002; and Canny 2001.

Harbor scene in Amsterdam. Colored copper-plate etching 1701

often former serfs, were granted freedom from feudal obligations in exchange for their effort to tame these uncultivated and uninhabited areas. The shrinking population from the mid-14th century onward, caused by the catastrophic plague epidemic that hit Europe around 1350, put an end to these colonizations and it was only in the 16th and especially from the late 17th century onward that the colonization of the last empty lands of Europe was resumed. These lands, like southern Russia, had never been occupied by farmers, or had been vacated due to war. In the Early Modern period these movements included more than one million migrants.

Another important colonization region was the shifting border between the Habsburg and Ottoman empires. When in the middle of the 16th century the expansion of the Ottomans slowed down in Croatia, the Austrian estates enticed colonists to settle in the (military) border region, granting them freedom from feudal obligations. This call was answered both by orthodox Catholics from the northern Habsburg regions and from the Ottoman-dominated south. The latter were known in 16th century sources as "Uskoks" (refugees), and came from the Dalmatian coastal areas (Kaser 2007).

When in 1672 the Ottoman empire had reached its zenith and the Habsburg rulers, with the help of numerous allies, had taken Hungary, a more general mercantilist

colonization of this area started. Thus, from the end of the 17th century onward, Hungarians, Czechs, Slovaks, Ruthanians, as well as Germans, colonized the territory taken from the Ottomans. The German armed peasants among them, known as the "Donauschwaben" (although only a minority actually came from Swabia), numbered some 150,000 to 200,000 in the years 1740–1790.

By far the largest colonization in the Early Modern period involved southern Russia. Earlier settlement schemes from the Muscovite core to the south, interrupted by the Polish-Lithuanian war, were resumed at the end of the 17th century to the detriment of the nomadic Bashkirs, Kirghizians and Kalmuks. Meanwhile the Ukraine had become Russian in 1645 and Russians had reached the Black Sea (1770), taking the last Turkish strongholds in 1783. Between 1670 and 1700, these new areas were initially populated by some 350,000 Russians among whom 200,000 were runaway serfs. Between 1762–1763 and 1804 (as well as after 1830), migrants from the west were attracted to the rural areas between the Dnjestr and the Donez, among whom 41,600 came from German states. Not all colonists were farmers, because in addition to the rural settlement schemes cities were also created and enlarged. Apart from the Habsburg and Russian empires, Prussia was also interested in what was then known as the "Peuplierungspolitik". In the Oder-, Warthe-,

und Netzebruch, much smaller than the areas mentioned above, no less than 300,000 new inhabitants were settled by the Prussian-Brandenburg rulers in the 18th century.

Much less is known about the colonization migrations in the Balkans sensu stricto, which were dominated by the Ottoman empire until the beginning of the 19th century (Sundhausen 2007). In general, population moves were numerous and followed the continually shifting borders between the Ottoman, Habsburg and Russian empires, as well as the Venetian, in this region. Regardless of whether territory was gained or lost, the new border regions were partly vacated and repopulated by the victorious party. With the gradual expansion of the Ottomans from the 14th century onwards, various colonists were attracted from Turkey and other regions. Well known examples are the Yürüks who came from Anatolia and settled in what later became Bulgaria, and Sephardic Jews who had fled Spain in the 15th and 16th centuries and in large numbers chose Constantinople (Istanbul), Edirne, and Thessaloniki as their new home. It should be mentioned, however, that expansion in the Balkans did not necessarily lead to refugee or forced migrations. The

The Russian Empress Catherine the Great recruited German settlers for the colonization of areas around the Volga and the Don. Copper-plate etching about 1790

Around the middle of the 19th century illustrated newspapers such as the "Leipziger Illustrirte Zeitung" and "Die Gartenlaube Illustrirtes Familienblatt" became fashionable. They showed rural life, customs and practices, cultural traditions, etc. in a highly romanticized manner, yet they had a circulation of around 380,000 copies. As the "Gartenlaube" (arbor) was read not only by families at home but was also available for reading in numerous public libraries and cafés, it is estimated that at its peak the actual readership was between 2 and 5 million. Formal dress of Saxons from Transylvania. Newspaper graphic 1844

from 1556), but emigration from England and Scotland intensified in the years 1610–1625 and then after 1641 under Cromwell, and finally under William III following the battle of the Boyne (1690) in the east of Ireland, where the Catholic army of James II was defeated by the new English king William III. In total, some 180,000 English colonists came to Ireland, especially in the 17th century. They were joined by 60,000 to 100,000 Scots, most of whom headed for Ulster. Finally, we should mention minor examples: the Dutch in Denmark (Amager) in the 16th century, Italians in Tuscany (Maremma), successful land reclamations in east Anglia and Holland in the 17th century, and a failed settlement of the Sierra Morena (southern Spain) by 7,800 German and Flemish Catholics in the years 1766–1769.

German Banats and Hungarians. Newspaper graphic 1850

Ottomans in particular were rather pragmatic at times and allowed the existing population to remain and granted them rights within the millet system (Adanir 2003; Hoerder et al. 2007). The legal status of Christians, Jews and Gypsies (Roma) may have been lower than that of Muslims, but they enjoyed protection by law and were often allowed a form of autonomy, providing they paid their taxes (at higher rates than Muslim co-citizens) and obeyed Ottoman authority. Moreover, many decided to convert to Islam, so that they could reap the benefits of Muslim status, as was the case with the Pomaks: Slavic-speaking people from the Rhodope region in present-day Bulgaria who islamized from the 17th century onward, and also settled in Greece and Macedonia.

In the much more densely populated western parts of Europe, colonization migration was insignificant, except for the English-Scottish settlements in Ireland. This island had already been conquered by the English in the 16th century (the first "Plantation" dates

Religious Upheavals

There are basically two reasons why people see themselves forced to migrate, or why they are displaced against their will: either forced by the state or forced by slave traders. States could expel inhabitants because of undesirable religious or political beliefs, or because of poverty. As for the activities of slave-merchants, these could be tolerated or condoned by the state or it could be the outcome of defeat when the victor state was able to enslave and sell its prisoners of war. Religious persuasions can result in forced emigration when people refuse to convert to the dominant or prescribed religion or when such a conversion is distrusted, as in the case with converted Muslims and Jews in 16th century Spain. In such cases, flight can be the only way out in order to lead a normal life, or even to save one's life, as in the case of pogroms. In general, however, many more people than is often acknowledged in such cases preferred conversion and stayed put.

Although also during the Middle Ages there were religious refugees – the most well-known example being the forced emigration of Jews from western Europe to Central and eastern Europe (especially Poland) following the pogroms during the crusades – Europe never saw more religious refugees than during the "long" 16th century. The shift to intolerance took place at the end of the 15th century.

In the very year Columbus discovered the Americas, Granada – the last remaining Islamic kingdom in the Iberian Peninsula – was conquered by the Spanish Catholic rulers, after which an elite group of some 6,000 people fled from Gibraltar to northern Africa. The bad treatment of the new Islamic subjects led to a first uprising (1499–1501) and in reaction the Catholic kings decided to break with the centuries-old tradition of the peaceful cohabitation of Christians, Muslims, and Jews. When in 1497 Portugal began evicting Muslims, Castile and Leon followed suit and from 1502 onward forced Muslims either to convert or to leave the country. A second uprising in Granada sparked off forced emigration of some 150,000 Muslims to Castile, where state and church closely cooperated in order to convert the so-called "Moriscos". In the end, however, even that was not deemed enough. Time and again their sincerity was questioned and between 1609 and 1614 the last "Moriscos" were forced to leave Spain: 64,000 from Aragon, 150,000 from Valencia and an unknown number from Castile. These hundreds of thousands settled in North Africa, from Morocco to Tunis.

The Catholic offensive in Spain and Portugal affected not only the Muslims, but also the Jews. When the kingdom of Granada was conquered, the Jews were also forced to convert to Catholicism (called "Conversos" or "Marranos") or to leave the realm (Coleman

2003). At first most of them went to Portugal, but in 1496–1497 they were subjected to the same regime as in Spain. Hundreds of thousands of Jews, many of whom were now labelled "Portuguese", emigrated to North Africa and the Ottoman empire, and smaller numbers to some Italian states and the Dutch Republic. In these new destinations, like the anti-Catholic Netherlands, many "Conversos" returned to Jewry (Bodian 1999).

The Spanish example of a unifying religion for all subjects of the state was imitated throughout Europe in the 16th-century wars of religion. Where the majority were Catholic, Protestants had to convert or to flee and vice versa. The only exceptions in Europe were the Ottoman empire and the Dutch Republic. In the rest of Europe the 1555 Augsburg principle ᾽for the German empire, "cuius regio eius religio", – subjects should follow the religious persuasion of their prince – was applied and resulted not only in mass forced conversions, but also in numerous forced migrations, both over long and

The Calvinist uprising in 1566 in a contemporary illustration by Franz Hogenberg (1535–1595). The then still Catholic William of Orange is riding a white horse and finds himself surrounded by a rebellious mob. In the background the insurgents demolish the entrance to the fortress with a battering ram. Franz Hogenberg lived in Cologne and was a famous copper engraver and artist working with etchings. His main works were maps and city scenes

"Inquisition in Spain", painting by Pedro Berruguete (16th century). The Court of Inquisition is elevated on a podium, in the right foreground two accused at the stake

short distances (as in Germany). It is hardly possible to quantify these migrations, because the historiography so far has concentrated on a few well-known examples. Besides, Protestant religious refugees have, for example, attracted much more attention than Catholics from Protestant states.*

The Dutch revolt against Spain started in the South, where in the middle of the 16th century the Reformation was most intense, but in the end was only successful in the North. southern Dutch who could or would not accept Spanish Catholic rule fled in massive numbers. Initially, when the outcome of the battle was uncertain, to England and some German regions (Emden, Palatinate) and later on in the northern Netherlands, where

some 100,000 settled in the urban western part (Davids and Lucassen 1995). It has largely been forgotten that in the same period many Catholics, especially clerics, left in the opposite direction.

Since the end of the 16th century, the Dutch Republic and France for some time followed the policy of tolerating religious minorities. In France the Calvinists were granted religious freedom with the Edict of Nantes (1598). Barely a century later, however, this Edict was revoked by Louis XIV. About one million French Calvinists (the majority living in the Dauphiné, the Midi and in western areas, like Poitou and Saintonge) faced the well-known choice between conversion, emigration with the loss of property, or open resistance. In the last two cases they risked prison, the galleys or even execution. The great majority chose conversion to Catholicism, but a minority clung even more stubbornly to the religion of their ancestors. In total, some 150,000 to 200,000, one in five French Protestants emigrated, about 50,000

---

*   Studies on the relationship between conversion and (non) migration are scarce. One exception is Martin 1986.

The World We Lost. European Migrations 1500–1830

17

The expulsion of Protestants from Salzburg. Newspaper graphic after a work by the historical painter Friedrich Martersteig, 1864

to the Dutch Republic, and the rest to Geneva, England and Brandenburg-Prussia. From there many Huguenots migrated further, from the Netherlands, for example, to Ireland and South Africa (Vigne and Littleton 2001).

Apart from the well-known examples of Calvinist refugees, we must also mention Hussites, Hutterites, Mennonites, Catholics, Lutherans, Puritans, Orthodox Christians, Jews, Muslims and Gypsies. The history of some of these groups, moreover, shows that many did not just settle in the place of their first new destination, but were forced to flee again (and again). One good example are the Swiss Mennonites, who arrived in the Palatinate in the middle of the 17th century, but half a century later saw their rights curbed and left for Galicia at the end of the 18th century (Beer and Dahlmann 2004).

Religious refugees also have economic considerations in their choice of destination. The mass emigrations from Ireland is a telling example. Large groups found employment as mercenaries in Spanish and French armies. But as Catholics looked for work away from their fatherland dominated by English Anglicans, Presbyterians from Ulster, originally immigrated from Scotland, had a good reputation as mercenaries in Protestant armies, especially in England.

A group of religious refugees that attracted a lot of attention throughout Europe were Lutherans from the Catholic prince bishopric of Salzburg in 1732. A year before, 19,000 adults – mostly farmers and workers from the salt mines – had offered a petition that demanded the freedom of religion or the right to leave the country. Invited by the King of Prussia, Friedrich Wilhelm I, the farmers went to the Lithuanian part of Prussia, the

salt workers to the Dutch Republic and North America. Moreover, Protestant salt workers from the neighboring Austrian region of Salzkammergut in the east and from the Bavarian Berchtesgaden in the west followed suit. The former were offered new opportunities in Siebenbürgen and Hungary, whereas the latter, about 1,000 men, went to Hanover (Haver 2007).

When the religious dust had settled in the course of the 18th century, ideological persuasions remained a cause for forced migrations. At the end of the Early Modern Period, during the Enlightenment, large numbers of political refugees became a new phenomenon. Until then political refugees were individuals or small groups who had tried in vain to dethrone a prince. The failed revolution by the so-called "Patriotten" in the Netherlands had a different effect (Rosendaal 2007). When stadtholder Willem V of Orange, assisted by his brother-in-law-Friedrich Wilhelm II of Prussia, regained control of the Republic in September/October 1787, it was not only the initiators of the Patriotten movement who were in danger. Banishment, persecution and

ransacking by Orangist mobs affected so many that more than 40,000 people (2 % of the population) left the country. Probably half of them returned quickly, but the rest left their fatherland for a longer period or for good. About 20,000 initially settled in the southern Netherlands (then under Joseph II of Austria), but after the failed Brabant rising in the northwest of France, a minority chose German destinations, like Hamburg and Münster, Denmark, Russia and the United States. It was only with the successful Batavian Revolution in 1795 that the Patriotten were able to return. This politically forced migration from 1787 was followed by many others in Europe, starting with the émigrés from the French Revolution, 129,000 nobles and clergymen, many of whom fled to Germany, Austria, and Switzerland.

Emergency bill issued by the city of Freren in the Emsland, from 1922. The picture shows a group of migrants going to Holland in the 19th century and reads: "When there was deprivation at home, money and bread were still to be had in Holland". In times of crisis, when legal tender was not readily available, emergency money was issued by states, communities or private enterprises. Migrants to Holland were seasonal itinerant workers mainly from North Germany who went there to cut turf and to make hay. Migration to Holland peaked in the early 19th century

Hollandgänger im vorigen Jahrhundert

75 75

War in der Heimat bittere Not,
In Holland gabs Verdienst und Brot,

In Search of Work and Wages Inside Europe[2]

Whereas refugees, religious and political, have attracted quite some attention from migration scholars, this is much less so for the much more common mobility of millions of workers, including seasonal migrants.

We define this labor migration as a form of mobility in which the migrant is more or less free and primarily economically motivated with the aim of settling somewhere else. We restrict ourselves here to those who remained in Europe and predominantly earned their money as artisans, workers or servants.

Apart from seasonal workers and servants who worked in rural areas, cities have always been the main pole of attraction for migrants – not only because urbanization from 1500 onward increased the share of city dwellers, but also because until the middle of the 18th century the urban death rate outstripped

---

2　For forms of temporary and seasonal labor, see Lucassen 1997 and Van Lottum 2007. For soldiers, see Kroener 2004, Czouz-Tornare 2007, Papenheim 2007a and Murdoch 2007.

fertility, so that cities – if only to prevent a demographic decline – constantly needed immigrants. Whereas cities grew all over Europe, urbanization was very uneven. Around 1500 the centre of gravity was around the Mediterranean, especially in Italy, with cities like Naples, Rome, Turin, Venice and Genoa, that sucked in tens of thousands of migrants. As Braudel and others demonstrated, in the 16th century the centre shifted via southern Germany to the Atlantic coast, with centres as Lisbon, Antwerp, Amsterdam, Hamburg and London. Around 1650 the significance of northern Italy had decreased markedly and cities like Madrid, Naples, but also the towns in southern Germany played a much less prominent role then before. Only southern cities that were linked to the northern European network, like Cadiz, Livorno and Malaga, were able to avoid stagnation. This unequal balance continued into the 19th century. A second feature of urbanization in Early Modern Europe is the distinction between monocentric and polycentric types of urbanization. Whereas England and to a lesser extent France (given the importance of Bordeaux and Lyon) were dominated by their capitals (London and Paris), in northern Italy, the Netherlands and Germany a

Cotton merchant, possibly from Germany. Picture on a Dutch playing card. Around 1820

more polycentric model prevailed, with many middle-sized cities.

In the period 1600–1750 cities that were both the capital and ports (such as London, Lisbon and Amsterdam) were particularly responsible for the rapid urbanization of Europe. Cities with only one of these functions were less successful in this respect, never mind other cities. This is especially true for cities outside north-western Europe, as is demonstrated by the low growth rate of many German residencies like Berlin, Dresden, Leipzig, Königsberg, Mannheim and Hanover (François 1990). The rapid expansion of industrial towns like Leiden and Lyon was an exception.

What all these cities had in common was the high share of immigrants, with an overrepresentation of women and an extremely high rate of mobility which surpassed net immigration by far. The main "push" factor was economic, but – especially in the 17th century – the devastating effects of war in the countryside also caused people to flock to the city. Well into the 18th century more than half of the inhabitants were born elsewhere, even in smaller towns. For the fast-growing

Street cleaners from Hesse in Paris. Photo around 1865

metropolis this could even surpass three-quarters. The mobility of temporary migrants, such as servants and journeymen, is difficult to measure, but was many times higher. The origin of all these migrants differed widely. In general we can say that the smaller the town, the shorter the distance traveled. Although a considerable part of the immigrants came from the immediate orbit (20–30 km), the so-called "demographic basin", in big cities the share of long-distance migrants was much higher, especially when they were important trading centres. One good example is Amsterdam, where in the 17th and 18th centuries the share of foreign-born inhabitants (especially from Scandinavia and Germany) was over 35 %. The appeal of monocentric cities, like London and Paris, was felt throughout the country. Thus, London recruited its population from throughout the British Isles, including Ireland, although the majority came from the region between 60 and 120 km from London (Van Lottum 2007: 111). In France, Bordeaux, Lyon and other cities also had a huge regional draw; nevertheless, Paris was still less of a strong centripetal force.

A third feature was that skilled migrants, predominantly men, but also the vagrant underclass, traveled long distances (Lucassen

1997). Furthermore, it has to be stressed that there was also a lot of migration between cities. For artisans in particular, the step-by-step migration from small towns to larger cities, along the urban hierarchy, was very common. Finally, we wish to point to specific cases in which industrial migration systems developed, mostly with textile towns as poles of attraction. These cities recruited workers from regions with a similar occupational structure (both urban and rural), as was the case with Leiden and Lyon in the 17th century. Thus towns with a cloth industry, like Verviers, Aix-la-Chapelle, Düsseldorf and Münster, saw many people leave for Leiden, at that time the most important producer of cloth in Europe (Lucassen and De Vries 2001).

Although the predominant pattern of migration in Early Modern Europe was from the countryside to the city, these were not two entirely different worlds. Smaller towns in particular functioned in close symbiosis with the surrounding hinterland (Clark 1995). Not only did migrants constantly travel between rural and urban areas (a pattern that remained important even until World War I), in the 18th and early 19th centuries the countryside spawned centres of production through the spectacular growth of the textile-dominated

Itinerant journeyman, lithograph from around 1850. Between 1827 and 1835 a blacksmith, for example, traveled from Linz in Austria via Munich, Ulm, Stuttgart, Heidelberg and Frankfurt to Cologne, then continued via Aachen, Liège and Reims to Paris, via Dijon, Besançon and Neuchâtel to Schaffhausen and then to Bregenz, Salzburg and Vienna and back to Linz

Arrest of a smuggler at the Dutch-German border near Gronau. A posed photograph, presumably before World War I

putting-out industry, with cities as centres of coordination. The result was migration to and within regions, some of which (Tilburg, Leeds, Birmingham, parts of the Ruhr) became industrialized in the process.

Closely connected to this development was the multiplication of smaller towns from the 18th century and the simultaneous levelling off of the metropolitan urbanization process that dominated the period 1600–1750. Later, in the 19th century, these smaller towns, but also the de-industrialising rural areas, again became the prime source of skilled workers to the big cities.

Although cities needed them, not all migrants were treated equally or given full

Tradesmen and manufacturers were predominant amongst the Huguenot emigrants to the Electorate of Hesse, Prussia and other regions in Germany. This copper-plate engraving (around 1770) shows tanners at work. The leather processing trade had been established around Clermont-Ferrand in the Auvergne; after their flight the Huguenots founded tanning works in, for example, Hofgeismar, near Kassel

citizenship. The poor in particular were excluded and had great difficulties attaining the status of citizen, as the elite wished to maintain their political power and the viability of the poor relief system. The distinction between the "good" and "bad" migrants was seen as vital for the functioning of the urban societal system, which has been characterized as miniature welfare states (Snell 1985). The exclusion from full citizenship also affected the indigenous poor, who found themselves in a similar position as many poor immigrants. Moreover, there were important differences between European regions in terms of settlement restrictions. German cities, for example, curbed the freedom of their inhabitants (as well as newcomers) by guild regulations and marriage bans, this in contrast to large Dutch cities, which did not have such stipulations and also made membership of urban institutions, like guilds and citizenship, much easier (Lourens and Lucassen 2000). Amsterdam even admitted poor migrants relatively easily to its social security system, which for many German migrants was one of the reasons to emigrate to Holland (Van de Pol and Kuijpers 2005).

Apart from political ones, there were also ethnic differences between immigrants and natives. In many cases newcomers moved in chains, so that people from specific origins settled in the same place, such as migrants from Calabria in Naples, from the Auvergne in Paris and East-Frisians in Amsterdam. These migrants often had the same occupations, lived concentrated in certain neighborhoods, and had their own institutions like churches, which often provided poor relief. In 17th century Naples for example there were twelve different churches for ethnic groups like the Castilians, Catalans, Genovese and Florentines (Papenheim 2007b; Musi 2000). The reach of these institutions was restricted as the children of the migrants used to assimilate quite quickly. Only in cases of dissenting and stigmatized religious groups, like Jews or Protestant and Catholic minorities, could isolation develop into a structural phenomenon.

As in the present, in the Early Modern period key institutions like states, universities and churches depended on highly skilled migrants, who were recruited on an international market. For most people these geographical moves meant a necessary step in their careers, and this form of migration can therefore be labeled as institutional career migration. The specific form of migration depended on the institution in question, but in most cases it involved multiple moves of men (women most often moved with their husbands) over large distances. Common to all three institutions, in particular in relation to states, is the rotation principle, which was deemed necessary to prevent corruption and overly friendly relations with inferiors.

Among higher ranking civil servants and army officers migration was the norm. Courts, state administrations, and central taxation offices all needed skilled personnel who were hired throughout the empire and sometimes from abroad. Composite states in particular, like the Habsburg (later Austria-Hungarian) and Ottoman empires, offered career migrants ample opportunities. One good example is the Spanish (from Catalonia and Aragon) and Genoese who dominated the governing elites of southern Italy during Spanish rule between the 15th and 18th centuries. As the highest ranking jobs in Naples and Sicily became hereditary, however, and Spanish families gradually integrated into local elites, the role of migration diminished (Papenheim 2007b). Other well-known centres of Habsburg power were Vienna and Brussels (18th century). Whereas the top jobs were reserved for the nobility, most work was done by well-trained civil servants. In the first half of the 18th century many lawyers from the southern Netherlands left for Vienna to work their way up in the bureaucracy. Later on there was a considerable movement of civil servants from Austria to Brussels, among them the sons of the erstwhile Belgian migrants. An interesting aspect of the rotation principle developed in the latter part of the 18th century, when in the Habsburg Empire civil servants were explicitly recruited from other parts of the empire in order to prevent nationalist tendencies (Zedinger 2000).

Furthermore, these civil servants had already migrated as students, many of whom attended several European universities (Leiden, Paris, Louvain) in order to learn the appropriate languages and skills before entering government service. Some universities, like Erlangen in the late 18th century, attracted significant numbers of Protestant students from areas without any significant centres of learning, such as Russia, Poland/Lithuania and the Baltic. As the case of Erlangen shows (Beyer-Thoma 2004), religion caused many students to travel to a university of their denomination. Thus Utrecht in the Netherlands pulled Calvinist students from Hungary and Siebenbürgen, whereas Catholics from the northern Netherlands chose Louvain and Rome. Universities were not only places that welcomed students from all over Europe, but were also important magnets for scholars, many of whom moved several times during their careers within the European university network. In some cases moves were caused by conflicts, but intellectual interests and job opportunities were more important. The Russian Empire, with no academic tradition to speak of, was largely dependent on foreign scholars. Thus the Russian Academy of Sciences, established in St. Petersburg in 1725, recruited more than half of its members from abroad during the 18th century. Most of these academics came from German university towns such as Halle, Leipzig, Tübingen, Basel, and Erlangen. Wages were high and many stayed for years at a time, whereas between 10 and 20% settled for good. Apart from Germans various Italian, French, and Scottish scholars took the road to St. Petersburg, most of them in science ("Naturwissenschaft"), followed by philosophy, law and the humanities (Dahlmann 2004).

Students with clerical ambitions also attended universities and after their graduation their career brought them to many different places. It was not only the Catholic Church that thus engendered migration, but less hierarchical religions, like Protestantism and Judaism, knew traveling scholars and priests as well. The most elaborate, international and largest pole of attraction were the Papal States, and in particular its capital Rome with the offices of the Curia Romana, dating from the 11th century and headed by the Pope. At the Vatican, both a political and a religious world centre, many different posts had to be filled (Emich 2001). Although from the 16th century onward in all ranks its personnel became increasingly Italianized (80% in the 18th century), and the Popes were exclusively Italian between 1523 and 1978 (Reinhard 1976), clerics from all over Europe (especially from France, England, Spain, and Germany) flocked to Rome. Apart from clerics, the Vatican also attracted diplomatic representatives from all over Europe.

Whereas Rome exerted centripetal forces, other institutions of the Catholic church can be characterized as centrifugal in nature. One good example is the Jesuits (Societas Jesu), established in the 16th century by Ignatius of Loyola. It was the aim of its members to spread over the world (in 1550 they were already present in Brazil, India, Japan and Central Africa), to convert heathens, but also to discipline the existing clergy and fight anti-Catholic tendencies. Starting out with

A "Frenchman's House" from 1688 in Mariendorf, a village founded by Huguenots near Kassel. Count Karl had granted the French religious refugees settlement rights. Photo from 1928

1,000 members in the mid-16th century, the order expanded to 14,000 in 1620 and almost 23,000 in 1750, of whom more than 3,000 worked in other parts of the world. Within Europe their presence was strong in Flanders, Spain, northern Italy and southern Germany. In most Protestant states, but in 1764 also in France, they were banned. Originally, many were recruited in Italy and Spain, but gradually countries where they were stationed "produced" their own members (Falkner 1997).

Settlement

In Early Modern Europe geographical mobility was to a certain extent intertwined with urbanization, but sometimes also with settlement policies for newly acquired "empty" lands. Whoever migrated to a city depended on the urban opportunity structure. Both the geographical, occupational and gender-specific selectivity was to a large extent determined by the occupational possibilities in a given place. Furthermore, the position of a given city in the wider urban network mattered and influenced the extent and nature of the immigration. Finally we should realise that population mobility was extremely high, as many newcomers only stayed for a short while. A widespread phenomenon was the migration of journeymen and servants, both in west as in Central Europe. In this paragraph we will deal both with permanent settlers and the more volatile part of the migrant population

For a systematic analysis of settlement processes we distinguish between factors that are determined by the receiving (local) society and the characteristics of the migrants themselves. Within these two perspectives we distinguish among three levels: individual, civil society and the (local) state. First of all we will concentrate on the economically motivated migration to largely autonomous cities in parts of Europe where free migration was the rule (the north-west and parts of southern and Central Europe).

City

In contrast to the modern era, aliens were locally defined and the distinctions between city dwellers and aliens were relatively small. In most cities, however, the legal differences between various categories of residents were considerable. Only a minority had full citizenship and could exert the rights attached to this status. The opportunities for immigrants therefore largely depended on their class position. Rich newcomers with sufficient money could buy their citizenship status and were automatically turned into full citizens, with considerably more rights than poor indigenous residents. Most immigrants had to accept a lower position. Moreover, urban authorities erected barriers to people with a different religious affiliation. Jews in particular, but also Catholics (in Protestant states), Protestants (the Huguenots in France) and Lutherans were confronted with this forms of systematic discrimination.

In general one can distinguish between two different settlement versions: 1) acceptance – without the granting of equal rights – of different religions, as in the Netherlands, Poland and France until the 17th century, and

Temporary buildings at a Dutch-German border crossing. The customs office had been destroyed by the explosion of a lorry laden with fire crackers. Photo 1922

workers. Furthermore we already mentioned the Huguenots, 20,000 of whom were settled by the Great Elector Friedrich Wilhelm I in Brandenburg (especially in Berlin). Other examples are the German, Dutch, English, and Finnish artisans and construction workers who were lured to Saint Petersburg by Peter the Great at the end of the 17th century. The dark side of this absolutist politics was that princes also forced people to settle, for example the Jews whom Catherine II at the end of the 18th century ordered to live in towns in present-day Ukraine and White Russia (the so called "Pale of Settlement").

Land

People not only left for cities, but also populated rural territories. The latter was highly regulated by the state, with all kinds of restrictions. From 1689 onward, the Habsburg rulers carefully selected settlers to populate the territory captured from the Ottomans. Hungarians were excluded, but German farmers and artisans, even if they were Jewish or refugees from the Ottoman empire, like Armenians from Wallachia and orthodox Serbs, were welcomed. Land was granted and artisans were forbidden to organise in guilds. Freedom of religion was granted, but the German language was given preferential treatment. Here, as in Russia, the new areas were very attractive for runaway serfs.

A decree by Empress Catherine II opened the southern Russian plains for settlement. Here, too, religious freedom, unprecedented in the Russian Empire, was allowed, even to Jews. Land of between 30 and 80 Desiatinas (1=2.7 acres) was parcelled out. Other benefits were freedom from military service and even autonomous rule. For the pacifist Hutterites and Mennonites the possibility to escape military service was of course a gift from God (Hellie 2002). In western Europe we have mentioned the settlement migration in the North of Ireland, especially in Ulster, enabled by the occupation of Ireland by the English crown. Around 1625 8,000 men and 6,000 women had settled down, followed by a second wave after 1633. Probably some 30,000 Scots made the journey, most of them small leaseholders from overpopulated

in the Ottoman empire. Residents of different religious affiliations were free to settle where they pleased under the same rule of law or, as in the Ottoman empire, in semi-autonomous millets. 2) attempts at forced conversion, sometimes with near-complete success, as in the Lutheran states in Scandinavia, in Catholic countries like Spain from the early 17th and France from the late 17th century, as well as in many German states (according to the cuius regio eius et religio principle), sometimes with partial success, as in England with its Anglican state church, which in theory covered the whole English population but had to admit that many Protestant dissenters and not a few Catholics continued their practices and were even able to flourish. In these countries occasionally "useful immigrants" of different religious convictions were allowed access, like Calvinist Huguenots and Lutheran refugees from Salzburg.

Of course the characteristics of migrants also determined their position in society. First of all this concerned categories like sex, class and religion, but also age, origin and occupational specialization. Women, for example, had very limited opportunities in the labor market, and also their chances in the marriage market lagged behind those of men, due to a surplus of women. As a result they were more dependent on poor relief, as shown for German

and Scandinavian migrants in 17th century Amsterdam (Van de Pol and Kuijpers 2005). Men, both immigrants and non-migrants, had far greater opportunities, but only a minority of them had an independent and good position as trader or artisan. In the guilds the number of masters was restricted and in most parts of Europe most journeymen were condemned to life-long proletarian status. For many journeymen and servants it was therefore almost impossible to settle for good, especially in German states with their very strict marriage restrictions. As a result, their (inter-urban) geographical mobility was high. Many journeymen traveled through chain migration networks, resulting in conspicuous concentrations of certain occupation and origins. Among well-known examples are the east Frisian bakers in Amsterdam, German furniture makers and construction workers from the Auvergne in Paris and Italian chimney sweeps in Vienna (Ehmer 1980). It seems, however, that this specialization was developed at destination, rather than in the source areas.

Although in general authorities did not interfere with the push and pull forces of the labor market, there were also cases in which the state intervened actively in attracting migrants. This was the case in many Dutch cities around 1600 who competed among one another for Flemish artisans and textile

areas. The Scottish peasants were deployed as soldiers to protect the English farmers from the "wild" Irish (Smout et al. 1994).

For the long-term settlement process there were great differences between rural and urban areas. Whereas in cities the assimilation of children and grandchildren was the rule, in rural territories a contrasting development could occur. The colonization of German speakers in the Balkans and in southern Russia, for example, led to linguistic and religious pockets which survived for centuries.

A Balanced View

The mapping of Early Modern migrations has started only recently. For a country with an impressive historical-demographic tradition like England, for example, emigration history still shows many lacunae and paradoxes, if only because of the coincidence of the Industrial Revolution and the concomitant economic growth and large-scale overseas emigration, coinciding with relatively low immigration (Van Lottum 2007). For other parts of Europe, like the Balkans in particular, only a first overview has recently become available (Sundhausen 2007). One conclusion, however, stands out very clearly now: migration history does not start with the so-called Industrial Revolution; neither does geographical mobility depend on modern means of traveling like steam trains or boats, nor is it inconsistent with servitude or proto-industry.

Although the actual state of research is still insufficient to make straightforward quantitative comparisons between sub-periods from 1500 until now, partial results already show that the relative mobility in the Early Modern period may have been more important than later on. Amsterdam is a good case in point: in the 17th century it had a higher percentage of immigrants than in the 19th and most of the 20th centuries. It is also safe to say that developments are not straightforward. The emigration from England to the Americas was more important in the 17th than in the 18th century. This not only goes for the migration process, but also for

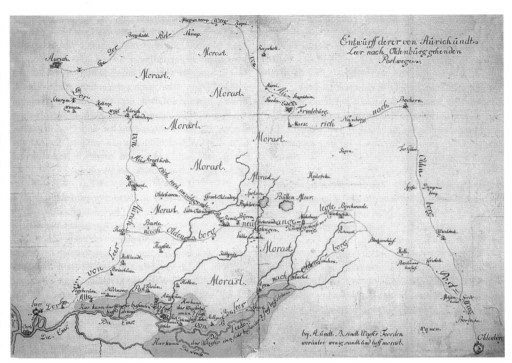

A map of postal routes from Aurich and Leer to Oldenburg with villages shown along the routes, 1720. Postal routes were important transport connections between regions, towns, villages and cultural areas

the settlement process and for tolerance vis-à-vis minorities: tolerance in medieval Spain was much higher than later on, and the same goes for Poland until the early 17th and France until the late 17th century. Besides, mass migration of political refugees is a phenomenon which dates only from the late 18th century.

This is of course not to say that through this "revolt of the Early Modernists" (De Vries 1994) we have suddenly discovered a golden age of free mobility and toleration long before modernity. It implies, however, that Europe has rapid much longer empirical evidence to offer for those interested in the historical backgrounds of the actual situation than was assumed until recently.

References:

Adanir, Fikret (2003). "Religious communities and ethnic groups under imperial sway: Ottoman and Habsburg lands in comparison." In: The historical practice of diversity. Transcultural interactions from the Early Modern Mediterranean to the postcolonial world, edited by Dirk Hoerder, Christiane Harzig and Adrian Shubert, 54–86. New York and London: Berghahn.

Bade, Klaus J., Pieter Emmer, Leo Lucassen and Jochen Oltmer (2007) eds. Enzyklopädie Migration in Europa vom 17. Jahrhundert bis zur Gegenwart, Paderborn/München: Schöningh Fink.

Bailyn, Bernard (1987). Voyagers to the West. A Passage in the Peopling of America on the Eve of the Revolution. New York.

Beer, Mathias, and Dittmar Dahlmann (2004), eds. Über die trockene Grenze und über das offene Meer. Binneneuropäische und transatlantische Migrationen im 18. und 19. Jahrhundert. Essen: Klartext.

Beyer-Thoma, Hermann (2004). "Netzwerke und Migration. Wanderungen von Gelehrten aus dem evangelischen Franken nach Russland im 18. und frühen 19. Jahrhundert." In: Beer and Dahlman 2004: 133–166.

Bodian, Miriam (1999). Hebrews of the Portuguese nation. Conversos and community in Early Modern

A "centsprent", a popular printed story in pictures, named after the price (one cent) one had to pay for it, from Amsterdam in the 18th century. "Look here young people, and note with amusement how Gretchen from Westphalia presented herself in Amsterdam." Such pictures illustrated farcical stage shows and street ballads performed at fairs and in public places. Numerous house maids from Westphalia and elsewhere migrated to Dutch cities

Amsterdam. Bloomington: Indiana University Press.

Canny, Nicholas (2001). Making Ireland British 1580–1650. Oxford: Oxford University Press.

Ibidem, 1994) ed. Europeans on the move. Studies on European migration, 1500–1800. Oxford: Clarendon Press.

Choquette, Leslie P. (1997). Frenchmen into peasants: modernity and tradition in the peopling of French Canada. Cambridge Mass.: Harvard University Press.

Clark, Peter (1995), ed. Small towns in Early Modern Europe Cambridge: Cambridge University Press.

Coleman, David (2003). Creating Christian Granada: Society and Religious Culture in an Old-World Frontier City, 1492–1600. Ithaca: Cornell University Press.

Czouz-Tornare, Alain-Jacques (2007). "Schweizer Söldner in Europa vom 17. bis zum 19. Jahrhunderts (Beispiel Frankreich)." In: Bade et al. 2007: 973–975

Dahlmann, Dittmar (2004). "Gelehrte auf Reisen." In Beer and Dahlmann 2004: 119–132.

Davids, Karel, and Jan Lucassen (1995) eds. A miracle mirrored: the Dutch Republic in European perspective. Cambridge: Cambridge University Press.

Ehmer, Josef (1980). Familienstruktur und Arbeitsorganisation im frühindustriellen Wien München.

Eltis, David (2002a). "Free and coerced migrations from the Old World to the New." In: Eltis ed. 2002b 33–74.

Ibidem, 2002b) ed. Coerced and free migration. Global perspectives. Stanford: Stanford University Press.

Emich, Birgit (2001). Bürokratie und Nepotismus unter Paul V. (1605–1621): Studien zur frühneuzeitlichen Mikropolitik in Rom. Stuttgart: A. Hiersemann.

Falkner, Andreas (1997). "Jesuiten." In: Kulturgeschichte der christlichen Orden in Einzeldarstellungen edited by Peter Dinzelbacher and James Lester Hogg, 204–241. Stuttgart: Kröner.

Fertig, Georg (1994). "Transatlantic migration from the German-speaking parts of Central Europe, 1600–1800." In: Canny 1994: 192–235.

François, Etienne (1990). "The German urban network between the sixteenth and 18th centuries. Cultural and demographic indicators." In: Urbanization in history. A process of dynamic interactions edited by Ad van der Woude, Akira Hayami and Jan de Vries, 84–100. Oxford.

Haver, Charlotte E. (2007). "Salzburger Protestanten in Ostpreussen seit dem 18. Jahrhundert." In: Bade et al. 2007: 935–938.

Hellie, Richard (2002). "Migration in Early Modern Russia, 1480s–1780s." In: Eltis 2002: 292–323.

Hoerder, Dirk (2002). Cultures in contact. World migrations in the second Millennium. Durham and London: Duke University Press.

Hoerder, Dirk, Jan Lucassen, and Leo Lucassen (2007). "Terminologien und Konzepte in der Migrationsforschung." In: Bade et al. 2007: 28–53.

Kaser, Karl (2007). "Siedler an der habsburgischen Militärgrenze seit der frühen Neuzeit." In: Bade et al. 2007: 985–990.

Kroener, Bernhard R. (2004). "Krieg und Karriere. Geographische Mobilität als Voraussetzung sozialen Aufstiegs in der militärischen Gesellschaft des 17. Jahrhunderts." In: Beer and Dahlmann 2004: 45–66.

Lottum, Jelle van (2007). Across the North Sea. The impact of the Dutch Republic on international labor migration, c. 1550–1850. Amsterdam: Aksant.

Lourens, Piet, and Jan Lucassen (2000). "Zunftlandschaften" in den Niederlanden um im benachbarten Deutschland." In: Zunftlandschaften in Deutschland und den Niederlanden im Vergleich, edited by Wilfried Reininghaus, 11–44. Münster: Aschendorff.

Porter from Lauscha, a glass blowing town in Thuringia, carrying glass tubes on his back, around 1920. Such porters were peddlers who carried a heavy basket or a pannier on their backs and covered distances of several hundred kilometres

Traveling town musician in Bremen-Blumenthal. Around 1900

Lucassen, Jan (1987). Migrant Labor in Europe. The Drift to the North Sea. London: Croom Helm.

Ibidem, 2004). "A multinational and its labor force: the Dutch East India Company, 1595–1795." International Labor and Working-Class History 66, No. Fall: 12–39.

Lucassen, Jan and Leo Lucassen (1997) eds. Migration, migration history, history: old paradigms and new perspectives. Bern: Peter Lang, 1997.

Lucassen, Leo (1997). "Eternal vagrants? State formation, migration, and traveling groups in western Europe, 1350–1914." In: Lucassen and Lucassen 1997: 225–252.

Lucassen, Leo and Boudien de Vries (2001). "The rise and fall of a west European textile worker migration system: Leiden, 1586–1700." Revue du Nord No. 15: 23–42.

Manning, Patrick (2005). Migration in world history. New York and London: Routledge.

Martin, Odil (1986). La conversion protestante à Lyon (1659–1687). Genève: Drost.

Moch, Leslie Page (2003). Moving Europeans. Migration in western Europe since 1650. Bloomington: Indiana University Press.

Murdoch, Steve (2007). "Schottische Soldaten in Europa in der frühen Neuzeit." In: Bade et al. 2007: 948–952.

Musi, Aurelio (2000). L'Italia dei viceré. Integrazione e resistenza nel sistema imperiale spagnolo. Cava de' Tirreni: Avagliano, 2000.

Papenheim, Martin (2007a). "Spanische Truppen in den Niederlanden im 16. und 17. Jahrhundert (Beispiel Geldern)." In: Bade et al. 2007: 1005–1007.

Ibidem, 2007b). "Verwaltungseliten in Süditalien und Sizilien unter spanischer Herrschaft in der Frühen Neuzeit." In: Bade et al. 2007: 1070–1071.

Pol, Lotte van de and Erika Kuijpers (2005). "Poor women's migration to the city. The attraction of Amsterdam health care and social assistance in Early Modern times." Journal of Urban History 32, No. 1: 44–60.

Reinhard, Wolfgang (1976). "Herkunft und Karriere der Päpste 1417–1963. Beitrag zu einer historischen Soziologie der römischen Kurie." Mededelingen van het Nederlands Historisch Instituut te Rome 38: 87–108.

Rosendaal, Joost (2007). "Niederländische Flüchtlinge ("Bataver") in Frankreich 1787–1795", In: Bade et al. 2007: 810–812.

Smout, T.C., N.C. Landsman, and T.M. Devine (1994) "Scottish emigration in the 17th and 18th centuries." In: Canny 1994: 76–112.

Steinfeld, Robert J. (1991). The invention of free labor: the employment relation in English and American law and culture, 1350–1870. Chapel Hill: University of North Carolina Press.

Sundhausen, Holm (2007). "Südosteuropa." In: Bade et al. 2007: 285–313.

Treadgold, Donald W. (1957). The great Siberian migration. Government and peasant in resettlement from emancipation to the First World War. Princeton: Princeton University Press.

Vigne, Randolph, and Charles Littleton (2001) eds. From strangers to citizens. The integration of immigrant communities in Britain, Ireland and colonial America. London: Sussex Academic Press.

Vink, Markus P.M. (2003). "The World's Oldest Trade": Dutch Slavery and Slave Trade in the Indian Ocean in the Seventeenth Century." Journal of World History 14, No. 2: 131–177.

Vries, Jan de (1994). "The Industrial Revolution and the Industrious Revolution." The Journal of Economic history 54, No. 2: 249–270.

Wokeck, Marianne S. (1999) Trade in strangers. The beginnings of mass migration to North America. University Park: The University of Pennsylvania Press.

Zedinger, Renate (2000). Die Verwaltung der Österreichischen Niederlande in Wien. Wien: Böhlau.

Poster announcing the sale of slaves, household goods, and a horse. A plantation owner in Surinam (Dutch Guiana) with a slave girl

Poster commemorating the 60th anniversary of Queen Victoria's term of government in 1897, which illustrates some significant technological developments: the invention of steam power, the revolution in the means of transport and the change of urban infrastructures

Brian Lambkin

Hallelujah, We're off to America!
The European Cultures of Origin in Western, Central and Northern Europe

Background

The explanation of why industrialisation should have started in Europe, and why in its north-western part and in Britain in particular, lies in a singular coincidence of ecological, economic, social, cultural and political circumstances that no other part of the world had experienced before. Out of this set of favourable conditions, through the exploitation of coal and iron and steam power, was generated the first transition to "modernity" – the move from a traditional, agrarian, peasant-based society, where the majority of people work on the land and produce their own food, to a modern urbanised and industrialised society, where most people earn their living in towns and factories. Already under way in the 18th century, industrialisation reached the point of "take-off" first in Britain in the 1820s and soon spread. By the middle of the 19th century it had achieved take-off in most of the countries of north-west Europe – first Belgium and Holland, then Prussia, Piedmont and France – and by 1900 Britain's lead was being rapidly overtaken by the recently united Germany and by the United States. There had long been a west-east divide in Europe but it had been largely religious and political in character. Now it took on an economic aspect as two distinct zones emerged: an advanced predominantly industrialised and modernised zone in the west, centre and north, and a backward, industrialising but largely un-modernised zone in the south and east.

The effect of the "take-off" of industrialisation in Europe is seen most starkly in the growth of its cities in relation to the population. Between 1800 and 1900 London had grown by 340 % to 6.5 million; Paris by 345 % to 2.5 million; Vienna by 490 % to about two million; and Berlin by a staggering 872 % also to about 2 million. In 1800, when Europe's population was about 200 million, 6 million (3 %) were living in its 23 major cities with populations over 100,000, but by 1900, when the population had reached 400 million, about 50 million (12 %) were living in 135 major cities. By 1914 there were a dozen million-plus conurbations in Europe with London, Paris, Berlin, Vienna, St Petersburg, and Istanbul having reached that status first, followed by Glasgow, Manchester, Leeds, Liverpool, Birmingham, the Ruhr, Hamburg, and Moscow.

A major component of this growth was internal and transnational migration within Europe (always more significant than emigration) that was highly complex according to the diversity of both the receiving and sending areas and of the causes and effects of the migration flows between them as changing cross-currents and counter-currents were driven by economic cycles of boom and bust and intermittent crises of famine and war. Towns and cities grew differently, as for example London and Paris whose proportions of growth due to in-migration in the second half of the 19th century were 16 and 64 % respectively. While all towns had service sectors of administration and commerce, they varied greatly in the relative importance of their primary and secondary manufacturing sectors. Predominantly service towns, like Amiens in France and Cologne in Germany, had low birth rates and grew mainly through in-migration, especially through women going into domestic service; textile towns, such as Manchester in England, Roubaix

Postcard of Plymouth, Dockyard Gates, undated (presumably 1890s)

PLYMOUTH. DOCKYARD GATES, KEYHAM.

Passenger list of the "Teutonic" (White Star Line) from Liverpool 1897, which had to be delivered by the captain to the New York port authorities, with predominantly Irish emigrants, the majority having boarded ship in Queenstown, now Cobh, near Cork

between 200,000 and 300,000 left each year. Not surprisingly, it was the countries of western, central and northern Europe which initially supplied the largest proportion of overseas migrants, especially Britain and Ireland. Of the 50 million or so Europeans who migrated overseas between 1800 and 1914 (40 million to the United States), about 10 million were from Britain (England, Scotland and Wales) and 6 million from Ireland, together accounting for over 30 % of the mass emigration.

Britain (England, Scotland and Wales)

In 1800 the population of Britain was about 10 million and by 1914 it had almost quadrupled to 36 million. Industrialisation had first developed in the regions of Lancashire (Manchester), Yorkshire (Leeds and Sheffield), the west Midlands (Birmingham) and Tyneside (Newcastle) in England, in the valleys of South Wales (Cardiff), and Clydebank (Glasgow) in Scotland. Ireland (considered separately below), which had been under complete British rule since the beginning of the 17th century and became part of the United Kingdom of Great Britain and Ireland in 1801, experienced comparable industrialisation only in the north-east in the Lagan valley (Belfast). As a result, the contrast between these mainly lowland industrialised areas and the outlying highlands and islands became even sharper. In 1800 about 30 % of Britain's population was living in towns of over 20,000 and in 1914 it was 80 %, with only about 12 % left engaged in agriculture and 15 % living in the Greater London area. For the first half of the 19th century there was a net inflow of migrants into England and Wales and even during the huge exodus of the 1880s the net outflow was no more than 2,000 per annum. Remarkably, Britain was able to export a large number of its people and sustain its population growth.

Although the growth of British industry generated high rates of internal migration to the towns, there were also high rates of overseas migration that increased steadily to the 1880s. Despite its high

in France, and Barmen in Germany, had high birth rates (decreasing after 1870) and high in-migration mostly from the immediate vicinity with a very high proportion of women; and coal and steel towns, like Sheffield in England and Duisburg in Germany, had the highest volume of in-migration with high birth rates and a very high proportion of men. Of course the migration process did not affect all parts of a country equally and therefore, as Dudley Baines has warned, the country may not be the appropriate unit of analysis because of the high degree of regional variation. In the survey that follows it is important to bear in mind that some countries, like Germany, were particularly large and heterogeneous to the point of developing different "cultures" of migration within them. In all

the European countries, even the smallest, some regions produced relatively large numbers of migrants while others produced relatively few, with sharp contrasts often observable down at the level of neighbouring sub-regions, and even between and within local communities. So as well as seeing the countries of western, central and northern Europe as "core" and the southern and eastern countries as "periphery" in the 19th century, we need also to be aware of both the "core" and "periphery" areas within the countries of western, central and northern Europe.

In the history of the migration streams between these areas lies the explanation for the "take-off" into high gear of mass overseas migration from Europe during the crisis years of the 1840s when

emigration rates, England was also one of the European nations importing workers in this period. Most of the immigrants came from Ireland, but, beginning about 1750 and increasing in the early 19th century, there was an influx of Germans, Lithuanians, and Italians; after 1850 there were also relatively large numbers of Russian and Polish Jews. The Jews settled in London and the other large cities, where there had been Jewish communities since the Middle Ages. There were also labour migrants from highly skilled trades who were attracted by the opportunity to improve their knowledge and technical qualifications in the advanced English industries. Therefore in England emigration, especially overseas emigration, and immigration developed in parallel, even though, unlike France, immigration was not of great importance to the Britain's economic development.

As the steam-driven industrial economy of Britain "took-off" in the 1820s, emigration moved up a gear. Between 1790 and 1815 about 150,000 had emigrated from England and Wales and about 33,000 from Scotland, but between 1815 and 1850 about 500,000 emigrated from England and Wales and 100,000 from Scotland. By 1870, migration out of England in one year was exceeding 100,000 at a rate of 3.5 per thousand of the population, which was probably the highest rate since the 1630s. In the second half of the 19th century as a whole, about 8 million left Britain and Ireland for destinations outside Europe. Of these, 52% were English and Welsh, 10% Scots and 38% Irish, with 66% going to the United States, 10% to Canada and 17% Australia and New Zealand. The rate for England and Wales was 1 per thousand, for Scotland 1.4, and for Ireland 3.1. While for England and Wales this represented only 9% of the natural population increase (that is, births over deaths), for Scotland it was 25%, and for Ireland much more. As English emigration rose in the 1870s and 1880s it nearly matched the Irish at over 640,000 per decade. Economic recession in the United States in the mid-1890s caused a drop back to 4 per thousand, but in the decade before 1914 it was up again to 6 per thousand.

As elsewhere, overseas migration from Britain after 1860 was basically a massive

Above: An English family. England continued sending quite a number of its subjects to the United States, even as late as the beginning of the 20th century. An Englishwoman with nine children poses on April 17, 1908. The family came to America on board the S.S. Adriatic, a steamer of Great Britain's White Star Line
Below: New Arrivals from Scotland line up for a family photograph at Ellis Island, 1905

expansion of older internal migration traditions. Also feeding into this was a long tradition of emigration in Britain, stretching back to the iconic sailing of the "Pilgrim Fathers" in 1620 from Plymouth to New England, of recruiting settlers and workers for the overseas colonies. About 1.5 million emigrated from Britain in the 18th century. The practice of indentured emigration, emigration under a work contract, was widespread and before 1770 only about 30% of emigrants paid their own passage. This system gave the impoverished hope — even if they couldn't improve their social

Emigration Depot at Birkenhead, with a Vessel on the wharf preparing for the voyage. The Illustrated London News, July 10, 1852. Birkenhead lies at the mouth of the river Mersey, opposite Liverpool. Unlike emigration to America, some to Australia and New Zealand was organized by the Emigration Commissioners. Those emigrants were accommodated at the depot before joining their ship and thus avoided the difficulty of finding accommodation in Liverpool and the danger of exploitation

status, in America there was at least some possibility of a secure livelihood. In comparison with Scotland, there were fewer indentured servants from England, where the typical emigrants were not the very poorest artisans or agricultural workers but rather people who saw emigration as the only way to avoid becoming completely impoverished. They were more willing to accept a limited (and hopefully temporary) loss of status in a society where they were strangers than at home. Agricultural change in Scotland in the second half of the 18th century resulted in forced migration, or »Clearances«, from the Highlands to the Lowlands. Many of the evicted moved on to the colonies. While many Irish poured into Scotland, Scots moved south to England, where in 1851 they formed 7 % of the population of Carlisle, 4 % of Liverpool, and 1.3 % of London. As elsewhere, poor harvests, falling crop prices, high food prices, and crises in particular industries led to surges in the tide of emigration with peak years in 1819, 1827, the early 1830s and 1842, and the rate kept climbing in the second half of the 19th century.

English migration was particularly urban in character. About 22 % of all emigrants between 1861 and 1900 came from London, of whom at least three-quarters had been born in London – a much higher proportion than other cities like Stockholm where only a quarter of emigrants were city-born. In the 1880s, 35 % of English emigrants came from London, the west Midlands and Lancashire, with another 25 % coming from other industrial conurbations. From the middle of the 19th century there was a greater openness to the prospect of emigration because living standards and wages in the United States and the colonies had overtaken those of Britain and Ireland. What helped make emigration attractive to many in the 1860s and 1870s when the price of a transatlantic crossing dropped by about 40 % was its relatively low cost: in 1870 a typical British worker paid about 5 to 6 weeks' wages for a ticket, whereas a German or Swedish worker paid at least 3 months' wages. The relative importance of British ports in transatlantic migration is indicated by the fact that in 1874 about 117,000 emigrants left from England, 21,000 from Scotland and 61,000 from Ireland, together with about 39,000 foreigners and 5,000 others not classified. Cornwall was top of the English emigration league table as its copper and tin industries went into steep decline. Of the English regions, the Cornish had perhaps the strongest sense of both community cohesion and of dispersion.

Scotland's overall contribution of 2 million to emigration from the British Isles in the 19th century might seem small when compared with about 8 million from England and Wales and about 6 million from Ireland, yet it represented a significant loss to a small country whose total population in 1914 was less than 5 million, so that the departure of 2 million was 42 % of the population as compared with 25 % in England and Wales. Of the Scottish emigrants, 44 % went to the United States, 28 % to Canada and 25 % to Australia and New Zealand. A further 600,000 moved south of the border to England, especially from the Glasgow region, as Scots voted with their feet against urban congestion and poverty at a time when there was relatively plentiful housing in central Scotland. In the ten years before the First World War the population of Scotland actually fell as Scots emigrated at almost twice the rate of the English.

Emigration from Wales in the 18th century had been more driven by religious than economic motives. In 1794, for example, there was a project to establish a Welsh colony, a "Beulah Land", in Pennsylvania that attracted hundreds of emigrants. After 1815 emigration increased, especially from the rural areas of Caernarvon and Montgomeryshire, to the point that by 1850 there were 30,000 Welsh-born in the United States with 90 % of them located in New York, Pennsylvania, Ohio and Wisconsin. Between 1871 and 1890 about 6,000 left Wales while 75,000 left Scotland, 380,000 England, and 365,000 Ireland.

Many British emigrants were industrial workers with redundant skills, or skills no longer useful where they were located. For example, the decline of hard rock mining in Cornwall resulted in Cornish emigration to the new mines of Mexico, Michigan and Australia. Skilled migrants transferred their skills, as in the pottery industry between Staffordshire and Paterson, New Jersey, and in textiles industry between Lancashire and New England, with the result that British skilled workers were to be found in many parts of the world involved in mines, ironworks and textiles. At the same time the rate of return of English and Welsh migrants in the second half of the 19th century was relatively high at 40% (35% in the 1880s and 60% in the 1890s). By 1914 English return migration was about 48% (compared with 20% of Germans and 16% of Irish). As elsewhere, those who returned were mainly men who had worked in construction gangs or factories for a few years and in the 1880s many were participating in a highly integrated international labour market underway, such as the British house painters and decorators who worked in America in the spring; in Scotland in the summer, when their upper-class customers were socialising in London; and then in London in the autumn, when rich Londoners went to Scotland for the hunting season.

Emigrants from across Britain spoke different dialects of English and some other languages that were still strong in western highland and island regions (Scottish Gaelic, Welsh and Irish Gaelic). As junior partners within the United Kingdom the Scots and Welsh could easily have found cause to resent English domination, as did nationalists in Ireland. However, comparable nationalist movements did not emerge in Scotland or Wales. Divisions between Gaelic-speaking Highland and Lowland Scots and English-speaking elements within Scotland impeded the growth of a common identity, as did the powerful attractions of British "Unionist" state nationalism, committed to the "union" of the kingdoms of England and Scotland (1707) and England and Ireland (1801) within the United Kingdom. Like Cardiff and Unionist-dominated Belfast, Scotland's principal city, Glasgow, benefited greatly from the economic success of the British Empire.

An indication of Britain's importance in Europe and world affairs was given by the British Foreign Secretary, George Canning, when he joined the President of the United States, James Monroe, in forbidding any sort of European intervention in the Americas, telling the House of Commons in 1826 that he had "called the New World into existence to redress the Balance of the Old". Since the 17th century, Britain had aimed at populating its colonies by inducing its emigrants to Empire destinations, by measures such as the Passenger Vessels Act of 1803. There had been deportation of convicts to the Americas in the 18th century and to Australia from the 1790s to the middle of the 19th century; and in addition, the poverty laws in effect between 1835 and 1850 granted government-paid transportation to welfare recipients going to Australia, South Africa or Canada. However, between 1846 and 1869 assisted emigration schemes accounted for only about 1400 people per year (7% of total). The Canadian government found it very difficult to recruit agricultural labourers in Britain in the 1860s and 1870s and even more remote Australia had to subsidise about 45% of all its immigrants before World War II. Trade unions generally had a positive view of emigration, hoping that a shrinking labour supply might help them negotiate higher wages. The overall impact of British emigration is indicated by the fact that of the foreign-born in the United States in 1890, 11% were from England and Wales, 3% were from Scotland and 20% were from Ireland.

Ireland

Although fully part of the United Kingdom from 1801 until 1921, when it was partitioned North (6 counties) and South (26 counties), Ireland requires separate consideration because its experience of migration makes it a special case in Europe as a whole. The island's population grew from 5 million in 1800 to 8.5 million in 1845. Its rate of growth from 1750–1845 was phenomenal at 1.3% per annum, compared with 1.0 in England, 0.8 in Scotland, and 0.4 in France. However, over the 19th century as a whole, during the rest of Europe experienced population growth, Ireland's was the only population to decline – from 8.5 million in 1845 to 4.4 million in 1914.

In the absence of any extensive deposits of iron or coal on the island, only two major

Photograph of emigrants passing through Liverpool, about 1900. This group of (possibly) eastern European emigrants was booked through the Cunard Line Steam Ship Company at whose hostel they stayed. They are on their way to the S.S. Lucania

conurbations developed on the eastern side of the island next to Britain, attracting internal migration from a generally poorer western zone. Between 1800 and 1900 the capital Dublin grew from 182,000 to 290,000, while Belfast, in the north-eastern region where Protestants were in a majority and textiles and shipbuilding were important, grew from 25,000 to 350,000, making it the fastest-growing city in the United Kingdom. It is only since the 1960s that more than 50% of the population has been living in towns and cities. The balance between immigration and emigration flows varied greatly in Ireland with immigration dominant in the first half of the 17th century; immigration and emigration almost in balance in the second half of the 17th century; emigration dominant from the 18th through to the late 20th century. In the 1860s, for example, natural increase in the population of Ireland was 8 per thousand with net emigration running at 12 per thousand.

The origin of Ireland's modern tradition of emigration can be traced back to the iconic moment in 1607 of the "Flight of the Earls', who departed Ireland for Spain and Rome in the hope of returning in force to retake their lands from the control of Protestant British settlers. Compared

Poor urban children, Kilkenny. Photograph about 1900

During the agricultural depression in Ireland in the 1880s tenants attempted to obtain a rent reduction. Landlords remained stubborn and demanded their rent, and were even prepared to evict their tenants. If tenants barricaded themselves, battering rams were brought into use, occasionally, as documented in this photograph

with other European countries, Ireland's population growth "took off" dramatically between 1750 and 1850 but migration was not the main factor driving it: paradoxically the increase took place in spite of net emigration. The immigration streams from Britain and Europe were so reduced that the Protestant community was scarcely able to sustain itself, with landowners replenishing their tenants by looking north to Ulster instead. Fundamental changes in the character of emigration were getting underway in the aftermath of the Seven Years War (1756–63) and before the American War of Independence (1775–82). After 1763 the importance of Britain and North America as emigrant destinations increased, as that of continental Europe declined. The "modern" practice of prior payment for transatlantic passage started to replace the "early modern" practice of indentured servitude, especially in Ulster and increasingly emigrants responded to the strengthening force of opportunities in the New World rather than to problems in the Old.

Between 1800 and 1850 Ireland became truly a country of "mass" emigration. As a destination for immigrants it was little more attractive after the Act of Union of 1801 than before. Most immigrants to Ireland came from Britain, but too few to promote any closer integration of the two islands. The population continued to grow dramatically and this, combined with slow economic growth, had the effect of entrenching structural poverty – indicated by the growing number of vagrants and beggars. Despite a surge of reforming energy, government had not come to grips with the problem before the catastrophic years of famine after 1845. Increasing numbers of temporary seasonal labourers joined departing emigrants on the new steam-propelled vessels plying between Dublin and Liverpool. Many families from the snug farming class took passages across the Atlantic via Liverpool, which had become the main emigration hub of Europe. Though many now entered the ports of British North America (Canada) their ultimate destination lay south of the 49th parallel.

The impact of the Great Famine with the failure of the potato crop in successive years (1845–9) was cataclysmic and the strength of the forces already driving internal migration and emigration was dramatically increased. Although traumatic in the extreme, this did not mark a complete break with the past because while new migration flows were started in some areas, well-established flows were reinforced in others. Insofar as they can be reconstructed, the individual migration stories of the Famine generation exhibit a broad diversity but all were affected by the general mood of panic and urge to escape. In popular imagination, the legacy of the Famine looms large over the entire Irish migration tradition, distorting the way many see both the century before and the century after. For example, replica ships of this period, such as the Jeannie Johnston, are assumed erroneously to be "coffin ships'; emigrant ancestors, who in fact left later or earlier, are assumed to be Famine victims; and the Irish diaspora is assumed to have been generated entirely by the Great Famine. This compression of memory has resulted in the "coffin ships" serving many Irish Americans as a convenient origin myth in much the same way as the Nina, Pinta and Santa Maria of Columbus and the Mayflower have served others. However understandable such over-simplification may be as a response by descendants to the trauma of ancestors, taking the long view of Irish migration we see how much more than this awful scattering explains the Irish presence in America.

The impact of the Great Famine echoed through the rest of the 19th century and into the 20th. Emigration persisted at a level higher than in any other country in Europe and, thought of as a "chronic haemorrhage', it resulted in steady population decline. Hugely augmented in the decade up to 1855, the Irish diaspora now exerted a stronger pull than ever on those remaining in Ireland. As well as the Famine's scarring psychological effect on them, recent research has pointed to its long-term physical damage, both in terms of those who were prevented from being born and those who were born damaged fundamentally by under-nutrition or by starvation. The spaces vacated by those who emigrated were never close to being filled by immigrants. Most who arrived in the later 19th century came mainly from eastern Europe and southern Italy, driven by oppressive force or severe poverty rather than attracted by the prospect of economic opportunity or an Irish welcome. As a result the streets of Irish cities remained remarkably homogeneous. While movement into them from the countryside continued,

especially into Belfast, most Irish migrants who made the transition from rural to urban living in this period did so through emigration, not internal migration as was the European norm. As elsewhere, the bicycle and the train transformed mobility and widened horizons. Contrary to what is still widely assumed, Protestants from Ireland continued to emigrate throughout the 19th century and into the 20th. Although a minority of the emigrant flow since about 1825, their numbers, compared to the 18th and early 19th century, were actually much greater. Viewed as part of the huge 19th century European diaspora of more than 50 million people, the Irish, Catholic and Protestant, stood out in the second half of the century because about half their emigrants were female (as compared with the European norm of males outnumbering females by two to one); because they were so much less likely to return (about 10 %) and because so many of them ritualised their leaving as if it were a death in the customary practice known as the "American Wake" (see Case Study on the Mellon Family).

Of all the countries participating in the great transatlantic migrations of the 19th century, Ireland was the first to reach its

Irish peat peasants, undated photo

Impoverished Irish peasants. Photo ca. 1880

peak, mainly because of the exceptional impact of the Great Famine. In the thirty years before the Great Famine of 1845–9, over one million left Ireland, most of them (about 900,000) for the United States and the rest mainly entering Britain as British emigrants were leaving. Emigration was removing only 7% of England's natural increase and 11% of Scotland's but 50% of that of Ireland. The contrast between the two islands could not be more starkly illustrated.

In the first half of the 19th century the majority of immigrants into the regions of recent settlement in the New World entered agriculture but the Irish were a notable exception in their urban preference. Between 1876 and 1921, 84% of all Irish emigrants went to the United States and only 8% to Britain, showing how, against the normal European pattern, transatlantic migration chains were more powerful than their internal counterparts. The greatest interregional and international mobility was experienced in Ireland. Ireland's population declined from 8.2 million in 1841 to 6.5 million in 1851: between 1845 and 1855 about 2 million people left the island, 1.5 million to United States and about 300,000 to Canada, about 250,000 went to England, Scotland or Wales, mainly the industrial regions in western England or south-western Scotland. In 1851 there were almost 730,000 Irish living in Britain, 806,000 in 1861 dropping to 632,000 in 1901. In all about 5 million Irish emigrated between 1840 and 1914, by which time two-thirds of all Irish-born were living abroad.

France

The contrast between the migration experience of Ireland and that of France was extreme. Having had only a moderate population increase in the 18th century, France had almost none in the 19th century. Whereas the population of Britain quadrupled between 1800 and 1914, that of France did not even double, growing from about 27 million to 42 million. Voluntary birth limitation, associated with later age of marriage due to a longer period

GIRL STOWAWAY, 15, LIKES 'GENDARME'

French Miss Slips In to See City, but Is Found Forlorn Standing in Doorway.

SHE CAPTIVATES A JUDGE

Justice Levy Gives Her a Present, but Sends Her to Ellis Island to Take Ship for Home.

Mlle. Michele d'Idier, 15 years old, of Grenoble, France, arrived on the liner Lafayette at 11:40 Thursday morning. She was a stowaway. About fourteen hours later, Patrolman Kenneth Waters saw a demure young woman in a blue silk dress, leather windbreaker and wrinkled

French Girl Stowaway. Stowaways arrived at Ellis Island in ample numbers. Aside from men and women, even boys and girls could often not resist the temptation to slip aboard ship without paying the fare, especially if their purses were empty. The girl in this piece, Michele d'Idier, 15, hailed from Grenoble, but was not successful in entering the U.S., she was deported. (New York Times, May 6, 1933)

of military service, high tax rates and laws forbidding those under the age of 15 to work which reduced the economic imperative to have children, made France also a special case in Europe. As the country of slowest population growth it was nevertheless amongst the first to industrialise. A stark regional divide emerged in France with the development of pioneer industrialising areas along the Paris-Lyons-Marseilles axis, with the mushrooming of these towns and also Bordeaux and Toulouse. The low birth rate led to labour shortages in the towns which generated high rates of internal migration, which affected about a fifth of all families. By 1914 the share of the population living in towns over 2,000 was 44%.

Despite having colonies and a liberal emigration policy, France was a country

of net immigration. From the 1840s immigration grew at a magnitude comparable to Irish migration to Britain, beginning with a flow from the southern Flemish areas of Belgium that had been hard hit by the collapse of the linen industry, crop failures and famine that was later joined by English, German, Swiss, Spanish, Italian, Polish and Russian immigrants, concentrated especially in construction and services. In the mid 1880s there were about 500,000 Belgians living in France. Whereas in 1851 Belgians had made up one-third of all foreigners, by 1911 when foreigners were 3% of the population, more than one-third (400,000) came from Italy. There were very few immigrants from the French colonies in Africa whose numbers did not increase until after World War II. About 40% of all immigrant workers were employed in industry and without them (in contrast to Britain) the rise of French industry would have been impossible.

Between 1850 and 1910 only 2 million left France, at a rate of less than 0.5 emigrants per thousand (compared with 6 per thousand in England and 6.6 in Norway). About 20% went to the French colonies in North Africa, the Caribbean and the Far East, and the rest in roughly equal proportions to other European countries and other overseas destinations. As in England, the peak years of emigration were the 1880s, but there was no mass emigration because the agrarian base remained stable for longer and the population grew relatively slowly.

There was a long tradition of internal migration in France, stretching back well beyond the 18th century, especially of migration to the Paris basin from the poor mountainous regions in the Alps, Pyrenees, the Massif Central and the Jura mountains. Immigrants to France settled mainly in the border regions: in the industrial regions of the north and north-west and in the wine-growing region of the south. However, this long tradition of internal migration did not develop, as elsewhere, into mass emigration.

Despite the high level of immigration to France, there was relatively little anti-immigrant friction. Although tensions were particularly high after the loss of Alsace and Lorraine in the Franco-Prussian War of 1870–71, when Germans in France were the victims of some xenophobia, and in the

1880s when immigration grew by 13%, on the whole the government policy of integrating foreign workers was successful. Although there were frequent proposals to limit the rights of immigrants, the period of residence required for naturalisation was actually reduced from five to three years in 1889 and citizenship was granted to all children born in France, enabling even late-arriving Polish migrants to integrate without too much difficulty. Active recruitment of foreign workers only became necessary during and after the First World War.

Poster of the leading French shipping company Compagnie Générale Transatlantique 1935. The "CIE. GLE. TRANSATLANTIQUE" commonly named "Transat", known overseas as the French Line, was established in 1861 as an attempt to revive the French merchant marine. Its first vessel, the S.S. Washington, undertook her maiden voyage on the 15th of June 1864

The Netherlands

Between 1800 and 1914 the population of the Netherlands trebled, from about 2 million to 6 million. Industrialisation, starting later than in Britain but much earlier than in Germany, developed along the Lille-Liège-Rotterdam axis, making the Netherlands the most densely urbanised area of Europe with almost 80% living in towns over 2,000 in 1869 and 90% in 1914. However, the provinces of Gelderland, Overijssel and Drenthe remained areas of strong out-migration. An indication of the huge pulling power of the industrialising Ruhr area of Germany is that it even drew some Dutch agricultural workers, especially after 1870 to cities such as Oberhausen and Essen, so reversing the traditional direction of labour migration flows. In the late 1880s around 20,000 men and women per year in Limburg alone went to work in the western provinces of Prussia and Belgium.

Unlike France, there was a mass migration from the Netherlands to North America in the 19th century, even though the number of Dutch immigrants was barely perceptible compared to other groups. The overall ratio of transatlantic migrants to non-migrants in the Netherlands was 1:15. The curve of Dutch emigration paralleled that of German emigration, except in that the absolute peak year for the Netherlands was 1847 when the potato crop failed (the worst year of the Great Famine in Ireland). The stream of emigration from southern and south-western Germany seems to have acted as a stimulus to Dutch emigration.

Again we can see the pattern of overseas migration developing from earlier patterns. As the Netherlands became the leading trading country in Europe in the second half of the 17th century, it developed a tolerant approach to its immigrants but sent relatively few emigrants to settle in colonies all over the world founded by the Dutch East India Company (1602) and the Dutch west India Company (1621). In 1624 Dutch migrants established the colony of Nieuw Amsterdam, New Holland, later renamed New York City and State. When forced to give it up to the British in 1664, there were only about 10,000 Europeans living in New Holland as compared with 30,000 in New England.

Dutch immigrant women in Ellis Island in costumes of their native country, 1902

Relatively few of the settlers in the Dutch colonies were Dutch, recruitment having been more successful in Germany and Scandinavia during Holland's so-called "Golden Age" when the rural population could earn a relatively good living from the fertile fenlands and new land reclamation schemes had provided additional living space for the growing population. This happy situation, combined with a policy of religious toleration for a population divided about evenly between Catholics and Protestants, meant that there was little impulse for emigration to the other Dutch colonies in Borneo, Java, Celebes, Ceylon and Cape Town. While Rotterdam and Amsterdam were major ports of embarkation for overseas migration, few Dutch joined that flow. There was some migration to the areas of proto-industrialisaion and in the border areas the Netherlands drew in seasonal migrants from neighbouring countries, including the "Hollandgänger" from Germany.

Religious dissent played a part in getting Dutch migration going to North America. The surrender of New Holland in 1664 had brought Dutch emigration to

Belgian refugees during World War I on their arrival on Ellis Island

a stop but the Labadists founded, albeit unsuccessfully, a Christian commune in Maryland in 1683 and between 1683 and 1690 about 300 Dutch Mennonites (most of whom had already migrated in a first stage to Krefeld and the Palatinate) joined the group led by the German Franz Daniel Pastorius in founding Germantown in Pennsylvania. In the 19th century the Separatist religious community made up an unusually high proportion of the Dutch emigrants but their reasons for leaving were more economic than religious: inheritance laws had led (as in Ireland) to the formation of very small farms through subdivision, to the point that they were incapable of supporting families; the industrial sector could not absorb the growing population; and the failure of the potato harvest 1845–6 gave many the final push to emigrate. The Separatists tended to emigrate in large well-organised groups and developed chains that brought out further emigrants. Largely as a result of this, the small numbers of Dutch immigrants in the United States were even more concentrated than the Norwegians with 56 % living in only 18 of the 2,300 counties in 1870, mainly in Michigan, New York, Wisconsin, Iowa, Ohio, Illinois and New Jersey.

Belgium

Belgium was established in 1830 as a constitutional monarchy from part of the former Kingdom of the Netherlands. Between 1800 and 1914, its population more than doubled, from about 3 million to 7 million. The majority (60 %) lived in the northern, predominantly Flemish-speaking part but industrialisation began in areas of the relatively sparsely populated south that formed the northern end of the Lille-Liège-Rotterdam axis. This southern region drew in migrants from the agrarian north and beyond to the new coal mines, metal and textile industries and sugar refineries. By 1900 by far the densest railway network had been built in Belgium (43 km of track per 100 km² as compared with 19 km in the UK and 17 km in Germany). By 1850 there were almost 100,000 foreigners living in Belgium and 250,000 in 1914 – about 3 % of the total population, as in France and Germany. As in France, active recruitment of foreign workers only began after the First World War. However, in the second half of the 19th century, Belgium was not able to absorb all its available workers and it became a country of net emigration.

Belgium had a well-established tradition of seasonal migration beyond its borders, where the migrants who went to France as harvest hands or as navvies on the roads, canals and railways were known as Franschmans – French-speaking Walloons from the south finding this seasonal migration easier than the Flemish-speaking majority from the north. With the collapse of the Flemish linen industry in the 1840s, men and women moved to work in French fields and industries. Although Antwerp was a port of embarkation for thousands of other Europeans, especially southern Germans going to North America, most Belgian emigrants did not go overseas but to neighbouring countries, especially as we have seen to France, planning to stay a few years and then return.

Illustration from "Über Land und Meer. Allgemeine Illustrirte Zeitung", 1887

Luxembourg

The Luxembourg "cultural area" of Europe provides a good example of the ethnic and linguistic complexity of Europe in the 19th century and a reminder of how the country may not be the most appropriate unit of study for understanding migration. Since the establishment of Belgium in 1830 it comprises the independent state of the Grand Duchy of Luxembourg, the Luxembourg province of Belgium immediately to the west, and also small parts of the Netherlands, France and Germany where the Germanic language of Letzebuergisch or Luxembourgeois is spoken – an area today of about 3,000 square miles and about 1 million people. Luxembourgers usually appeared in national immigration and emigration statistics under the category of "other nationalities" or were lumped together with either French or German migrants on the basis of language.

The population of the Grand Duchy increased from 175,000 in 1839 to 210,000 in 1890. Before its industrial "take-off" in the 1870s, about 80 % of Luxembourgers were engaged in agriculture and 10 % of the population were reckoned to be in long-term poverty. Between 1870 and 1914 the rich "Minette" deposits in Luxembourg-Lorraine were developed to form one of the main iron-mining centres in Europe and the Grand Duchy became an industrial power whose annual iron and steel production ranked immediately after that of Britain, the United States, Germany, France, Russia and Belgium.

As Luxembourg industrialised, it was a country of both immigration and emigration as poor peasants who refused to work as miners or steelworkers preferred transatlantic migration. Between 1840 and 1890 about 70,000 Luxembourgers emigrated, most going to France and the United States. Outside Luxembourg, they tended to settle in Letzebuergisch-speaking areas, such as Thionville and Arlon, and also Bitburg and Trier. In the United States, where 30,000 settled between 1836 and 1888, they tended to concentrate in distinct settlements in Wisconsin (Belgium, Holy Cross and Port Washington), Iowa (Dubuque, Luxembourg and St. Donatus) and Minnesota (Rollingstone and St. Cloud). There was also a stream to South America and to Brazil and Argentina

The Science Fiction journal "Amazing Stories" was founded by immigrant Hugo Gernsback from Luxembourg, the first publication of this genre

"Homeless". Woodcut after a painting by A. Heyn, 1877. Already in 1822 the Brockhaus Encyclopedia stated that the final reason for people to emigrate was "the hopelessness that things will ever improve"

as well as in the Bohemia-Vienna-Budapest core of Austria-Hungary, leading to a strong contrast between industrial western and central Germany and the mixed agrarian-commercial regions of south-western Germany and agrarian Bavaria. The transition, from an agrarian state with a strong industrial sector to an industrial state with a strong agricultural base, "took-off" in the 1890s. In Prussia two-thirds of the population were living in the countryside as late as 1867 but by 1910 the rural-urban balance had been reversed with two-thirds then living in the towns.

By 1900, Germany (in contrast to Britain) had become a country of net immigration with one million foreign workers in 1914. In the decade before the First World War Germany was second only to the United States as "the greatest labour-importing country in the world'. In the peak years of 1816 and 1817 after the Napoleonic Wars, about 20,000 German-speaking people left for North America (while similar numbers left from Ireland) and then for a while numbers decreased, with only 3,000

in particular. In the two years between 1888 and 1890 enthusiasm for overseas migration, Argentinienfieber, took hold to the extent that more than a thousand (0.5 % of the total population) left for Argentina.

For most Luxembourgers the port of departure was Antwerp, close to the former Luxembourg province of Belgium and the western and southern parts of the Grand Duchy, from which came most of the emigrants of the 1840s. Overpopulation, partible inheritance, floods and crop failures, high taxes, and conscription into foreign armies (between 1845 and 1860 the main threat was from recently independent Belgium and between 1861 and 1875 from Germany) drove the emigration stream. As elsewhere, it was not usually the poorest of the rural population that left since overseas emigrants needed at least a few acres of land to finance the journey and for this reason the less fertile and upland region of Oesling in the northern half of Luxembourg hardly contributed any early settlers to the emigration stream.

The German-Speaking Countries

Before the unification of Germany in 1871, Prussia and Austria were the leading German-speaking countries of Europe but there were also 35 small and very small German states, similar to Luxembourg, numerous free cities, and several Swiss cantons where German was the official language. Despite their common language and many historical connections, there was, unlike Scandinavia, great political, economic, and religious diversity between them. Between 1800 and 1914 the population of the area that became Germany more than doubled, from about 25 million to 59 million, with the most remarkable growth in Prussia where the population increased from about 10 million to 40 million. In 1800 there were only two metropolitan centres, Berlin and Hamburg, but by 1914 there were 45. Between 1850 and 1910, for example, the Ruhr and Rhine cities of Essen and Düsseldorf grew from 9,000 and 27,000 to 295,000 and 359,000 respectively. Industrialisation developed along the Rhineland-Ruhr-Berlin-Saxony-Silesia axis,

At the emigrant agent's. Newspaper illustration after a painting by Austrian artist Hans Pöck. Probably 1880s

transatlantic emigrants leaving in 1820. However, from the 1830s it rose continuously with the United States accounting for almost 90 % of total German emigration, the rest going to Canada, Brazil, Argentina, Australia and South Africa. Between 1820 and 1879 about 3 million Germans went overseas, and by the end of the 19th century another 2 million had followed. In the peak years, including the 1880s, about a quarter of the total number of German emigrants came from west Prussia and Pomerania. After 1890 there was a marked decline in emigration due mainly to the rapidly increasing urbanisation of the Ruhr region and Saxony. Emigration from western Germany then virtually ceased and most migrants from east of the river Oder moved internally.

Three main phases of transatlantic emigration from the German-speaking regions can be distinguished. Before 1865, mainly independent peasants and artisans emigrated; they came for the most part from south-western and southern Germany and travelled in family groups. In the second phase, between 1865 and 1895, the rural poor of northern and north-eastern Germany began to leave home, and more and more of the emigrants left as individuals. In the third phase, from 1895 to the First World War, individual men and women emigrated from all parts of the German-speaking area. These migrants hoped to earn a living in America as workers or in domestic service in the cities, rural settlement being feasible then for only relatively few emigrants. After the Civil War, the Homestead Act (1864) still encouraged emigrants to settle on the land, but by the 1880s at the latest the available land had been taken, and America needed workers on the railroads and in the factories.

In this third phase, emigration to North America was paralleled by intensive rural-urban migration within Europe as landless peasants sought employment as factory workers in nearby cities, and young women took positions as domestic servants in urban middle-class households. In Austria, for example, Vienna had an attraction for the rural population much like that of North America with thousands migrating in from Bohemia, Moravia and Silesia. However, after the 1880s when the dream of one's own farm could not longer be realised in Germany or America and industrial work

in the United States was not much better-paid than that in Germany, there was an industrial boom in the German cities in the 1890s that lasted until the First World War. This attracted landless workers from north-eastern Germany to the extent that out-migration from these agricultural areas left acute labour shortages. The drop in grain prices and increasing mechanization of agriculture had led many of the large landholders to switch to sugar beets as their primary crop. The introduction of this labour-intensive crop stimulated new seasonal migration patterns such as the Sachsengängerei ("going to Saxony") with Russians and Galician Poles being recruited and soon agriculture could not function without them. Poles were also recruited to the industrial cities of the Rhineland and especially in the Ruhr, but they came mainly from the Prussian part of Poland and so could not be treated as foreigners. The situation was similar in most large European cities. Many of the young independent jobseekers attracted to them later moved on

to the United States, joining others who had decided to go there directly, perhaps in the hope that in America they could avoid what many considered a downward step into the life of a factory worker.

The roots of German transatlantic migration went back beyond the 18th century and were entangled with Europe's internal migration patterns. We have already referred to the long-established North Sea system of seasonal migration that in 1800 still saw large numbers of Hollandgänger moving annually from northern and western Germany to the Netherlands to engage in peat cutting or harvest work but there were also long-established patterns of migration into Germany. As early as 1600, for example, almost 40 % of the population of Frankfurt am Main was made up of "foreigners". Of about 20,000 inhabitants, several thousand were journeymen; about 3,000 were Protestants who had left the Spanish Netherlands for religious reasons, and about 2,500 were Jews, living in a ghetto under varying degrees of tolerance. These

Caricature (title: Causes for Emigration, lithograph by W. Stock, about 1849), characterising the relationship between the authorities and poor peasantry: "Bailiff: 'But, folks, is there nothing that can make you stay!' Old peasant: 'Oh, yes, if you leave, then we'll stay'"

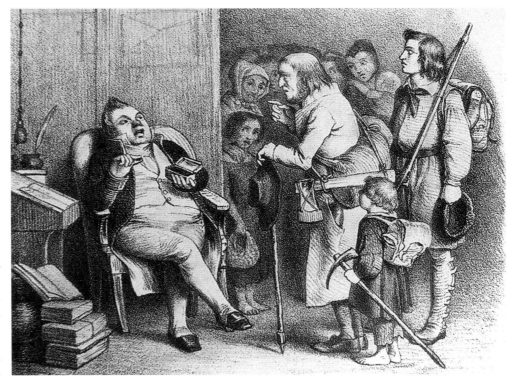

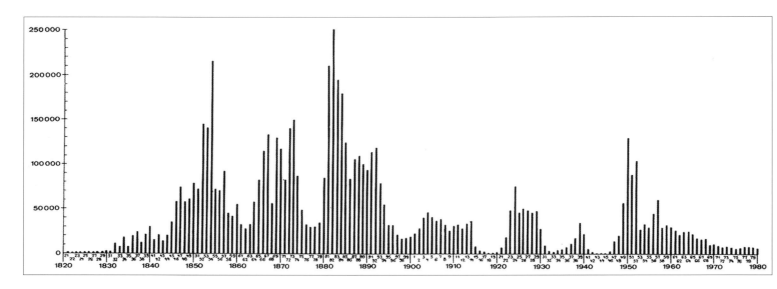

German Immigration to the United States from 1820 to 1980

earlier migration movements had resulted from either force of some kind, expulsion by government authority, or economic recruiting campaigns and voluntary, individual decisions had only rarely played a role. Along with the Dutch Protestants already mentioned who fled to Germany from the Netherlands to escape persecution by the Spanish Catholic authorities, also important to the economy were the 500,000 Huguenots who arrived from France, expelled after

the revocation of the Edict of Nantes in 1685. Many of them were skilled craftsmen or merchants and were welcomed in the German states and cities. The same was true of the 20,000 Austrian Protestants who settled in east Prussia, having been expelled by the archbishop of Salzburg in 1731, many of them later to emigrate to North America. Group migration driven by religious intolerance had played an important role throughout the 17th and 18th centuries and even

into the early 19th century. What changed in the middle of the 19th century was the collapse of the agrarian North Sea System centred on the Netherlands and its replacement by a system based on migration east to the industrialising Ruhr area of Prussia.

In south-western and southern Gemany, the effects of strong population growth and the economic problems of the subdivision of land to the point that farms became "dwarf farms" (Zwergwirtschaften) were strongly evident in the 18th century. At the end of the 18th and beginning of the 19th century, the poorest peasants were granted the status of free men, but this led to increasing indebtedness: for many peasants the payments owed to the landowners in the place of the feudal obligations were so burdensome that any failed harvest or economic crisis could force peasants to give up their farms. Also related to the emancipation of the peasants was the enclosure of common land (Allmenden). The loss of grazing rights that this entailed put further pressure on poorer farmers, especially those closest to the poverty line. At the same time, the newly granted freedom to practice the trade of one's choice and the strict protective-tariff policies adopted by many governments made many craftsmen economically insecure as well. There seemed to be little economic chances left for such people, or for farmers who had already lost their land or were faced with

Hessian handloom weaver, painting by J.H. Hasselhorst, about 1865

Emigrant's Joys in America – Emigrant's Sufferings in America; Neu-Ruppinger Bilderbogen, ca. 1839, also published in "Fliegende Blätter", a humorous, richly illustrated weekly, which appeared in Munich from 1844 to 1944

inevitable impoverishment, and for artisans who were experiencing or who foresaw an economic crisis due to increased competition or a loss of buying power among the general population. For them emigration, within Europe or beyond, seemed a realistic alternative to impending poverty. So such German-speaking areas of the southwest and the south proved fertile recruiting grounds for those seeking settlers for eastern Europe and for North America. The first large-scale transatlantic emigration movements were from the Palatinate in 1709 (some of whom migrated in stages via Britain and Ireland), from Württemberg in 1717, and from Baden in 1737. From these areas, and later from the Austrian provinces of the western Tyrol and Vorarlberg and the infertile parts of Switzerland the emigrants had a good travell route along the Rhine to the ports of Antwerp, Rotterdam and Amsterdam. In the 18th century at least 125,000 German emigrants had settled in North America, with about 17,000 of those who had fought on the British side in the American War of Independence staying on after the American Revolution.

Deteriorating demographic and economic conditions gradually caused mass transatlantic emigration to spread to other regions of Germany, from the south to north. In Rhine-Hesse and the areas west of the Rhine, the introduction of partible inheritance had come later, as part of the French Code Civil during the Napoleonic occupation and this had meant that the rapid population growth of the period had not lead to widespread poverty as quickly as in the pioneer regions of mass migration.

There was also more industrial development, beginning as early as the 1850s, which had been able to absorb at least some of the landless rural population and so substantial transatlantic emigration from this area did not begin until the middle of the 19th century and remained relatively small.

In Bavaria east of the Rhine, in Tyrol and Salzburg, and in north-western Germany, impartible inheritance was the rule, so that farms were inherited intact. There the typical farm was larger, and members of the sub-peasant class could get by working as farm hands, although they usually needed

supplementary income of some kind (for example, from domestic work in the textile industry or, in north-western Germany, from seasonal work in Dutch brickworks). However, the cottage textile industry was soon unable to compete with cheap imported English manufactured goods, and after the division of the Netherlands in 1830 seasonal migration to Dutch factory jobs dropped sharply, and was completely forbidden by the Dutch government a few years later. In this situation, day labourers, farm hands, and non-inheriting children of farmers – those who owned no land and had no chance to earn any supplementary income – saw themselves forced to emigrate.

Conditions were different again in Schleswig-Holstein, Mecklenburg, and Prussia east of the Elbe, where peasants were dependents of a very small number of estate owners. In Schleswig-Holstein peasants had held their farms under inheritable leases since the 18th century and were for the most part exempt from performing feudal services. Extensive development of the land made it possible to absorb the surplus population for a relatively long time and therefore transatlantic emigration from the area began late and did not reach significant proportions. In Mecklenburg, by contrast, there were hardly any free peasants, most of the rural population being made up of day-labourers and domestic servants working on a small number of large estates. They were without hope of buying land and did not even own their own homes, receiving instead temporary leases from the estate owners. It was the responsibility of the landlords to care for the poor, but this duty was also dependent on residence and landlords could block marriages by denying the right to a homestead, since marriage without proof of a legal residence was not permitted. The peasants' near absolute dependence and above all the absence of any prospect of circumstances changing led to massive emigration of the rural population around 1850.

In Prussia east of the Elbe, there was a sharp increase in population during the first half of the 19th century, but it was for the most part absorbed by the rising need for workers as a result of liberal agricultural reforms. In the 1850s, Polish agricultural workers were even recruited on a seasonal

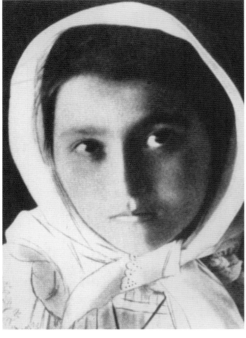

Above left: A Swiss Girl. This picture of a Swiss immigrant girl dates from about 1905. More than 1,000 immigrants from Switzerland passed through Ellis Island

Above right: A Girl of Alsace. Dressed in the costume distinctive to her province, at the time of her emigration Alsace was a part of Germany's Kaiserreich. Most notable is her elegant headdress, which is characteristically Alsatian

Below left: A Swedish Girl. Her conical hat and the style and design of her dress reveal her origin as from Rättvik in the province of Dalarna, in west-central Sweden

Below right: A Scottish lad and lasses, with their kilts and adornments. These three are probably siblings

basis, much as Irish workers had been in Britain. The situation changed in the 1860s and 1870s as population pressure increased even more. There was a severe general crisis in agriculture in the 1870s and 1880s due to cheap grain imports from an expanding European market and from overseas. Structural poverty in the rural underclass in these regions soon led to transatlantic emigration, as it did for similar reasons in the German-speaking cantons of Switzerland where farming in the fertile valleys had become unprofitable.

Switzerland was one country where emigration received particular official encouragement in the form of foreign military service since it generated a significant income. A kind of "enlistment fever" led to about 80,000 young men being abroad as mercenaries each year. In the 1880s Switzerland became a country of net immigration with in-migration mainly to construction, textiles, trade, tourism and domestic service. By 1914 almost 15% of the total population of about 4 million were foreigners (80% Germans and Italians) as compared with 3% in France and Belgium and 2% in Germany.

With the advance of industrialisation and the descent of many artisans and small businessmen into the urban lower classes, the character of emigration from the entire German-speaking region changed at the end of the 19th century. Fewer family groups and more single individuals were leaving, including increasing numbers of single women. The advent of the steamship meant that, as Europe, emigrants no longer saw transatlantic emigration as a final irreversible decision, but rather as a sort of extended seasonal migration. In the long-distance east-west migration of Poles from east Prussia, Gelsenkirchen functioned as a kind of "New York" for new arrivals who went straight to "their" districts in the city's cultural mix and "their" plants of the coal and steel industry.

Like other European countries, all of the German-speaking areas still had more or less strictly enforced bans on emigration in the early 19th century. Nevertheless, there had always been some migration within countries, within Europe and to some extent even overseas. An early example of regulation was that of the internal European migration of journeymen by

Paintig by Benjamin Blessum from 1914, titled: "Restauration forlater Stavanger 5. juli 1825" "Restauration" sails from Stavanger July 5, 1825). First in a series of three paintings commissioned specially for the exhibition "Emigrated Norway", held in Oslo during the summer of 1914 in connection with the centennial of the Norwegian constitution. The sailing of the "Restauration" in 1825 is generally taken to date the beginning of organised Norwegian emigration to America

languages, with the exception of Finnish were mutually comprehensible, at least at a basic level. There were well developed patterns of internal migration and emigration to neighbouring countries as well as movement from the land to the small regional towns. Despite restrictive emigration policies (enforced more loosely, as in Germany after about 1840), migrants from the Scandinavian countries had been attracted to the towns and countryside of the Netherlands, and also to London, Hamburg, and St Petersburg, since the 16th century. In the 19th century, internal migration connected the Scandinavian countries as Norwegians sought work in the iron industry of Sweden and on the large estates of Denmark and northern Germany, where many Swedes were also employed. Swedes also took jobs in Norwegian fisheries or as workers in the Lübeck area, and Swedish domestic maids found positions in Hamburg and Copenhagen. Finns moved from the countryside to Turku and Helsinki, but they also joined the fishing fleets of Norway or Russia, or became workers in St. Petersburg or in the Swedish woodworking industry.

trade guilds that required travell as part of the professional qualification process. Journeymen had to travell for two or three years, and for this purpose they received from the authorities a "Wanderbuch" which was also valid as a passport. Every master was obliged to take a journeyman into his shop for a certain period or, if this was impossible, to give him expense money to travell on to the next town. In this way the journeymen helped spread technical knowledge all over Europe, along with information about the living conditions and job opportunities in other areas. Thousands of other people were encouraged to leave home by recruiters working for foreign governments. Highly skilled craftsmen were especially sought after at European courts – so much so that many states enacted strict bans on emigration for these occupations. Also active, for the most part illegally, were military recruiters; they were also subjected to especially close control by the authorities. An extension of this kind of migration in the late 19th century was that of skilled workers in the wine industry moving from southern

Germany to Argentina. At the same time, Prussia (in contrast to France) enacted anti-Polish immigration and labour policies, despite pressures from industry and large landowners who desperately needed foreign labour. This security policy, concerned with Polish nationalism and the possible threat of a resurrected Polish state (uniting the Poles of eastern Germany, Austria and Russia), was continued after the First World War, its consequences for integration being felt even to the present.

Scandinavia

Although the political configuration of the Scandinavian countries (Norway, Sweden, Denmark, Finland and Iceland) was considerably adjusted in 1815 by the Congress of Vienna, the economy of the whole area remained based on farming, fishing and timber. Most of the population were Protestant and most of their

Clang Peerson, leader of the first Norwegian Quaker emigrant group leaving Norway on the "Restauration" in 1825

Reapers in the fields of an estate in Lolland, Denmark, about 1880. These people were hired for the harvest season only

Scandinavian historians in studying changing patterns of migration in relation to the development of towns have been to the fore in pioneering the concept of "urban influence fields" and analysis of the forces operating between towns and their hinterlands, particularly those of Bergen and Oslo (Norway), Stockholm, Göteborg, Malmö and Norrköping (Sweden), Copenhagen (Denmark) and Helsinki, Tampere and Turku (Finland). As elsewhere in western Europe, long-established patterns of internal migration became extended to transatlantic migration, although much later than in Britain and Ireland and Germany. Apart from a small group of Swedes and Swedish Finns from Värmland who founded the successful colony of New Sweden in Delaware in 1638, and some Norwegian and Finnish sailors who jumped ship in American ports, there was no significant Scandinavian transatlantic migration before the 19th century. However, between 1800 and 1914 there were about 2 million emigrants from Scandinavia with the peak period between 1880 and 1900, except for Finland, where the transatlantic pattern more resembled that of eastern Europe than the other Nordic countries. As elsewhere also throughout the 19th century, agricultural workers with little prospect of advancement, tenant farmers in danger of losing their land, and non-inheriting farmers' sons made up the greater part of the migrants to America. Land ownership was generally very important in the farming communities of Scandinavia as the main way of providing for economic security and an opportunity for advancement. For this reason family emigration with the aim of homesteading remained dominant for much longer in Scandinavia than in other European countries. As in Scotland, Scandinavian overseas emigrants were most likely to come from the highlands and islands, especially the highlands of south-central Norway and south-central Sweden and the Danish islands of Bornholm and Lolland-Falster and the Öland Islands. Only after 1880 did a gradual structural change set in as the number of unmarried single male and female migrants under the age of 25 increased, who were usually well informed about conditions in the American labour market and sought wage work in cities on the east Coast. They too came mainly from the country but had often travelled first to a Scandinavian city to look for work and this step migration was especially typical of young women, again demonstrating the link between internal and overseas migration. With the shift from sail to steam in the 1860s, improvements in the rail and ship transportation network led to an increase in the rate of return migration. There were years of economic decline in the United States like 1894 and 1898 when return migration suddenly shot up to 70 % of the emigration rate, showing how quickly labour migrants were able react to unfavourable changes in economic conditions. Return migration also played an important part in the "American fever" that swept parts of Norway and Sweden in the 1850s and 1860s that had a multiplier effect on emigration and the Scandinavian rate of return overall remained comparatively low at about 20 %.

Norwegian emigration from 1846 to 1930

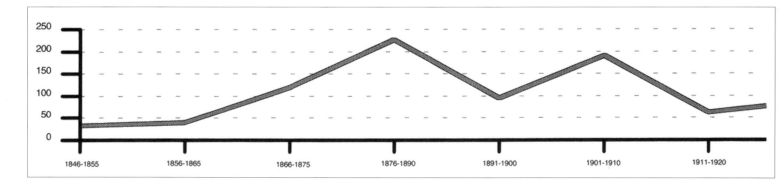

Norway

The population of Norway more than doubled between 1800 and 1914, from just under 1 million to almost 2.5 million. Three-quarters of the land was agriculturally worthless and even the cultivated land was heavily forested. Nevertheless, as late as 1865 about two-thirds of the population lived from farming or the timber industry, with 15 % engaged in mining and industry and the rest of the employed population divided among fishing, commerce and shipping and only 15 % living in towns. This pattern changed only slowly as industrialisation got under way in the second half of the 19th century mainly in wood- and metal-working, so that by 1900 just under 50 % of the population were still engaged in agriculture, with only 28 % living in towns and 23 % engaged in mining and industry. In the second half of the 19th century Norwegians were the most likely overseas European migrants with an annual average of about 6.5 persons per thousand, and the census of 1920 showed in some parts that as many as one adult male in four had spent some time in the United States.

The transatlantic movement from Norway, almost exclusively to North America, began with the sailing in 1825 of the iconic ship Restauration from Stavanger to New York with 52 people on board. It grew to a steady stream by the 1850s, spread to Sweden and Denmark about ten years later, and reached Finland in the 1880s.

Although serfdom had been abolished in Scandinavia since the 18th century, in many cases the farmers' political position did not match their economic importance.

The strongest and most independent groups were the so-called bonder, who in 1845 made up 58 % of the total population. With the right to vote and after 1837 some local autonomy, they formed a kind of peasant aristocracy. As in Ireland and in southern Germany however, repeated sub-division of land in many parts of Norway had produced "dwarf farms". As a result, the number of farmsteads grew from about 79,000 in 1800 to more than 135,000 in 1860, with the biggest jump between 1820 and 1845 (from about 93,600 to almost 113,000) – only a very small part of the increase was the result of clearing previously uncultivated land. The number of dependent farmers, day labourers, tenant farmers, and hired hands also grew rapidly, rising by almost a third between 1825 and 1855 from 49,000 to 65,000.

Since most Norwegian districts were very isolated, migration was difficult, and more and more of the nominally free farmers became economically dependent on large landowners. Nevertheless, of all the Scandinavian countries Norway had the earliest and strongest emigration relative to its population density. In 1825, the pioneer group of 50 Quakers and Pietists on the Restauration, led by Cleng Peerson, had settled near Rochester, New York. The motive for their emigration was mainly the intolerance of the official Norwegian Lutheran church, but economic considerations also played a role. Although only a few other Norwegians followed them across the Atlantic in the next ten years, this first Norwegian settlement in North America marked the beginning of an ever-increasing movement. Only 300 emigrated in 1840, but through the crisis years of the 1840s, during which Ireland and other parts of Europe were so badly affected, the number increased and in 1849 there were 1,600 emigrants. These pioneer migrants often belonged to organised groups, sometimes under leaders like Peerson who had made the transatlantic journey several times and were consciously setting up and maintaining a chain migration process.

The first wave of mass migration from Norway was between 1856 and 1865, with almost 40,000 emigrants going to the United States. In the following decade the number of emigrants rose to 120,000. By 1900 320,000 more had gone, including 106,000 in the peak years between 1880 and 1885 (many driven by the failure of the potato crop in 1883 which led to a serious famine). Between 1900 and 1914, a further 235,000 Norwegians left. The large majority went to the United States and Canada with hardly any going to other non-European countries. Notwithstanding mutual comprehensibility at a basic level between most speakers of the Scandinavian languages, the geographic isolation of many Norwegian districts resulted in the development of particular traditions and dialects which stood in the way of communication with Norwegians from other areas and for this reason their preference in settling in the United States was often to stay close to people from the same region. As late as 1910, 70 % of Norwegian immigrants in the United States were found in only six states: Wisconsin, Illinois, Iowa, Minnesota and the Dakotas.

Sweden

In Sweden the population rose by more than 10 % per year between 1815 and 1865, from almost 3 million to 4 million. As late as 1870, the proportion of the population engaged in farming, the timber industry and fishing was 72 % with only 13 % engaged in coal and iron-based industries or trades and about 5 % each in commerce and transportation, government jobs, and domestic service in the towns. In 1850 there were only four towns with populations greater than 10,000 (Norrköpping, Karlskrona, Gothenburg and Stockholm).

Emigrant agent from Frankfurt, Michigan, advertising in Sweden. Oelrichs & Co in New York was an agent of Norddeutsche Lloyd, Bremen, associates were Edwin Oelrichs and his brothers

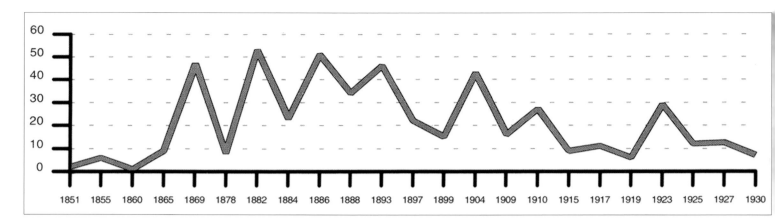

Swedish emigration from 1851 to 1930

The proportion living in towns in 1800 was 10 % and by 1900 this had only increased to 15 %. The exploitation of one of Europe's most important deposits of iron in northern Sweden and the gradual development of industry, mainly in metal-working, helped bring about a further increase in the proportion living in towns to 26 % by 1914. This was reflected by the fact that although Belgium had the densest railway network, by 1900 Sweden had made by far the most extensive network (27 km per 10,000 inhabitants as compared with 12 km in Belgium). Nevertheless, the economy was still predominantly agricultural with over two-thirds still living in the countryside. A study of Västnorrland had shown that returnees were disproportionately destined for rural areas and mostly for their original home areas, despite the fact that Sweden was becoming urbanised. Like temporary migrants over the centuries, many Swedish used migration as a way of staying on the land and returning to move up the social ladder.

The long-established tradition of inheritance of land by the eldest son was reformed in 1827 when the division of farms was legalised. As elsewhere, small subsistence-level farms were pushed to the limits of viability with the result that large parts of the rural population became wage earners as day labourers. In 1860, almost 50 % of the male population of Sweden belonged to this lowest social class. The transatlantic movement to North America, which had begun in Norway in 1825 and

grown to a steady stream by the 1850s had spread to Sweden and Denmark by the 1860s, and Finland by the 1880s. The iconic start of Swedish emigration to the United States was made in 1845 by a group of 25 (out of a total of 65) that went to Iowa and founded the settlement of "New Sweden" that attracted hundreds of others in the following decades. The desire to own their own farms was the main motive for most of these people. Many other Swedes left home because of conflict with the strict and authoritarian Swedish Lutheran church as the

number of independent churches grew rapidly in the 1840s and 1850s. About 14,500 people left Sweden before 1854, and only about 4,000 more followed in the next five years – a temporary decrease related to economic crisis in the United States. The dream of owning land, encouraged by the Homestead Act of 1864 in the United States, and crop failures in Sweden leading to famine in 1867 and 1868 led to a sharp increase in numbers leaving. Between 1868 and 1873, as the American economy recovered, 103,000 emigrants left for America, 32,000 in 1869 alone.

A day labourer in front of his cottage (photograph about 1880). During the 1850s there were around 150,000 farmhands in service. The meagre wages offered no possibility of buying one's own land. On top of this the work was hard and the labourers were subject to domestic discipline. The master had the right to punish his servants if he thought it necessary

Some of them became involved in the famous example of assisted migration by which railroad companies attempted in the 1860s and 1870s to divert Swedes from Iowa to settle them in northern Minnesota. The peak period came between 1879 and 1893 when almost 500,000 emigrated, with an absolute peak in 1887 of 46,500. Most were single males and females rather than farming family groups, seeking jobs in the construction industry and in factories. Although the United States remained the main destination, smaller flows of emigrants in these years headed for Latin America, mainly Brazil, and, as the search for land continued, Canada became a more important destination.

Denmark

The population of Denmark tripled between 1800 and 1914 from about 1 million to 3 million. Like Sweden, about 70 % of the population were still living in the countryside in 1900 and the pace of industrialisation was similarly slow. However, by 1914 Denmark had a higher proportion living in towns (40 %), mainly around Copenhagen and due in part to in-migration of north Germans, Swedes and Poles. Danish farms were typically large and subdivision was prevented by the introduction of a minimum legal size for farms in 1819. The large estates had long specialised in labour-intensive grain production, providing employment for many tenant farmers and day labourers. Then a widespread shift from grain to dairying and cattle-raising between the 1860s and 1880s helped Denmark withstand the agricultural crisis which struck many European countries when cheap imported grain, mainly from the United States, flooded the market. Although this type of agriculture also required many workers, they could more easily be replaced by machines. Until 1866, only landowners had real political rights in Denmark. The struggle for parliamentary democracy resulted in landless day labourers and tenant farmers getting the right to vote but many felt intimidated because of their high economic dependency on conservative estate owners who feared the growth of the liberal party. Male and female farm workers in general were poorly paid and servants, still without voting rights, were required to carry a certificate of good conduct from their employers and the government also imposed restrictions on freedom of movement. With no alternative employment available, non-inheriting sons and daughters of small farmers had to take work as farm hands and domestic servants. Added to this was the pressure of new Germanisation policies in Schleswig after 1864 that required use of the German language and service in the Prussian army. For many, escape from such conditions of dependency seemed only possible through emigration.

The transatlantic movement to North America got underway in Denmark in the 1850s. Settler migration still accounted for half of all emigration in 1870 and for 25 % in 1890. Before the First World War the emigration rate from Denmark was 2.8 per thousand (compared with 10.8 for Italy and 0.1 for France).

Iceland

Following the division of Denmark-Norway into the separate kingdoms of Norway and Denmark in 1815, Iceland remained a Danish dependency. Its population grew from about 40,000 in 1800 to 60,000 in 1850. Mass emigration in the second half of the 19th century, mainly to Canada, was caused by deterioration in the island's climate and, as elsewhere, population pressure on limited agricultural resources. In the 20th century the population increased, reaching 313,000 in 2007.

Finland

Between 1800 and 1914 the population of Finland (like Denmark) tripled from about 1 million to 3 million. Unlike Norway, Sweden and Denmark, there was virtually no industrial development in Finland before 1914 and the economy remained based on farming, timber, fishing and shipping. Apart from Helsinki, there were only small regional capitals like Viipuri (Vyborg), Pori and Jyväsklä. In Finland, as well as Sweden, laws governing the inheritance of land led to a rapid rise in the landless rural population in the first half of the 19th century. Since there was no industry to absorb the non-inheriting children of farmers, this social problem was an important motive for emigration which got underway in the 1880s. About one-third of all Finnish emigrants came from the one province of southern Ostrobothnia (the area around Seinäjoki).

Conclusion

The diversity of the picture that emerges of West, Central and northern Europe is so great that there may be a danger of it obscuring the fundamentally common, shared process of mass emigration. For example, the relationship of emigration to industrialisation and urbanisation in England and Scotland, where emigration increased as the country became more urban and urbanised, was opposite to that of Germany. Although the German economy

Finnish emigrant family at Ellis Island, 1900

Letter from America (1875), James Brenan, Crawford Municipal Art Gallery, Cork. Brenan's painting suggests a representative narrative. The envelope of the letter from America, possibly from a relative, lies on the corner of the table. The father sits, holding in his left hand the pre-paid ticket that has arrived, possibly from Five Points, New York City. He listens intently as his younger, barefoot daughter reads. The family group is framed between the pot of potatoes on the left (a reminder of the Great Famine) and the open door, leading to the railway station and port
James Brenan (1837–1907) was an internal migrant from Cork, where he was head of the Cork School of Art, to Dublin, where he was head of the Dublin Metropolitan School of Art

was growing faster than the British in the late 19th century and so jobs in the urban areas in Germany were created at a faster rate, this does not seem to be the explanation. Earlier patterns and "chains" were still exerting pressure on migration and in England in a way that led to emigration being perceived by many as more attractive than internal migration, even when the additional risk and cost was taken into account. England's early industrial development of course made it a special case: in 1900 only 12% of its population was engaged in agriculture compared with 40% in Germany (having dropped from 75% in thirty years) and 37% in the United States. We also need to take into account the other special cases, including France with its extremely low population growth and Ireland with its extremely high rate of female emigration.

Diversity is also indicated by the "iconic" moments that mark the origins of the modern tradition of overseas migration from these countries, such as England's "Pilgrim Fathers", Ireland's "Flight of the Earls (1607) and Norway's "Restauration" (1825). One way of interpreting this diversity is to see the mass emigration from Europe in the 19th as a series of waves, but following Klaus Bade we may also see it as series of fluctuations of "one large emigration wave" that was interrupted by various obstacles such as the American Civil War. All the countries of west, central and northern Europe eventually shared in creating and sustaining the transnational network that brought emigrants to the great ports of embarkation such as Liverpool, Hamburg and Bremerhaven, and they all participated in the shift from migration that was predominantly in family groups to predominantly individual migration. There was to be no such "folk" or family group stage in the later migration from the countries of southern and eastern Europe that became dominant in the first decade of the 20th century. By then the large share of German emigrants in the flow to the New World had shrunk to about 2%, with West, Central and northern Europe as a whole accounting for only a third, while the rest came from southern Europe (40%), and eastern, eastern-central and south-eastern Europe (25%).

References

Bade, Klaus, J. (2003), Migration in European History, Blackwell, Oxford

Baines, Dudley (1991), Emigration from Europe 1815–1930, Cambridge University Press, Cambridge

Barton, H. Arnold (1994), A Folk Divided: Homeland Swedes and Swedish Americans, 1840–1940, southern Illinois University Press, Carbondale

Beibom, Ulf (ed) (1993), Swedes in America: New Perspectives, Swedish Emigrant Institute, Vaxjö

Norman Davies (1996), Europe: A History, Pimlico

Harper, Marjory (2003), Adventurers and Exiles: The Great Scottish Exodus, Profile Books, London

Harper, Marjory (ed.) (2006), Emigrant Homecomings: The Return Movement of Emigrants, 1600–2000, Manchester University Press

Hatton, Timothy, J. and Williamson, Jeffrey G. (2005), Global Migration and the World Economy, MIT Press, Cambridge, Massachusetts

Hoerder, Dirk and Page Moch, Leslie (eds) (1996), European Migrants: Global and Local Perspectives, Northeastern University Press, Boston

Larsen, Birgit Flemming and Bender, Henning (eds) (1992), Danish Emigration to the U.S.A., Danes Worldwide Archives, Aalborg

Manning, Patrick (2005), Migration in World History, Routledge, New York

Page Moch, Leslie (1992, 2003), Moving Europeans: Migration in western Society since 1650, Indiana University Press

Richards, Eric (2004), Britannia's Children: Emigration from England, Scotland, Wales and Ireland since 1600, Hambledon and London, London and New York

Semmingsen, Ingrid (1978), Norway to America: A History of the Migration, University of Minnesota Press, Minneapolis

Wey, Claude (2003), "Luxembourgers in Latin America and the permanent threat of failure', Journal of the Association of European Migration Institutions, Vol. 1, 94–105

Wyman, Mark (1993), Round-Trip To America: The Immigrants Return to Europe, 1880–1930, Cornell University Press, Ithaca

Ticket of the Hamburg-Amerikanische Packetfahrt-Actiengesellschaft (HAPAG)

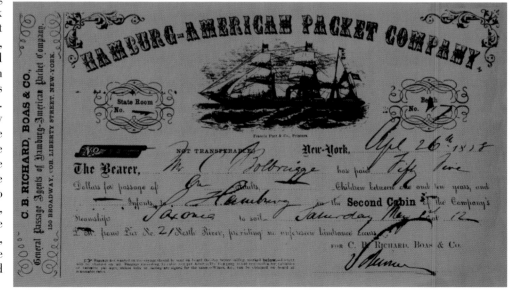

This photo from around 1895 shows the author's great grandfather, Ernst Heinrich Kamphoefner, and his wife Klara Elsabein, née Rölkers, both almost 80 years old. They are seen together with their daughter and son-in-law Theilmann and their grandchild in front of the log cabin which (with extensions and improvements) was their home throughout their lives in America

Walter Kamphoefner

From Tenant to Farm Owner:
The Life of Ernst Heinrich Kamphoefner –
One German-American Story Among Many

Ernst Heinrich Kamphoefner and his family were quite undistinguished, but also quite typical immigrants of the mid 19th century. The only surviving document in his own hand is a naturalization petition in shaky German script, so much of his life story has to be pieced together from entries in parish registers and census documents. One thing can be said for certain: the precarious economic situation of his family played a major role in their decision to emigrate.

The first thing that one notices about the Kamphoefner family is their geographical mobility, or better said, instability. But until their journey across the Atlantic, they never got very far, literally or figuratively. The family had no deep roots in the area of Melle and Buer—or maybe they did after all. Ernst Heinrich and all of his siblings were born in the Bauernschaft or neighborhood of Düingdorf in the parish of Buer, which borders on the parish of Melle. All the church records list their parents as Heuerleute (tenant farmers), but the mother is also listed once as a spinner, which indicates that they followed the traditional side occupation of the rural poor of the region, linen weaving. But Ernst's father, Johann Heirich Kamphöfener (as the name was written then), was born on March 7, 1781 in Ennigloh near Bünde, a dozen km eastward in Prussian Westfalia. Perhaps he came as a young farmhand to Buer, for he was married there on October 13, 1809, to Maria Elsabein Stamm, a native of Düingdorf born on January 14, 1781. Johann and Maria died in 1834 and 1837, only 53 and 55 years old respectively, before any of their children had emigrated. Also in the previous generation, there is evidence of local mobility: Johann Heinrich's parents were Caspar Heinrich Kamphöfener, (1742–1805), who died in Neuenkirchen near Melle. His wife, Anna Luise Wreden, was born in 1741 and died in 1803 in Gevinghausen near Bünde.

By the time Ernst Kamphoefner and his brothers started thinking about emigration, America was no longer terra incognita. Families from the vicinity of Melle had arrived in Missouri by 1835, and the settlement had experienced a rapid influx in 1839 with the arrival of what I have designated the "New Melle Mayflower," actually the bark "Alexander," with some 20 families totaling 70 persons, who were among the founders of a transplanted village called New Melle, Missouri. In 1842 there was another huge wave of emigration from Melle and Buer, with many emigrants bound for Missouri and others for Cincinnati, Ohio, or to nearby areas of Indiana.

The weekly German-language county paper, the St. Charles Demokrat, reported on Sept. 14, 1857 about New Melle:

The name is taken from the Hannoverian town of Melle, the area from which most of the inhabitants in and around New Melle immigrated. [...] The settlement in the area started in 1838, and within a few years, the whole area which up to then had been uninhabited was taken up by settlers. A church and school were soon established and a teacher supported. A few years ago, part of the congregation's land where the church stands was laid out in lots. Last year it got a Post Office, [...] with mail delivery three times per week. [...] The land in the vicinity is second class, but lies fairly level, which has the advantage for farmers that it can be easily improved. [...] The settlement consists almost exclusively of North Germans. The diligence and thrift of the inhabitants has made it, despite the stepmotherly treatment of nature, into a thriving settlement.

The immigration from "Old" to New Melle was so intense that 70% of the Germans in this village and surrounding Calloway Township (a land unit about 10 x 10 km), nearly 300 people by 1860, were natives of the Kingdom of Hannover, the great majority of them from Melle and vicinity.

But New Melle was not the only destination for emigrants from Melle, as the following example shows. The first in the Kamphoefner family to emigrate was Johann Heinrich, born in 1815, who in 1842 set out not for Missouri but for Indiana. His journey to America and through life are well documented. In the Osnabrück archives it is reported that he obtained a six month furlough from the army of Hannover in order to get married. His wife requested and obtained an emigration permit on July 14, 1842, with the provision that "Husband: Kampfhöfener, Johann Heinrich, is not coming along. Her husband must remain behind until he has completed his military service." But a different story is told by the passenger lists, and by a joint obituary of the couple, who both died within nine days of each other in 1895. They arrived together in Baltimore on October 10, 1842, on the ship "Ann," and after a brief sojourn in New York and Cincinnati, they settled on a farm in the village of Farmer's Retreat, Indiana, near Cincinnati, along with many other former neighbors from Buer.

Five generations later, it is impossible to say how much contact these Kamphoefners had with their other siblings, but when brother Ernst Heinrich set out for America two years later, his destination was New Melle, Missouri. Two more brothers followed him there. Finally in 1866, Johann Heinrich and his whole family moved from Indiana to Missouri, but we do not know what role the other siblings played in the move, or whether they were even still in contact by then. One thing that speaks against this is the fact that they settled in an entirely different area of the state, Waldron in Platte County on the western border of Missouri near Kansas City, whereas the other Kamphoefners lived in and around New Melle, St. Charles County, on the eastern edge of the state near St. Louis. Johann and his family spelled their

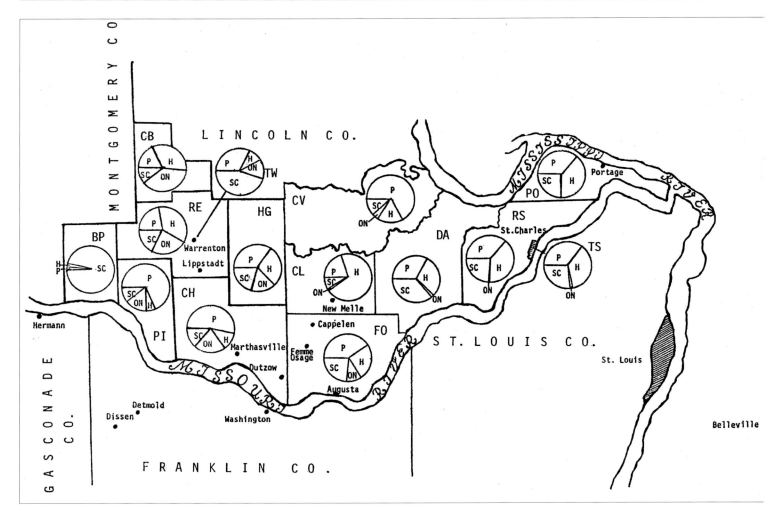

Areas settled by emigrants from Melle and Cappeln

name Kamphefner, and some of their descendants still live in the immediate vicinity of Kansas City.

Ernst Heinrich was thus the second brother to emigrate. He applied for permission on August 11, 1844, the same day that the farm owner Johann Heinrich Welker and his family of Düingdorf made his application, with the remark that they were taking along a fortune of 3,000 Talers ($2100). In one document Kamphoefner is listed with a fortune of 250 Talers, an amount that seems implausible given the economic situation of the family; in another document, no money is mentioned. As direct neighbors in Düingdorf (Welkers owned the farm No. 5; Kamphoefners were tenants of No. 2 or 3), it is highly probably that they traveled together to America. But since the New Orleans passenger lists from this era are

poorly preserved, it is impossible to say for sure.

Perhaps at the same time as Ernst, but probably somewhat later, a third Kamphoefner brother, Caspar Heinrich, (born on Christmas day, 1812), came to Missouri. His immigration is recorded neither in German nor in American records. Since his wife gave birth to a daughter on December 1, 1844, it seems likely that Caspar departed sometime after this date, leaving his wife and daughters behind for the time being. This and other clues between the lines point to bitter poverty. When their daughter was born they were tenants on farm No. 3 in Düingdorf; at an earlier birth in 1839 they were tenants of No. 2. Before her emigration in 1849, Caspar's wife lived in Bulsten, another village or Bauernschaft in the Melle parish. When she and her three daughters applied for an emigration permit on July 20,

1849, it was noted in the document, "The husband lives in America and has sent the passage money." They arrived in New Orleans on October 31, 1849 on the ship "Julius" from Bremen. Caspar lived until 1879; his gravestone stands on the cemetery of St. Johannes Evangelical Church in Cappeln, Missouri not 10 km from New Melle. His wife lived till 1888 and is buried on the Evangelical cemetery in Alhambra, Illinois, where a daughter lived as a pastor's wife. Caspar had only one son, named Ernst, who also settled in this area of Illinois. He had male descendants living there until 1990, who spelled their name "Kamphoeffner"; a woman with this maiden name still lived at Alhambra in 2006.

The last of the Kamphoefners to come to America was Heinrich Mattheus, along with his wife and daughter. They arrived in New Orleans on the ship "Carl" on October 29

1860, and settled near Augusta, Missouri. There they became members of the Lutheran church that was founded as a daughter congregation of New Melle. Heinrich died only two years after their arrival, and his widow remarried on October 14, 1863. Her second husband was Friedrich Wilhelm Wissman, also a native of Buer. One son, August Kamphoefner, is buried on the Lutheran cemetery in Augusta, and several descendants named Fuhr are still members of that congregation.

Only one brother remained in Germany; after World War II, his descendants re-established contact with Hermann Kamphoefner, Ernst's grandson, in New Melle, and were supplied with CARE packages for a while. In the 1980s, Hermann's daughter, Alberta, and her husband Frank Toedebusch (also with roots in Melle), looked up the family in Germany. This developed into a transatlantic friendship and a number of visits in both directions with her distant cousin Friedhelm Kamphöfener and his family in Gelsenkirchen.

Ernst Heinrich Kamphoefner appears for the first time in American records on May 9, 1846, when he married the widow "Mary E. Meyers" (according to German records, Clare Elsabein nee. Rolkers, born January 21, 1817, near Melle). She had been married the first time in Germany to Johann Heinrich Meier on August 20, 1842, shortly before they left for America. By March 6, 1843 they had bought a 24 ha plot of land near New Melle. They had one son, named Johann Heinrich (Henry), who may have been born after his father's death. In fact, it appears possible that Rolkers and Kamphoefner were already cohabiting when the child was born: he was baptized in the Lutheran church with the name of Johan Heinr. Kamphoefner, with no record of his parentage but with his uncle Adam Meier serving as godfather. In some censuses he appears as Henry Kamphoefner, in others as Meyer, but Ernst Kamphoefner's will lists him as a stepchild. He was apparently somewhat retarded, could neither read nor write, never married, and signed with an X. Adam Meier also served as godfather for the first child that Kamphoefner and Rolkers had with each other, my great grandfather Johann Friedrich (Fritz), born August 15, 1847.

Ernst Heinrich and his wife had seven more children together, among them two sons who lived to adulthood: Casper Wilhelm, born June 6, 1851, and Herman Heinrich, born June 18, 1855. But Casper moved to

The Lutheran Church in New Melle. It was built by parishioners during the 1850s using local materials. Entries in the parish register date back to 1840. A pastor was appointed in 1844

Douglas County, Oregon, reportedly because of a disappointment in love, and changed his name to "William Kamp." As late as the 1960s he still had descendants in Oregon, though none by the name of Kamp, much less Kamphoefner. Hermann Heinrich moved to

St. Louis, became a partner in the grocery business with one Frederick W.R. Jungling, and also boarded in his household. After Jungling's death, Hermann married his widow, Anna, and had several children with her. Their grocery business went under in 1896

The German Protestant Church of St. John in Cappeln was built in 1863, at the height of the American Civil War. The stone work is worthy of note

in the midst of a depression, and from then on until his death in the late 1920s he worked as a common laborer, night watchman, and chauffeur. He had one surviving son, Fred W., who worked as a driver and later as "traffic manager" for the Knollman Co., and shows up for the last time in the St. Louis city directory of 1952, spelling his name "Kamphafner". I have corresponded recently with descendants but none survive who bear his name.

Ernst Kamphoefner appears in an 1875 plat book with a farm of 110 acres (ca. 44 ha) directly to the south of New Melle, including 60 acres which his wife and her first husband had bought, and 40 acres of "Government land" which he purchased in 1853 for $50. The next farm over belonged to J.H. Welker, his old neighbor from Duingdorf. In 1883 Ernst bought another 40 acres, bringing his total landholdings to 150 acres oder 60 ha. Kamphoefner's increasing assets were recorded in the census: in 1850 his farm was valued at only $190; ten years later he showed $500 in real estate and another $200 worth

of personal property. In 1870 his farm was valued at $1,000, with an additional $1,000 in personal property–all in all not bad for someone who had started as a tenant farmer in Germany and would have probably remained one all his life if he had stayed there.

Ernst and his wife lived for the rest of their lives in their original log cabin (which may have been built by Meier, since it was on his original land purchase), made more comfortable with weatherboarding and a frame addition. They died in 1897 and 1896, both nearly reaching 80, having lived to see their golden wedding anniversary. Perhaps that was the occasion for a photo taken near the end of their life, reproduced at the start of the chapter. It shows them with their youngest daughter Anna, her husband Heinrich Theilmann, and their son (Johann) Hermann, who lived together with them. Hermann was a bright young man and studied agriculture at the University of Missouri, which offered him a job as an instructor. But he had psychological problems, and in the aftermath of the

sudden death of both his parents in 1928, he lived a hermit-like existence in the original Kamphoefner house, milking goats and raising vegetables, until he was found dead there on March 7, 1969. The abandoned house was still standing in the early 1980s, when I photographed it.

Ernst's son, my great-grandfather Johann Frederich "Fritz" Kamphoefner, worked as a blacksmith's apprentice for Conrad Weinrich in New Melle and then married his daughter Wilhelmina on March 16, 1871–just in the nick of time. Their first child, christened Conrad Friedrich Kamphoefner, was born three weeks later on April 9, 1871, but he only lived to be 14 months. In the summer of 1870 Conrad was serving as a representative in the State Legislature in Jefferson City, and apparently could not keep his eye on things back home. Both Conrad and Fritz, and also Fritz's father Ernst, fought for the Union in the Civil War, Conrad as the organizer and then captain of a Home Guard and State Milita company.

Most of the earliest houses, like the first Lutheran Church, were log cabins. This one was built around 1840 by Friedrich Diekmann, an emigrant from Tecklenburg. Originally there were two cabins linked by a covered walkway, known as the "dog trot". The gaps between the wooden beams were in-filled with clay

Fritz Kamphoefner spent the rest of his life in New Melle and gradually took over the blacksmith shop from his father-in-law Weinrich. He also build a new brick house, which now, recently restored, houses the Boone-Duden Historical Society which is devoted to local history. Weinrich probably provided financial support for the house construction, since he built himself a nearly identical residence just down the street. In all Fritz and Wilhelmina had eleven more children, including three sons who lived to adulthood: Ernst Johann, my grandfather (May 4, 1879–October 14, 1954); Hermann Heinrich (April 28, 1885–Nov. 4, 1968), father of Alberta Toedebusch; and Friedr. Johann Heinr. (October 20, 1890–April 12, 1939), whose daughter, Leanna White, as the last of her (fourth) generation

survived into the 21st century. Fred worked for a few years as a blacksmith in New Melle, before he married into a farm in the vicinity.

The two eldest sons, Ernst and Hermann, took over the blacksmith shop in New Melle from their father, and ran it in close cooperation with the adjacent wagon making shop of the Aupings (whose ancestors arrived on the "New Melle Mayflower"). When a new county road was being built, they would go out to the construction site in the evenings in order to shoe the broncos, captured wild horses, that were used to pull the scrapers. But in the long run, this road construction helped the main enemy of the village blacksmith– the automobile. With the end of horse and buggy days, the blacksmith shop could no longer support two families. So Ernst began to work at the "car shops" of

American Car and Foundry in St. Charles. I still have an heirloom from him, a little model anvil of brass about 4 inches long that he made on a lathe, perhaps an expression of frustration on the part of a skilled craftsman who was now reduced to doing routine, repetitive factory work. Ernst and his wife Lydia lived out the rest of their life in a rented house on Sixth Street in St. Charles. Brother Hermann married a pastor's daughter (her father, Rev. Falke, was a Saxon immigrant who until his retirement in New Melle in 1928 preached only in German) and continued to work as a blacksmith until his retirement. When he died in 1968, there was for the first time in 124 years no Kamphoefner living in New Melle or belonging to the Lutheran congregation there.

The home of Thomas Mellon, 401 Negley Avenue, Pittsburgh, Pennsylvania, built 1850–51. Close by lived other members of the Mellon family on what was known locally as "the Mellon patch"

Brian Lambkin

The Mellon Family of Castletown, Omagh, County Tyrone, Ireland

There are many documentation centres and museums in Europe and overseas that are concerned with archiving records of migration. Migration museums in Europe that specialise in vivid reconstructions of individual migration stories include the award-winning Deutsches Auswandererhaus in Bremerhaven and BallinStadt in Hamburg, Germany, the Norwegian Emigrant Museum at Ottestad and the Ulster American Folk Park, near Omagh, in northern Ireland.

Featured in the outdoor museum of the Ulster American Folk Park is the story of the Mellon family. The central exhibit is the original family farmhouse, still on its original site, from which the last of the Mellon family emigrated to the United States in 1818. This was during the agricultural depression that followed the end of the Napoleonic Wars in 1815. We may take the story of the Mellon family as standing in some respects for the thousands of families who left Europe at this time for the

New World, although in other respects, of course, their story was not typical, even of emigration from Ireland, or from its northern province of Ulster.

The key figure in the story of the Mellon family is Thomas Mellon (1813–1908), who in old age wrote his autobiography and had it privately printed. He was only five years old when his parents, Andrew and Rebecca, took him with them to the United States in 1818. They sailed from the port of Derry (Londonderry), about

The Mellon family home in Castletown, near Omagh, County Tyrone, still on its original site and now part of the Ulster American Folk Park

Replica of the first log cabin house in which Thomas Mellon and his family settled on arrival in Pennsylvania

thirty miles north of their home. The ship that took them to St. John's New Brunswick was fairly typical of the 1810s and 1820s: about 300 tons, registered to carry 160 passengers. But their voyage was untypical in taking twelve weeks instead of the more usual six weeks, due to exceptionally bad weather. On arrival in Canada, they took another ship south to the United States, arriving in Baltimore after a further two weeks. From Baltimore, they traveled on to western Pennsylvania by Conestoga wagon, taking three weeks to arrive in Westmoreland county, where they settled on a farm at Poverty Point. This destination was no accident. Thomas's father, Andrew, had brought his wife and son deliberately to this curiously named place in order to join his own father and mother and brother, who had settled nearby two years earlier. A life-size reconstruction of their first home, a log cabin, is on display on the New World side of the outdoor museum at the Ulster American Folk Park.

Also on display in the Ulster American Folk Park is a reconstruction of the six-room, two-story house at Duff's Hill, built by the Mellon family on land bought from a German immigrant, Jacob Kline. Thomas Mellon as a young boy had to fight hard to persuade his father that he did not want to inherit the family farm and to send him to be educated at Westmoreland County Academy, Greensburg. He graduated in 1837 from the western University of Pennsylvania (now the University of Pittsburgh) where he then taught Latin for a few months. In 1838 he began studying law in the office of Judge Charles Shaler in Pittsburgh, was appointed assistant chief clerk of the Courts of Common Pleas in March and was admitted to the bar in December. In June 1839 he opened his own law office in Pittsburgh and quickly developed a prosperous practice. He began investing his savings judiciously in real estate, coal, mortgages and loans, becoming the trustee of many estates, the operator of coalmines and an owner of extensive real estate. By 1859 he

had become the legal adviser to many prominent members of the rapidly growing business and financial community in Pittsburgh, some of whom persuaded him to stand for election as judge in the Court of Common Pleas of Allegheny county. He served as judge for ten years, earning a reputation for wisdom and integrity while maintaining his business activities and becoming president of the People's Savings Bank in 1866.

In 1843 he married Sarah Jane Negley, daughter of Jacob Negley, land surveyor and mechanical engineer of east Liberty, Pennsylvania, and Anna Barbara Winebiddle. Mellon's wife was a descendant of German immigrants on both the Negley and Winebiddle sides of her family. In 1848 Thomas moved his family out of Pittsburgh to the nearby village of east Liberty. He resided at 401 Negley Avenue from May 1851 until his death.

Having reached the age of fifty-five, Thomas Mellon had been more successful than most immigrants from fairly humble farming stock, but he was to go further. In 1869, he abandoned his legal career to devote himself to business and finance and in January 1870 he established the banking house of T. Mellon & Sons, as a one-room business in Smithfield Street, Pittsburgh, with his sons Thomas Alexander and James Ross as partners. A replica of the bank is on display in the Ulster American Folk Park. During the post-Civil War boom, the bank developed through shrewd investments in various real estate and business and financial enterprises (such as lending money to Henry Clay Frick – a descendant of German Palatine immigrants – to buy coal fields and to establish his first coke ovens) into one of the most important financial institutions in western Pennsylvania. The bank was forced briefly to suspend payment of deposits during the financial

"crash" of 1873 but came through with its reputation intact.

In 1877 Thomas purchased the failing Ligonier Valley Railroad putting his sons Thomas Alexander, Richard Beatty and James Ross in charge of its ultimately successful development. He also became the owner of an iron foundry and a large stockholder in traction lines in Pittsburgh and vicinity. In 1880 he was elected to the Select Council of Pittsburgh, serving until 1887. He officially retired from business in 1882, leaving his son Andrew in charge of the bank. With Sarah Jane he had eight children: Thomas Alexander (financier); James Ross (financier); Sarah Emma, Annie Rebecca and Samuel Selwyn (these three died in infancy); Andrew William (financier and secretary to the treasury 1921–32 under the Presidents Harding, Coolidge and

Hoover, founder of the National Gallery of Art); Richard Beatty (president of the Mellon Bank) and George Negley Mellon. By 1936 the Mellons were considered one of the four wealthiest families in the United States, along with the Rockefellers, DuPonts and Fords.

In 1885, Thomas Mellon completed his autobiography, Thomas Mellon and His Times. This is one of the very few accounts written by the great American entrepreneurs of the 19th century (another is that by Mellon's friend Andrew Carnegie, who had been born in a weaver's cottage in Dunfermline, Scotland and had emigrated with his parents to the United States in 1848, aged thirteen). It is both a well written and detailed source for economic and social history. It includes, for example, Mellon's boyhood memory of the "last look"

Replica of the two-story hewn log house built by the Mellons a few years after they settled in Greensburg, western Pennsylvania

Replica of the first Mellon bank, opened at 145 Smithfield Street, near Sixth Avenue, Pittsburgh in January, 1870

of his grandfather at "the place of parting" when he emigrated in 1816.

This was the last point from which the old homestead could be seen: a homestead which had sheltered the family and their ancestors for so many generations. It was sad to look back on it for the last time. After a great deal of tear shedding and hand shaking, and good wishes and blessings, the kind hearted crowd turned homeward, and the little emigrant party continued their solitary way onward with sad hearts.

How many other families, in Ireland and elsewhere, must have departed from their homes in this way? Many emigrants from Europe brought with them to America particular objects as "souvenirs" of old home. Few such migrant objects now survive in the collections of migration museums but one such, now on display in the Ulster American Folk Park, is a walking stick. As Thomas Mellon explained in his autobiography, it had originally belonged to his earliest known ancestor, who had arrived in Ireland from Scotland about 1660, and, having been passed down the generations in Ulster, it was brought by the family with them to America.

Of course Thomas Mellon was exceptional in the way that he succeeded in realising the "American Dream" that he shared with so many other immigrants. Starting in a log cabin he made it, if not to the White House, then right to the top of Pittsburgh's millionaire elite. However, the trajectory of his migration story is in some ways typical: in the cause and manner of his family's departure from their small farm, through their transatlantic crossing from the nearest port about thirty miles distant, to their arrival via Canada in rural Pennsylvania, followed by their internal migration to another part of the state, and then his internal migration from the countryside into the rapidly industrialising town of Pittsburgh.

Thanks to Mellon's autobiography, which is a model for family historians, we know the wider context of his family's migration story. His father's earliest known ancestor had migrated to the northern part of Ireland from Scotland in the second half of the 17th century. His mother's earliest known ancestor (her maiden name was Wauchob) had migrated there in the 1690s from the Netherlands as a soldier in the army of King

William III of Orange. As we have already noted, Thomas's father, Andrew, was not the first of his family to emigrate to the United States. He was the third of seven brothers and two sisters and all of them were already in the United States. His father, Archibald, had emigrated two years previously with the other children, apart from the two sons who had emigrated in 1808 to join their uncle who had emigrated in 1796. Here we see chain migration at work. One uncle proved particularly successful as a merchant, first in Philadelphia, and later in New Orleans. In Ireland, the Mellon family lived within the "urban field" of the port of Derry. The decision to emigrate in 1818 was most likely influenced by the crisis of 1816–17: the extremely cold and wet year of 1816 resulted in minimal harvests throughout Europe and was known as "the year without a summer". It had been triggered by the eruption of the Tambora volcano on Java in 1815, which caused a kind of "nuclear winter" in the "summer". It is not entirely a coincidence that two of the other emigrants featured in the Ulster-American Folk Park, Hugh Campbell and John Joseph Hughes (later Archbishop of

New York) both also emigrated in 1818, one of the peak years of emigration from Europe.

The reasons Thomas gave in his autobiography for his family's emigration were echoed around Europe, especially in the German-speaking areas: Times were bad then in Ireland, and the hardest on the middle class which had been known for a generation or more. The protracted wars in which England had been engaged had rendered taxation oppressive. Every method was resorted to [in order] to raise revenue. Every hearth and window and head of livestock, and every business transaction was separately and oppressively taxed; and after paying the rent and taxes, little was left to the farmer.

Interestingly, Mellon was proud of describing his own and the neighboring families amongst whom he grew up in Pennsylvania as "Scotch-Irish". He distinguished them from their English and German ("Dutch") neighbors, referring to a "Scotch-Irish standard of morality" which, he alleged, was superior to the German standard in respect of "sexual intercourse and religious observances"!

Unlike most Irish emigrants in the 19th century, Thomas Mellon made one return visit back to "Old Ireland". In contrast to the sailing ship on which his family had emigrated in 1818, he returned from New York to Queenstown (near Cork) in August 1882 on the steamship "Celtic". The "Celtic" was 4,000 tons with 850 passengers and the voyage took nine days. This "liner" was one of several "new and splendid vessels" of the White Star Line, which, as the advertisements of the time boasted:

Reduce the passage to the shortest possible time, and afford to Passengers the highest degree of comfort hitherto attainable at sea. Average passage 8 days in Summer, 9 days in Winter. Each Vessel is constructed in seven watertight compartments. The STEERAGES are unusually spacious, well lighted, ventilated, and warmed, and Passengers of this class receive the utmost civility and attention. An unlimited supply of Cooked Provisions. Medical comforts free of charge. Stewardesses in Steerage to attend the Women and Children. Steerage fare as low as by any other Line (Armagh Guardian, 23 April 1875).

Arrived in Cork, Mellon took the train north to Omagh via Dublin and spent a whole day visiting the farm where he had been born followed by a weekend staying with his mother's surviving relatives at Kinkit about ten miles to the north. The day he spent revisiting his birthplace he experienced as particularly satisfying: Before coming I had supposed that I should want to stay or return here for several days; but I am satisfied: what more could I see or know if I returned again? So farewell to the home of my childhood. Adieu to the reality of its beautiful presence, but its sweet memory will remain to the last!

The sense of satisfaction described here has something to do with the idea of completing unfinished business. There is no question in this case of the returned emigrant wanting to remain permanently in his country of origin. It is clear from Mellon's account that he thought of himself at the time first as a "Yankee", but also as an "Irishman", and as a "Scotch-Irishman". What he was particularly concerned about on his return visit was to see for himself whether or not the "photographic" memory of his childhood home, which he had carried with him all his life, was exactly as he remembered it. He also had a strong sense that he was revisiting the family home for the sake of his deceased father and mother and uncles – something that they had not been able to do for themselves. Descendants of emigrants as "roots tourists" report a similar sense of acting on behalf of ancestors who had never managed to return themselves, despite the promises they had more than likely made on their departure, and renewed repeatedly in reply to letters from the "Old Country".

Although the migration story of the Mellon family is in some respects typical of emigrants from Europe, it is far from representing their huge diversity. As Donald Akenson reminds us, Europe's emigrants "have for the most part been capable of strong and conscious decision making and were not mere passive bits of flotsam on some alleged historical tide". We need therefore to "grant integrity and authenticity" to the decisions of the millions who emigrated. As well as explaining their behaviour in terms of the large-scale economic and political structures and forces that set the limits to what was and was not possible for them, we need also to understand their particular human situations, if possible in as much detail as Thomas Mellon provided of his family. An important task for our migration archives, libraries and museums remains to reconstruct as many individual migration stories as possible, in order that we may better understand the big picture of Europe's great emigration.

Cane or walking stick brought by the Mellon family from Ireland to the United States. It belonged originally to Archibald Mellon, their earliest known ancestor (died c. 1700) and is now in the collection of the Ulster-American Folk Park

פתחו
שערים
ויבוא
גוי צדק

פתחו
לי
שערי
צדק

America opens the door to freedom for eastern European Jews escaping the pogroms. Colored illustration 1906

Adam Walaszek

Do Ameryki za chlebem: Central-Eastern Europeans Cross the Atlantic

In the 19th century the region described here – Central and eastern Europe – embraced territory of two empires: the Russian Empire (spreading from the Urals to the partitioned Polish lands in the west, including what was called the Kingdom of Poland, an area inhabited by various nationalities – Poles, Ukrainians, Lithuanians, Byelorussians, Jews); and the Austrian Empire (Austro-Hungarian after the 1867 compromise between the Habsburgs and the Magyar rulers, which divided major political control with the Magyars supreme in Hungary), a multilingual and multi-national state (with Czechs, Slovaks, Poles, Carpatho-Rusyns, Ruthenians, Magyars, Croats, Slovenes, Jews, Germans, and the other nationalities living within its territory). The groups, cohabiting these lands since the early modern period, had linguistic, cultural, and religious differences but also shared some common features.

Demography

In the second half of the 19th century the region experienced an unusual demographic explosion, which peaked between 1860 and 1890 (in Hungary between 1875 and 1885). Birth rates were rising. In European Russia in 1870 the rate was 49.2 per 10,000 people, 50.3 in 1890, and 49.3 in 1900. In Austria-Hungary in 1870 it was 39.8 per 10,000, in 1890 36.2, in 1900 35.0. At the same time death rates were falling. In European Russia the rate was 35.0 per 10,000 in 1870, 36.7 in 1890 and 31.1 in 1900. In Austria-Hungary they were 29.4, 29.1 and 25.2, respectively.

The population of the Hungarian part of the Austro-Hungarian Monarchy (including Croatia) rose from 15.5 to 20.9 million between 1870 and 1910. The conquest of infectious diseases contributed to the decline in the death rate, although epidemics could still occur. Cholera brought from Russia struck in 1848–49, 1852–1855, 1866, and 1873. Allegedly, it took 9,000 lives in Hamburg in 1892. Natural disasters, such as droughts and economic crises, at the end of the 19th century added to the causes of migration.

Agriculture

The production of foodstuffs, raw materials, and raw agricultural products remained basic to Central Europe's economy. The percentage of people associated with agriculture was higher than elsewhere, in Austria-Hungary 65 %, in Russia 78 %; 80–85 % of the Hungarian and 65–80 % of the Lithuanian and Latvian population worked in agriculture.

Post-emancipation villages were characterized by overpopulation and land hunger. Emancipation, the abolition of serfdom and the alienation of manorial farms, took place in Austria in 1848, in Russia proper in 1861, and in Russian Poland in 1864. In the Polish lands 72 % of peasant holdings were very small. Village proto-industry disappeared and rural handicraft disintegrated. The number of village proletariat rose everywhere. In the 1860s and 1870s the mining industry in Slovakia faced deep crises. Croatia, Slovenia, and Serbia with traditional agriculture had a smaller number of village proletariat but Croatian and Slovene villages also experienced indebtedness, poverty and economic stagnation. For centuries the Croatian agrarian population worked on landholdings of extended families, the economic, social, emotional, and biological system of zadruga, which in the middle of the 19th century broke up under the pressure of economic and legal changes. The traditional division of labor and egalitarianism in consumption was disrupted. The new practice of individual ownership eroded the zadruga and soon led to fragmentation of the land. The smallest landholdings existed in Dalmatia. Most Dalmatians worked on contracts for others, or paid high rent, and so transatlantic migration here started earlier and had particular intensity. Dalmatians used also their skill as fishermen, so many of them settled on the west Coast.

After emancipation, peasants lacked both wealth and ready cash. Money became a new reality and a new value in the life of the peasantry. But it was difficult to acquire money in the countryside. Everywhere credit conditions were bad or nonexistent. For example, the indebtedness of Galician villagers increased twelvefold between 1885 and 1905. (The term Galicia refers to the Polish lands that came under Austrian rule, with the eastern border of the province marked by the River Zbruch.) "The peasantry is going bankrupt," noted the contemporary sociologist Ludwik Krzywicki, pointing to one reason for migration from the Polish lands. In Hungary reforms lead to bankruptcy of the peasantry and the aristocracy as well. Reports highlighted the misery of large groups of peasants in the eastern parts of Hungary. In Hungary a few thousand families controlled more than 50 % of the land. 70 % of peasants lived on dwarf lots and parcels of land which could hardly feed them. In Slovakia 1 % of the population held 46.3 % of all arable land, a fact which without additional comment explains the economic reasons for migration. In the 1890s the agrarian proletariat increased from approximately 111,000 to 147,000. In practice, enfranchisement of the peasants meant accelerated partitioning of holdings. Peasant holdings were divided into increasingly small fragments. In Galicia, in the year 1902, 44 % of farms consisted of two hectares (1 hectare equals 2.471 acres),

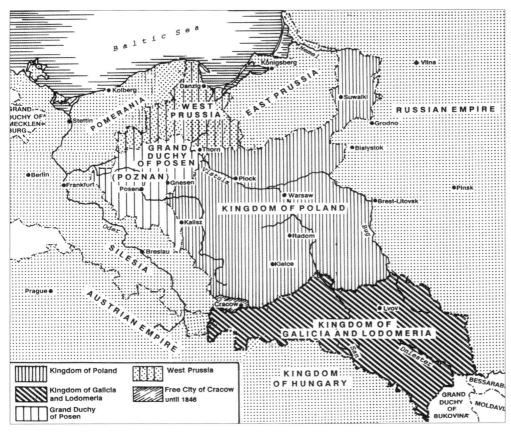

The partition of Poland after the Congress of Vienna 1815

to the decision to migrate. The first significant waves of Czechs arriving in the United States are associated with the "Spring of Nations" (the European liberal, labor and national turmoil of 1848–1849). Political and national suppression played a role in the decision of emigrants, predominantly of artisan, worker and intellectual background. The post-1848/1849 revolution emigration of some activists from Hungary was similar. Later, at the end of the century, the ruling Magyars in Hungary introduced a policy of Magyarization (implemented e.g. in the educational system) which Slovaks, Serbs (mostly from Croatia, and the region of Voivodina in particular), and Croats strongly opposed, demanding legal status for their languages and political and cultural freedom. Political oppression could be a motive for migration, nonetheless it should not be overstressed. The biggest centers of Slovak emigration were in the regions, where nationalist feelings were not the strongest. Among Slovak migrants to the U.S. there was a very high rate of return, despite the fact that the political situation and the policy of Magyarization did not change before World War I.

37% 2–5 hectares, 18% 5 to 20 hectares and only 1% more than 20 hectares, so the majority of farms were not self-sufficient. Peasants sold their products individually at low prices. The cost of living grew faster than wages. Only the southern Hungarian Military Border Zone, abutting on to the Ottoman Empire, enjoyed special regulations until 1881, because it had to meet particular military requirements the fragmentation of land was restricted and geographical mobility limited.

Migration

The process of incorporation of these territories into the economic system of the Atlantic world affected not only the flow of capital and materials but migration as well. "Migration, like any other social phenomenon with an economic background, is conditioned by a rise of new needs among people, and by a

knowledge that these needs can be fulfilled," wrote Florian Znaniecki at the end of the 19th century.

Migration derived from a desire (if not a need) to improve peoples' economic and social positions. It was an act of struggle against fate but sometimes also a revolt against one's way of life, against oppression, the authorities, and family, and the elderly as well. Someone recalled: "Finally I revolted against my fate and my parents… I escaped from the house." Those leaving their countries could be the most dissatisfied, and at the same time the most courageous people. Memoirs of the migrant Władysław Wiśniewski, a wanderer from the western part of the Kingdom of Poland (Russian Poland), and the memoirs of other migrants support this thesis. Teenagers could emigrate illegally, to avoid military service (in both empires. This was often one of the reasons for which people sailed to America). Finally, sometimes the literature also mentions political circumstances and tensions. The rise of national awareness led to conflicts which could contribute

Destinations

The various types of migratory movements were a remedy for overpopulation in regions that could not feed their populations. People could migrate internally, work seasonally within shorter distances, or go abroad, to work either in agriculture or in industry. Moreover, with time, they could choose between European or overseas destinations, where they also could move permanently or temporarily. They had various options and possibilities. The expanding transnational and transatlantic economy modernized and expanded local industry, which in some territories could compete for the labor force, but new industries depended on western capital, lacked impetus, and could not absorb the masses of people seeking employment.

Internally, seasonal agricultural migrations within some regions had long traditions. Unskilled workers were hired on the local labor market, skilled and qualified workers (e.g. supervisors, skilled servants, cooks, butlers) in more distant markets. In addition, in Galician villages, "almost each peasant… kept servants" Jan Słomka recalled in his memoirs. At the beginning of the 20th century Franciszek Bujak, economist, sociologist and historian, wrote that at that time peasants had "quite broad" contacts with the outside world: "significant liveliness of labor migration after the emancipation proves that people living on the river in Ropczyce County [in Galicia – AW] were familiar with far-away destinations and knew how to reach them." Peasants' horizons and world views broadened. During fairs and other celebrations one could hear about migrants' adventures and the miracles of the distant world. Migration was a topic of lively conversations in village taverns. The Polish peasant leader noted: "Soldiers on leave… would tell of marvels they had seen and of things they usually did not understand… They reported houses made of glass, golden churches, tenement houses as high as our Tatras [mountains in southern Poland], cows with stomachs ten times as big, with such an abundance of wine that people wash and bath themselves in it, instead of using water." And peasants decided to seek out new opportunities. Seasonally Poles worked in agriculture in Saxony, Brandenburg, Mecklenburg, and even in the Hamburg region. According to some sources during the season of 1912–1913, 149,000 people, who originated in Galicia and the Kingdom of Poland, worked in the eastern provinces of Germany. People circulated between Galicia and Saxony as early as the 1840s (the practice was called obieżysastwo, or Sachsengängerei). The sugar beet fields of Denmark appeared as another destination at the end of the century. At that time the movements accelerated and European destinations "competed" with the American ones. Migration to different destinations was also correlated. During cyclical economic depressions in America (e.g. in the years 1885, 1894–1895, 1904, 1907–1909) seasonal migration to Germany grew, providing an additional safety exit for wage seeking Austro-Hungarians (Poles, Slovaks, Jews, Czechs, Russians). During the long and dramatic coal miners strike of 1902 return migration to Austria-Hungary reached 50 % – Poles, Slovaks, and Hungarians depended so heavily on the work in Pennsylvanian coal mines.

Slovaks, particularly people from Šariš Hung. Sáros) and northern mountainous regions, worked seasonally in Hungary and Transylvania since the 18th century. In

Female Polish seasonal workers at a railway station in Berlin. Photo around 1907, on their way to the large Saxon estates in the west, for instance to the fertile plains around Magdeburg, where they worked in the sugar beet fields. Many industrial enterprises also recruited male and female workers at railway stations in Berlin

1845 crop failure and hunger pushed them again to seek work in the Great Hungarian Plain (Nagy Magyar Alföld), and each year harvesters from eastern Slovakia traveled to the Alföld. In 1910 approximately half a million people from Croatia-Slavonia, Bukovina, Transylvania and Slovakia worked in Hungary. Another destination was Austria proper.

Thus, migrating agricultural workers or déclassé craftsmen faced a palette of options. Władysław Wiśniewski, the worker from the Kingdom of Poland mentioned earlier, had such choices and used them well. He not only migrated short distances locally within the Kingdom of Poland but also went to Mecklenburg, Westphalia, Hanover, Denmark, Russia proper, and finally crossed the Atlantic to the U.S.

Macroeconomics mattered in the decision making processes. Migration traditions and established social networks were important as well. Some researchers maintain that Germany was a popular destination because the country offered important advantages, despite the fact that the standard of living was problematic. Seasonal work in spring and summer obviously paid better than e.g. in Russian Poland and allowed easy and cheap

return with one's savings. The emotional cost of separation from relatives was smaller than in the case of migration to America. Finally, in Germany it could be easier to cope with various difficulties. A large Polish migration stream was associated with the industrialization of the Ruhr district. The industrialized territories of Austria-Hungary became another destination for Croats, Slovenes, Czechs, and Jews.

The dual monarchy was economically and nationally one of the most complex European states. Some parts of it (Bohemia, Moravia, Austrian Silesia, Vienna, Upper Austria, Upper Styria, Budapest) became sites of booming industrial development and there immigration prevailed over emigration. The other provinces ranked as the most remote agricultural peripheries. Because of such social and economic dualism the country attracted migrants and was sending others abroad at the same time. Statistics show that people from Galicia, Bukovina, and Dalmatia more often migrated to foreign states, while Poles and Ruthenians chose western Europe or the Americas. In the monarchy's other lands the tendencies were reversed and internal migration prevailed.

Market day in Strij, Galicia, 1905. Between 1880 and 1924 more than one million immigrants, mainly Poles, Ukrainians, and Jews from this very poor region in the Austro-Hungarian Empire, went to America

Wojciech Łagowski was, in the 1880s, the first resident from Krzywa, a Galician village in Ropczyce County, to cross the Atlantic. "There was so much talk in the village, so much fear. A year later the second, and then a third one left, and after these sent back a few dollars to their families a real hysteria started, everybody borrowed money wherever they could, and left for the golden country." In Hungary (but on Polish lands as well) the pioneers departed mostly in family units.

The Example of One Village

"Emigration attacked the village from its periphery," wrote the sociologist Krystyna Duda-Dziewierz, describing the situation in the village of Babica in Rzeszów County, some 15–20 km from the city of Rzeszów, between Kraków in the west and Lvov in the east of western Galicia. Four km west of the village was a small agrarian town Czudec, the site of the parish to which Babica belonged. In (the year) 1890 the railway linking Rzeszów and the eastern town, of Jasło opened. The railroad passed through the village, conveniently placing it on the main Galician transportation route from Germany to Lvov (Lemberg, Lwów, Lviv) and further east.

At the turn of the century Babica was basically divided into two socially and economically different parts: the core (consisting of two districts) and the peripheries (composed of a few districts). Social, economic, and topographical divisions between village districts were essential to migration patterns in the region. They provided a context in which migration decisions were made.

The core of the village, composed of two parts – Dół (Lower Part) and Góra (Upper Part), stretched on both sides of the road located along the Wisłok River, which linked Babica with Czudec and Rzeszów. In Dół wealthy peasants (kmiecie) owned farms of considerable size, and their situation differed significantly from that of the poor zagrodnicy (people who simply possessed just a house) or navvies. Towards the north west, closer to Czudec, existed a hamlet called Budy (Shanties), and towards the east two other hamlets Dział I and Dział I (Division or Section I and II).

Pioneers in America

After the 1870s and 1880s, the inhabitants of central-eastern Europe discovered distant destinations. Once villagers "discovered" America, migration streams started to flow without interruption. The United States was the main and most popular destination in this part of Europe.

Historians have made some interesting observations regarding these movements. It is very difficult to establish why some "pioneers" decided to take a long and risky journey to America. Micro studies suggest that most likely the first persons who left for America were people loosely associated with village communities, who had only recently settled in a village or marginalized agricultural laborers.

The first emigrants from Babica originated from Budy and Dział. Pioneers of migration to America were not village natives: they married "into" the village, were agrarian proletariat, navvies or small owners, loosely connected with the rest of Babica, but they had the experience of living outside of the village. It was in the peripheries where American migration started. The location of Budy facilitated the decision as well; here people often met merchant-peddlers and heard travelers' stories about the world in a local inn (karczma, situated on the road to the south).

In the first period of American migration (1883–1900) village peripheries sent seventeen, people across the ocean – poor owners, laborers, servants, disinherited people: one from Dół, three from Budy, three from Dział I and two from Dział II. From Góra eight people migrated (among them six originating from Góra's poor periphery). Budy and Dział I and II established their own roads for communication with neighboring towns. To reach Czudec (and the broader world), the inhabitants of Budy used a different path from the ones used by the core (the shorter road crossed land of the manor). Going to Rzeszów people from Dział I and II also used

A group of Bulgarian emigrants posing for the camera in front of the Holland-America Line (HAL) office in Tarnopol, Bulgaria. They had to travel by train to Rotterdam first, where they then boarded steamships for America. More then one million people emigrated to the USA with HAL before World War I. Photo about 1910

At the end of the 19th century between 35 % (Silesia) and 45 % (Russian territory) of the land in Poland was in the hands of big landowners, although they comprised only between 0.5 and 1.4 % of landowners as a whole. The proportion of small farmers with up to five hectares of land (about half of what a family needed to survive) was between 35 % in Upper Silesia and 79 % in Galicia. Rural scene near Cracow. Photo around 1900

different routes. "The hamlets are not linked organically with the village center, and have different ties with local economic centers as well," summarized Duda-Dziewierz. Because of topography, the people of the hamlets participated to a lesser degree in the village's social life, such as community meetings etc. Children from Budy did not attend school in Babica but enrolled in the one in Czudec.

It was Paweł Dudek who in (the year) 1883 left for America: his wife and two sons followed him in 1886. In 1894 the second emigrant, Jędrzej Sołtys, crossed the ocean and afterwards migration to America became popular. Paweł Dudek, a carpenter, was born in Nowa Wieś, so he himself was an immigrant in Babica, married to a widow from Budy (primo voto Wójcik) who owned 3 morgas of land (Austrian morga, or Joch, equalled 5,755.4 square meters, one Polish morga equalled 5,598.7 square meters). The Dudeks decided to migrate when a suit they had brought against Michał Molenda (also an inhabitant of Budy) about the boundary strip of land almost ruined them. When Dudek's cow had been sequestered to cover the cost of the suit, a son of Dudek's wife from her first marriage burned Molenda's barn. Then their financial situation worsened

considerably. The Dudeks lost most of the land they owned, borrowed money and left for America. They did not have relatives in America, but in the family there was a tradition of migration. To escape from serfdom Dudek's father-in-law had migrated to Hungary. In 1898 the Dudeks moved to Detroit. The next year a few other poor people from Babica followed them, among them relatives of Ludwik Pasternak (an impoverished kmieć from Góra, a "leader" of an anti-Dół faction within the village). Jędrzej Sołtys, the second migrant, was born outside Babica as well (in the village of Baryczka). An agricultural laborer, he married Angela Papciak, a servant working in villages and towns. Although she was born in Dół, her parents belonged to the poorest segment of the population. They owned only a primitive cottage with no chimney. Jędrzej served in the army. After their marriage (in 1889) he spent five years working in mills in Budapest, thus, the couple had migration experience as well. The Sołtys returned to Babica and in the year 1894 left for Detroit, without knowing anyone there. The Missler travel agency of the shipping company Norddeutsche Lloyd in Bremen arranged the passage. After three years they returned to Babica, bought

Advertisement for emigrants in Poland before World War I

seven morgas in Dział, and soon returned to America. Their relatives took care of the land. They made this journey accompanied by a few other migrants (including members of the Pasternak family).

Franciszek Bujak, an economist, historian and sociologist, while describing emigration from the Galician village of Maszkienice, has shown how transatlantic movement simply added to the repertoire of historical migration patterns. In 1899 landholders could not earn a living and were forced to earn money outside. Men could work along the railway line which linked Kraków and Lvov; 40 % worked seasonally in Vienna, Ostrava or in the beet fields of Denmark. They had heard about America earlier but only in 1899 did they begin to travel there. After the first Maszkieniczaner went to Pennsylvania, the floodgate opened in earnest. In 1911 the number of migrants heading for the U.S. grew fourteenfold. 20 % of the migrants from this village in Brzesko County worked on the other side of the ocean. The number of people working in Germany remained unchanged.

Regional Patterns of Migration

In the case of America a "positive motivation" always existed. People were drawn not only by the need for a better life but also by the desire for social improvement. The notion of advancement – a better future, prestige – was, of course, understood in the context of their own culture. For better or worse, work in the fields provided a living. Using cash received from outside the village, migrants could build a house, achieve greater authority, and buy more land. Emigration created a chance, the means toward a personal career. The expanding economic situation in the United States at the end of the 19th century offered peasants an opportunity to fulfill "their aspiration for social advancement defined by their own hierarchy of values." They saved, worked like oxen, and became members of the proletariat – all in order to buy land. During two weeks in America one could earn as much as during a whole season in German or Hungarian agriculture.

In order to survive and to achieve their goals migrants slowly formed intricate organizational and institutional networks (at first through mutual assistance with other groups – Germans, Rusyns, Lithuanians, Slovaks). During the first phase of migration to America people originating in a particular region formed their own districts. Cleveland attracted people from the Karlovac region, Gorski Kotar, Žumberok, regions which bordered on a Slovenian area, from which Slovenes also traveled to America. Undoubtedly Slovenes informed Croats about American possibilities. Slovaks and Magyars from the northeastern county of Abauj and Zemplén also traveled to Cleveland. Emigration was typically organized by families, relatives or friends. Recent emigrants to America invited their relations and friends to follow in their footsteps. Close ties existed between those who left for America and those who remained in European villages. Letters were constantly crossing the ocean. The everyday dialogue was conducted at a very great distance with the help of those who were

Departure of Polish emigrants via Bremen to New York. These caricatures are from an album entitled "Emigration to America" by the Polish caricaturist and painter Jósel Kruszewski (1853–1920) from Cracow. The text was in three languages: German, Polish and Hungarian

able to write letters. The migrants not only sent money to the old country, but they also gave advice and persuaded their friends that they, too, should leave. "And if you are going to lease the land, then let the lessee have it, but for years; and let him pay for the lease in advance if he can… And if you have straw to sell, leave it on the land and the dung as well. Tear down the fence and chop it up for firewood unless he wants to pay you for it," one man wrote to his wife. And the most common statement was: "I will send you a steamship ticket if you wish." Possibilities and dangers were considered in these "conversations": "As regards Władek, I'd like to ask you to help him come overseas, as you are his uncle, and I will try to get a steamship ticket for him if he sends the money. For one must have at least 40 rubles for this journey; for the trip to Cleveland, one may need over 47."

Regional variations in migration trends were also associated with the ethnic composition of the peripheries of the empires. Mass migration to America started in areas ethnically mixed and in the borderlands. In Hungary Slovaks started it; Poles followed Germans in Oppeln Silesia, migration waves later spread in Prussian Poland, east Prussia and northern Russian Poland.

The western part of Slovakia (belonging to Hungary) was economically the most developed part. In Hungary migration to the U.S. started in the north-eastern counties with a predominantly Slovak ethnic population, which also had long traditions of seasonal migration to agricultural work in Alföld, such as Spiš (Hung. Szepes), Šariš (Hung. Sáros), Zemplín (Hung. Zemplén), Abauj (Hung. Abaúj), Borsod, Užh (Hung. Ung), Satu-Mare (Hung. Szatmár), and Szabolcs: forested regions with poor agriculture and some mining industry. Between 1899 and 1913 31 % of the people leaving the Hungarian part of the dual monarchy originated there. Starting in the 1860s emigration to America was heaviest from the counties of Šariš, Spiš, and Zemplín. Between 1881 and 1910 half the population of Šariš county left. 90 % of Slovak migrants traveling to America came from the eastern counties. Magyars were leaving the same region and neighboring counties. In Transylvania the movement of Saxons caused Romanians to migrate; in Croatia-Slavonia Slovenes transmitted the emigration fever to the Germans, Croats and Serbs. In Austrian Galicia gorączka emigracyjna [emigration fever] had started in the middle of western Galicia, soon spreading to the east and west, but the inspiration probably came from Slovakia. Migration waves coming from the west and south encouraged the movement of various national and cultural groups (Poles, Lemkos, Ukrainians, Armenians, Jews, Germans). Poles, Jews, and Germans traveled at the same time. Migration regions were not evenly distributed. In the diocese of Tarnów in Galicia the heaviest migration to Germany was observed in the northern part. From the other regions people were going to Austria, Germany, and Hungary to seek employment in agriculture or industry. The historical literature suggests that the poorest people, who could not afford money for travel to America, migrated shorter distances.

Left: Ludmilla K. Foxlee worked on Ellis Island for the Young Women's Christian Association (YWCA) to assist newly arrived immigrants. She herself came from Czechoslovakia. Here, she is seen with three children in the early 1920s. They all wear Bohemian dresses, herself included
Right: Lewis Krauss (at the age of 15) in Russia around 1908. Like many other young Jews he made his way to America alone in order to escape the brutal anti-Semitic pogroms in Russia at that time. Lewis became an American citizen in 1916

Volume of American Migration

It is estimated that 450,000 people from Prussian Poland, 900,000 from Austrian Poland, and 950,000 from Russian Poland left for the United States (when we consider the high return migration the number will be smaller, 1.3–1.5 million altogether). Until World War I approximately 1.8 million Jews, 300,000 Lithuanians, 250,000 Ukrainians, 100,000–150,000 Ruthenians, Byelorussians, and Ukrainians (who could call themselves Galicians, Bukovynians, Carpatho-Rusyns, depending on the region where they originated) were also distinguished by their religion: some from eastern Galicia were predominantly Uniates or Ukrainian Greek Catholics, while minorities from Volhynia and Bukovina belonged to various Orthodox churches. In the United States and Canada they formed the Ukrainian Greek Orthodox church.

According to the careful estimates of Juliana Puskás for the period between 1861

and 1924 4,116,988 people left the Austro-Hungarian Monarchy for the U.S., including: approx. 684–728,000 Slovaks, 758–767,000 Poles, 381–390,000 Jews, 544–568,000 Croatians-Slovenes, 526–549,000 Magyars, 434–442,000 Germans, 169–175,000 Bohemians-Moravians, 261–267,000 Ruthenians, 93–98,000 other South Slavic groups, and 153–154,000 Romanians. They could also be differentiated by their religion, because there could be Catholics, Protestants, Orthodox, and Uniates among them.

In Austria-Hungary various regions had different rates of migration between 1881 and 1910. In the first decade (1881–1890) the highest rate was observed in Kraina, then Bohemia and Dalmatia. During the next decade (1891–1900) the number steadily rose and Kraina was followed by Galicia and Moravia, whereas between 1901 and 1910 Galicia had the highest emigration rate, followed by Kraina, Dalmatia and Bukovina.

The movement to America was to be temporary in nature. Before World War I return migration and transatlantic circulation

of migrants were common phenomena. 19% of Slovaks, and 11% of Magyars who migrated to the U.S. between 1899 and 1910 had been there previously, according to the U.S. Immigration Commission publication for the year 1911. Research conducted earlier in Hungary in the years 1895–1896 established that 23% of emigrants had visited that country before. A significant proportion of Polish migrants, perhaps the majority of them, intended their stay in America to be a temporary one. People went there, like the mountain dwellers of the Tatra Mountains, "to make their pile of krutzers" in order to "buy a farm to run" in the homeland. In their intention to return, Poles were not different from many other groups migrating to America in the 1880s, 1890s, and ensuing years. In the United States, these people were then labeled "birds of passage." If we place them in the context of the Atlantic economy we might better call them "migrant workers". Indeed many people returned. In the case of Austria-Hungary on average 17–27%, but for some ethnic groups estimations were higher: for Croats 33–40%, for Magyars 46.5 (but between 1899–1913 on average 24.3% of emigrants returned), for Lithuanians 20%, for Slovaks between 20–36%, while Polish returnees amounted to nearly 30% of the total emigration population. As mentioned above, decreases in the arrivals and increases in returnees were significant at the time of American economic crises. In 1907 22,000 Croats arrived in the U.S.; in the following year only 2,800.

Jews

After the three partitions of Poland the largest number of Ashkenazi Jews lived in the so-called Pale of Jewish Settlement in the Russian Empire. In the 19th century 5 million out of 7 million east European Jews lived in Russia. They also experienced a remarkable population explosion. In 1816 in the Kingdom of Poland Jews composed 8.7% of the entire population, in 1865 13.5%. Jews were concentrated in big cities, small towns and countryside villages, in the famous shtetls. Social and economic changes, urbanization, and pauperization hurt them equally as much as the Christian peasantry.

Furthermore, in the Russian Empire their legal status was restricted. Since 1835 their presence was limited to the Pale (that is to Lithuania, Belarus, Ukraine, and the Kingdom of Poland). Pushed towards the west, Jews created a large group of urban proletariat, craftsmen, and petty merchants. Their internal mobility within the Kingdom of Poland was very high, much higher then among gentiles. Poverty (in 1898 the existence of one-fifth of Jewish families depended on charity), discrimination, and finally the wave of pogroms and persecutions created a climate conducive to emigration. The anti-semitic atmosphere and evident persecutions were often stressed to argue that Jewish migration experience was different from that of other migrants from a given country. After the assassination of Tsar Alexander II on March 1, 1881 Jews were accused of conspiracy, and in Russia violence broke out against the group in the years 1881–1884. The May Laws of 1882 established Jewish quotas in particular professions. Minister of Internal Affairs Count Nikolai Pavlovich Ignatiev's Laws forbade Jewish rural settlement and work on Sundays and during Christian holidays. Pogroms occurred later – the most infamous in 1903 in Kishiniev – and others during the 1905–1907 revolution.

In the case of the Jews compulsion and free decisions to migrate could mix. east European Jewry left their countries afraid

Extended family of Jews from Russia. More than 1.8 million Jews came to the U.S. via Ellis Island, most of them from Tsarist Russia. Photo around 1910

to lose their positions but also "poisoned by the ideology of freedom." At least since Lloyd Gartner's 1960 publication (supported later by the works of Simon Kuznets, John D. Klier and others), the exceptionality of Jewish emigration and the role of the pogroms has been questioned. According to recent literature Jewish emigration (at least until the year 1903) is to be explained from the perspective of economic transformations, urbanization and social changes which regionally coincided with the pogroms in Russia. Jewish emigration started earlier, before the first wave of pogroms. When the anti-Semitic incidents occurred (e.g. in 1883 in Yekaterinburg and Nizhny Novgorod), Jewish emigration to America actually diminished. Also, emigrants were recruited from the north-western part of the empire, which until the 20th century was not plagued with anti-Jewish riots. Thus, one of the arguments goes, it was rather the crises in agriculture, the pauperization of the peasantry (clients of Jewish merchants and craftsmen), crop failures, and hunger in the years 1869–1870, and 1891–1892 which explain the exodus. Of the few new social movements which appeared among Jews (the Haskalah, Zionism, socialism) mass migration was by far the greatest and most popular answer to distress. Finally, before the year 1903 22 % of Jewish migrants returned home; in the 1890s the percentage was even higher at 26 %.

Between 1800 and 1880, 250,000 Jews left eastern Europe, between 1881 and 1900 the figure was 1 million, and between 1901 and 1914 approximately 2 million. Two-thirds originated in the Russian Empire, where the situation of

Rural scene in the Burgenland, eastern Austria. Undated photo (probably before World War I)

the group was the worst. Jews had better conditions in the Austro-Hungarian Monarchy, where according to the Act of 1867 they enjoyed legal protection. But Jewish emigrants were leaving Galicia, northern Hungary (Slovakia), Hungary and Romania. Their picture of the American Goldene Medine (New York) was more realistic, based on a hope of work in the textile industry. There was anti-Semitism in Hungary, visible in the 1870s. The infamous trial about ritual murder in 1882, however, did not provoke a social reaction and did not lead to mass migration.

The situation in Romania was different. There pogroms started in 1895 and,

as a consequence, between 1881 and 1914 19.6 % of Romanian Jews left (mostly for America).

The United States of America was the main destination of Jewish overseas migrants. But there were others as well. Before World War I a few thousand reached Canadian towns (Montreal, Toronto, Winnipeg). Larger and more significant were Jewish colonies in Argentina (Russian Jews predominated in the group of 100,000 European Jewish immigrants there). More than 40,000, mostly Lithuanian Jews, settled in South Africa. The Zionist idea also attracted some settlers to Palestine in the first three aliyahs (Jewish migration waves to Palestine).

Travel and Train

In addition to the main "push" factors mentioned above, some efforts at modernization also facilitated geographical mobility in Central and eastern Europe. In the second half of the 19th century it was the construction of railway systems. In Galicia in 1851 the Charles Ludwig Railway linked eastern and western Galicia with Vienna, Prague, and Germany. Cost barriers fell, when prices did. Travel became faster, safer, and cheaper. "The South Railway" connected Ljubljana (Laibach, Slovenia) with Vienna from 1849, and after 1857 with Trieste. Later other lines linked Slovenia and Croatia with Budapest and Italy, providing easy connections to the ports of Le Havre, Antwerp, Rotterdam, Bremen/Bremerhaven, and Hamburg. Travel from Ljubljana to Vienna was cut from 10 days to 12 hours. Trains facilitated long-distance migration, providing easier access to labor markets but they also provoked curiosity about the distant world. "This passing train... tells us... that the world is different, bigger, better," said someone in Galicia. In isolated eastern regions (e.g. Polesie, or Horodło county in Podolia in Russia) long distances to the railway resulted in weak migration. At the same time steamships made transatlantic travel cheaper and faster as well.

Persecution of Jews in Russia – Jews escaping from a Podolian village in the border region between the Ukraine and Moldavia. This dramatized newspaper illustration highlights the wave of pogroms between 1881 and 1884 following the assassination of Tsar Alexander II

Travel and Border Crossings

Emigrants from Galicia (Ruthenians, Poles, Ukrainians, Jews) usually crossed the Austrian-German frontier at the border station in the city of Myslowitz. From the Hungarian part of the monarchy, Slovaks, Jews, and Magyars could transfer to trains in Budapest or Vienna destined for German ports, or sometimes Antwerp. southern Slavs also used this route, but of course Slovenes, Croats, Dalmatians, and others could also choose the ports of Trieste or Fiume (Rijeka). In 1904 the Hungarian government signed an agreement with the Cunard Line, according to which the shipping company would transport Hungarian emigrants overseas from Fiume. Nevertheless, people were still choosing the rather well known and established routes to German ports.

Migrants from the Kingdom of Poland, as well as citizens of the Austro-Hungarian Monarchy, had to obtain official permits in order to cross the Prussian border. To avoid this requirement people from northern Russian Poland pretended that they were going to the nearest German town or market. Crossing was difficult. People, usually walking or riding in carts, had to bribe the gendarmes or soldiers. Sometimes, when they were turned back at the border posts, they tried again the next day. On the Russian side of the border they had some connections and were quite well informed by letters from their relatives or acquaintances what to do and how to behave: "if they ask you about the passport, you should say you're from here", wrote someone. In taverns near the border there was always someone providing assistance, or smuggling people across the border. "When you are in Prussia and when they ask you where you come from, you should tell them you come from some

Passport cover advertising the Friedrich Missler Agency with headquarters in Bahnhofstr., Bremen, 1905. Friedrich Missler was the main agent for North German Lloyd who built up an extensive advertising network for emigrants in east and south-east Europe. He made use of clever advertising material such as visiting cards, stationary, etc. People traveled "with Missler" to the USA

little town or village in Prussia; thanks to that, you will have an easier journey... Only ask God that the Lord Jesus will allow you to cross the border safely so that they will not catch you", someone advised in a letter. People traveling without passports from Galicia took longer, less convenient routes.

They traveled from Kraków to Prague, and crossed the border in Bodenbach, were control was more relaxed and guards less watchful. Ukrainians or Jews from the Russian Ukraine usually traveled to Brody, the closest town to the Austrian-Russian border, and a center for emigrants or Jewish refugees. From Brody they continued to travel further west in Austrian trains.

Migrants from the Kingdom of Poland most often chose the route to Bremen or Hamburg. On the German side travel was easier but full of other dangers as well. People had to change trains in Berlin, exchange money, pay for a night, and find agents but there were also many "touts" and swindlers waiting for them at the stations. Migrants carried necessities (alcohol, bread, lard, a spoon, a bowl) with them. A husband instructed his wife before the trip: "You should take with you on the trip thick bread, smoked dried fatback, sugar, and vinegar... take the nicer pictures out of their frames and bring them with you; sell the frames and glass... Take the iron with

Schematic illustration of control and registration stations for emigrants at the borders of the German Empire

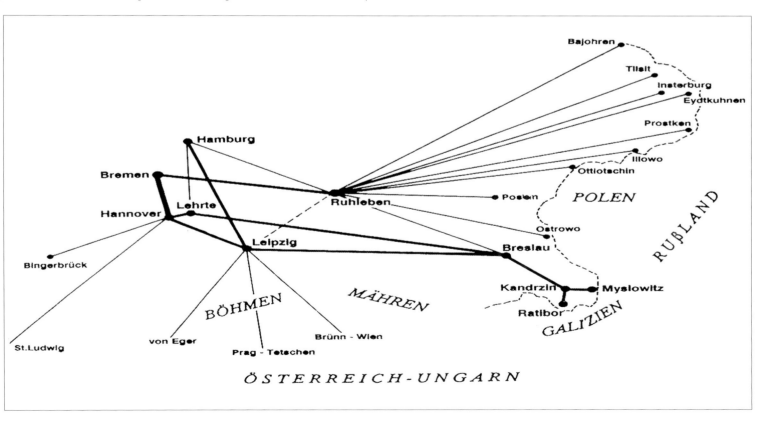

Romanian peasant family on Ellis Island, photo ca. 1905. Shepards, agricultural day laborers and small farmers constituted to a large extent the work force of American industries

you, the large pieces, too. But do not waste space on the bedding." Hotels in Bremen or Hamburg were often prepaid, or places to stay overnight had to be found. Red information flyers put on their hats helped people to be recognized by the representatives of the agents.

Czech craftsman, later famous businessman, Frank Vlchek from Bydyn, a village in the Pisek district in Bohemia, who had worked and apprenticed in many Austrian towns, decided in 1889 to seek work across the Atlantic. His sister lived in Cleveland, so with the help of a travel agent in Pisek he arranged the passage to go there. Vlchek failed to obtain a passport allowing him to travel legally, but decided to continue with his original plan. With two other Czechs he traveled to the German border, where a travel agent arranged train tickets for the onward journey and assisted him to the carriage. All three men arrived in Bremen via Berlin, stayed overnight and boarded a ship.

Agents

When in the 1840s news about emigration to America first reached the Kingdom of Poland, the authorities were alarmed that even priests propagated the movement from the pulpits. Tavern (karczma) keepers who read German newspapers promoted migration movements as well. Here and there agitators and agents appeared. Forty years later, everywhere in central-eastern Europe agents were blamed for the rising waves of migration. Some contemporary commentators were of the opinion that eliminating the agents' posts and offices would successfully stop migration hysteria. Agents' activity, however, was not the sole cause of migration: the presence of representatives of shipping companies, intermediaries, and subagents facilitated departures. The Austro-Americana (AA) shipping company provides an example of such activity. AA had its main offices in Trieste. In Galicia and Bukovina the general agent of AA was Goldlust and Co. The company had numerous official branches

in the countryside, semi-official and unofficial ones as well, and also sub-branches and "touts" who acted on behalf of AA. In the cities and travel offices the telegraph also made travel planning easier. In Ljubljana, on Railway Station Street, at the end of the 19th century, there were several emigration agencies and other facilities (such as bars, restaurants, inns, and shelters) helping emigrants. Before World War I nine shipping companies were active in the city through their representatives: Norddeutsche Lloyd, Hamburg America Line, Companie Général Transatlantique, Cunard Line, Red Star Line, Austro-Americana, White Star Line, American Line, and Holland America Line. Other agencies were located in the smaller towns and the countryside. The majority of agencies operated in the name of big European companies (located in Germany, Italy, Belgium, Britain etc.).

The biggest and the most famous of all was J. F. Missler's agency in Bremen, which operated through sub-agents in this part of Europe. The address of Missler's bureau (No 30 Bahnhofstrasse in Bremen) was widely known in Central European villages. His annual income was 180,000 marks and outside Bremen his main agencies were in Prague, Vienna, Budapest, Zagreb, Bucharest, Temesvar, Hermannstadt, Riga, Kovno, and Moscow. Several thousand sub-agents worked in Galicia alone. Between 1885 and 1923 Missler provided services to 1.8 million people. Jan Bukowski, who migrated with his family from southern Galicia to Pennsylvania in 1899 arrived in Bremen. Later he recalled meeting the famous agent: "Here reigns Missler, God of emigrants. His offices cannot house so many people, they send them to the other lodgings. Finally we are admitted by this Missler. I wanted to meet him very much in person and achieved this. He talked with people in a very friendly manner and advised everyone well. He was quite a nice man, restless, with white hair and beard, and of medium height."

Travel and company agents and bureaus also distributed literature promoting overseas destinations. Brochures, posters, and leaflets portrayed big ships on calm waters, taking people safely and quickly to America. Shipping companies and travel agencies advertized widely in newspapers. For those who decided to go they also sold textbooks for learning English, examples of conversations, guides to the country, and information of all sorts. Austria-Hungary and Russia were flooded with such materials printed in national languages.

Everywhere agents and intermediaries also tried to cheat potential emigrants. Some cases, such as those of Josip Paulin from Ljubljana and Zofia Biesiadecka in Galicia, became quite famous. Malpractices and cheatings of various sorts led to the loss of licenses to sell tickets or provide other travel services (Paulin lost his license twice, in 1889 and 1893) or, sometimes, to trials and imprisonment. Such actions had no effect and did not diminish the wave of migration either.

Going Elsewhere Overseas

In contrast to most of the migration to the U.S., the movement to some other overseas destinations was – from the very beginning – planned as a permanent one. Such was the settlement of Poles or Ukrainians on farms in the American states of Wisconsin or Nebraska, or – later – in the Argentinean province of Misiones, or in Canada. Settlers came to the peripheries of the industrial Atlantic world (such as the pampas in Misiones or southern Brazilian lands).

Between 1860 and 1910 Argentina (with a population of half a million people) was transforming itself into a modern and important nation. It systematically tried to populate the country according to the slogan "gobernar es poblar" (to govern is to populate). Among the immigrants were people from Austria-Hungary – 31,000 Ruthenians and Poles, although they did not necessarily clearly identify themselves as such. The distinction between polacos and rutenos appeared later. They formed agricultural settlements in the Misiones province (Apóstoles, Azara, San José and Corpus), and smaller worker enclaves in Buenos Aires, Rosario, Tucumán and the province of Corrientes.

Among 4 million immigrants who between 1888–1939 reached Brazil, Poles constituted 4.7 %. In the late 19th century, Brazilian authorities tried to form farms and attract newcomers to the valleys of Iguaçu and Parana. This policy, and

Hester Street, the center of the Jewish immigrant quarter on the Lower East Side, New York, with the cultural attributes typical of Jewish life. Photo around 1890

legends circulating about the country's wealth, attracted approximately 100,000 Poles, peasants from Oppeln, Silesia (in Prussia), the Kingdom of Poland, and Galicia before World War I. It is worth noting that the news was not always so appealing – here is a Polish beggar's song about Brazil: "Also a Christian./ But, God, mercy, what a man!/ Sleeps and works fully armed./ All around are hanging knives./ Which they use to kill their wives. / When at children he gets mad, / Chops heads off, such a dad." Immigrants arrived during the so-called "Brazilian fevers" – the first from Russian Poland in 1890–1891, a second from Galicia in 1895–1896, and the third in 1907–1908 from both Russian and Austrian Poland. The emigration was planned as permanent and peasants settled on farms in Parana, Santa Catarina and Rio Grande do Sul, where people received land under cultivation. However, the task was very difficult. Polish agricultural practices were irrelevant in the new surroundings. Settlements were peripheral and isolated. Ukrainians and Rusyns from east Galicia and Bukovyna caught the "Brazilian fever" as well. Polish emigration to Brazil was not as big as we might expect. In general approximately

80,000–100,000 Polish people settled in South America before World War I, half of them in Parana.

Until 1914 Polish emigration to Canada was neither large nor significant. In 1858, Kasubians (a distinctive ethnographical and linguistic group living in Pomerania, in the northern region of Prussia, close to the Baltic Sea) started to emigrate to Canada and soon numbered around 20,000 there. In the 1880s they were joined by Poles from Greater Poland (Prussian Poland) and Galicia. In Canada the newcomers either worked as agricultural laborers, railway

View of the Argentine pampas 1938

workers, or independent farmers. Stronger before World War I was the Ukrainian presence in Canada, since 1895 approximately 180,000 Ukrainians and Carpatho-Rusyns arrived as farmers in Manitoba, Alberta, and Saskatchewan.

Political Opinions About Migration

In the regions migrants had left, interest in migration rose when the group dominating a territory felt endangered. Originally departures were presented in a very negative light, as a problem. It was argued that emigration weakened the "demographic potential" of a country, that emigrants were exposed to assimilation abroad.

Polish writers and publicists condemned emigration. Józef Ignacy Kraszewski, a writer, presented it as "a crime," "desertion," "a misfortune." Eliza Orzeszkowa used even stronger words. Losing national identity in a foreign surrounding was described as "a Polish drama." Public opinion in Hungary was identical. Politicians were supported by poets: "Hungarians will perish as if they had never existed," wrote Ady Endre. The Croatian weekly "Sabor" in 1903 wrote: "If the mass exodus goes on, the very existence of the Croat nationality will become uncertain."

In Hungary Count Kuno Klebesberg, Under Secretary of State in the year 1902, suggested that the emigration of non-Hungarian nationalities could be an advantage in building the Hungarian national state. He wrote: "… smaller ethnic groups have recently been awakening to an ever increasing national consciousness, it is hardly possible to count any further on more extensive assimilation […an] important new factor [is] the mass emigration of the non-Hungarian population."

In the Polish lands it was often believed that peasants and members of the lower classes, who mostly took part in migrations, were "ignorant," illiterate, nationally unaware. Indeed, deep inside their hearts, migrants still belonged to their villages, towns, or "private homelands," as sociologist Stanisław Ossowski has aptly called them. Migrants often considered themselves rather to belong to regional,

village communities, "private homelands" not to any larger structures. Thus, though they had known and missed their "private homelands", in the new and alien cultural and linguistic surroundings they discovered supra-local links. The original concerns faded away. Some commentators said that migration was not harmful because the movement to America was temporary in nature. Nonetheless, there still was a belief that in distant territories people could lose national awareness. That ties between emigrant communities overseas and the Old Country should be strengthened, was a belief among Polish politicians. Furthermore, the Commercial-Geographical Society in Galicia (organized to provide help to migrants) propagated emigration to Parana. Joseph Siemiradzki called the state of Parana "New Poland" tout court. "Polish emigration" should thus change its form from the one "for bread with butter" to conscious "colonization" efforts. Emigrants' settlements were now seen as a chance for a new dynamism for nationalist efforts. And since, indeed, migrants were acquiring rather than losing national awareness, emigration from the nationalist perspective, should be supported. The Hungarian politician Mihály Károlyi said that "great Hungarian colonies in America" were ideally "suited for the propagation of our ideals." In the 20th century Slovak nationalist politicians also said that in America Slovak nationalism had good prospects for development. Ukrainian politicians – on the contrary – opposed the movement, which would weaken the Ukrainian/Ruthenian presence in Galicia.

Migration movements were thus – in Hungary, among Polish or Ukrainian politicians – evaluated first of all from the perspective of national identity or the formation of national states.

Bibliography

Bodnar J., The Transplanted. A History of Immigrants in Urban America, Bloomington: Indiana University Press, 1985

Brinkman T., "Jewish Mass Migrations between Empire and Nation State," Przegląd Polonijny (Kraków), 31(2005), No 1, 99–116

Brożek A., Polish Americans 1854–1939, trans. W. Worsztynowicz (Warszawa Interpress, 1985)

Drnovsek M. "Ljubljana and Emigrant Agencies at the Beginning of the Twentieth Century," AEMI Journal (Stavanger), 1(2003), 47–55

Duda-Dziewierz K., Wieś małopolska a emigracja amerykańska. Studium wsi Babica powiatu rzeszowskiego. Warszawa-Poznań 1938, Biblioteka Socjologiczna nr 3

Erickson C., "Jewish People in the Atlantic Migration 1850–1914," in: Patterns of migration, 1850–1914. Proceedings of the International Academic Conference of the Jewish Historical Society of England and the Institute of Jewish Studies, University College London, London 1996, 1–20

Fassmann H., "Emigration, Immigration, and Internal Migration in the Austro-Hungarian Monarchy 1910," in: Roots of the Transplanted, Vol. 1, 255–267

Hoerder D., Blank I., eds., Roots of Transplanted, Vol. 1: Late 19th Century east Central and south-eastern Europe, Boulder-New York 1994, 201–252

Hammack D.C., D.L. Grabowski, J.J. Grabowski, eds., Identity, Conflict, and Cooperation. Central Europeans in Cleveland, 1850–1930, Cleveland 2002, 185–248

Hoerder D., "The Traffic of Emigration via Bremen/Bremerhaven: Merchants' Interests, Protective Legislation, and Migrants' Experiences," Journal of American Ethnic History, 13(1993, no 1, 68–101

Kula M., Assorodobraj-Kula N., Wtulich J., eds., Writing Home, Boulder-New York : Columbia University Press, 1987

Moch L.P., Moving Europeans. Migration in western Europe since 1650, Bloomington-Indianapolis 2003

Morawska E., Insecure Prosperity. Small-Town Jews in Industrial America, 1890–1940, Princeton: Princeton University Press, 1996

Morawska E., "Labor Migrations of Poles in the Atlantic World Economy, 1880–1914," Comparative Studies in Society and History 31(1989), 237–272

Morawska E., "East Europeans on the Move," in: R. Cohen, ed., The Cambridge Survey of World Migrations,

Arrival of the "Kaiser Wilhelm II" express steamer in Bremerhaven. Postcard 1910

Cambridge: Cambridge University Press, 1995, 97–102

Morawska E., For Bread with Butter: The Life-Worlds of east Central Europeans in Johnstown, Pennsylvania, 1890–1940, New York-Cambridge 1985

Nugent W., Crossing. The Great Transatlantic Migrations, 1870–1914, Bloomington-Indianapolis: Indiana University Press, 1992

Puskás J. ed., Overseas Migration from East-Central and south-eastern Europe, 1880–1914, Budapest: Akadémiai Kiadó, 1990

Puskás J., "Overseas Emigration from Hungary and the National Minorities, 1880–1914," in: Ethnicity and Society in Hungary, Ferenc Glaz ed., Budapest 1990, Études Historique Hongroise 1990 publiée a l'occasion du XVIIe Congrès International des Sciences Historique, Budapest: MTA Történettudományi Intézet, 1990, 281–302

Puskás J., Ties That Bind. Ties That Divide: 100 Years of Hungarian Experience in the United States. Translated by Zora Ludwig, New York: Holmes and Meier, 2000

Walaszek A., "Preserving or Transforming Role? Migrants and Polish Territories in the Era of Mass Migrations," in: D. Hoerder, J. Nagler, eds. People in Transit.

German Migrations in Comparative Perspective, 1820–1930, Cambridge: Cambridge University Press, 1995, 101–124

Emigrant agent's office in the Austrian region of Burgenland. Photo ca. 1905

"DUILIO"
"GIULIO CESARE"
I DUE MAGGIORI VAPORI
in servizio tra
L'EUROPA E il SUD-AMERICA

SEZIONE TRASVERSALE

27.000. Tonnellate di dislocamento
194. Metri di lunghezza · · ·
23. Metri di larghezza · · ·
29. Metri di altezza · · · ·
20. Nodi all'ora di velocità·

Cross section of an Italian emigrant ship on the route Europe-South America, poster 1920. The "Giulio Cesare", the first of two 27,000-ton steamships built by the Navigazione Generale Italiana – the other was the "Duilio" – was used on Genoa-Naples-South American voyages but also served North American ports. It could accommodate 256 passengers in first class, 306 in second class, and 1,800 in third class

Marina Maccari-Clayton/Maddalena Marinari

Emigration from Southern Europe to the United States (1830–1914)

In 1911, the United States Immigration Commission published a 41-volume report on the impact of the recent wave of immigration on American society. The Commission's findings introduced for the first time the distinction between "old" immigrants (those from north-western European countries) and "new" immigrants (those from eastern and southern Europe). Greeks, Italians, Spaniards, and Portuguese all fell into the latter group. About 17 million Europeans had migrated to the United States between 1831 and 1880, but less than 2% of them had come from southern Europe. The following 35 years witnessed a dramatic shift toward Greeks, Italians, Spaniards, and Portuguese, who came to represent over 20% of all the migrants arriving from the "old" world.

A Quantitative Exploration

In absolute numbers, the increase in emigration from southern Europe was largely driven by Italian migration. During the first fifty-year period (1831–1880), 80,838 immigrants arrived in the United States from the Italian peninsula (0.9% of total immigration from Europe). In the last two decades of the 19th century (1881–1900), the number of Italian migrants increased to almost one million (12%), and the figures tripled in the following 14 years (1901–1914), when Italian emigration came to account for 25% of all European emigration and 87% of the southern European flow. Greek emigration also increased significantly during the same period. The number of Greek arrivals in the U.S., which was little more than a statistical curiosity between 1831 and 1880 (0.004% of total European migration for the period), grew to be over a quarter of a million in the opening years of the 20th century (8% of all emigration from southern Europe). Proportionally, the growth of Greek emigration was even more impressive than that of Italians. While the magnitude of the Greek flow swelled by over three hundred times from 1831–1880 to 1881–1914, the Italian flow increased by twenty-one times over the same time span.

Spain and Portugal experienced a similar increase from the late 19th century onward but at a slower pace. Between 1831 and 1880, Spaniards and Portuguese accounted for 0.3% and 0.2% respectively of the total flow from Europe. The numbers for Spain remained essentially the same (0.33%) for the following 35 years, while Portuguese emigration to the United States increased to 0.8%. These numbers, however, should be taken with some caution. When compiling their statistics, U.S. immigration officials classified immigrants based on the country of last residence. Hence, the figures above only reflect arrivals directly from the Iberian Peninsula. Many Portuguese and even more Spaniards who entered the United States before World War I, however, did so from third countries, namely from Latin America and the Caribbean. Over 1.2 million Spanish migrants went to Cuba

Greek, Italian, Portuguese, and Spanish immigration to the U.S. by decade (1831–1914)

	Greece	Italy	Portugal	Spain
1831–1840	49	2.253	829	2,125
1841–1850	16	1,812	550	2,105
1851–1860	31	9,289	1,048	9,403
1861–1870	72	11,725	2,658	6,697
1871–1880	210	55,759	13,624	5,266
1881–1890	2,308	307.309	16,978	4,419
1891–1900	15,979	651,893	27,502	8,726
1901–1910	167,519	2.045,877	69,149	27,935
1911–1914	106,324	889,296	43,673	25,159

Emigrants in Genoa the night before going on board, undated, probably around 1900

One last quantitative factor to take into consideration when analyzing southern European emigration to the United States is the staggering return migration numbers for most of the southern European migrants, especially for the two largest groups. Despite the significant spikes in their emigration rates to the New World, in fact, 63% of Greeks and 58% of Italians eventually returned to their respective homelands.

Why Did They Leave?

The late 19th century marked a watershed in the history of European migrations, as southern and eastern Europe came to replace the north-western European countries as the main areas of origin of the emigrants. Population growth, the persistence of traditional economic structures in a rapidly industrializing world, and, in some cases, internal political developments were all factors that contributed to the surge in emigration from southern Europe. In the last quarter of the 19th century, cheap wheat imports from the United States and Russia flooded European markets and presented agricultural laborers and small landowners with an almost impossible challenge. The emergence of a global market hit the southern European countries especially hard. Their economies were still largely pre-industrial, their agricultural production relied on inefficient methods, and modern manufacturing was taking off slowly and only in limited areas (north-eastern Italy, Catalonia). In addition to declining opportunities for employment and profits in agriculture, Italy and Portugal faced a population boom that further saturated the labor market. The Italian population, which numbered slightly above 26 million at the time of unification in 1861, passed the 34-million mark by the beginning of the 20th century. The Portuguese population almost doubled in 50 years, rising from about 3.8 million at the middle of the 19th century to about 5.5 million by the opening of the 20th century. Moreover, the years 1830–1914 were also a period of political turmoil in all the countries of the Mediterranean basin. The Carlist Wars in Spain, the growing strength of republicanism in Portugal, the instability in the Balkan areas, and the social problems confronting

between the last two decades of the 19th century and the end of the 1910s. An undetermined number of them then moved to the United States, especially following the Spanish-American war in 1898 when Cuba ceased to be part of the Spanish Empire. In a similar fashion, many Portuguese entered the United States from the former colony of Brazil.

From the 1880s onward, more Greeks, Italians, Portuguese, and Spaniards went to the United States than ever before. The increase in U.S. immigration from these countries took place in the context of an overall rise in emigration from the Mediterranean basin. When considered within this broader framework, the United States emerges as just one destination among many others available to southern European emigrants. In fact, of the about 14 million Italians who emigrated between 1876 – the first year for which official statistics are available – and 1914, about 28% chose the United States as their destination; of the almost 1.5 million Portuguese who emigrated between 1855 and 1914, about 12.3% went to the United States; and of the over 3 million emigrants who left Spain between 1882 and the outbreak of the First World War, only 2% emigrated to the United States. For these three groups of emigrants, European (France, Switzerland) and South American (Argentina, Brazil) countries were the main destinations in the 19th century and remained important receiving countries throughout the first decades of the 20th century.

he new Kingdom of Italy all contributed to social upheaval across southern Europe. As economic conditions worsened, as population growth put a heavier burden on unskilled workers, and as political conflicts emerged, more and more Greeks, Italians, Portuguese, and Spaniards, decided to migrate, attracted by the higher wages available in the industrialized nations of north-western Europe and overseas.

If southern Europe lagged behind industrialized nations and saw its relative economic power stagnate, north-western Europe and the United States witnessed a second wave of rapid and large-scale industrialization. The United States quickly emerged as one of the world's leading industrialized economies. During the Progressive Era (ca. 1890–1913), its economic boom fueled massive demands for cheap and unskilled labor for the mines and the factories of the great urban centers in the Northeast and the Midwest. Furthermore, the concentration of industrial production led to urbanization, which in turn stimulated the growth of the construction sector. Finally, as the American economy took off, the building of infrastructure, especially the extension of railway lines, intensified (The Great northern Railroad, Canadian Pacific Railway, etc.). At the same time, improvements in transportation and the opening of new steamship routes between southern Europe and North America facilitated the diffusion of information about employment opportunities in the New World and provided prospective migrants with faster, cheaper, and safer passage across the Atlantic. These simultaneous changes convinced many southern European agrarian laborers to leave home to find jobs as factory workers, day laborers, miners, and construction workers in the United States. As their communities in America grew, many began to work in the service industry as well, opening restaurants, banks, grocery stores, and cleaners that catered to their countrymen.

As the first significant groups of Greeks, Italians, Portuguese, and Spaniards settled in the United States, they played a crucial role in attracting more immigrants from their respective countries. The letters and remittances they sent to friends and relatives back home contributed to the creation of the myth of America – the country where streets were paved with gold. Their savings provided the capital necessary to sponsor the trips of those family members who could not afford the cost of the journey across the Atlantic. And those who decided to settle permanently in the United States sent for their wives and children that they had left behind in the "old" world.

Southern European Immigrants in the United States

The Greeks

Before the wave of mass migration that began in the 1880s, only a few Greek cotton merchants, sailors, gold miners, and students had left Greece to settle in the United States. By 1860, only about 328 Greek migrants lived in the United States, and they resided mostly in Arkansas, California, Massachusetts, and New Jersey. Greek immigration to the United States took off in the 1880s, when poor economic conditions, repeated crop failure, and rapid population growth prompted many to leave Greece to head to the United States, attracted by reports of a rapid American economic expansion and of available job opportunities.

An estimated 800,000 emigrants left Greece for the United States during the great wave of migration between 1890 and 1924. The exact number of Greeks who migrated to the U.S. is impossible to determine as Greece was part of the Ottoman Empire until 1821, and it acquired its current borders only after World War I. U.S. official statistics also ignore Greek expatriates from the surrounding Balkan countries Cyprus, Egypt, and Turkey and the number of Greek immigrants who entered the United States illegally. Over half of them eventually returned to Greece, but the numbers are equally unreliable because many of those who repatriated often returned to the United States or crossed the Atlantic a number of times over their lifetime.

The first sizeable group of Greek immigrants arrived in the United States in the 1880s from the region of Laconia, particularly from Sparta. In the 1890s, they were followed by a migratory flow from Arcadia, which eventually provided the largest number of Greek immigrants in the United States. Emigrants from central Greece, Crete, the Aegean and Ionian Islands, and the Dodecanese Islands, joined the first two groups shortly afterwards, together with Greek

View of Naples, undated picture postcard

Greek miners in Clear Creek, Utah, pose for a photograph to send to relatives in Crete, ca. 1915. The bottles and guns are perhaps signs of affluence

immigrant communities and opened restau rants, candy stores, bootblack and sho repair stores, dry cleaners, florists, bars taverns, and grocery stores.

The Portuguese

The origins of Portuguese emigration ca be traced back to the great explorations o the 15th and 16th centuries, but it was onl around the middle of the 19th century tha departures from Portugal became a "mass phenomenon. The majority of the Portugues emigrants went to Latin America, especiall Brazil and Venezuela. Yet, the 19th centur also witnessed the beginning of a signif icant flow to the United States. Most o these migrants did not come from Portuga proper but hailed from the Azores, wher overpopulation, the land-tenure system, and geo-climatic conditions precluded youn adults from finding stable employmen

nationals from Turkey, Cyprus, the Balkans, and Egypt. Greek emigrants represented a fairly homogenous group from a cultural standpoint. The majority of them spoke standard Greek, had very few years of schooling, and adhered to the Greek Orthodox faith. Most of them were unskilled males from rural areas, who spoke no English and knew very little about the country to which they were going. The few Jews, Slavophones, and Romanians coming from Greece proper never became part of the Greek-American community.

Except for a small minority of urban and educated Greeks who left Turkey to flee the persecutions of the Turkish government and for some young males who desired to avoid compulsory military service, the majority left for economic reasons and hardly ever intended to settle permanently in the United States. They planned to migrate temporarily in order to take advantage of the higher wages available overseas to improve their lives and those of their families upon their return to Greece. The aspiring emigrants usually bought their passage to the United States by selling their land or borrowing money, either by mortgaging family property or by using future wages as collateral if an agent or their prospective employer agreed to do so.

Upon their arrival in the United States, Greek immigrants settled in the industrial cities in the Northeast and the Midwest. New Hampshire, Massachusetts, Pennsylvania, Illinois, Ohio, and Wisconsin were the states with the highest concentration of Greeks. New York City, however, soon emerged as the urban center with the largest Greek community. Another group of Greek immigrants spread across the South, settling in Galveston, Texas; Atlanta, Georgia; or Tarpon Springs, Florida, where a prosperous Greek community grew around the sponge diving business. Fewer numbers of Greeks opted for Colorado, California, Idaho, Nevada, and Wyoming, with the biggest settlement being in San Francisco.

Similarly to the other immigrant groups from southern Europe, Greek immigrants in the Northeast found employment as unskilled industrial workers. In New England, they worked in textile and shoe factories. Outside the factories, they found jobs as busboys, dishwashers, bootblacks, or peddlers. On the west coast, on the other hand, they worked for railroad construction companies or in mining. As their numbers grew, many Greeks started businesses that specifically targeted the members of their

Portuguese sporting club in Toronto, Canada. The poster advertizes a fishing competition on July 10, 1988

People from the eastern Mediterranean Sea also set off for the United States. All the members of this group, posing ca. 1917, emigrated from the village of Machgharah, Lebanon, and settled in Methuen, Massachusetts. Many of them belonged to the same extended family

Many single men were also leaving to avoid the mandatory military conscription that the Portuguese government had introduced at the beginning of the century. As Portuguese emigration to the United States steadily increased in the last years of the 19th century, the early Azorean migrants were joined by a flow originating in Portugal proper. Similar reasons to the first Azorean emigration lay behind this second flow: population pressure, unemployment, and a regional imbalance in economic development, with the districts of Lisbon and Oporto experiencing significant industrial growth during this period while the rest of the country lagged significantly behind.

Overall, the modern Portuguese migratory experience to the United States consisted of four different streams. The first, and quantitatively most significant, involved Azoreans recruited as crew members on American whaling expeditions departing from New England. This initial form of temporary recruitment gradually led to the establishment of a steady migration flow between the Azores and the east Coast of the United States, further encouraged by the establishment of American mercantile houses on the Portuguese islands. In the 1870s, as these first Azorean settlements grew, their friends, relatives, and family members began to arrive, especially after the growth of direct shipping between Boston and the port of Horta in the Azores provided a direct and more effective

means of transportation. The second largest group of Portuguese immigrants settled on the west Coast during the California gold rush of the mid-19th century. Most of them arrived from New England or Hawaii. The number of Portuguese in California rose from 109 in 1850 to over 8,000 in the 1880s. With the abating of the gold rush, the majority of these Californian Portuguese entered farming or found employment once again in the whaling industry.

The remaining two flows of Portuguese migration to the United States went to Louisiana and Hawaii at the end of the 19th century. Neither group went to its destination spontaneously; rather they arrived as contract workers for the sugar plantations. In Louisiana, they were employed as a substitute for slave labor, and a group of runaways from Louisiana subsequently established the first Portuguese settlement in Hawaii. Of the two flows, Portuguese migration to Hawaii was quantitatively more relevant. At the end of 1880, over 800 Azoreans lived in Hawaii, and their number increased after 1882 when the Portuguese and Hawaiian governments (Hawaii became part of the United States in 1898) signed a commercial treaty that also included provisions concerning emigration. Portuguese migrants to Hawaii provided the workforce to counteract the islands' persistent labor shortage and helped limit the hiring of Asian migrants. The Hawaii Sugar Planter's Association offered

Portuguese immigrants three-year contracts, which included food, lodging, medical care, a garden plot, and a monthly wage of ten dollars. The Company also encouraged the immigration of entire families by providing the full cost of passage for each man and child and half the cost for each woman. This policy marked a decisive shift in the composition of the Portuguese community on the island, which went from being prevalently male in 1878 to achieving a more balanced ratio already by the early 1890s. Between 1878 and 1913, approximately 18,000 Portuguese migrated to Hawaii, bringing the percentage of the Portuguese on the island from one to 15% of the overall Hawaiian population. The flow of Portuguese migrants to Hawaii ended abruptly in 1914 when the sugar planters began to recruit laborers from other regions of the world.

Most of the Portuguese from the Azores, Madeira, and continental Portugal, however, migrated to the U.S. mainland. Responding to repeated economic crises and persistent political turmoil, they soon joined the mass migration to the United States at the turn of the 20th century and reached a peak in 1920. As their predecessors, they continued to settle primarily in California and New England. Portuguese from the Azores moved to California to join the older Azorean communities to work as entrepreneurs or employees in the farming, dairy, and fishing industries. Portuguese

Italian emigrants on the steamer « La Champagne » on the way to Rio de Janeiro. Dramatizing representation, newspaper graphic ca. 1898

from Madeira and continental Portugal joined the uninterrupted flow of Azoreans who had settled on the east Coast. The new arrivals took jobs as unskilled laborers in the New England textile mill towns. Portuguese emigration to the United States slowed down significantly after the passage of the literacy test requirement in 1917 and almost completely stopped with the ratification of the quota system with the 1924 Immigration Act. Between 1900 and 1920, 25% of the Azorean migrants in the U.S. mainland left to return to their homeland. Many of them would eventually return to the United States to leave once again afterwards. An estimated 94% of those who returned later left again in less than ten years.

The Spaniards

Many of the causes that motivated Portuguese to leave also caused their next-door neighbors to emigrate. Similar to Portugal, 19th-century Spain was a country in crisis – both politically and economically. The loss of most of its empire following colonial wars of independence (1808–1829) deprived Spain of the main source of its riches and reduced it to a second-rate power. Spanish migration had a long-established tradition dating back to the Age of Exploration in the late 15th century. The 19th century, however, witnessed the beginning of a new kind of emigration from the Iberian Peninsula. No longer conquistadores or exclusively colonial settlers, many Spanish emigrants of the 19th century became

an integral part of the population movement that linked the impoverished laborers of the southern European countries to the employment opportunities available in the industrial centers of north-western Europe and the Americas.

Approximately 5 million Spaniards emigrated between 1882 and 1947. Very few Spanish migrants arrived in the United States directly from Spain, however. Many of them went elsewhere first. Half of those who left after 1882 went to Argentina, which at the time was actively pursuing European immigrants to implement its populationist policies. Many of the remaining migrants went to Brazil or to Cuba while it was still part of the Spanish Empire. When Cuba became independent after the Spanish-American war of 1898, a significant number of them moved on to the United States. Although the tension between the United States and Spain that preceded and followed the war diminished the flow directly from Spain to the United States, more Spanish migrants continued to enter the United States from the other Latin and South American countries where they had previously settled.

Many of the Spanish migrants came mostly from four different areas and, similarly to the rest of southern European emigrants, they left with the hope to save enough money to return to their native village to acquire property and improve their social status within the community. The majority of those who left for the United States were young men from Galicia and areas of Old Castile touching its southern borders. Both areas were isolated, prevalently agricultural, and among the poorest in the country. Galicia's stringent inheritance laws further hindered the economic prospects of many Galicians, as they either prescribed the fragmentation of family property into smaller and economically non-profitable plots of land among all the siblings or stipulated the granting of the inheritance to first-born children only. Later on, Asturias became another Spanish region to send many emigrants to America. Emigrants from this area were more highly skilled than other contemporary southern Europeans as they had often previously worked in the region's emerging coal mining, ship building, and metal working industries. It was their presence in the United States that gave Spanish migrants a reputation for being highly skilled workers. Smaller numbers of Spanish migrants also left from Madeira, Granada, Almeria, and the Canary Islands. In these regions, the slow industrialization, rural poverty, and agricultural problems combined with the existence of large latifundia – the control of large estates by few families – forced many to leave to look for a job on the other side of the Atlantic. Finally, many of the Spanish migrants who left for the United States came from the Basque Country, where the devastation that followed the Napoleonic and the Carlist Wars added to the already precarious living and working conditions of the region.

Most of the Spanish migrants in the United States settled in California, Florida, the Mountain West, New York, and industrial cities in the Midwest. The biggest Spanish community in the United States was in New York City, especially in Brooklyn.

From here, many of them later moved to New Jersey or Connecticut. Because of its connections with the Cuban cigar industry, Florida soon became home to the second largest Spanish community in the country. Many of the cigar factory owners were originally from Asturias, had moved to Cuba through the late 19th century, and then relocated to Key West and Tampa, bringing many of their Spanish workers with them to their American factories. Spanish migrants who settled in California joined earlier Spanish communities of pineapple and sugar cane growers who had resettled in the United States from Hawaii, where they had migrated during the first decades of the 19th century. Others moved to San Francisco or went to work in the heavy industry in southern California.

The Italians

Between 1886 and the outbreak of World War I, about 4 million Italians migrated to the United States. However, small contingents of Italians had been migrating to the United States well before the 1880s. Before the Civil War, most of the Italian migrants who left for the United States were mostly intellectuals, revolutionaries, artists, artisans, or skilled farmers from economically developed areas in northern Italy. Many of the skilled farmers from Liguria and Piedmont settled in California and established prosperous wine and citrus enterprises or moved to New York to become prominent fruit merchants. Hundreds of others left to participate in the 1849 Gold Rush in California, to take advantage of the job prospects for seamen in the

During the peak immigration years, the facilities on Ellis Island, the immigration station in the New York Bay, were so overcrowded that newcomers such as this Italian family might have had to wait several days on their ship before a ferry could even bring them to the island. Photo 1905

Italian posters advertizing sailings to the United States and South America 1906. Trieste was the largest port in the Austro-Hungarian Empire at that time, although over two-thirds of the residents were Italian. The shipping companies also advertized emigration insurance, which would reimburse the emigrant did he fail to be admitted. Travel advantages such as medical dare, electric light and ventilation were also emphasized

port of New Orleans, or to work as artisans for Casper Hennecke, a statuary maker in Milwaukee. Yet, Italian emigration to the United States began in earnest only in the 1880s, when its numbers grew exponentially. Almost 40% of all Italians who left between 1901 and 1914 went to the United States. This substantial transatlantic emigration to the United States coincided with a larger emigration flow out of Italy that saw Italian emigrants spread in four other major destinations across both sides of the Atlantic in addition to the United States, namely Argentina, Austria-Hungary, Brazil, and France.

A complex web of factors lay behind the age of Italian mass emigration. In the late 1880s, three major economic setbacks forced many Italians to seek work abroad: the United States cut its imports of Italian citrus fruits because of the improved production in Florida and California; plant lice destroyed thousands of Italian vineyards; and France established high tariffs that curtailed the export of grapes from Apulia, Calabria, and Sicily. In addition to these serious economic setbacks, other factors that contributed to the high emigration rates out of Italy during the last decades of the 19th century included low wages, rapid population growth, the introduction of the military draft, poor health conditions, repeated crop failures, heavy indirect taxes, the absence of a responsive and attentive national government, corruption among local government officials, and the control of most of the land available by exploitative wealthy landowners. As in the case of the other groups examined so far, a small percentage of the Italians who left did so for political reasons. After the debacle of the Fasci Siciliani – a movement that developed in Sicily between 1891 and 1894 that sought to organize farmers, workers, and miners – many of the Sicilians who took part in the movement left to escape the political and social repercussions of the aftermath. In addition to economic and political motivations, reports of opportunities for economic improvement and upward mobility in the Americas as well as the transportation revolution further reinforced Italians' desire to seek their fortunes elsewhere.

Most of the Italians who left between 1880 and 1920 came from poor agricultural areas in Abruzzi, Campania, Apulia, Basilicata (Lucania), Calabria, and Sicily. Many of them were unskilled men between the age of 16 and 45 who emigrated to work abroad to save as much money as possible and then to return to Italy to purchase their own plot of land and provide for their families. Similarly to other southern European migrants, Italian emigrants hardly ever left with the intention of settling in the United States permanently. Many of them traveled to America in the early spring, worked seasonal jobs until late fall, and returned to their families in Italy at the beginning of winter. For them, trips to the United States represented the extension to the other side of the Atlantic of a long-established radition of temporary labor migration. talians believed that the United States was not a land where migrants went to stay and viewed it as a means rather than an end. As a testament to this belief, between 1899 and 1924, these "birds of passage," as Americans called them, reached a peak of 3.8 million, but some 2.1 million returned to Italy during the same period. The problems with integration that many Italian migrants faced once in the United States as well as the negative stereotypes that mainstream America had of them effectively delayed the desire for many of them to settle permanently in the New World. The gender ratio among Italian migrants began to shift only at the beginning of the 20th century when a growing number of men began to settle permanently in the United States and to send for their families to join them.

Central to the initial phases of Italian emigration to the United States was the padrone system. Subsequently outlawed by the United States government, the padrone system saw previously established Italians acting as intermediaries between American employers and the newly arrived immigrants. The padroni found employment and paid for the transatlantic ship fare, but they asked aspiring emigrants to pay them back exorbitant amounts of money, exploited their labor, and forced them to cope with sub-standard working conditions. Expecting their stay in the United States to be only temporary, many Italian migrants often lived as inexpensively and frugally as possible under conditions that many Americans viewed as intolerable.

Once in the United States, most Italian migrants concentrated in major industrial areas in states on the east Coast, namely New York, Connecticut, Massachusetts, Rhode Island, and Pennsylvania, or went westward to work in Illinois or California. During the era of mass migration, an estimated 97% of Italians landed in New York City, making it the city with the largest Italian community in the country. They often worked as factory workers, peddlers, ragpickers, manual laborers, miners, or street workers; however, approximately half of Italian emigrants in the United States at the end of the 19th century took heavy construction jobs. They built bridges and roads, dug tunnels, laid railroad tracks, and erected the first skyscrapers. As they began

to settle permanently in the New World, Italians created ethnic neighborhoods that expanded the range of job opportunities as some of them opened small businesses that catered to their fellow countrymen.

Selected Bibliography

Baganha, Maria Ioannis Beni. Portuguese Emigration to the United States, 1820–1930. New York: Garland Publishing, 1990.

Bertagna, Federica, and Marina Maccari-Clayton. "Italian." In: Enzyklopädie Migration in: Europa. Vom 17. Jahrhundert biz zur Gegenwart, edited by Klaus J. Bade, Pieter Emmer, Jochen Oltmer and Leo Lucassen, 205-219. Paderborn and Munich: ferdinand Schoningh and Wilhelm Fink, 2007.

Emmer, Jochen Oltmer and Leo Lucassen 205–219. Paderborn and Munich: Ferdinand Schöningh and Wilhelm Fink, 2007.

Bevilacqua, Piero, Andreina De Clementi and Emilio Franzina, eds. Storia dell'Emigrazione Italiana – Partenze. Rome, Italy: Donzelli, 2001.

Bevilacqua, Piero, Andreina De Clementi and Emilio Franzina, eds. Storia dell'Emigrazione Italiana – Arrivi. Rome, Italy: Donzelli, 2002.

Carreras, Albert and Xavier Tafunell, eds. Estadísticas Históricas de España – Siglos XIX-XX, 2nd edition. Fundación BBVA, 2005.

Carter, Susan B., Scott Sigmund Gartner, Michael R. Haines, Alan L. Olmstead, Richard Sutch, Gavin Wright, eds. Historical Statistics of the United States. Millennial Edition. Cambridge: Cambridge University Press, 2006.

Fernandez-Shaw, Carlos. The Hispanic Presence in North America from 1492 to Today. New York: Facts on File, 1991.

Friedman, Max Paul. "Beyond 'Voting with Their Feet:' Toward a Conceptual History of 'America' in European Migrant Communities, 1860s to 1914." Journal of Social History, Vol. 40, No. 3 (Spring 2007): 557–575.

Gabaccia, Donna R. Italy's Many Diasporas. Seattle, WA: University of Washington Press, 2000.

Harvard Encyclopedia of American Ethnic Groups. Cambridge, MA: Harvard University Press, 1980.

Hatton, Timothy and Jeffrey G. Williamson. The Age of Mass Migration. Causes and Economic Impact. New York: Oxford University Press, 1998.

ISTAT, Sommario di Statistiche Storiche dell'Italia, 1861–1875, 1976.

Luconi, Stefano and Matteo Pretelli, L'immigrazione negli Stati Uniti. Bologna, Italy: Il Mulino, 2008.

Moya, José. Cousins and Strangers. Spanish Immigrants in Buenos Aires, 1850–1930. Berkeley, CA: University of California Press, 1998.

Moskos, Charles C. Greek Americans: Struggles and Success, 2nd edition. New Brunswick, NJ: Transaction, 1989.

Salutos, Theodore. The Greeks in the United States. Cambridge, MA: Harvard University Press, 1964.

Scourby, Alice. The Greek Americans. Boston, MA: Twayne, 1977.

Wyman, Mark. Roundtrip to America: The Immigrants Return to Europe, 1880–1930. Ithaca, NY: Cornell University Press, 1993.

Italians arriving at the Emigrant Aid Society in Naples before embarking for the United States. Many Italians, as well as Greeks and Slavs, followed a pattern of migration that brought them to the United States in the spring and returned them home in time for Christmas. Immigration officials called them "Birds of Passage"

Poster advertising Oelrichs & Co, the Bremen emigration agency
for North German Lloyd in New York, 1875

Horst Rössler

"The Time has Come, We are Going to America." The Main Travel Routes and Emigrant Ports

The 19th century (1815–1914) was the century of mass European overseas migration, the destination being, for the most part, the United States of America. Around 1850, the most important European emigration ports had emerged: the so-called "western Ports" of Le Havre, Antwerp and Rotterdam on the Atlantic; Bremen and Hamburg on the North Sea coast; and London and Liverpool in Great Britain. Only after 1880 did Genoa and Naples in Italy also gain importance as ports of departure for overseas migrants.

In 1851, 3,000 Germans left their home via Rotterdam and 9,200 via Antwerp. In that year, 18,000 overseas migrants were registered in Hamburg and nearly 38,000 in Bremen (mainly German). Le Havre was by far the most important continental European embarkation port at this time. Around 72,000 emigrants were counted here in 1852, of whom more than 45,000 came from Bavaria, Baden, Hesse and other German states. English, Scottish and Irish emigrants were in the majority at the British ports. Until 1850, London was the most important emigrant port in the United Kingdom; later, Liverpool took the lead. In 1851, 160,000 passengers left from there for New York. The city on the Mersey also became the most important embarkation port for Scandinavian overseas migrants from Sweden and Norway. A considerable proportion of German migrants emigrated via England, too. In 1853, approximately 30,000 Germans are said to have traveled via London and Liverpool. Overall, until the mid-1850s, the majority of German overseas emigrants left their home from non-German ports, Le Havre being of exceptional importance in this regard.

The volume of travel via these ports increased steadily during the second half of the 19th century. After 1855, however, Bremen and Hamburg replaced Le Havre as the most important ports for German emigrants. European emigration peaked in 1913, just before the beginning of the First World War, when 240,000 people left the Old World via Bremen alone – 190,000 from Hamburg and 160,000 from Le Havre. In fact, Bremen had developed into the leading emigrant port from continental Europe, just ahead of Hamburg. After 1890, the migrants came mainly from eastern and south-eastern Europe, including many Jewish emigrants, who left the continent for the USA and other foreign regions via the German ports or from Le Havre. Le Havre also attracted a large number of Italian emigrants at this time. The majority of the Italian overseas migrants, however, left home from Genoa and Naples, bound both for the United States and for Latin America, in particular Argentina.

The Journey to the Seaports

During the early stages of overseas mass migration, the migrants used the traditional overland routes, as developed in the 18th century, to reach the emigrant ports. Thus, for German emigrants, Strasbourg and later Mannheim were the most important gathering points on the Rhine, from where emigrants from the south-west of Germany began their arduous journey by freight-wagon via Paris to Le Havre, a journey which often lasted several weeks. Wagoners from Le Havre and Paris, who transported freight to Strasbourg, took the migrants with them on the return journey. But emigrants also banded together in their hometowns, formed groups, hired wagoners there or bought horses and carts and set off together. The emigrants then sold the carts and the horses in Paris, and undertook the last stage of the journey to Le Havre by boat down the Seine. Less well-off emigrants continued to use this route around 1850.

Before the middle of the 19th century, those migrating to America from north-east and east German regions were reliant for the most part on the difficult overland journey. The "America emigrant" Heinrich

Emigrants from Hesse making their way on foot and by cart to Bremen. Oil painting, Carl Rhode. Titled: Emigrants from Hesse passing the city of Kassel on their way to Bremen, 1824

Hauptmann told of his journey of more than two weeks from Saxony to Bremen in 1833: "The first day we only got as far as Langwolmsdorf (author's note: near Stolpen, not far from Pirna, approx. 30 km away from Dresden) and on the second day we only caught up with Jokiesche's family in Dresden. They were already on the carts. They wanted to leave and I traveled with them that day as far as Meißen… Our wagoner drove very fast, and it was very good, there were little inns everywhere where we spent the night. We even had to sleep in byres and barns. On the fourth day we arrived in Leipzig… The journey went well, we had good weather for the first ten days and on the others it was stormy and it rained. On the 19th day we arrived in Bremen. We had survived the overland journey."

Often the journey to the emigrant ports was a combination of overland and river travel. Wherever possible, rivers were used as transport routes, as this increased the travel tempo noticeably, thereby dispensing with some of the difficulties. For decades, the Rhine, with its tributaries the Neckar and the Main, was the most important travel route for emigrants from southern and south-western Germany. In addition to travel by boat, the massive Rhine rafts were also used until well into the 19th century. These were able to transport up to 800 people. However, the journey on the raft from the mouth of the Neckar to the coast lasted around six weeks! In Rotterdam the emigrants were then able to transfer to the transatlantic ships or travel on by boat to Le Havre, and depart the Old World from there.

Because Hamburg properly entered the emigrant market only at the end of the 1840s, the Elbe did not play a large role as a migrant transport route. This was not the case for the Weser, which for centuries had enabled the merchants from Bremen to access the hinterland. Although it was not nearly as easy to navigate as the Rhine, in the early phases of migration to America, the Weser was nevertheless of great importance for the journey overseas from Bremen. On 9 May 1833, the miller and Mennonite preacher Jakob Schwartzengruber left Hessen-Waldeck with his family and a group of other emigrants, to move to Pennsylvania. After they left, they traveled by cart first via Kassel to Münden, where the group arrived on May 10th and were able to board a Weser "Bockschiff", a small hooker with one sail usually used for

Those who wanted to emigrate legally from Germany in the 19th century were often faced with bureaucratic chicanery. Different legal stipulations applied in practically each small German state. The photo shows a passport issued by the Free Hanseatic City of Bremen in 1858 to the shop assistant Friedrich Wilhelm Corßen. This document entitled him to emigrate "free and unhindered" to Lima in Peru and it instructed all "civil and military authorities" to grant him protection and assistance

In the village of Schweinsberg near Gießen, in Hesse, the name of the "Zur Stadt New York" inn drew attention to the fact that its owner, Christian Klötz, was also an agent for North German Lloyd in Bremen and sold tickets for the passage across the Atlantic. Scene from a postcard, around 1895

transporting goods. Hindered by sandbanks and fog, it took five days for the groups of emigrants to get some distance downstream, where more emigrants from south-west Germany boarded.

On May 15th, the travelers reached "late in the evening the town of Hamelin, where we spent the evening. We had been joined on our ship by a group of 18 people from Württemberg, including a pregnant woman, who survived the birth of a boy, stillborn. This caused great delay the next day, which was the 16th, Ascension Day, for the child first had to be buried, and this took so long that we were able to leave only around ten o'clock."

Early in the day on May 17th the group reached Minden, via Vlotho. That evening the boat did not stop at a town or village, "instead we had to sleep in the open country by a large dairy pasture. We departed early on the 18th and came through Nienburg even before everyone was awake. We had hoped to reach Bremen that same day, but, because of the stormy weather, we were not able to travel ar. Here, too, there were places in the Weser where the skippers had to be very careful not to be pitched overboard, taking all of us with them. Thus, every time we met another ship, they had to throw anchor three or even four times to reach the other bank and a safe place, and this delayed us considerably so that we were not able to travel far on that day. While we set off early the next morning, that of the 19th, or the Sunday before Whitsun, we had to battle unfavorable winds and thus we were unable to reach Bremen. But on the 20th, at 10 o'clock in the morning, we arrived here." The journey on the overcrowded boat from Münden to Bremen, battling bad weather and high winds, had lasted ten days.

Not until the reduction of customs barriers within Europe (in the late 18th century from Strasbourg to the Dutch border 32 customs posts had to be crossed!), as well as the introduction of steam navigation and the construction of railway lines around 1830, was there any noticeable improvement in travel conditions. In 1827 the "Rheinisch-Preußische Dampfschiffahrtsgesellschaft", a Prussian shipping company operating on the Rhine between Cologne and Mainz was established, which later expanded its business as far as Strasbourg. In 1838 the shipping company "Dampfschiffahrtsgesellschaft für den Mittel- und Niederrhein" was set up in Düsseldorf in competition with the Cologne company and the Dutch companies. In 1842 in Hameln the "Vereinigte Weserdampfschiffahrtsgesellschaft auf der Oberweser", a shipping company offering transport on the river Weser, was created. As a result of the concurrent development of steamship and railway transport, the journeys that previously had lasted many weeks were reduced to just a few days. This made travel to the emigrant ports more predictable and less gruelling, and ultimately also less expensive, since the emigrants were able to save on the costs of board, lodgings and other travel costs.

In addition to Strasbourg and Mannheim, Basel, Frankfurt, Mainz, and above all Cologne, later Leipzig and Berlin became important gathering points for the emigrants. As early as the 1840s, Cologne was already connected with Rotterdam, Antwerp, and Le Havre by steamship and railway lines. The connection of Bremen and Hamburg to the railway network in 1847 was of great importance for German emigration to America. The Hanseatic towns could now be reached from Cologne in 12 or

Emigrants leaving on an Atlantic steamship board directly from the Compagnie Générale Transatlantique's emigrant train in Le Havre. Newspaper graphic entitled: "Arrival of an emigrant train", 1886

24 hours, respectively. This created the conditions necessary for a re-routing of German emigration from the "western Ports" to the North Sea ports of Germany – a process that was intensified through the rapid expansion of the railway lines throughout all of the German states. After 1850, the railway made Hamburg accessible from Pomerania, Lower and Upper Silesia as well as Mecklenburg. From the south of Germany, emigrants could reach Bremen or alternatively Hamburg, direct by train from Munich via Augsburg, Nördlingen, Nuremberg, and Bamberg.

In 1880, the European rail network was so well-developed that emigrants from Belgrade, Vienna, and Budapest, Prague, Kiev, Minsk, and St. Petersburg were all able to reach the North Sea ports via Berlin without difficulty. The railway was also very important for "indirect" overseas emigration from the continent via the English ports. Steamship routes connected Rotterdam and Hamburg with London and Hull. From London, emigrants could travel to the United States or to the British colonies. By preference, German emigrants to America chose the route via Hamburg to Hull, from where they were quickly brought by train to Liverpool. Slower steamship travel was ultimately not able to compete with the expansion of the rail connections and, following a brief boom

in the second half of the 19th century, it gradually lost its importance for emigration. The completion of the Paris–Strasbourg railway line in 1851 attracted the majority of emigrants away from the steamships of the Rhine onto the railway, which covered the same distance in 30 hours.

In peak times of mass overseas emigration, the European railway companies offered reduced ticket prices and discounts on luggage and used special trains, in which the emigrants were transported to the emigrant ports with limited stopovers. In the beginning, the emigrants were packed into wagons that were more like cattle trucks than passenger carriages. Until well into the 1860s, passenger carriages on the German trains had neither lighting nor heating and it was not customary for there to be toilet facilities, but these conditions gradually improved. From 1880, the French "Compagnie Générale Transatlantique" (CGT), which ran both a transatlantic shipping line and a railway line, used carriages tailored specifically to the needs of the emigrants on its emigrant trains. These were fitted with bunks and sufficient storage space and also provided food and coffee for their passengers.

The expansion of the railway and a network of highly-competitive emigration agencies went hand in hand. The shipping clerks and agents

Hôtel des Emigrants

A large Emigrants' House was established in Le Havre just before the start of World War I, coinciding with a dramatic decline in overseas mass migration into the USA. Photo around 1925

found the passengers for the ship-owners and shipping companies. Usually in the traditional areas of emigration, sub-agents such as innkeepers, bakers, grocers or merchants, who carried out this brokerage on a part-time basis, played a lead role. Despite increasing state regulation in the form of the granting of franchises and statutory monitoring, trade was characterized for many decades by unscrupulous commercial practices and fraud. This was not remedied until the establishment of large agencies that were active Europe-wide, cooperating directly with the major emigrant shipping agencies and with professional employees on site. But even this was not able to prevent the deplorable state of affairs still in evidence around the turn of the century, particularly in the highly-competitive eastern European "emigration market".

However, thanks to a continually expanding and interconnected web of agencies, the transport of millions of people who were "tired" of Europe was not only brought under control but also simplified, so that by about the turn of the century, the journey overseas became almost routine, even from the most remote areas of Europe. Before the World War I, there was a gathering point for south-eastern European emigrants in Ljubljana in Slovenia, with ten major emigration agencies, including representatives of the leading German,

French, Dutch, Belgian, and British shipping companies, advertising departure from Bremen, Hamburg, Le Havre, Rotterdam, Antwerp, and Liverpool.

Albin Kunc from Ljubljana, who, prior to his emigration to the United States in 1903, worked for several months for the Rommel emigration agency in Basel, provides in his memoirs a striking description of how he and his fellow countrymen, who came from the Austrian region of Krain, undertook the first stage of their journey to the New World by train. Although the Slovenes preferred to emigrate via Bremen/Bremerhaven or Hamburg, in the decade preceding the First World War, the French route via Switzerland, operated by CGT, was also very popular. When the train arrived in Basel from Ljubljana, the emigrants were welcomed at the station by the agents. "Every passenger had a badge affixed to his chest, so that each agent could immediately recognize "his" people. As we reached the station exit, the porter from Rommel & Cie. and a lady who worked at the company as an interpreter shouted: "hup, hup, everyone to this side". It was a terrible cry, which gave me a very unpleasant impression of this business, as I saw how the poor people were treated as soon as they arrived in Basel, as if the emigrants were just livestock."

The extra trains usually arrived in the morning in Basel, where food was provided for the emigrants. In the early evening, the journey continued to Paris, where the travellers were met the next morning at the eastern Station by a CGT employee and led by him to another station. Before the journey continued the emigrants were again provided with food and drink (this was included in the ticket price) and were able to rest in large waiting rooms. The journey to Le Havre continued by night, and they reached the coast in the early hours of the morning. "The sea air also became apparent... some emigrants began to feel a little strange and many were afraid of the sea. A lot of the women began reciting the rosary, praying for safe sea passage…a short time later the extra train stopped directly at the docks of the Compagnie Générale Transatlantique. The carriage doors were opened and the passengers disembarked onto solid ground for the last time before the long journey across the Atlantic Ocean. Around 30 metres from the train, the lovely big high speed steamship "La Savoie" was moored."

In the Emigration Ports

In no other embarkation port was the emigration business as important for the economic development of the entire town as in Bremen where, from the 1820s onwards, it was mainly local merchants trading with the USA who provided passenger transport in their ships. With the increasing importance of emigration, temporary intermediary decks were fitted in the cargo holds of freight ships, where passengers were accommodated and shipped across the Atlantic as profitable export goods. In return, stackable goods such as tobacco, rice or cotton were imported from the New World. At the beginning of the forties, three quarters of all trade between Germany and North America was controlled by Bremen. It was primarily merchant shippers who profited from the emigration business, as well as brokers, shipping clerks and agents, innkeepers and retailers, who provided the emigrants with the necessary travel equipment.

This is despite the fact that for many years Bremen was at a disadvantage compared with the other European embarkation ports in terms of its location: the actual overseas port was 60 km downstream from Bremen, at the mouth of the Weser. Upon

Warnung.

Die Auswanderer werden vor **Bauernfängern** (namentlich Kartenspielern), **Taschendieben** und solchen Personen, die sich ihnen auf der Straße, in fremden Wirthschaften u. s. w. zum Geldwechseln oder zum Ankauf von **Schiffskarten** aufdrängen, gewarnt. Auswanderer, die in irgend welche Schwierigkeiten gerathen oder Auskunft bedürfen, mögen sich sofort an den **Wirth**, bei welchem sie logiren, an das **Nachweisungsbureau für Auswanderer** am Bahnhof oder an das nächste **Polizeibureau** wenden.

Die Polizeidirektion.

In 1851, an "Information Office" for the protection and care of emigrants was set up in Bremen at the Chamber of Commerce in the city center, at the main rail station and at the jetty of the Oberweser Steam Shipping Company. These offices had warnings posted throughout the city against ticket touts and pickpockets

reaching the Hanseatic town the emigrants faced a troublesome onward journey on open barges to Bremerhaven, founded in 1827; this journey took a further two to three days. While the use of steamships improved the situation considerably, only in 1862, when Bremerhaven was connected to the railway, which covered the distance to Bremen in one-and-a-half to two hours, did this disadvantage vis-à-vis the other emigrant ports lose its importance once and for all.

In no other harbor town was emigration attributed such importance by the state authorities as in Bremen, where an emigration act (Ordinance Concerning the Emigrants Travelling on Domestic or Foreign Ships) was passed as early as 1832. This was intended on the one hand to protect Bremen from destitute emigrants, and on the other, to protect those passing through the city against people taking unfair advantage of them and to prevent suffering in the town and on the ships. Above all, minimum standards were set for the accommodation and provision of food aboard ship and later, medical examinations were also regulated. Over the decades,

the Bremen emigration legislation was continually revised and improved. While from the middle of the century onwards, the government also monitored transit migration via the English ports, there was no specific legislation governing the "western Ports" of Rotterdam, Antwerp, and Le Havre, which were far more important for German emigration until around 1855. Hamburg, on the other hand, which in the thirties was not yet particularly interested in the business of overseas migration, in 1850 had emigration laws based on the Bremen provisions. Only in 1897 was emigration via the German ports codified in a nationwide emigration act.

Until that time, from 1868 the Hamburg legislation also governed indirect emigration from the Hanseatic town on the Elbe via England. In 1854 this method of travelling to the United States reached its highpoint, with a 36% share in overall emigration from Hamburg. Indirect emigration was attractive in particular for those emigrants with less money, since the passage to the USA from London and Liverpool was less expensive than from the German ports. The indirect

route was, however, more arduous, due to the more frequent changes. The journey on the steamers from Hamburg to England was particularly controversial, since, according to reports, the emigrants were treated like "livestock" on the ships, which initially were by no means equipped for passenger transport. Such drawbacks were, however, for the most part done away with by the mid-seventies, ultimately thanks to the Hamburg ordinances.

Even on the journey to the embarkation ports passengers could expect to be taken advantage of at the various gathering points, by wagoners, innkeepers or agents. In 1851, for example, the agent Geilhausen, together with the captain of a Rhine steamer tried with all his might to convince a group of emigrants from southern Germany to travel to Antwerp and to sell them passage via the Belgian port, despite the fact that the travelers had already agreed passage with a Bremen company. Geilhausen insulted Bremen, saying it was a "bad port", where emigrants to America were "treated like dogs". In 1854 the agent was given a prison sentence for various fraudulent activities, which he managed to avoid by emigrating to the USA!

This kind of treatment continued in the ports on the Atlantic, the North Sea coast and in England: the trade in "emigration fever" was lucrative not only for ship-owners, shipping clerks, brokers and agents, and business was characterized by various irregularities until the middle of the 19th century. Emigrants suffered far more due to the fact that mass emigration was a very profitable business for retailers in the harbour towns, characterized by fierce competition. Innkeepers tried by any means to persuade travelers to lodge with them; their servants, known in Bremen as "Litzer", in Hamburg as "Buttjer" and in Liverpool as "man-catchers" or "runners", brawled over the arriving travelers, trying to entice them to stay at lodgings or visit moneychangers or agents, or to conclude transactions, whereby commission payments and bribes were passed on to the emigrants by way of inflated prices. Prohibitions and writs were not initially able to counter this. Georg Brandt, traveling from Hanover to New Orleans in 1841, noted in his diary upon his arrival in Bremerhaven: "Fraud is customary trade here; anyone who does not have his wits about him is likely to be conned."

In the German ports the establishment of "Information Offices for Emigrants" helped

White Star Line poster 1918

HAPAG poster around 1870

to a certain degree. Here, too, Bremen led the way. In 1851, at the suggestion of the Chamber of Commerce, an office was established by ship-owners and brokers, with the aim of making Bremen and Bremerhaven even more attractive as an embarkation port through closer monitoring of compliance with the emigration acts. The office informed the travelers about the provisions of the emigration laws and the activities of the most important German immigrant aid organizations in the USA. In addition, emigrants were provided, free of charge, with lists of addresses of licensed shipping agents and clerks and innkeepers, including a price list for food, lodging and the transport of luggage to the inns. Furthermore, the office provided information on the average cost of the most important equipment necessary for the Atlantic crossing (such as mattresses, blankets or metal cutlery) and directed emigrants seeking advice to trustworthy moneychangers. Above all, the office acted as a central ombudsman to which the emigrants could turn. A similar institution was established in Hamburg in the same year.

In England it was the charitable organization established in 1806, the "Society of Friends of Foreigners in Distress", which took

care not only of immigrants but also of transit migrants, who passed through Hull, London or Liverpool in huge numbers on their way to the USA. Despite the international aims, this society offered help – in the form of clothing or medicine – primarily to needy travalers from Germany. In extreme emergencies, the Society even provided financial support to fund the return journey to the continent or the passage to America, whereby, due to the limited funds available to the "Society", only a very small number of emigrants were lucky enough to receive this support. In 1865 in Liverpool, 45 out of a total of 1,500 applicants received a subsidy for the journey across the Atlantic, and a further 56 for their return journey to Hamburg, Bremen, and Le Havre.

Providing accommodation for the migrants, who, according to the season and the economic situation, arrived in batches in the harbor towns, was a big problem. In the early phase of overseas emigration this often took dramatic turns. If the ships had not yet docked due to bad weather or if the cargo had to be unloaded first, the emigrants often had to wait a very long time – up to four weeks. Large groups often amassed, for which there was not nearly enough or adequate accommodation available. So, in the first half of the 1840s German

emigrants camped outside in tents erected as a temporary measure on the dockside and along the roads leading to Le Havre. When, in 1847, emigration via Bremerhaven reached a volume never before seen, with more than 33,000 people, many travalers had to be accommodated in lofts, byres, barns and on barges with completely inadequate hygienic provision and beggarly food. Even towards the end of the 19th century, disused train stations, ballrooms, and storage halls or older transatlantic steamers were used as makeshift emergency accommodation in Bremen and Hamburg.

Usually, however, throughout the 19th century, the emigrants passing through the European ports were, for the most part, accommodated in a multitude of guest houses and inns, of which there were, in Le Havre for example, around 100 in 1850, and more than 160 in Bremen in 1852. As late as 1904, more than 3,500 emigrants stayed at 52 inns in the Hanseatic town on the Weser. Grievances were the order of the day. With the establishment of "Information Offices" in Bremen and Hamburg, controls on lodgings became more stringent. Despite all efforts, however, the complaints did not let up. A police report from 1868 in Bremen states: "In the Segelkeschen Haus there are around 15–20 beds for emigrants. Mrs. Segelke estimated the number of emigrants residing in the house at around 150–160… the lounge was packed full of people, not on beds or mattresses, but on tables, chairs and on the bare floor. On the floor, where there were some beds, male and female persons were lying in a jumble entirely obscuring the floor, on straw sacks… – Mrs. Segelke continued to lie when she claimed that she took only 10 silver coins; on closer questioning it was revealed that she had consistently taken 17 ½ silver coins."

Inflated prices, crowded rooms and extremely poor sanitary facilities characterized guest houses and inns at the high point of mass European emigration overseas. In 1883 in Hamburg, inns were licensed for a total of 2,000 emigrants. When this was no longer enough due to the influx of travalers coming into the town, the Senate permitted overoccupancy of up to 50%. Not until 1900 was this rule abolished in view of the unacceptable conditions found in many lodgings.

Larger establishments, run either privately or partly by the state, were set up to accommodate the increasing transmigration in many European emigration ports. The first of these

Old harbor in Bremerhaven, painting from around 1837

was the "Auswandererhaus" ("Emigrants' House") in Bremerhaven. Against the opposition of the local innkeepers, and financed by Bremen merchants, it was opened in the spring of 1850. The Senate of the town supported this project by providing the land at a cheap price. In return, it reserved the right to supervise the institution, which did in fact represent a huge improvement in the accommodation available to emigrants in the port town.

Having visited the "Emigrants' House", contemporary writer Hermann Allmers confirmed that with its "great simplicity" it nevertheless had an almost "palatial character." In the basement of the building he found the kitchen, in which, by using a steamer, food could be prepared for 3,500 people. This was said to be inexpensive and "most splendid, and many a poor emigrant is unlikely at home in his hills (!) ever to have tasted such robust soup, such good vegetables, such fat meat and thick bacon." The storage rooms for the luggage (which could be stored free of charge) were also in the basement, while on the two upper floors there were lodgings and dormitories for more than 2,000 emigrants. Allmers' conclusion: "No other port of emigration, be it Hamburg, Antwerp, Ostend, or Le Havre, is lucky enough to have a similar or even slightly similar institution."

In the mid-1850s, the "Emigrants' House" was used by over 60% of the transmigrants. It was often overcrowded and the ventilation was just as poor as the hygienic conditions,

but these problems were solved over time. Due to the short-term downturn in mass overseas migration at the end of the fifties, however, running this lodging house proved to be less and less profitable. From the 1860s, travalers came from Bremen, where they had stayed for a few days and were accommodated in inns, by train to the harbor town, where now

increasingly often they were able to transfer directly to the overseas steamers, which left punctually. This robbed the "Emigrants' House" in Bremerhaven of its purpose and it closed its doors.

A similar institution was not initially established in Bremen and in the other embarkation ports it took several decades until larger projects to accommodate the migrants were implemented. This did not change until the mass influx of eastern and south-eastern European emigrants into the ports after 1890. In 1892 the shipping company "Hamburg-Amerikanische Packetfahrt-Aktiengesellschaft" (HAPAG) set up dormitory housing on the "America Quay", above all to cope with the dramatic increase in transmigrants from Russia, Poland and Galicia, as well as Jewish emigrants. The "emigrant barracks" provided very basic accommodation for 1,400 people and encompassed not only dormitories, waiting rooms and dining rooms, but also bathing rooms and disinfection cells. For steerage passengers from eastern Europe to the USA it was mandatory to stay in these lodgings. Even before the cholera outbreak in Hamburg in the summer of 1892, HAPAG together with the local police and health authorities did everything possible to isolate the transmigrants from the local population,

Between the end of the American Civil War, in 1865, and 1890 more than 9 million people came to the USA. Settlers and workers were needed there. In comparison with Europe, wages were higher. In particular, women were recruited, on the one hand for the expanding textile industry and on the other as farmers' wives. Here, a father, brother or lover tries to prevent a woman from emigrating. Copper-plate engraving, undated

Left: Only at a relatively late stage did the major churches become involved in looking after emigrants in a systematic way; they established a presence not only in the emigration but also in the main immigration ports. A Protestant emigration mission was set up at 22 Georgstraße in Bremen which cared in particular for women traveling alone. Photo around 1900

Right: For the proprietors of restaurants and lodgings the feeding and housing of emigrants was a profitable business which was, however, subject to fluctuations in the number of emigrants at any given time. Here, a lodging house for emigrants in Hamburg. Photo around 1900

since the migrants from eastern Europe were generally under suspicion of introducing contagious diseases to the ports.

In 1901 HAPAG went a step further and opened more generous accommodation, now described as "emigrant halls", initially intended for 1,000 emigrants but expanded in 1906/7 to accommodate 4,000 to 5,000 people. Separated from the surroundings by a picket fence, the area virtually formed a separate little town. The emigrants were housed in 15 buildings, according to their ethnic origin and religious beliefs. In addition, there was not only a disinfection station, but also a bandstand. The area had its own train station and, after a brief stay, the emigrants' journey continued from the emigrant halls directly to the ship without any immediate contact with the city of Hamburg.

Other continental European emigrant ports also reacted. Thus, the leading Dutch shipping company, the "Nederlandsch-Amerikaansche Stroomvart-Maatschappij" (NASM), established a large "emigrant hotel" for Dutch and eastern European emigrants in Rotterdam in 1893. In Le Havre, the "Compagnie Générale Transatlantique" also established an "Hôtel des Emigrants" in 1910, with a canteen kitchen that specialized in the

requirements of Jewish emigrants and offered kosher meals in a separate dining room. In Bremen in 1907, "Norddeutsche Lloyd" (NDL) together with its general agent, Friedrich Missler, built "emigrant halls" close to the train station which could accommodate a total of 3,100 people. These were exclusively for non-German emigrants from Russia, Poland and Galicia as well as or those from Slovakia and Slovenia for Romania and Croatia.

In the first half of the 19th century, the medical care of the transmigrants in the various European embarkation ports was entirely inadequate. The situation was particularly dire for those leaving their homeland via Bremerhaven, since there was no hospital in the town. The emigrants were often in poor health following the arduous journey to the port. The situation improved only when the "Emigrants' House" opened its doors. This had three sick bays with a total of 35 beds. In the years 1854 and 1855 alone, more than 700 patients were treated here. In addition to sickness and diarrhoea, the travalers were suffering mainly from remittent fever, pneumonia and pleurisy, as well as measles.

From the mid-1850s the Bremen Senate appointed doctors who regularly visited the "Emigrants' House" to check food and

supplies, supervise the sick bays and ensure that the rooms were not overcrowded. Their responsibilities also included the inspection of the cabins and the "tween decks of the ships" and examining the health of the passengers. Yet only in 1868 did an obligatory medical examination of the emigrants prior to the ships' departure become a fixed component of both the Bremen and the Hamburg emigran legislation. Due to the sheer number of the emigrants to be examined within a short space of time, however, the medical care was often of only a perfunctory nature. Overall, however the Bremen emigrant ships recorded lower mortality rates during this time than those from other European countries. Thus, according to reports of the New York Immigration company for example, mortality rates on ships that set sail from the Weser between 1865 and 1867 were at 0.47 to 0.70 %; on those leaving from English ports, it was 0.38 to 1.57 % and on ships sailing from France it was 0.5 to 1.60 %. The Dutch ships had the highes mortality rates, with 5.45 % of the passengers dying in 1867.

In fact the inadequate care continued on the ships. For decades, the emigrants were provided with medical care by the captain alone, who, as complaints show, found it difficult to fulfil these tasks and often simply ignored his medical duties. Not until 1868 did the Hamburg emigration legislation require that a special medical orderly had to accompany the ship, as was customary on the English ships. Then, in 1870, at least on the ships from Bremen and Hamburg, the establishment of a "hospital" was ordered. This had to have four beds per 100 steerage passengers and be separated from the rest of

HAPAG emigrant halls in Hamburg, providing lodgings for transatlantic emigrants. Photo 1920s

Main building of the emigrant halls of the NDL Missler General Agency in Bremen which offered cheap accommodation to eastern and southern European emigrants. Under the windows notices in several eastern European languages. Around 3,000 people could be accommodated in these emigrant halls. Photo 1907

the ship, an attempt to isolate emigrants with contagious diseases from the other passengers. There was not, however, any kind of qualified treatment.

In the course of the growing mass overseas migration from eastern and south-eastern Europe, however, medical care of the transmigrants was afforded ever-greater importance by the harbor towns on the German North Sea. At least since the outbreak of cholera in Hamburg in 1892, this meant first and foremost medical check-ups. The state authorities feared the introduction of diseases and the shipping companies were worried about having to return at their own costs the sick migrants who were refused entry to the USA. As a result, the Prussian state government, the NDL and HAPAG agreed in 1893 to channel and control the transit journey by setting up registration stations at the borders. A total of eleven such stations financed by NDL and HAPAG were set up as a result; there was a central control station in Ruhleben near Berlin and one each in Hamburg and Bremen.

Medical examinations were carried out at the checkpoints, where the sick were placed in quarantine in sick bays, while their luggage was disinfected and the travalers were bathed. Mary Antin, a Jew from Lithuania, who emigrated to the United States in 1894, recalls in her autobiography her experiences in Ruhleben: "There was such confusion in the luggage store, into which we were

directed. Trunks and crates, baskets, sacks, suitcases and large items that were impossible to identify were thrown around by the baggage porters and other people, who sorted everything and with the exception of those packages containing food, marked them with tickets. The others were opened and hastily checked."

The ticket collector then ushered the emigrants "out into the spacious courtyard. There, we were met by a horde of men and women all dressed in white… we were led into a small room, in which a large cauldron stood upon a small stove. We were undressed and a slippery substance, that could have been anything, was rubbed on our bodies; without warning, a warm shower sprinkled down on us. Then we came to a small room where we had to sit and wait, huddled in woollen blankets, until large, rough sacks were brought in and emptied… we had to find our clothing from among this huge heap of clothes, almost blinded with the steam. We were almost suffocating, coughing and begging the women to give us more time. But they were insistent with their "hurry, hurry! Otherwise you will miss the train!" Aha, so they didn't want to kill us after all! We were just being prepared for the onward journey, cleansed of all imaginable germs." The journey to Hamburg continued on the emigrant train.

In the Hanseatic towns, eye examinations and vaccinations awaited the emigrants. The metal worker Fritz Kummer, who traveled

to the USA from Bremen in 1907, observed at the main train station that "from time to time… people came out of a side building screaming, sometimes also with their chests bared. Anyone who wanted to know what had happened was told in sign language that they had been inoculated. Small bloody scratches could be seen on the upper arms. This was to prevent the steerage passengers from contracting pox or similar diseases during the passage… the way it (i.e. the vaccination) was carried out must have been humiliating for many."

Upon leaving their home the emigrants reached an important turning point in their lives. In this situation they were particularly reliant on religious support. In the harbor towns such as Le Havre or Liverpool the local expatriate community took care of the German transmigrants, but, in general, religious care of the emigrants was for many decades of a sporadic nature, at best. Special spiritual care was provided initially only in Bremerhaven, since the "Emigrants' House" there also had a chapel with a capacity of 300 to 400. Religious services for Catholics usually took place twice a month on the ships' voyage days; prayers for Protestants on the

Aid associations played a major role for settling emigrants in the new country. An introductory card supplied by the Catholic St. Raphael Association gave addresses of intermediary agents in the emigration ports on the reverse side. The Leo-Haus in New York opened in 1888 as a hostel for Catholic immigrants and by 1901 had taken in over 10,000

Above: Irish emigrants in Cork: newspaper graphic from The Illustrated Times, May 1851. Between 1830 and 1860 around 2 million Irish made the perilous journey across the Atlantic to America to escape hunger and misery at home. The posters advertize not only New York but also Boston and Quebec as destinations

Below: Emigrants on the deck of a sailing ship. Newspaper graphic entitled "The Departure" shows how overcrowded these sailing ships were on the Atlantic passage. The Illustrated London News, July 1850

other hand were held daily. Furthermore, for the Protestants there were also special weekly farewell services. This was why there were various complaints from the Catholic overseas emigrants, most of whom came from southern Germany, and who saw this as discrimination against them.

After Bremerhaven lost its importance as a place to stay for emigrants during the 1860s, pastoral care for the travalers was provided first and foremost in Bremen. Then the major

churches began to expand their emigrant work in a targeted fashion. In 1871 the "St. Raphael Association for the protection of Catholic German Emigrants" was brought to life and in 1872 a branch was set up in Hamburg, in Bremen in 1873, and in Antwerp, Rotterdam, Le Havre, London, and Liverpool in 1877. Later, branches of the association were also set up in the most important arrival ports, in New York and Baltimore, as well as Rio de Janeiro and Buenos Aires. In this way, a network of

trustworthy people who took care of the travalers was set up. The support encompassed not only actual spiritual guidance, but the association also provided advice and information on travel options, recommended lodgings and warned against swindlers.

From the 1870s the Protestant church also increased its activities. In 1873 the "Evangelisch-Lutherische Auswanderermission" (Lutheran Emigrant Mission) was set up. This collaborated with the Association of Home Missions and the Catholic associations to provide spiritual and practical support. Employees of the Bremen Emigrants' Mission collected the emigrants from the train station, took them to their advisory office, visited them in the various lodgings and organized religious services. Around 11,000 emigrants attended these services in the space of 13 months in the years 1881/1882. After the turn of the century, first the "St. Raphaels-Verein" and later the "Evangelische Auswanderermission" established their own "emigrant chapels" in Bremen. In Hamburg, a church built in the grounds of the "emigrant halls" served the religious needs of both Protestants and Catholics, and there was even a synagogue for Jewish emigrants. The latter was originally created on the initiative of the Central German Committee for Russian Jews. This committee, as well as other Jewish aid organisations, supported Jewish transmigrants from eastern and south-eastern Europe, above all financially.

At the end of the 19th century, the "Evangelische Mission" and the "Raphaels Werk" also took care primarily of women traveling alone and developed a highly specialized aspect of their work. The emigrants usually took their monetary funds with them in cash. Losses due to theft or when exchanging money were all too common. For this reason, the mission allowed the transmigrants to lodge their money with the advisory office in return for a receipt. In the New York Lutheran emigrant house, which the Mission cooperated closely with, the emigrants were paid their money in American currency. A total of seven million Reichsmark crossed the Atlantic in this manner between 1884 and 1900. The "St. Raphaels-Verein" operated a similar system of money transfer. In addition, the Protestant Mission also organized the provision of "pre-paid tickets", i.e. tickets for the crossing that the emigrants from the USA sent to their relatives and friends at home to allow them to travel overseas.

The Atlantic Crossing

On the sailing ships that set sail from the various European ports around 1850, each steerage passenger had 14 square feet to himself, as required by the American immigration authorities. This was also set forth in the Bremen and Hamburg emigration acts. This area corresponded roughly to the size of a bed. Stacking two bunks made of raw wooden planks one on top of the other – usually five people per bunk – made it possible to keep free half of the floor space, which was at a premium. Even this was far from effective in preventing overcrowding of the 'tween deck. The steerage was at the same time a dormitory, dining room and common room. There were no tables or chairs and the aisles between the bunks were furthermore blocked with the migrants' luggage. There was very little light below deck and the ventilation was poor, since the steerage area could be aired only through the small number of hatchways and one or two stairways to the upper deck. Bad weather and sea-sickness heightened the already desperate conditions and made much of the Atlantic crossing a trial.

The food provided on board was also an ongoing bone of contention. While until 1855 the passengers on the ships that set sail from the English ports and from the "western ports" had to organize their own board in full or in part, this was prohibited in both Bremen and Hamburg. Often, due to inexperience, lack of money or false economy, the emigrants brought too little or unsuitable (perishable) foodstuffs for the journey overseas. In order to counter this, from the outset, the Bremen emigration laws required the shipping companies to supply the ships with sufficient provisions for whatever the number of passengers traveling for 90 days, whereby a crossing to the USA took an average of 60 to 70 days.

Nevertheless, even on the ships leaving from the North Sea ports, the quantity and quality of the food by no means corresponded with the criteria set forth in the migration ordinances. Furthermore, the crew's treatment of the emigrants repeatedly gave rise to complaints. One complaint in the spring of 1851 from emigrants who contacted the "Information Office" upon their arrival in New Orleans from Bremen read as follows:

"The undersigned passengers of the ship the 'Olbers', master, Captain Fechter, feel they have cause for bitter complaint about the food and treatment on board. They have been treated like livestock, compared to dogs, the 'tween deck was referred to as "the byre" and, with the exception of some ordinary seamen, the passengers were treated extremely roughly and brutally by the ship's crew, the captain and the ship's mates, even threatened with violence, and some people were in fact beaten.

The food was very poor, the preparation even worse, the bread had probably been on several journeys and only during the last 8 days, when it was finished, were we given something that tasted better. The pork served to the passengers was totally off, in spite of the availability of better; only in the last 8 days did we get good pork. The cooking water was like liquid manure in terms of dirtiness, color and smell and it must have been off when it was taken on board, since the drinking water stayed good; but each person only got ¼ quart of that each day …

If these grievances are not remedied, we cannot recommend the passage via Bremen to our successors."

Often, the emigrants' complaints were well-founded. On the ships, which were, in actuality, freight ships, the emigrants were

Above: Farewell scene at the Columbus Quay. Photo 1911
Below: Steamship with four funnels in the Bremerhaven Kaiserhafen. To the right, processing areas of North German Lloyd. Photo around 1910

Steerage passengers on a transatlantic steamer prepare for their arrival in New York. Photo 1905

Above: Oppressive confinement, crowded sleeping areas, no fresh air, no toilets and bad food – this was life between-decks on a sailing ship. Graphic from the "Leipziger Illustrirte Zeitung", 1849 – Samuel Hop emigrant ship
Below: Third class on the transatlantic steamer S.S. Hellvig Olav, 1904. The typical between-deck area was a huge open dormitory with hundreds of bunks. There were no separate areas for men, women and children. Note the doctor in his white coat in the center

confronted with a ships' crew that had no skills in dealing with passengers. In the absence of knowing any better, or due to lack of experience, the captains usually countered the almost-unavoidable chaos in the steerage with quasi-military disciplinary measures, which understandably heightened the passengers' resentment. On the other hand, the provision of food on board was indeed problematic. In view of the very limited means of preserving food on the ships, there was not only always either salt junk or smoked bacon; on very long journeys, it could be the case that food had gone bad but had to be handed out regardless. Furthermore, now and again, the ship-owners insisted, in order to make an additional profit and in contravention of the required checks, on serving the foodstuffs left over from a relatively short transatlantic passage to the emigrants on the next crossing, albeit in a more or less tainted condition.

A radical improvement in the transatlantic crossing did not come until sailing ships were replaced with passenger steamships. At the end of the 1860s three-quarters of

emigrants crossed the Atlantic on such ships. In 1875, emigration transport by sailing ship from Bremen came to a complete halt, while the last sail-boat transporting emigrants from Hamburg left the port in 1879. The steamship crossing of the Atlantic had started earlier in Great Britain. After 1880 monopolistic structures began to emerge in overseas passenger transport from the European ports. The large number of shipping companies profiting from the emigration business disappeared, to be replaced with large market-dominating companies such as the CGT in Le Havre, the NASM in Rotterdam, and the "Red Star" in Antwerp, as well as the "Cunard" and "White Star" lines in Liverpool. In Hamburg, HAPAG dominated the field, in Bremen it was the NDL, both of which developed into the largest emigrant shipping companies in the world. Thus, in 1891, Norddeutsche Lloyd also set up a route Genoa-Naples-New York, in order to profit from the growing Italian emigration to the United States.

With the rise of passenger steamship travel, the duration of the crossing to America decreased to 14 days and even less. This removed many of the difficulties that were typical of transport on the sailing ships. The medical care of the emigrants improved, since ship's doctors had been employed on the steamers from the 1860s. Although there was

still crowding in the steerage, the ventilation was better, there was lighting and there were also fewer problems with the food provided since it was now possible to bake and to slaughter on board. Furthermore, it was possible to give the children fresh milk every day and to prepare kosher meals for the Jewish emigrants.

In 1906 the German Member of Parliament, Liborius Gerstenberger, traveled on the NDL steamer "Bremen" to New York. During the journey he also had a look at the steerage: "The Germans have the best area directly by the ventilation shafts. The dormitories are… segregated according to gender… There are about 1,500 iron beds down there double bunks each… From the iron beams of the ceiling hang the tin containers that the people use to get their food… the passengers place clothing and hand luggage on their bed, the rest of the luggage is kept in a special room. – Along the walls of the ship there are narrow tables upon which the emigrants can rest their eating receptacles. The shipping company provides the blankets, tin containers and spoons, but the passengers have to provide their own knives." One flight of stairs lower, the eastern European emigrants were accommodated: "The air there is thicker, the heat greater; the portholes are closer to the water and cannot be opened as often… The ood for the steerage passengers is simple and good... in the morning there is coffee and a piece of bread; at lunchtime there is soup, meat and pieces of potato and in the evening another meal, e.g. cabbage with meat and potatoes. People are given as much as they can eat and they are allowed to have two or three helpings."

Unlike the first class passengers, however, the journey on the modern steamers was by no means a pleasure trip or a jaunt for the emigrants. Often the 'tween decks of the steamers were overcrowded, and life on board was not always easy. The Dutchman Dirk Pieter van den Bergh, who left his home in 1906 via Liverpool, told of his journey on the "White Star" steamer "Celtic": "We got up at 6.00 o'clock in the morning, the wash rooms were totally overcrowded – no chance of getting in there. Breakfast was peeled, boiled potatoes with meat and fresh bread. Too many people were fighting for a seat at the table. It was impossible for a whole family to sit together at once. So we men tried first, while the women took care of the children. We would find places for them when they were ready."

Arrival and Onward Journey

In the first half of the 19th century, Baltimore, New Orleans, and New York became the most important immigration ports in the New World of America. After 1850, New York took a pre-eminent role: around 75 % of all immigrants entered the United States through this city, where, from 1855, a central point of arrival was created, "Castle Garden". This was on the one hand a registration station and on the other a place where the new immigrants could spend the night and change their money with reputable moneychangers. Information offices provided the emigrants with advice on the options for onward travel and, last but not least, "Castle Garden" also acted as an employment office.

As a result of the dramatic increase in immigration from the traditional western European and the newly added eastern and south-eastern European emigration areas from 1880 onwards, "Castle Garden" increasingly proved to be too small and was replaced in 1892 with a massive complex on "Ellis Island", a small island directly facing Manhattan. However, "Ellis Island" also marked the end of more or less free

New York, painting 1850. Battery Park on the southern tip of Manhattan, Broadway in the center of the picture, Trinity Church clearly visible, on the opposite side Wall Street. To the left of the southern tip, Castle Garden in the water. Battery Park had not been completely filled in. Castle Garden, built in 1807, had originally been part of the fortifications constructed in preparation for the war against England in 1812

and unhindered immigration. Conditions for admission into the country were made more stringent, and the aim now was increasingly to control the flow of immigrants. Pierina Gasperetti, who in 1912 left her small village in the Pavia province and traveled from Genoa to New York, recalled many years later her experience of arrival and registration: "They wanted to know a whole bunch of things: why did we come to America, how much money we had with us (because, at that time, you had to have a certain amount in Lira, to be allowed in). Why? I still don't know. Probably they were afraid that I wasn't even able to buy myself a piece of bread... Ah yes, I remember something else: they stuck a label on us, here, with my name on it, like for livestock."

The formal checks also included an additional medical examination. Ultimately the ill or those with no money, anarchists (if they let themselves be known as such!) or the infirm could be refused entry to the USA. Only steerage passengers had to undergo the complicated procedure of registration. A total of approximately 16 million European migrants were processed through Ellis Island between 1892 and 1924 – around 5,000 to 10,000 thousand a day. Two to 3% of them were sent home, having never set foot on the soil of the New World of North America. For them, Ellis Island became the "Island of Tears".

Once the new arrivals left the arrival ports, conditions similar to those they had already been confronted with in the emigration ports and other gathering points awaited them. The "Buttjer" or "Litzer" of the North Sea ports, were in New York (as in Liverpool) the "runners", who tried to entice the travelers into overcrowded lodging houses or to pass them on to agents who sold the immigrants extortionate "tickets" for riverboats and trains or even worthless shares in real-estate companies. Both the "Commissioners of Immigration of the State of New York" (established in 1847) and special aid organisations for emigrants, such as the "German Societies" of New York and New Orleans attempted to protect the immigrants from such practices.

The members of the "German Societies" were recruited for the most part from the economic elite of German-America, with Hanseatic merchants particularly well represented. They traded primarily with Germany and, as ship-owners, were often also directly involved in the emigration business. Encouraging immigration and facilitating the move into the New World (by supervising emigrant protection provisions etc.) was one of the central concerns of these societies. They also helped in the search for employment and housing and supported fellow countrymen who had fallen on hard times. At the same time, they were clearly against the immigration of professional beggars, work-shy vagabonds, the

Above: Castle Garden, the first immigrant station at the southern tip of Manhattan, established in 1854; in the background the Statue of Liberty. Photo 1911. Below: When the immigrants had been medically examined they waited anxiously in the registry room to be questioned by immigration officers (at desks beneath the American flag). Photo 1905

en masse. The employees of this company attempted to find employment and housing for the newly-arrived Jews. In 1889, they established a place of refuge, the "Hebrew Sheltering House Association", which offered destitute emigrants a place to sleep, as well as food and clothing. From 1892, HIAS employees collected the immigrants on Ellis Island. As well as acting as translators, they helped the immigrants to deal with the first hurdles of immigration formalities. They were also able to prevent "unwelcome" Jewish immigrants from being sent back to the Old World.

For two-thirds of the immigrants, the immigration ports were purely transit stations on their way inland. For many of the remaining migrants, Baltimore or New Orleans or New York was merely a stopover on their way to the West. Thus, Klaus Hinrich Viebrock who came from a small town between Bremen and Hamburg, told the local authorities when asking for emigration papers in 1871 "Initially I think I will take some suitable work in New York, and as soon as I have earned sufficient funds to travel onwards, I will continue my journey and find a suitable job in the country, perhaps as a farm hand."

Until around 1880, the majority of immigrants, in particular the Germans, settled in the States of the mid-west. By 1850 two main travel routes had evolved along which the immigrants continued their journey. On the one hand, from New Orleans with the relatively inexpensive paddle wheel steamer up the Mississippi, whereby the journey to St. Louis lasted around seven days. On the other, those who landed in New York traveled by steamship and railway to the Erie canal completed in 1825, on which they traveled to the Great Lakes and then on to the settlement areas of Mississippi and Missouri by steamship. The onward journey westwards was undertaken for many decades by wagon trains pulled by oxen. By about 1840 the construction of the railways had already begun. In 1869 the transcontinental railway line was completed and by around 1880, all states were connected by an extensive railway network. For the immigrants' onward journey to their destination this was of the utmost importance, particularly from 1870 when, as in Europe, special trains were used for immigrants in the USA. Once the rigors of the journey had been overcome, filled with new hope, the immigrants could begin to build a new life in the "land of the free."

ill and those with a criminal background. More important than these organisations, however was an informal network of relatives and countrymen who had emigrated previously, and who provided the new immigrants with the most essential information.

There were many other aid organizations such as the "Hebrew Immigrant Aid Society" (HIAS), which was set up in the 1880s in New York. This organization was of paramount importance for the Jews from eastern Europe, who began traveling to the United States

View of the New York skyline from Ellis Island, Photo 1905

Literature

Arno Armgort, Bremen – Bremerhaven – New York 1683–1960. Geschichte der Auswanderung über die Bremischen Häfen, Bremen 1991.

Jean Braunstein, "L'Émigration allemande par le port du Havre au XIXe siècle", Annales de Normandie (1984): pp. 95–104.

Heike Brück, "Die Verbesserung der Hinterlandsbeziehungen zu den Auswandererhäfen im frühen and mittleren 19. Jahrhundert. Wechselwirkungen zwischen Auswandererströmen und Verkehrseinrichtungen", Deutsches Schiffahrtsarchiv, 7 (1984): pp. 213–221.

Martin Drnovsek, "Slowenische Auswanderung vor 1914 über Hamburg, Bremen/Bremerhaven und Le Havre nach Ellis Island", in: Karin Schulz (Hg.), Hoffnung Amerika. Europäische Auswanderung in die Neue Welt, Bremerhaven 1994, pp. 103–118.

Rolf Engelsing, Bremen als Auswandererhafen 1683–1880, Bremen 1961.

Birgit Gelberg, Auswanderung nach Übersee. Soziale Probleme der Auswandererbeförderung in Hamburg und Bremen von der Mitte des 19. Jahrhundert bis zum Ersten Weltkrieg, Hamburg 1973.

Ulrike Kirchberger, Aspekte deutsch-britischer Expansion. Die Überseeinteressen der Deutschen Migranten in Großbritannien in der Mitte des 19. Jahrhundert, Stuttgart 1999.

Jean Legoy, Hier, Le Havre, Fécamp 1997.

Georges Perec, Robert Bober, Geschichten von Ellis Island oder wie man Amerikaner macht, Berlin 1997.

Gordon Read, "Transithafen Liverpool. Die Europäische Auswanderung über England nach New York, 1870–1913", in: Schulz, pp. 151–162.

Horst Rössler, "Bremen-Bremerhaven als Transitstation für Auswanderer aus dem Rheinland im 19. Jahrhundert", in: Schöne Neue Welt. Rheinländer erobern Amerika, Vol. 2, Kommern 2001, pp. 151–184.

Jürgen Sielemann, "Haben alle Passagiere auch Geld? Zur Geschichte der Auswanderung über den Hamburger Hafen 1892–1954", in: Schulz, pp. 81–102.

Immigrants with their covered wagons on the arduous journey to the West. Photo around 1890

Barry Moreno

The Devil's Isle

In 1910, a journalist wrote an article for a publication named *Answers* that was saved by Commissioner William Williams and is currently held in the archives of the New York Public Library. It described conditions at Ellis Island under that commissioner's management in these unflattering terms:

"Devil's Isle" – The American Immigrants' Inquisition Scandal
Map-Makers write it down Ellis Island but immigrants to New York call it "Devil's Isle" – appropriately, as I can testify, writes an *Answers* reader. For, having to visit the State at a time when practically every berth in every transatlantic liner was taken, I was forced to travel as an immigrant. I trust that I shall never again have to submit to such indignities as I was subjected to on my arrival across the "Pond."
Before being officially received on American soil, immigrants to New York are taken over on steam-packet to Ellis Island. When this vessel arrives alongside the liner, loud orders are given to the immigrants: *All form in line for the shore! Close up! Step this way with your green health-cards handy! Bring all your hand baggage with you!*
Each immigrant has been given a green health-card by the ship's doctor after examination. These cards are now to pinned on a conspicuous part of the person.
Once disembarked on Ellis Island, we move along in single file till we pass through the portals of an immense hall, divided by stout wire netting into alleyways and pens like cattleyard. This intricate mass we traverse several times, getting shuffled up with the passengers of French and German boats. Suddenly, there is a cry of *Halt!* And then a specialist examines us for trachoma, folding back each eyelid in a very rough manner. Next, proceeding in single file, we are individually chalked. My brand is a capital S, which, I suppose, stands for *senile*. P means *pulmonary*; Ex means *excema*. A man chalked Face had a large wart thereon. *Gait* is lame; *Vision* wears an eyeglass.

The rams are now separated from the ewes, the men filing to the right, the women to the left. What happens to the ladies, I do not know; but it is not pleasant, to judge by the squealing, crying, and protesting we can hear.
I find myself one of fifty white, black, red, and yellow immigrants. *Strip!* comes the order. *Take everything off and line up as you were born!* I protest. I am a Britisher. No matter! comes the answer. *Line up naked like the rest!* We strip and, one by one, pass up for inspection. I am tested and told to *Cough! Cough again!* And then, as something is written on my paper, to *Pass along and dress! Take this report with you!*
The ladies join us and we kick our heels for a space. Then our papers are taken from us and copies in a letter-press, the originals being filed for further inspection. Next, a strip of paper, with the word *Certificate* is pinned on our shoulders. Some have already passed along; but just as my turn arrives the officials tell us that they are going to knock off for one hour for lunch, and walk through the folding glass doors marked No Admittance puffing their cigarettes.
I begin to light up. *No smoking allowed!*, snaps an attendant. I ask for a drink. *First to the right, first to the left!* I follow these directions and find an iron pipe without a nozzle. There is no glass. The water flows, and you just put your mouth to the pipe.
When the hour has expired the officiating medico resumes his chair. *I am asked, Are you married? Where is your wife? What have you come to America for? What do you intend to do now you're here?*, etc. Then the certificate is torn from my shoulder and I march along to the last pen, cheerfully marked *Hospital Cases*. Here I remain for another hour and a half.
Altogether I spend four and a half hours at Ellis Island. Once outside the *Hall of Tears*, I inquired for my cabin trunk. I was told to go to the nether regions; so, mentally consigning the said trunk to that warm place, I went across myself to South Ferry, New York.

Barry Moreno

The Question of Race and Ethnicity: Doctor Folkmar's Solution

From the moment Ellis Island opened, the public and the press frequently enquired about the racial and ethnic background of the massive numbers of newcomers. In order to get information on this point, the Bureau of Immigration added a racial category to their annual statistical tables in 1898. But identifying the major "races and nationalities" proved to be a difficult proceeding. Aside from directly asking foreigners their ethnic background (and often getting inconclusive or unhelpful responses), officials could also turn to cultural clues: family names, given names, native languages and dialects spoken, and a person's religion. The United States, then a predominantly WASP – white, Anglo-Saxon, Protestant – nation, was deeply sensitive when it came to race. Anxious for more guidelines and information on the question, Congress commissioned an anthropologist to undertake a careful study of the immigrant races.

In 1911, Dr. Daniel Folkmar's findings were published in book form by the Government Printing Office bearing the title, *The Dictionary of Races or Peoples*. Filled with descriptive entries of each ethnic group, this volume served as a handbook for immigrant inspectors. It followed the standard classification of races known to educated Americans at the time: Caucasian (white), Ethiopian (black), Mongolian (yellow), Malay (brown), and American (red). Next, it examined ethnic groups within that classification. Thus in the Caucasian race, it dealt with Semites, Nordics, Aryans, Slavs, Alpines, Latins, and so forth. The greater part of the dictionary's entries, however, focused on national ethnic groups of various countries, such as the English, Irish, French, Germans, Hebrews, North Italian, South Italian, Magyars, and Greeks. In accordance with the concern for physical verification of ethnic stock, the dictionary described the races by craniofacial anthropometry. In addition, Doctor Folkmar (1861–1932), who was himself of Danish ancestry, included information on the ethnic groups' average height and build, hair and eye color, various racial or ethnic mixtures or strains, and their settlement patterns within the United States. In carrying out his research for the book, Folkmar was assisted by his wife, Dr. Elnora C. Folkmar, a physician, and to a lesser degree by the economist, Dr. Jeremiah Jenks. *The Dictionary of Races and Peoples* was published as the fifth volume in the U.S. Immigration Commission's 42-volume series on immigration.

Hester Street,
New York.

New York's Jewish neighborhood, 1905. Hester Street in the Lower East Side was its center, with thousands of peddlers and push carts. Upon arrival immigrants often went to where they found familiar things in a strange New World: the language, religion, and ways of life of the old country, provided by the ethnic neighborhood

Suzanne M. Sinke

Re-Envisioning the United States in Migration History

For the first 150 years of the existence of the United States, migration connected the country to global developments in a variety of ways. People entered, people left, and people moved around within the expanding borders of the young nation. In this period the United States began articulating a vision of belonging that would welcome and embrace some, but exclude or reject others, meaning migrants helped define the amorphous concept of "American." Immigrants linked the U.S. directly to economic, political, and religious currents in other parts of the world. At the same time, the vision of the United States – "America" – became an international mantra for opportunities and freedom. The United States rose to occupy an important role in the realm of international migration.

At the founding of the nation the United States had no immigration policy, though there were some preferences related to local or state poor laws. For the most part the country welcomed newcomers, whom it sought to people the countryside. In the vision of the day more population, particularly more people of European background, would strengthen the country and increase its standing on an international scale. Through the 19th century this vision prevailed, growing stronger with territorial acquisition. As transportation improvements in the form of railroad lines and steamships cut the time and cost of migration, more people joined the migrant streams, which grew to millions. Over time fewer migrants sought land or a less developed way of life, and more helped fuel industrialization in the United States. Like Canada to the north, and Argentina and Brazil much farther south, the U.S. developed major migrant streams from Europe. Numerically lesser streams from Asia came into being as well. Like many European countries in the same period, the U.S. attracted large numbers of migrants to its industrial cities. By the early 20th century the United States boasted the largest numbers of immigrants of any country, though not the largest proportion[1]. It became the quintessential immigrant country primarily because it defined itself that way.

Some voices always opposed migration, most notably those of the original inhabitants, American Indians, who faced expulsion and extermination. And from the start the country sought to limit certain groups both from migration and from incorporation. The first naturalization law of 1790 stipulated that "free white" people could gain citizenship, and race remained a major determinant of migrant acceptance. The end of the slave trade cut one major category of immigrants. Further restrictions on migration later in the 19th century targeted Chinese migrants and diminished that migrant stream. At the turn of the century increasing numbers of people sought to cut the migration not just of those from Asia, but also the multitude of migrants from southern and eastern Europe. The First World War limited feasibility of migration, and thereafter the National Origins Acts officially cut the numbers. This ended, at least for a time, the perception of the open door to the United States. "America" still had cachet as a land of freedom and opportunity, but it had lots of competition.

The signing of the American Declaration of Independence 1776 with its promise of "life, liberty and the pursuit of happiness," painting by John Trumbull

The Early Years

Abd Abd ar-Rahman was hardly the image of a typical immigrant. A Muslim, who reported speaking Bambara, Mandingo, and Jallonke, in addition to literacy in Arabic, he left his home in the Futa Jallon region of west Africa when captured in battle and transported to Spanish New Orleans as part of the slave trade in the 1780s. The formal political shift of his new domicile first to French and then to U.S. sovereignty in 1803, did not change his status as a slave. Though an involuntary migrant, he still faced many adjustment issues common for any newcomer. His loss of status, from the son of nobility to slave, made this transition particularly difficult at first. Within a few years he "married" a local woman, also enslaved, and they had a family of nine children. When he gained his freedom in the 1820s, he and his U.S. wife, Isabella, made their way around the north-east, raising funds and organizing, and then back to Africa, specifically to Liberia, where a colony for former slaves was in the making.[2]

The slave trade, a major part of colonial migration to North America, dropped precipitously along with most other migration during the U.S. War for Independence, but rose afterwards, and Abd ar-Rahman was part of that upsurge. In the final years before it adopted the ban on the international slave trade, U.S. slave imports reached their highest levels. In all, around 100,000 slaves entered North America in the years after independence, helping (together with natural increase) to grow the slave population from under one million in 1800 to over a million and a half in 1820.[3] The slave trade numbers paled in comparison to imports for Brazil or parts of the Caribbean, where the majority of slaves disembarked, but nonetheless helped set up a particularly important racial dynamic that would shape U.S. history for centuries to come.

The end of the international slave trade in 1808 became the first major restriction on immigration to the United States. Thereafter natural increase and the internal slave trade took on much greater importance. African roots, so important for Abd ar-Rahman, became more difficult to sustain with each new generation born in the U.S. The closing of this migration meant a shifting into a black American existence, one of decidedly lesser standing than that of Whites. "Return" migration in the form of colonization in Africa became one solution, albeit for only a small group, to the dilemma of where free African Americans might fit.[4] Just as the 1790 law limited naturalization to "free white" people, even sympathetic Whites often hoped that free Africans would no stay in the United States.

Though the slave trade continued fo decades, immigration to the United State after independence shifted from predomi nantly a trade in unfree labor to more fre immigration. In particular, the convict an indentured servant trades, which had bee major streams of labor under colonial rule did not revive to any significant degree. And despite the initial increase in th slave trade, the majority of migrants cam as free people. This was the U.S. version c what one historian termed a much broade global trend from widespread acceptanc of the slave trade in the 1700s to mora disdain for slavery and the embrace of fre migration in the 1900s, with a small segu through distaste for contract labor in th intervening period.[6] Contract labor did nc take hold in the United States, except i the imagination of those trying to limit th migration of particular people – a story t which we will return.

Free migration ruled. Free also mean unregulated, to the extent that the Unite States government passed few laws regard ing free immigration until 1819, and kep few records beyond passenger lists there after for decades. Any control rest wit individual states, but in general por authorities welcomed all but those wit obvious illness or infirmity who migh become a public charge, with slight excep tions in times of war. The largest number came from Britain and Ireland, adding up to nearly 300,000 prior to 1820.[7] Som came via Canada, where the border wa particularly porous.

While European-descended immigra tion was free, European development motivated the Federalist Party in the 1790 to limit the acceptance of immigrants int the polity of the United States. With th Alien and Sedition Acts it raised residenc requirements for citizenship from two t fourteen years, and required the registr of all incoming immigrants and of alien already resident in the U.S. It even allowe for the apprehension and deportation o aliens. The outcry at this anti-immigran shift helped crystallize ethnic suppor for the Democratic-Republican Party which won the subsequent election. Whe revised in 1802, naturalization law settle on a five-year residency requirement tha

Engraving of Abd ar-Rahman Crayon. Drawing by Henry Inman, New York 1828, from the Colonization and Journal of Freedom, Boston 1834; document stating that Abd ar-Rahman wrote the Lord's prayer in Arabic and recounted to the undersigned "the circumstances of his abduction"

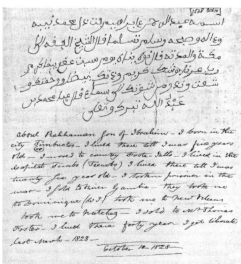

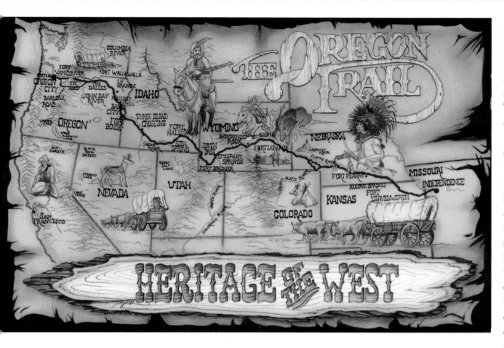

The Oregon Trail; the Lewis & Clark expedition of 1804 paved the way for the westward exodus of an estimated 300,000 pioneers by wagon train along what became known as the Oregon Trail; commemorative postcard 1994

would remain standard thereafter (to the present).[8]

Land and labor opportunities, along with familial obligations, led the list of motivations for free migrants to the United States. But open borders also meant options for people with other motivations for coming. The Revolution in Saint Domingue (Haiti) in 1791 sparked the sudden exodus of many plantation owners, who often brought at least some of their slaves.[9] The impetus to flee from war or from other forms of persecution continued over the years. State churches invariably faced opposition, sometimes armed. Irish Catholic migrants, particularly those active in challenging Anglican rule, sometimes sought refuge across the ocean.[10] Protestant religious revivals in areas such as the Netherlands in the 1830s led to the creation of new or splinter denominations, unwelcome by state churches. In general adherents to minority faiths tended to be more likely to emigrate than others.[11] The United States, with a reputation for relative religious freedom, became a beacon in this ocean of religions.

The United States not only attracted immigrants, it also produced them. Those seeking relief from debts after the 1821 panic as well as some interested in trade or finding new lands headed for the newly independent country of Mexico.[12] Fugitive slaves continued the pattern started under Spanish rule of escaping to this area in order to gain their freedom. Mexico's laws were ambiguous on slavery at first, particularly in the Texas region, so some moved further south. Meanwhile land companies and railroads vied for newcomers – particularly those with landholding ambitions. A few migrants to Mexico, such as Carl Blümner, who made his way from Brandenburg via Missouri to Santa Fe, intermarried into the local population.[13]

Other immigrants opposed Mexican rule, particularly its provisions outlawing slavery or supporting Catholicism as the state religion.[14] These Anglos and their allies fought and won independence for Texas. They then set the stage for subsequent annexation into the United States.

Another group went to Mexico under quite different circumstances. As the United States took over American Indian lands and forced the native population onto reservations, various individuals as well as groups fought their loss of territory and rights. The Indian Removal Act of 1830 set the stage for moving Indian nations of the south-east to reservation lands west of the Mississippi. Coacoochee, a head man of the Seminoles and military leader from the Second Seminole War, took his followers to Indian Territory in 1841, where he challenged first Cherokee and then Creek rule. Next he and "Gopher John" Cowaya, a black Seminole, took a group to Texas and then on to Mexico, where they became citizens and received land.[15] The "removal" of American Indians meant they lost possession to millions of acres in the United States. The land lost by the Seminoles and other indigenous peoples became the land available for international as well as internal migrants through most of the 19th century. Freedom and opportunity, in other words, applied to some people more than others, largely based on race.[16]

For groups such as German speakers, information on where one might want to go came in many forms as chains of migration formed. In addition to official recruitment propaganda from railroads and states, potential migrants sometimes relied on word of mouth by returned migrants,

Left: Log cabin, North Carolina, around 1890. Settlers preferred a home of this type if wood was available as building material
Right: Dugout, around 1890, settlement of the first immigrant generation in the North American plains

personal letters, reports to local newspapers, and guidebooks. Positive images such as Gottfried Duden's 1829 account, or Traugott Bromme's multi-volume and multi-edition handbook for emigrants, tended to increase migration.[17] As infrastructure such as the Erie Canal made travel easier, migrants moved farther west, creating ethnic enclaves such as the Over-the-Rhine neighborhood in Cincinnati, which began major expansion in the 1820s. These early groups set the stage for later migration.

Mid-Century Shifts

Several international events shifted U.S. immigration patterns in the 1840s: war and its aftermath in China, famine and political unrest in Europe, and war and land losses in Mexico. The earlier patterns of people moving for land and labor, and as part of families, continued even in these circumstances, but natural disasters and political persecution motivated many to leave. The massive addition of territory to the U.S. south-west in the wake of the Mexican-American War meant the border crossed thousands of former Mexicans, who now became part of the United States. The discovery of gold in California created a mad rush across internal as well as national borders from all directions. Growing debates about slavery also sparked migration. Few immigrants from outside the United States chose to move to slaveholding areas in the years leading up to the Civil War, but many slaves fled, moving to areas of freedom such as northern states, and then, especially after the Fugitive Slave Law of 1850, to Canada. The outbreak of the Civil War put a damper on international migration, though like most wars it mobilized a young male group to unprecedented mobility. International migration resumed higher levels again after the war, spurred by land availability.

Vicente Pérez Rosales typified gold rush migrants in some ways. He took a ship from his native Chile to California late in 1848. The Pacific coast trade made it possible for those in port cities of Chile to get the news and make the journey to California faster than many in the eastern

Construction of the St. Paul, Minneapolis and Manitoba Railroad, Minnesota, 1897. The Irish and Chinese contributions to building the transcontinental railroad during the 1860s are legendary, but by the turn of the century, rail crews were generally made up of many nationalities

United States. As one might expect Pérez first tried mining, but not for long. Gringos had little respect for Chileans or any other Spanish-speakers, and lawless greed tended to exacerbate prejudice. With first-hand experience of attacks on the rise, Pérez shifted from mining to a variety of other jobs. Eventually he started running a restaurant with some fellow Chilenos, finding that providing services for the swelling migrant population was more lucrative than looking for gold, particularly given the skewed sex ratio. In an area without many women, providing food, lodging, and laundry became men's work. After a fire in San Francisco destroyed the restaurant, he returned to Chile in 1850, where he became – among many other things – an immigration agent attracting Germans to that country. Male, without family, hoping to get rich quickly in 1849, and not particularly committed to staying, Pérez fit the image of many gold rush migrants. Yet in other ways he did not. His elite Parisian education set him far apart academically, as did his close political ties to Chilean independence, and his age,

early forties when he arrived in California made him older than many in the gold camps.[18]

Thousands of Chinese men and handful of Chinese women followed a pattern similar to Pérez in making a journey to what they termed "gold mountain". Like the ports of Chile, the Pearl River Delta region of China, which became the base for much of the migration to the United States (until after World War II), was well-connected to trade routes and merchants and wage-laborers there heard the news of the gold rush earlier than others. A longstanding tradition of migration to other parts of Southeast Asia meant that the option of a man going for a time to another location seemed normal. Various local conditions made migration attractive at mid-century: the aftermath of the Opium War, famine, and flood. But it was as often those with previous contact with U.S. merchants and missionaries and a sense of opportunity who most often decided to risk the trip.[19]

The Chinese migration picked up rapidly in the early 1850s, and by 1870

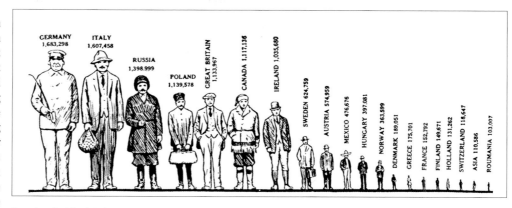

Countries of origin of the immigrants to the USA 1920

he census reported 63,000 Chinese in he United States, the vast majority in California.[20] Many went to the mines, but s with Pérez, prejudice made it difficult o continue, more so as the state passed aws taxing foreign miners and forbidding on-Whites to testify against Whites. Some Chinese moved into other business, selling oods to miners, providing restaurant or aundry services. The Central Pacific Railroad hired many to build through he Sierra Nevada, involving much more lasting and bridge construction than the astern segments of what would become he first transcontinental railroad.[21] Many Chinese migrants in the United States lanned to return to China after making ome money, and they gained the reputa- on of being "sojourners," though as the Pérez case showed, people from many laces fit this category. As a mindset, emporary migration meant less likelihood f setting up or sending for a spouse or hildren. It meant that community organi- ations tended to focus in slightly different irections than for groups who arrived with n idea of permanence.

nti-Chinese caricature in "The Illustrated WASP," 1877, which as published in San Francisco

The late 1840s and early 1850s also witnessed massive migration from Ireland. Though migration from Ireland to North America had long roots, it took on differ- ent proportions during the potato famine of the late 1840s. A shift in rural family patterns to late marriage and high rates of celibacy, meaning lower fertility rates, was already beginning to take hold prior to the massive population loss.[22] During the famine both mortality and emigration rates rose dramatically, with roughly one million lost to death and another two to migration, which went in several directions: England, Canada, and the United States. The U.S. recorded close to 800,000 arrivals from Ireland in the 1840s, and over 900,000 in the subsequent decade. Even Irish who came from meager circumstances in these years of hunger and who settled in Five Points, the most notorious of New York's slums, did relatively well in a rather short period of time. Living conditions in the slum were better than prior to migrating, and it was possible to earn money.[23] Not only did they amass savings, but they also made their way into the political landscape, becoming citizens and voting in numbers that soon attracted attention. During the famine migrants often blamed the British government for the poor conditions. Long after the famine, migrants still placed the onus on British rule for the motivation to migrate.[24] Over time many more Irish came to the United States after the famine than during it, but the stereotype remains in U.S. popular culture that all Irish, whether

they arrived in 1830, 1890, or 1905, came because of the famine. Irish women, who outnumbered Irish men among migrants later in the century, carved out a niche as domestic servants. Though an unattract- ive occupation by many standards, service in the U.S. typically offered better condi- tions than in Ireland or England, and Irish immigrant women used their wages for a variety of purposes from conspicu- ous consumption to charity contributions to amassing a dowry.[25]

Many other European groups migrated to the United States during the mid-19th century. In terms of numbers, German speakers were the most common after British and Irish migrants. To a greater extent than the Irish, Germans tended to head for potential farmland. Increasing population on agricultural land in the German states meant shrinking farm sizes and increasing numbers of landless labor- ers there. Cottage industry added income, but became less profitable as urban indus- trialization increased.[26] Potential migrants weighed many possible locations as options. Some moved within Europe, particu- larly eastward. Others, beginning in the 1820s, headed for Brazil, where a substan- tial ethnic population developed. A few made the trek to Chile (for which Pérez was doing some recruiting), and others moved in limited numbers to various other South American countries.[27] Those who came to the U.S. could draw upon the human capital that came with being ethnically associ- ated with a group already established since

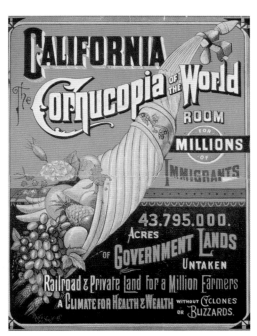

Published in 1885 by the California Immigration Commission of the Central Pacific Railroad, this booklet describes California as "not only the land of promise, but the land of real fruition," capable of "supporting easily and prosperously 4,000,000"

the colonial era. As the group moved into regions of the Old Northwest – what would become the Middle west – German patterns of farming, particularly the contributions of wives and children to fieldwork, tended to promote permanence to a greater degree than those of "Yankees."[28]

Yet another strand of German migration at mid-century had its origins in the liberal revolutions of 1848. A number of leading figures involved in these uprisings made their way to the United States. Almost by definition intellectuals, this group fit the model later termed refugees, fleeing imprisonment or worse across a variety of countries. Of them, Carl Schurz earned the greatest national recognition, serving within a few years of his arrival in the U.S. as an ambassador and Union general, gaining election as senator, and garnering an appointment as secretary of the interior. In comparison to migrants from other backgrounds, many U.S. leaders embraced Schurz despite his foreign birth, and he could play upon both the German and U.S. aspects of his identity.[29] Likewise, German migrants could and did

promote separate ethnic neighborhoods and German language schools, more often chosen rather than imposed, as was the case with immigrant and ethnic groups considered non-white.

The 1840s also witnessed a paradoxical stationary migrant group – those who lived in parts of northern Mexico. Whatever their political leanings, the border crossed them, shifting their national location with a stroke of the pen. In the wake of the Mexican-American War, residents of the newly incorporated southwest region supposedly got to choose their political affiliation, though by default it assumed U.S. citizenship. Official words and actual deeds conflicted, however. Latinos faced a situation where the government officially stated it would recognize them as citizens possessing all the rights related to that status, yet socially few Anglos accepted them in this role. U.S. residents challenged previous land rights based on Hispanic jurisprudence, whether contesting boundaries or denying a right to water or free range for cattle.[30] To be socially brown was to encounter increasing prejudice in this era.

The United States had a population of about 23 million in 1850, and it was growing at a rate of almost a million people per year – most from natural increase, but somewhere between 30–40 % due to net migration gains. Net migration gain encompassed many newcomers from Europe, but it also masked the loss of certain groups. With the passage of the Fugitive Slave Law of 1850 free Blacks in non-slave regions of the United States feared for their freedom. Though the overall numbers of both slaves and free Blacks increased in the subsequent decade, some sought greater assurances of freedom in Canada or Mexico. The Underground Railroad led to places such as Buxton, Ontario, a successful all-black community of the era.[31] Other African Americans sought out opportunities in the west.

Just as slavery raged in public debate, so too, the question of immigration began to take on political implications. In public perception masses of poor Catholic migrants from Ireland and beer-drinking (and anti-prohibition) German speakers, also predominantly Catholic, would shift the culture of the United States away

from what some "Native Americans" felt were the founding Protestant virtues of the republic. Though nativism always existed in the mid 1850s it became a potent political force as groups coalesced around the American Party and elected candidates for a number of state and local offices. Much of this impetus disappeared with the election of Lincoln and the beginning of the Civil War, though opposition to immigration, or at least to the immigration of certain groups, would recur sporadically in subsequent decades.

The political upheaval associated with the Civil War allowed the passage of one of the most momentous pieces of legislation in terms of immigration: the Homestead Act of 1862. Under the provisions of this law, U.S. citizens AND those intending to become citizens could file a claim for 160 acres of government land. If the person stayed on the land for five years and "improved" it through building a dwelling and planting crops, the individual could get title to the land after that time for a nominal registration fee. The land was, at least for most intents and purposes, free. Not surprisingly, this drew large numbers of people not only from the eastern states

"Fear of Swamping with Foreigners," nativist, anti-immigrant caricature, 1888

ut also from other countries, who sought
and. It added pressure on the American
ndians of the plains, who faced increas-
ng numbers of "settlers" moving further
nd further into their territory. It fueled
ne construction of railroads and transpor-
ation hubs. It connected U.S. agricultural
arkets increasingly with global ones, and
s U.S. grain came into competition with
uropean products, more small farmers of
ae Old World found their own economic
velihood threatened, meaning greater
acentive to move.

Shifting Gears

he railroads that brought immigrants and
thers to parts of the U.S. plains were just
ne part of a growing industrial transpor-
ation network. Steamships increasingly
eplaced sailing vessels in oceanic trans-
ortation, cutting both time and the cost
f coming to North America. Railroads
xpanded into various regions, making the
ansport of people as well as goods more
easible across long distances. Industrial
obs attracted migrants to various locations
n many countries. The late 19th century
epresented a major era of migration on an
aternational scale. Migrations went from
aral areas to cities (and back), across
orders (and back), across oceans (and
ack). The combination of industrializa-
on, significant natural resources, avail-
ble land, and an open policy regard-
ag most migration meant that the United
tates expansion welcomed massive
umbers of immigrants in these years.
hae Chan Ping was not one of them.

Chae Chan Ping arrived in California in
875, not an auspicious year to be Chinese
a that location. Anti-Chinese agitation
ad been rising since the days of the gold
ash. Just in terms of formal measures it
acluded: the foreign miners tax of 1850, a
alifornia Supreme Court decision of 1854
aaking it impossible for a Chinese person
o testify in court against a white, and a
ouple of attempts to stop the "coolie" trade
a 1862.[32] The year Chan Ping arrived,
875, the U.S. Congress passed the Page
aw, outlawing the migration of prosti-
ates and specifically targeting women

Ellis Island Immigrant Station, founded in 1892

arriving from Asia. Two years later Denis
Kearney, an Irish immigrant, founded the
Workingman's Party in California, which
then campaigned on a platform of "the
Chinese must go." In the context of reconstruction after the Civil War Congress
passed a law allowing for naturalization
of persons of African descent. California's
Supreme Court soon ruled that Chinese
immigrants were neither white nor black,
and hence could not naturalize, so though
Chan Ping resided in California for twelve
years continuously, he had no option to
become a citizen. Neither would it have
been easy to find a spouse had he wanted
to given the tremendous sex ratio imbalance in the migrating population (due
in part to the Page Law) and to an anti-
miscegenation measure of 1880 that
prohibited "Mongolians" from marrying Whites.[33] Chan Ping became part of a
bachelor society, one largely restricted to
Chinatown.

In 1882 the U.S. Congress acceded to
the nativist demand, passing the first of
a number of Chinese Exclusion Acts that
would bar the migration of laborers from
China. Another measure, this one aimed
at contract labor, passed a couple of years
later. Still, the laws and treaty rights

between the U.S. and China provided for
some migration, and for return visits by
those already in the United States provided
they organized certificates of return before
departure. Following these provisions,
Chae Chan Ping left for a return visit in
1887. He was on a ship headed back to San
Francisco when Congress passed the Scott
Act, eliminating the option of return – and
invalidating return certificates for those
out of the country. Chan Ping, like many
Chinese immigrants, fought for his rights

New York labor agency, around 1900, offering – among other
things – jobs in construction and coal mines

Chinese settled in the Mott Street/Pell Street area of New York City in the 1870s. This general store was established in 1890 and served many functions; it was a shop, a trading center, a bank, a money transfer institution, and a social center

railroads and other transportation link brought many parts of eastern and south ern Europe as well as Mexico into a we of connections. As they spread, so did th likelihood that people would gain opportu nities to migrate. Added to this transporta tion revolution was an increase in literac in many regions. One did not need to rea in order to migrate, but it helped facilitat the process.

The United States became the larges magnet for international immigration in th late 19th century, but hardly the only one Italians, united politically from 1870, face various options for migration. Some move internally to industrial opportunities suc as the silk mills of the north-east. Othe moved across the northern border to tak advantage of better wages or more consiste employment in France or Belgium. Some the largest groups headed for Buenos Aire where they constituted a major compe nent of the Argentine population. Other particularly from the southern provinces Italy, might come to the United States. I later years many would head for Canada Australia.[37] There was no dearth of poss ble options, and relatively low transporta tion costs meant that many would return Moreover, the migration changed not onl those who went, but also those who remaine behind. People who spoke back to the bosses, or felt they had a right to service in a bank, or changed their consumptio

through the court system.[34] Eventually the U.S. Supreme Court denied his appeal, and authorities in San Francisco for cibly placed him on a steamer bound back for China. The New York Times reported he tried at length "to force his unwelcome presence upon the citizens of this fair and free country."[35]

The United States took greater inter est in immigration as the century went on. The most obvious manifestation of this interest was the construction of a major entrepôt at Ellis Island, which opened its doors in 1892. This was part of a broader move to bring immigration under federal auspices, and New York served as the gateway for the majority of Europeans coming to the United States. More than 12 million immigrants would pass through Ellis Island before it closed its doors in the mid-20th century. Most could do so relatively quickly, particularly compared to arrivals at Angel Island, which opened in 1910 and served as the point of entry for San Francisco for perhaps 300,000 people.[36] Of the 92 million people living in the United States in 1910, roughly 13.5 million were foreign-born. Many more had at least one parent born in another land.

There were still significant numbers of immigrants headed for rural areas and for agricultural opportunities, more after the Indian Wars of the 1870s "freed" up these lands for non-indigenous newcom ers. Other opportunities beckoned in trade, service, and industry. The reach of

Chicago was founded as a small rural settlement in the 1830s and had two million inhabitants by 1900, definitely a symbol of a rapid process of urbanization and industrialization, postcard 1910

patterns, could all be "American" in addition to those who actually spent time across the ocean.[38]

In the period from 1908 to 1923 the U.S. government estimated that 60% of southern Italians who immigrated to the United States went back. Some eastern European groups had rates reaching close to 90%. This was, in other words, a temporary migration for many. Go, earn some money, return and use the money to buy land or improve a home: these were typical goals. Here the pattern of the gold rush, and the imposed pattern of Chinese migration, applied to large numbers of relatively free migrants. Even among the groups with longer histories in the U.S., such as the English or Germans, 20% rates of return were normal in this period. The major exception was for "Hebrew" migrants, because with the imposition of czarist pogroms, few eastern European Jews wanted to return to active persecution.[39] For those Jews who came to the United States, the immigrant population clustered in one location, New York, and particularly the lower east Side of Manhattan, though smaller contingents went to a variety of other locations, not just to major cities, but also to less urban areas from Johnstown, Pennsylvania, to homesteads in rural North Dakota.[40]

Another group of Asian migrants also began coming around the turn of the century. With the Meiji restoration Japan resumed more contacts with other parts of the world, and this included migration. The United States, Canada, Peru, and Brazil served as destinations beginning in the 1890s[41]. The Japanese government set standards for those who would leave, and chains of migration developed.[42] Within the United States, anti-Asian sentiment rose rapidly. Just as Japan proved its military prowess in the Russo-Japanese War, the school board in San Francisco sought to relegate Japanese American children to "Oriental school" there. Both the local Japanese American community and the Japanese government strongly opposed this action. A major international incident ensued, ending in the Gentlemen's Agreement, by which Japan would largely limit migration of new laboring men beginning in 1908, a model also adopted in Canada. Because the previous migrants

tended to be young men, one of the questions remained if they could marry. Like Chinese men before them, they could not marry white women. But Japanese law allowed a man to marry without being present and hence men sent for "picture brides" from their homeland. The couples sometimes exchanged pictures as part of the marriage arrangement. These photographs served not only to assess basic characteristics, but also as a record for immigration authorities, who expanded the use of photography to control not just the Japanese, but migrants more generally. Journalists published photographs of large groups of Japanese wives coming to join husbands in the U.S., adding fuel to anti-Asian sentiment.[43]

As the United States rose in international stature, its military adventures and colonial activities fostered migration in unexpected ways. The Spanish-American war led to U.S. control of Puerto Rico, Guam, and the Philippines, as well as a particularly fraught relationship with nominally independent Cuba. To these the United States also added Hawaii, much to the chagrin of the local nobility, and to the glee of U.S. sugar planters. In this newly formed political landscape, "nationals" in colonial territory could and did migrate back and forth to the United States. When other migration waned during World War I and thereafter, these links remained.

Another major stream of migration formed just prior to World War I. Railroads linked Mexico on a north-south axis to the United States in the late 19th century. When the revolution broke out in 1910, many Mexicans fled northward. For the 75,000 U.S. citizens living in Mexico wartime also proved dangerous, as their property, if not their lives, was threatened. Many returned, often with the help of the U.S. government.[44] Mexican migrants also came in significant numbers and went into a variety of occupations. Prior to the revolution many sought jobs on ranches or in mines, and some tried to continue in these areas. With the revolution and later, more became part of agricultural and construction work gangs.[45] The major reorientation of U.S. migration patterns to a north/south, rather than east/west axis, was underway. As migration restrictions came into play, migration from Canada and Mexico continued with relatively few limitations.

Above: Attired in the customary dress of his native country (Bavaria or Austria), a "New American" poses proudly at Ellis Island, 1898

Below: Two young arrivals at Ellis Island, tagged and waiting for further processing, 1905

Closing Doors

By the 1910s sentiment was building to cut immigration levels in the United States. With the coming of World War I, the United States faced difficult decisions regarding both alliances and migration. World War I closed many migration streams, and allowed the strains of nativism to come to fruition. First a literacy test, then more stringent controls on political activists (including deportation), and finally the implementation of quotas based on national origins, these measures put the brakes on a migration already slowed by wartime disruption. By the mid-1920s the United States revamped its immigration statutes to a much more restrictive regime, at least in terms of European migration. In these years it established an Asian barred zone – eliminating all migration from this region of the world.

Proportionately the United States experienced the greatest population growth due to migration around 1850 and 1880, but by the 20th century the association of population with strength had to compete with a version of strength based on reproducing the "right" people. This racialized ideal existed in a world where ethnicity could mean life or death.

It did for Veron Dumehjian. Her prosperous childhood ended when the Young Turk government of the Ottoman Empire began a systematic attack on the Armenian ethnic group in 1915. Dumehjian's family fled their home as the massacres got underway. They traveled from place to place as refugees. Cholera swept one camp where they resided, killing most of her family. When she finally was able to rejoin her father and grandmother they faced expulsion from another town by the Turkish army. More deaths followed. Dumehjian continued moving from place

Growth from immigration, 1790–1930

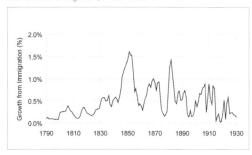

to place, eventually ending up in Athens. Diasporic communities developed in various locations in Europe. Left without means and without a homeland by the persecution, at age sixteen she agreed to an arranged marriage with an Armenian man she did not know, a man twice her age. Many Armenian women refugees looked to marriage as a way out of impossible conditions. For Dumehjian the offer led to the United States. Large numbers of Armenian women went to Canada, some to the United States, and a few to Argentina. In these lands of immigration the marriages meant balancing out sex ratios and an opportunity to rebuild an Armenian life.[47] At least some felt the responsibility to reproduce their ethnic group to counter the massive loss of lives suffered prior to migration.

Dumehjian was fortunate, for though U.S. federal authorities had initially labeled Armenians "Asiatics," by 1909 a court in Massachusetts ruled they were white, and another court upheld this decision in 1925. The fact that people brought cases meant there was some ambivalence, but overall Armenians could make the argument that they were white and there was no automatic racial association that would challenge them. As white, Armenians could migrate, could own land in California, could become citizens, and could effectively plead for assistance for other Armenian refugees.[48] Further, Armenians could practice picture marriage without the stigma or the public outcry that the Japanese faced.

The examples of Abd Abd ar-Rahman, Vicente Pérez Rosales, Chae Chan Ping, and Veron Dumehjian should suggest that an image of the United States as a country which welcomes immigrants ignores quite a number of variations, and that the history of migration in the United States involves complex patterns. When Israel Zangwill created the 1908 play about the melting pot, it was Europeans who entered the pot and came out waving American flags. The U.S. offered some people many opportunities, in part based on economic conditions, in part based on political philosophy, and in part based on a tradition of religious freedom. In comparison to many countries these could mean quite a bit – a land of freedom and opportunity, for some. Yet, immigration drove others from

the land, and was forced upon both group and individuals. Migration could be i one direction only, or it could be back an forth and around. It could take place for few years, or for a lifetime. Overall migra tion connected the United States into th global world in many ways.

Literature

1   See Walter Nugent, Crossings: The Grea Transatlantic Migrations, 1870–191 (Bloomington: Indiana University Pres 1992), p. 164–165.

2   Allan D. Austin, African Muslims i Antebellum America: Transatlanti Stories and Spiritual Struggles (Ne York: Routledge, 1997), p. 70–72.

3   David Eltis, "The Volume and Structur of the Transatlantic Slave Trade: , Reassessment", William and Mar Quarterly 58, No. 1 (January 2001 45; Michael R. Haines, "Population by sex and race: 1790–1990." Tabl Aa145–184 in Historical Statistics c the United States, Earliest Times to th Present: Millennial Edition, eds. Susa B. Carter, Scott Sigmund Gartne Michael R. Haines, Alan L. Olmstead Richard Sutch and Gavin Wright (Ne York: Cambridge University Pres 2006). http://dx.doi.org/10.1017 ISBN–9780511132971.Aa110–683.

4   This also led to death rates not know until then, see Antonio Mc Danie "Extreme Mortality in Nineteent Century Africa: the Case of Liberia Immigrants", Demography 29, No. (November 1992): 581.

5   Aaron S. Fogelman, "From Slave Convicts, and Servants to Fre Passengers: The Transformation c Immigration in the Era of the America Revolution", Journal of American Histor 85, No. 1 (June 1998): 61.

6   David Eltis, "Introduction", Coerced an Free Migrations: Global Perspective ed. David Eltis (Stanford: Stanfor University Press, 2002), p. 18.

7   Hans-Jürgen Grabbe, "Europea Immigration to the United States in th Early National Period, 1783–1820 Proceedings of the America Philosophical Society 133, No. 2 (Jun 1989): 194.

Left: Coal Miners, ca. 1910. At this time nearly half the coal miners in America were foreign-born, with Poles, other Slavs, and Italians the most numerous. The miners worked ten hours a day, six and a half days a week. The work was grueling, dirty, and highly dangerous. In 1907, over 3,000 miners died in job-related accidents
Right: "Knee pants" at forty-five cents a dozen, sweat shop, Ludlow Street, Lower east Side, New York City, photo ca. 1890

8 Douglas M. Bradburn, "'True Americans' and 'Hordes of Foreigners': Nationalism, Ethnicity, and the Problem of Citizenship in the United States 1789–1800", Historical Reflections 29, No. 1 (2003): 19–41; see: http://www.uscis.gov/files/nativedocuments/Legislation%20from%201790%20-%201900.pdf (05.03.2009).

9 Rebecca J. Scott, "The Atlantic World and the Road to Plessy v. Ferguson", Journal of American History 94, No. 3 (2007): 727; Gary B. Nash, "Reverberations of Haiti in the American North: Black Saint Dominguans in Philadelphia", Pennsylvania History 65 (1998): 44–73.

10 See the example of the Devereux Family in: Kerby A. Miller, Arnold Schrier, Bruce D. Boling und David N. Doyle, eds., Irish Immigrants in the Land of Canaan: Letters and Memoirs from Colonial and Revolutionary America, 1675–1815 (New York: Oxford University Press, 2003), p. 41–43.

11 Robert P. Swierenga, Faith and Family: Dutch Immigration and Settlement in the United States, 1820–1920 (New York: Holmes & Meier, 2000), p. 16–17.

12 Jorge A. Hernandez, "Merchants and Mercenaries: Anglo-Americans in Mexico's Northeast", New Mexico Historical Review 75, No. 1 (2000): 43–75; Mark E. Nackman, "Anglo-American Migrants to the West: Men of Broken Fortunes? The Case of Texas, 1821–1846", western Historical Quarterly 5, No. 4 (1974): 441–455.

13 Walter D. Kamphoefner, Wolfgang Helbich und Ulrike Sommer, eds., News from the Land of Freedom: German Immigrants Write Home (Ithaca: Cornell University Press, 1991), p. 111–121.

14 Sean Kelley, "Mexico in his Head: Slavery and the Texas-Mexico Border, 1810–1860", Journal of Social History 32, No. 3 (2004): 716.

15 Susan A. Miller, Coacoochee's Bones: A Seminole Saga (Lawrence: University of Kansas Press, 2003): passim.

16 See Paul Spickard, Almost all Aliens: Immigration, Race, and Colonialism in American History and Identity (New York: Routledge, 2007), p. 153–157.

17 Richard L. Bland, "Michigan in 1848: as described by Traugott Bromme in his handbook for German emigrants", Michigan Historical Review 31, No.

2 (Fall 2005): 49; Jerry Schuchalter, "'Geld' and 'Geist' in the Writings of Gottfried Duden, Nikolaus Lenau, and Charles Sealsfield: A Study of Competing America Paradigms", Yearbook of German-American Studies 27 (1992): 49–73.

18 Vincente Pérez Rosales, Times Gone By: Memoirs of a Man of Action (New York: Oxford University Press, 2003), p. xv.

19 Yong Chen, "The Internal Origins of Chinese Emigration to California Reconsidered", western Historical Quarterly 28/4: 522–523.

20 Ronald Takaki, Strangers from a Different Shore: A History of Asian Americans (New York: Penguin Books, 1989), p. 79.

21 See dazu Public Broadcasting Series Transcontinental Railroad: http://www.pbs.org/wgbh/amex/tcrr/peopleevents/p_cprr.html, 12.03.2009

22 James H. Johnson, "The Context of Migration: The Example of Ireland in the Nineteenth Century", Transactions of the Institute of British Geographers 15, No. 3 (1990): 265.

23 Tyler Anbinder, "From Famine to Five Points: Lord Lansdowne's Irish Tenants

Above left: "Give me your tired, your poor, your huddled masses, yearning to breathe free" – welcome to the land of liberty, newspaper etching 1887
Above right: Newly arrived immigrants wait for processing at Ellis Island and, eventually, for entry to their new home, 1902
Below left: Interior of a German restaurant in New York, wood engraving in the Hamburg-Altonaer Illustrirte, between 1880 and 1890
Below right: Detained children posing for a photograph in rooftop playground of main building, Ellis Island ca. 1910. Seated in an "Uncle Sam" wagon and holding the Stars and Stripes, they have already begun the process of americanization

Encounter North America's Most Notorious Slum", American Historical Review 107, No. 2 (2002): 353, 376.

24 Kerby A. Miller, "Emigration as Exile, Cultural Hegemony in Post-Famine Ireland", in A Century of European Migrations, 1830–1930, eds. Rudolph J. Vecoli und Suzanne M. Sinke (Urbana: University of Illinois Press, 1991), p. 339–340.

25 Hasia Diner, Erin's Daughters in America: Irish Immigrant Women in the Nineteenth Century (Baltimore: Johns Hopkins University Press, 1984).

26 Steve Hochstadt, "The Socioeconomic Determinants of Increasing Mobility in Nineteenth-Century Germany", in European Migrants: Global and Local Perspectives, eds. Dirk Hoerder und Leslie Page Moch (Boston: Northeastern University Press, 1996), p. 154–157.

27 Anja Alert, "Mecklenburger Auswanderung nach Südamerika", Asien, Afrika, Lateinamerika 26, No. 4 (1998): 455–466.

28 Jon Gjerde, "Prescriptions and Perceptions of Labor and Family among Ethnic Group in the Nineteenth Century American Middle-West", in German-American Immigration and Ethnicity in Comparative Perspective, eds. Wolfgang Helbich and Walter D. Kamphoefner (Madison: Max Kade Institute for German-American Studies, 2004), p. 120–121.

29 Hans L. Trefousse, "Carl Schurz and the Politics of Identity", Yearbook of German-American Studies 31 (1996): 1–11.

30 See z. B. Michael C. Meyer und Michael M. Brescia, "The Treaty of Guadalupe Hidalgo as a Living Document: Water and Land Use Issues in northern New Mexico", New Mexico Historical Review 73, No. 4 (1998): 321–345.

31 Michael R. Haines, "Population, by sex and race: 1790–1990." Table Aa145–184 in Historical Statistics of the United States. http://dx.doi.org/10.1017/ISBN–9780511132971.Aa110–683;

zu Buxton see John Hope Franklin und Loren Schweninger, In Search of the Promised Land: A Slave Family in the Old South (New York: Oxford University Press, 2006), p. 142–144.

32 Franklin Odo, ed., The Columbia Documentary History of the Asian American Experience (New York: Columbia University Press, 2002), p 86–88.

33 Martha Menchaca, "The Anti-Miscegenation History of the American Southwest, 1837–1970. Transforming Racial Ideology into Law", Cultural Dynamics 20, No. 3 (2008): 294.

34 Lucy E. Salyer, Laws Harsh as Tigers. Chinese Immigrants and the Shaping of Modern Immigration Law (Chapel Hill: University of North Carolina Press, 1995), p. 21–23.

35 "Chan Ping Leaves Us", New York Times, (2 September 1889). http://query.nytimes.com/mem/archive-free pdf?_r=1&res=990DE6DF1130E6 33A25751C0A96F9C94689FD7C1 (05.03.2009).

36 Robert Barde und Gustavo J. Bobonis "Detention at Angel Island: First Empirical Evidence", Social Science History 30, No. 1 (2006): 106.

37 Donna R. Gabaccia, "Is Everywhere Nowhere? Nomads, Nations, and the Immigrant Paradigm of United States History", Journal of American History 86, No. 3 (1999): 1115–1134.

38 See Linda Reeder, "When the Men Left Sutera: Sicilian Women and Mass Migration, 1880–1920", in Women, Gender, and Transnational Lives: Italian Workers of the World, eds. Donna Gabaccia und Franca Iacovetta (Toronto: University of Toronto Press, 2002), p. 45–75.

39 Mark Wyman, Round-Trip to America. The Immigrants Return to Europe 1880–1930 (Ithaca: Cornell University Press, 1993), p. 11.

40 Ewa Morawska, Insecure Prosperity. Small-Town Jews in Industrial America 1890–1940 (Princeton: Princeton University Press, 1996); J. Sanford Rikoon Rachel Calof's Story: Jewish Homesteader on the northern Plains (Bloomington: Indiana University Press, 1995).

41 Ulrich Mücke, "Aus einer anderen alten Welt. Asiatische Einwanderer in der

Amerikas, ca. 1850–1945", Periplus: Jahrbuch für Außereuropäische Geschichte 14 (2004): 117–142.

42 Yuzo Murayama, "Information and Emigrants: Interprefectural Differences of Japanese Emigration to the Pacific Northwest, 1880–1915", Journal of Economic History 51, No. 1 (March 1991): 125.

43 Kei Tanaka, "Photographs of Japanese Picture Brides: Visualizing Immigrants and Practicing Immigration Policy in Early Twentieth-Century United States", American Studies [Korea] 31, No. 1 (May 2008): 29, 38.

44 David H. Grover, "Gringos go Home: west Coast Seagoing Evacuations of Americans during the Mexican Revolution, 1912–1916", southern California Quarterly 82, No. 2 (2000): 169–192.

45 Josef Barton, "Borderland Discontents: Mexican Migration in Regional Contexts, 1880–1930", in Repositioning North American Migration History: New Directions in Modern Continental Migration, Citizenship and Community, ed. Marc S. Rodriguez (Rochester: University of Rochester Press, 2004), p. 160–161.

46 David Kherdian, The Road from Home: The Story of an Armenian Girl (New York: Greenwillow, 1979); this is a fictitious story which is based on the true story of Kherdian' mother.

47 Isabel Kaprielian-Churchill, "Armenian Refugee Women: The Picture Brides, 1920–1930", Journal of American Ethnic History 12, No. 3 (1993): 3–29.

48 Ian Haney-López, White by Law: The Legal Construction of Race (New York: New York University Press, 1996), p. 91–92.

Poster in World War II which promises European refugee children safety in America

Barry Moreno

The Strange Journey of Ignatz Mezei

The little cabinetmaker seemed an unlikely spy, but the attorney general of the United States, thinking otherwise, held the fellow at Ellis Island on suspicion of subversion for more than three years. Ignatz Mezei (1897–1976) came to this country from a Hungarian community Romania in 1923. He settled in Buffalo, New York, followed his trade, married, and had four children, but like many immigrants, never became a United States citizen. His future immigration hassles seemed to have stemmed from his membership in the International Workers Order, a fraternal and insurance organization with Communist ties (around the year 1936, Mezei had served as the president of the Buffalo lodge's Hungarian section). In 1947, the International Workers Order was placed on the FBI's list of subversive organizations, at which time it also ceased to exist. The next year, Mezei received word from Romania that his mother was gravely ill and dying. Alarmed at the news, he notified the Immigration and Naturalization Service of his intention of going to visit her. But on his arrival in war-torn eastern Europe, he found things awkward: he was barred from crossing the Romanian frontier and wound up stuck in Hungary. To make matters worse, he had to wait for nineteen months before getting a visa to return to his home in the United States.

When Mezei arrived back in New York in February 1950, he was detained by immigration inspectors and taken directly to Ellis Island. The Immigration and Naturalization Service, backed by the attorney general, kept the reasons for Mezei's detention a dark secret, simply saying that he was being held for security reasons, which was another way of saying that they believed him to be a subversive. After a deportation warrant was issued against him, Mezei applied to 15 different foreign consulates and embassies for permission to emigrate to their countries, but each request was denied; apparently no one wanted a subversive cabinetmaker. This prompted Mezei to file an appeal against the deportation order, but the Supreme Court ruled in favor of the Justice Department in 1951. So, with no nation willing to grant him a passport and visa and the federal government refusing him permission to leave Ellis Island and reenter the United States, Mezei was stuck in a legal limbo: it looked as though he might be kept in detention for the rest of his life. But, finally, in 1954, an immigration service board of special inquiry finally had a change of heart and quietly recommended that Mezei be allowed to reenter to the United States. On August 9, 1954, Attorney General Herbert Brownell paroled Mezei and released him from Ellis Island, ending the detention of the man whom *The New York Times* had dubbed "The Man Without a Country." A few years later, Mezei returned to Hungary.

Barry Moreno

The Deportation Express

In the years between the two world wars (1919–1941), the deportation of aliens from the United States was systematized and became a common practice; it attracted widespread interest from the general public as well as from the newshounds of the press. During the 1920s and '30s, hundreds of such persons were brought every four to six weeks to Ellis Island on trains that usually set out from San Francisco and Seattle. Passing through rural and urban America, they would pick up more immigrants for the unpleasant journey east. Aboard the sealed cars, immigrant inspectors supervised the party and were staffed with armed guards and matrons. A private physician was also in attendance. (One such medical attendant, Dr. Leo L. Stanley, accompanied three deportation parties, one each in 1920, 1921 and 1922; while on board the train, he kept a diary, which is now in the collections of Stanford University.)

The policy of deporting foreigners in large parties (sometimes numbering 300 or more) originated during the Red Scare (1919–1920) when hundreds were rounded up nationwide and brought by train for deportation to Russia and other countries. The anarchists Emma Goldman and Alexander Berkman were among those apprehended. Most subsequent deportees were not expelled on political grounds; their troubles were more commonplace: illegal entry, no passport, no immigrant visa, moral turpitude, having criminal convictions, or having fallen into poverty and become a public charge. For instance, Anna Sage, known as the "Woman in Red" for her assistance to the F.B.I. in finding the notorious bank robber John Dillinger, was deported in 1936 on the grounds of having run a brothel, which made her guilty of the crime of moral turpitude.

The steps to deport someone began when the Immigration Service issued a warrant of deportation. However, there was one hitch: no alien could be deported without a valid passport. Now if the immigrant didn't have a passport – which was all too common – the Immigration Service had to contact the alien's embassy or consulate and request one. This often caused delay and even occasional resistance on the part of diplomats from the immigrant's homeland. At Ellis Island, a passport office was opened in the 1920s to handle these requests.

Deportation trains left from the west Coast to the east coast and vice versa on a regular timetable; along the way, some had to be enlarged by adding more railway cars to accommodate new passengers. Eastbound trains dropped off deportees heading for Toronto at Chicago and those bound for Montreal at Buffalo, while the remaining deportees (usually the majority) continued on to Ellis Island, so that they could board ships bound for Europe, Latin America, the Near East, and other foreign destinations. When the trains reached their terminus in Jersey City, New Jersey, deportees were transferred to Ellis Island via barges. At the island, prostitutes were sent to separate waiting rooms and quarters from the other deportees. The Deporting Division also kept the undesirable aliens well away from other detainees. Although conditions in much of Europe and the Far east during World War II curtailed the numbers of deportees to those regions, deportation parties bound for Canada, Mexico, and Latin America kept the Immigration and Naturalization Service busy. Following the war, deportations and repatriations to Europe and the Far east resumed.

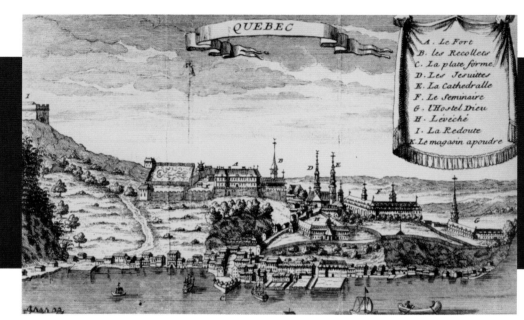

QUEBEC

A . Le Fort
B . les Recollets
C . La plate forme
D . Les Jesuittes
E . La Cathedralle
F . Le Seminaire
G . l'Hostel Dieu
H . L'eveché
I . La Redoute
K . Le magasin apoudre

Quebec, 1722

Valerie Knowles

'In Search of Fame, Fortune and Sweet Liberty" – European Emigration to Canada, 1830 to the Present

Emigration to British North America, as Canada was known before Confederation (1867), was overwhelmingly British. Not only was it predominately British, it had the distinction of being part of what has been called the western world's "greatest folk movement" of modern times.

This movement got underway in the decade following the conclusion of the Napoleonic wars in 1815. Initially it saw thousands, then tens of thousands, and eventually hundreds of thousands of people leave continental Europe and the British Isles in search of new homes in South America, Australasia, South Africa, and North America. By the closing years of the 19th century, the annual exodus numbered well over a million individuals.

Misery in overpopulated, oppressed Ireland and unemployment in England and Scotland, coupled with work and land-owning opportunities in Britain's northern colonies, fueled much of this emigration to British North America in the decades immediately following 1815. In the 1830s, there were also additional factors at work: the uneasiness triggered by the Paris and Belgian revolutions of 1830 and a depression that began in the 1830s and continued intermittently for ten years.

Nowhere was this depression felt more keenly than in such English manufacturing centres as Liverpool, Leeds, and Manchester. In these cities rampant unemployment, flyers advertising opportunities in the colonies, remittances of money from family members and friends, and the enticing pitches of shipping agents combined to persuade many English to emigrate.

The year 1830 marked both the start of a new decade and a surge in the overall volume of British emigration to British North America. Indeed, the early and middle years of this decade witnessed the largest emigration yet to Britain's northern colonies, which

then consisted of Upper Canada (present-day southern Ontario), Lower Canada (present-day southern Quebec), and further east, Nova Scotia, New Brunswick, Prince Edward Island, and Newfoundland.

Between 1829 and 1830, the number of Britons who gave British North America as their destination rocketed from 13,307 to 30,574, while the number of recorded arrivals at the port of Quebec, the largest receiving center, jumped from 15,945 to 28,000. It's a moot point as to which set of figures is more reliable. What is significant is the impressive increase in numbers, which, as it turned out, was not an isolated case. In fact, annual increases of comparable magnitude were experienced between 1833 and 1834, and between 1835 and 1836.

This upswing in British immigration occurred at a time when the colonizing views of the social reformer, Edward Gibbon Wakefield, were gaining in popularity. These views were inspired by Wakefield's three-year sojourn in Newgate Prison, following his abduction of a 15-year-old heiress, Ellen Turner.

Shocked by what he learned in notorious Newgate of the penal system at home, the budding reformer concluded that systematic colonization could solve much of the poverty and crime resulting from Britain's steep rise in population and overcrowding. Land in Britain's colonies, he argued, should be sold at reasonable prices, not given away, and the proceeds, along with a tax on rent, be used to transport deserving individuals to a new life abroad.

Before Wakefield began promoting his ideas by means of the Colonization Society he established, people had looked upon life in the colonies as demeaning and having a lot in common with penal transportation. With the spread of his teachings, they began to regard emigration to British North America and

other imperial outposts as a means of both improving their prospects and strengthening the Empire.

Interest in and support for emigration was also whipped up by extensive parliamentary debate on the topic during the 1820s and by the findings of select committees of the British House of Commons. One of these, the Select Committee of 1826, concluded that the grossly underpopulated colonies could provide gainful employment for Britain's excess workers. Even more significant was the work of the wide-ranging 1830 House of Commons inquiry into the condition of the Irish poor. Its findings produced a recommendation that large-scale emigration be used as a remedial measure for Ireland's many social ills.

Recommendations such as these reinforced the British government's interest in promoting emigration to British North America, especially that of the poverty-stricken Irish, who, it was feared, might

Cultural traditions continue to be preserved by the immigrant communities well into the present. German culture in Edmonton, Alberta, 1985

one day swarm into Britain in unprecedented numbers. To encourage emigration to British North America, the government routinely made the passage to that part of the world cheaper than to American ports, and provided free transportation in barges up the St. Lawrence River to poor newcomers who declared their intention of settling in Upper or Lower Canada.

Even before the Great Famine of 1846–51 Irish made up by far the largest part of those emigrants striking out for British North America, where Irish settlements had already been established around Peterborough and between Perth and the Ottawa River in Canada West. Estimates in these years indicate that about two-thirds of those individuals who staggered onto the docks of Quebec City were Irish; two-thirds of the remainder were from England, while approximately one-tenth of all the new arrivals hailed from Scotland.

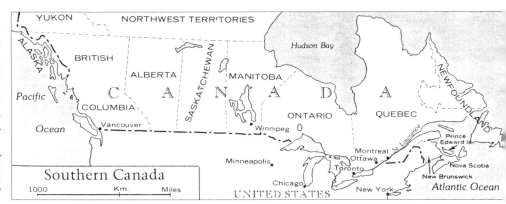

Map of the southern part of Canada

Indian woman from the north of Alberta. Photo around 1900

No matter what their origin, however, about four-fifths of them were destined for Upper Canada, although it should be noted that much of the immigration that made it to the Canadas kept right on going until it reached the more prosperous United States. This diversion or loss of immigration to Canada's southern neighbor would be a recurring theme in 19th-century Canadian history. From the 1860s to the closing years of the century, in fact, more people would leave Canada than enter it.

During the 1830s, immigration largely bypassed the Maritime colonies. Immigration to Nova Scotia, for example, began to fall off after 1838, because by that time most of its last frontiers had become pretty well occupied. In the immigration that took place between 1831 and 1836 (11,000), Scots formed the largest component. Scots had earlier emigrated in impressive numbers to tiny Prince Edward Island, but that province, like Newfoundland, which was chiefly populated by Irish and English from the west of England, did not share in the large British immigration of the 1830s. Only New Brunswick received significant numbers of immigrants in the 1830s (31,000 between 1831 and 1836 alone) and most of these were Irish.

British North America may have inspired many dreams and hopes in these years, but harsh reality caught up with the emigrants as soon as they embarked on the Atlantic crossing. This took from to one to three months, usually on a 300 to 800-ton wooden sailing vessel that had been used to transport timber and general imports and that lacked sophisticated fire-fighting equipment and navigational aids.

Although well-off emigrants could have a cabin, the overwhelming majority of them traveled in unventilated, cramped, filthy steerage, where berths were merely spaces on small wooden bunks built into the ship's timbers on either side of the hold. In addition to a lack of space and light, passengers also had to contend with meager rations, and bad food and water. Conditions in steerage, in other words, were ideally suited to the spread of dysentery, typhus, and cholera, which were brought aboard by passengers and sometimes crew members.

One of the largest influxes of immigrants in the 1830s occurred in 1832 when almost 52,000 immigrants arrived at the port of Quebec. What made this year so memorable, however, was not the immigration total, but rather the large number of people struck down by cholera, a bacterial infection of the small intestine, acquired by swallowing contaminated food or water. A regular visitor to the Canadas in these years, it arrived early in June on one of the overladen immigrant ships that docked at the port. Before the epidemic had run its course in October, it had killed approximately one-twelfth of the newly arrived immigrants and thousands of residents of Lower and Upper Canada.

In addition to causing thousands of deaths, the epidemic unleashed turmoil among French-Canadians, who had long equated immigration with disaster. Just as today many Québecois harbor deep fears for their survival and integrity as a cultural community so did many of them as far back as the first decades of the 19th century. Although numerically superior in these years, they regarded themselves as under constant threat from Lower Canada's

English-speaking minority which ran the economy and the executive branch of the government and controled the Legislative Council.

These insecurities led to some hysterical behavior in 1832. Thinking that cholera represented a deliberate attempt to exterminate their people, crowds of French-Canadians lined the shores of Lake Champlain that July, weapons at the ready, threatening to fire on any vessels that did not turn back.

Although it was appalled by the plague, Upper Canada continued to welcome all the immigrants it could receive – provided they were British. Americans were definitely not welcome. Nobody did more to court Britons than the province's lieutenant-governor, Sir John Colborne, who initiated an organized campaign to attract British immigrants and strove unceasingly to reduce obstacles to settlement by building roads and bridges. Thanks to his vigorous promotion of immigration and public works, the province witnessed a 50% increase in population between 1830 and 1833.

The late 1830s experienced a downturn in immigration, largely because of political unrest in both the Canadas, where constitutional breakdown, recurrent outbreaks of violence, rioting and military confrontation began in the autumn of 1837 and continued until the early months of 1839. When it realized just how serious popular discontent was in the Canadas and how ineffective colonial government was in both provinces, the British government decided to initiate a thorough overhaul of the Canadian state. To this end, it dispatched Lord Durham, a diplomat, politician, and colonial administrator, to the colonies to conduct an inquiry into the causes of the rebellions.

Since it was the crisis in Lower Canada that was principally responsible for bringing him to this side of the Atlantic, the radical Whig devoted most of his five-month sojourn in British North America to studying the situation in that colony. His report, therefore, dwelt at length on the perennial feud between the English and the French, whom he considered an uneducated and unprogressive people.

To resolve this problem, Durham recommended that municipal institutions and a judicious program of immigration be implemented in the province. He also urged the adoption of qualified responsible government and the union of the two Canadas, believing

British immigrants on their way to settlement in Upper Canada; engraving ca. the end of the 18th century

that the French-Canadians would be submerged in an intercolonial union. Of these two recommendations, only the second one found favor with the British government, which created the United Province of Canada in 1841.

Lord Durham's provocative assessment of the problem in Lower Canada and his two key recommendations for the Canadas – union and qualified responsible government – have often deflected attention away from two other themes raised in this state document: immigration or "emigration," as it is labeled, and the disposal of public lands. According to Durham, the disposal of public lands in British North America had so many shortcomings that it not only hindered settlement and discouraged immigration it actually promoted emigration to the United States, which, unlike British North America, boasted a highly efficient land-granting policy.

The 1840s: A Decade of Contrasts

Although immigration to British North America plummeted in 1838 because of the rebellions in the Canadas, it soon gathered momentum, with fairly equal numbers of English, Irish, and Scots reaching the colonies in the first half of the next decade. Because they provide a fascinating study in cause and effect, two years in particular stand out in the first half of the decade: 1842 and 1843.

In February 1842, the governor general of British North America, Sir Charles Bagot, advised Britain's colonial secretary that there would be plenty of work for unskilled laborers in the Province of Canada the following summer. Accordingly, the Colonial Office, promoted emigration and over 44,000 people sailed for Canada, many anticipating employment in canal building. Regrettably, Bagot's predictions were off the mark, and when much of the work he had promised failed to materialize, hordes of newly arrived immigrants became destitute. Many, despairing of finding employment in Canada, made their way to New York, hoping to find jobs there, but to no avail. Disillusioned and discouraged, some 9,500 Britons returned to their homeland from New York in the autumn and winter of 1842–43.

The following year immigration was down, with less than half the new arrivals being

Danish-Canadian farm in Dalum, Alberta. Top: First settlement late 19th century, bottom: expansion a few decades later (around 1930). Danes started coming to Canada in the late 19th century and they continue to immigrate to this country. As early as the 1920s, even the older settlements began to experience a loss of Danish culture

Irish. Still, the immigration of that year was long remembered in New Brunswick and the Province of Canada as one that was a real asset to the colonies. Quite different, though, would be the memories of the "famine" immigration that transformed the character of immigration in the second half of the decade and triggered a groundswell of opposition in the colonies to the dumping of paupers in their midst.

In the 1840s, a decade of heavy immigration, one year stands out above all the others: 1847, the year when a mammoth tide of penniless and starving immigrants arrived on Canada's shores, many suffering from typhus and dysentery.

During the memorable spring and summer of 1847, Canada's first and largest quarantine station, Grosse-Île (located 46 km downstream from Quebec), processed approximately 100,000 boat passengers, most of whom were Irish. Of these, approximately 5,000 died on the island, described by one official as "the great charnel-house of victimized humanity." Indeed, so many emigrants succumbed that year to typhus or other diseases either on the voyage to Canada, on Grosse-Île,

or inland that 1847 would be known as Black '47.

The toll was also impressive in the Maritimes, where in Miramachi, New Brunswick alone, hundreds of passengers and crew members of "emigrant" ships were carried off by disease in the autumn of 1847.

Of the hordes of emigrants who sailed that year from English, Scottish, and Irish ports for British North America, nearly all were Irish fleeing the ravages of the Great Famine of 1846–51, caused in part by the failure of the potato crop, which had been destroyed by a fungus. The potato crop failed not only in Ireland but also throughout the rest of northwestern Europe, but because it was the basic food staple in Ireland its failure represented a huge catastrophe in the British possession.

Irish immigrants accounted for most of the over 400,000 people who sailed from Britain to British North America between 1846 and 1854, the peak immigration years in pre-Confederation Canada. So many Irish were attracted to Canada west (present-day southern Ontario) in these and the pre-famine years that two-thirds of the people living in Ontario at the time of the first Dominion

census (1871) classified themselves as Irish. Contrary to popular perception, two-thirds of these were Protestant and over three-quarter of those who described themselves as Irish lived in rural areas.

Sheer numbers alone, however, account for the shift in political power that occurred as a result of the Irish influx in the late forties and early fifties. In 1848, Canada west boasted 57,604 persons of Irish birth while in 1851–52 the census reported an equivalent statistic of 179,963. This increase of 118,358 in the number of Irish-born was just enough to shift the population balance and hence the balance of political power between Canada west and Canada East, their respective populations numbering 952,004 and 890,261 in 1851.

Thanks to the revival of trade in the United Kingdom and the demand for men to serve in the Crimean War, British immigration to British North America dropped dramatically in 1855. Not until after Confederation would it resume on the same scale and then it would be very different in character from the "famine" emigration.

Although Blacks had lived in Canada since the French regime, by far the largest number arrived in this country in the mid-years of the 19th century. These were the American Blacks who escaped north of the border using a network of secret routes known collectively as the "Underground Railroad." It is estimated that some 40,000 Blacks made their way to Canada before the outbreak of the American Civil War, many settling in southern Ontario. Another destination was British Columbia, which, in 1858, received approximately 800 Blacks who had immigrated from California.

The slump in British immigration, the continuing loss of large numbers of newcomers to the United States, and the exodus of increasing numbers of French-Canadians to that country in search of work led the Province of Canada to embark on a modest immigration promotion program in the 1850s. In the 1840s, the colony's principal concern had been its lack of control over the quality of immigrants pouring into it. Now its main preoccupation was the overseas recruitment of immigrants, particularly suitable British ones. To this end, beginning in 1854, the province began to assign a small amount of money to advertising its attractions in England and on the Continent, relying

nly a small number of French settlers came to Alberta from France. Among their ranks was a group of former cavalry officers who establish- ranches at Trochu, north of Calgary. Several appear here in 1904 at the Ste. Anne ranch

chiefly on pamphlets distributed by agents of the Department of Agriculture, which had responsibility for immigration.

A landmark step in the active recruit-ment of immigrants was taken in 1859 when Canadian official, A.B. Hawke, opened an office in Liverpool, England, and began promotion work in the United Kingdom. The following year, William Wagner was dispatched to Germany by the Crown Lands Department. He was armed with literature on the province and instructed to promote the migration of small farmers and agricultural laborers.

The work undertaken by these immigra-tion salesmen foreshadowed the activi-ties carried out by the network of immigra-tion agents established after the Dominion of Canada came into being in 1867. Like their predecessors, these agents targeted Britons, especially British agriculturalists. British immigration had done much to stamp the character of the colonies in the earlier decades and it would continue to play a notable role in Canadian society in the years immediately after Confederation.

Although Irish, English, and Scottish immigration predominated in the years prior to Confederation, other immigration took place as well. By far the most signifi-ant category of non-British immigration was German-speaking in origin. Large numbers of these people emigrated from Europe to the western states of the United States of America between 1830 and 1870, and since part of this movement made the trip by way of Montreal and Canada West, impressive numbers of these immigrants stopped off in Canada West. Others — many of whom were German Catholics and Amish people — arrived directly from Europe.

Berlin (which was renamed Kitchener in 1916 as a result of anti-German agita-tion during the First World War), became an area of concentrated German settlement and from this part of south-western Canada west German-speaking settlers spread to Perth, Bruce, Huron, and Grey Counties. Then, in the 1860s, as a result of the American Civil War, America-bound Germans headed for the wilderness lands of the upper Ottawa Valley, where some 12,000 Germans, chiefly from Prussia, settled by 1891.

Some 200,000 people of German origin settled in Canada by the time of Confederation, principally in Ontario. Approximately 1,500 lived in Quebec (mainly in Montreal), and 47,000 in the Maritime provinces.

By comparison, the first Dominion census (conducted in 1871, it refers to only the four original provinces of Canada) reveals that

German immigrants in Edmonton, 1902. Most people of German origin in pioneer Alberta went to farming areas, but a small class of successful German entrepreneurs emerged in Edmonton and surrounding towns

Finnish cowboys in Ontario. Photo 1900

Canadians of French origin comprised the largest group in the Canadian population. They numbered 1,082,940. The Irish, numbering some 846,000, made up the second largest group, followed by the English, who numbered about 706,000. Altogether some 2,101,946 Canadians were of British origin in 1871. With the exception of the Germans, other groups, such as the Dutch, Scandinavians, and Italians, were much smaller.

Immigration in the Macdonald Years

From the time of the publication of Lord Durham's Report (1839), British politicians regarded the union of British North America as a realistic target. By the 1850s, visionaries even envisaged a transcontinental union. Confederation did not become a practical option until the 1860s, however, and then largely because of the continental crisis provoked by the American Civil War and truculent American foreign policy.

Following three conferences, and with the approval of the British government, Confederation finally became a reality on July 1, 1867 when the new Dominion of Canada came into being, its entry on the North American stage celebrated by fireworks and parades. Composed of Nova Scotia, New Brunswick, and the provinces of Quebec and Ontario, it was dominated by the larger-than-life image of Sir John A. Macdonald. Sir John had opposed the idea of Confederation when it first took concrete shape in 1864. But as an eminently practical, skillful politician he finally embraced the idea and ran with it. And it was Sir John, a Conservative, who emerged as the first prime minister of the new, sparsely populated Dominion of Canada, which, in 1871 would record a population of 3,689,257. Three-quarters of it lived in southern Ontario and Quebec, over 90% in areas occupied since 1851.

For the first three decades after Confederation, large-scale immigration was a dream rather than a reality. This was not, however, because Sir John A. Macdonald and the Conservatives, who were in office most of the period, did not attach a high priority to luring new settlers to this country. They did, especially Sir John, the nation-builder, who dreamt of a vibrant Canada extending from the Atlantic to the Pacific.

When the new federal union came into official existence, Macdonald and the other Fathers of Confederation could pat themselves on the back for having accomplished a great deal. Nevertheless, the largest part of their program had yet to be realized: the coaxing of Prince Edward Island and British Columbia into the union, and the deciding of the future of the Red River settlement and Rupert's Land (the vast territory granted to the Hudson's Bay Company in 1670).

By far the most important of these considerations was the future of the west because failure to include it in the new union would have dealt a severe blow to the expansionist urge that had figured so prominently in the Confederation movement. As far as Macdonald and the Conservatives were concerned, the west had to be brought into Confederation as quickly as possible because of the threat posed to it by the imperialist ambitions of Canada's neighbor to the south.

This sentiment was voiced by a leading Father of Confederation, George Brown, who declared in 1865, "Double our population, and we will at once be in a position to meet promptly and effectually any invader who may put his foot with hostile intent upon our soil."

The race to incorporate British Columbia and the Hudson's Bay Company domains into the fledging dominion therefore became the most urgent task facing the government in Ottawa, the country's capital. And closely allied with this was the need to promote large-scale immigration into the vast, thinly settled plain that stretched from the Lakehead to the Rocky Mountains. As never before, immigration would receive top billing, but despite this it would not rate a department of its own. Between 1867 and March 1892, immigration would come under the Department of Agriculture and from 1892 until October 1917 under the Department of the Interior.

No sooner had the fledgling dominion come into being than the federal government began establishing a network of emigration agents to advertise this country's attractions to prospective immigrants. Until the advent of the First World War, these immigration salesmen would target farmers with capital, agricultural laborers, and female domestics, preferably from Great Britain, the United States, and northern Europe, in that order. In the picturesque words of one assistant superintendent of immigration, those sought were "men of good muscle who are willing to hustle." Not so welcome were individuals with professions, clerks, or other prospective newcomers of sedentary occupation. These were actually discouraged from emigrating to Canada, while artisans, mechanics, and tradesmen, if not discouraged from doing so, were certainly not courted.

Before the first agents could be appointed, the federal and provincial governments had to decide how to share the joint responsibility for immigration conferred on them by section 95 of the British North America Act, now known as the Constitution Act, 1867. With a view to deciding how to share this responsibility, a federal-provincial conference convened in 1868 to define respective spheres of action in the field of immigration promotion. As a result of the delegates' deliberations, it was decided that Ottawa would open an emigration office in London and one on the Continent, followed by other agencies when the need arose. The provincial governments were to be free to appoint their own agents as they saw fit.

Almost immediately a federal agent set up shop in London, England. His appointment was soon followed by the installation of an emigration agent on the Continent and by the appointment of other permanent agents located in Glasgow, Belfast, and Dublin.

It didn't take long, however, for the carefully formulated plans for immigration romotion to unravel. An immigration onference that convened in 1874 quickly oncluded that separate and independent action by the provinces in promoting immigration had led to waste and inefficiency and, in some cases, to actual conflict ith the federal government. Accordingly, e participants decided that henceorth the federal minister of agriculture ould assume full control of all immigraion promotion in the United Kingdom and urope and that "independent agencies r any of the provinces [would be] iscontinued."

In 1869, one year after the opening of the ondon office, Parliament passed Canada's rst act dealing with immigration matters. eflecting as it did the prevailing laissezire philosophy of the time, it said nothing bout which classes of immigrants should e admitted and which categories should e proscribed. Not until 1872 was the act nended to prohibit the entry of criminals d other "vicious classes" into this country d not until 1879 was an order-in-council assed excluding paupers and destitute migrants.

With the introduction of these amendments, the pattern was set for future Canadian immigration policy: it would be evolutionary and implemented largely by amendments to the current immigration act. In this way the government could avoid the difficult and time-consuming job of introducing new acts and be in a position to put new policies into effect quickly. Authorization for such amendments is provided by the Immigration Act, which delegates power to the cabinet to make rules and regulations in the form of orders-in-council, designed to adapt the act's broad provisions to changing circumstances.

The Opening of the West

One of the federal government's most urgent goals was realized in 1869 with the Hudson's Bay Company sale of Rupert's Land (an area covering present-day northern Ontario, northern Quebec, all of Manitoba, most of Saskatchewan and much of the northwest Territories) to Canada and the creation

the following year of the "Postage Stamp Province" of Manitoba. When Canada's westernmost province, British Columbia, comprising Vancouver Island and part of the mainland, was wooed into Confederation in 1871 with the promise of a railway from central Canada, several of the Conservative government's expansionist goals were met.

With the acquisition of this huge expanse of new territory, the whole question of immigration was thrown into sharp focus. Indeed, only a populous west under the plough would ensure the economic viability of the projected transcontinental railway and safeguard the 49th parallel against encroachment from Canada's rapacious neighbor, where at least one state legislature (Minnesota) had cast covetous eyes on the Red River district. Large-scale colonization of the west would also provide a domestic market for the products of Quebec and Ontario's factories, a development envisaged by the Conservatives' National Policy, introduced in 1878.

It was estimated that total Canadian immigration between 1861 and 1871 was 179,000, while natural increase was estimated to be 550,698. Although this represented a rate of increase of only 14.2% as against 32.6% for the previous decade, it was nevertheless a good rate of growth. Still, it was obvious that immigration had to be promoted as never before if the dominion's new lands were to be filled with people and its resources sufficiently exploited to justify such a daring and costly undertaking as a transcontinental railway to British Columbia.

With this in mind, the government staged the first of a series of immigration conferences in Ottawa in 1871. Then, to encourage settlement in recently acquired Manitoba and the north-west Territories the Conservatives introduced the Dominion Lands Act (1872). This act, which was modeled on the United States Homestead Act of 1862, granted 160 acres of free land to any settler 21 years of age or older who paid a ten-dollar registration fee, lived on his quarter section for three years, cultivated 30 acres, and built a permanent dwelling.

By anyone's standards, including the Americans', this was a most generous offer. However, not many newcomers from outside Canada were tempted by it in the 1870s and 1880s. In fact, for the first three decades after Confederation, large-scale immigration

group of immigrant land seekers at Rivers, Manitoba, during their trip out to western lands. Photo early 1900s

Lumberjacks in Canada. Undated photo

was never realized. The colonization of the west merely limped along, the majority of newcomers arriving from within Canada itself, especially from Ontario.

So many land-hungry sons and daughters of Ontario farming families migrated to Manitoba in the 1870s that the province acquired the nickname "Ontario West." Maritimers and English-speaking Quebeckers also journeyed to the west as did French-Canadians. But the French-Canadians came in significantly smaller numbers. For them, the major attraction was New England, located on Quebec's doorstep and a ready source of factory and laboring jobs. Indeed, from the 1840s on, so many French-Canadians fled Quebec for such New England factory towns as Manchester, Lowell, and Suncook that these manufacturing centres became known as the "Little Canadas."

With only a small number of people from outside Canada trickling into the west in these years, Alexander Mackenzie's Liberal government (1873–78) decided that another approach was needed to attract settlers to the Prairies. Although colonization companies had failed in the past, the government decided in 1874 to amend the Dominion Lands Act in such a way as to encourage the establishment of colonization companies

that would settle lands at no expense to the government.

Regrettably, numerous colonization schemes and companies launched under the new regulations met with resounding failure. Thoroughly disillusioned, the government decided, in 1877, to abandon the practice of surrendering large tracts of land to colonization companies. Four years later, however, the Macdonald Conservatives, back in power, decided to allow the establishment of colonization companies composed primarily of the friends and supporters of the government willing to invest capital in public improvements designed to attract settlers to the West. Even this approach proved ineffective as only one company fulfilled its promises punctually; the remainder of the 20 or more companies defaulted or were liquidated. As a result, this approach was discontinued, not to be revived until after Wilfrid Laurier and the Liberals were swept into office (1896).

Among the small number of newcomers from outside Canada who did enter the west in the 1870s and 1880s was a group of Mennonites, an Anabaptist sect that spoke a Low German dialect and embraced pacifism and a simple lifestyle. Their search for a new home was triggered by the introduction of a policy of russification in the schools of the Ukraine, where they lived, and by the

implementation of universal conscription which went against their pacifist beliefs.

In response to generous concessions and offers from the Canadian government, some 7,500 Mennonites journeyed to Manitoba in the 1870s. There they settled on two tracts of land, one located south-west and the other south-east of Winnipeg, Manitoba's capital. Since the former reserve was located on open prairie, the Mennonites acquired the distinction of being the first post-Confederation European immigrants to farm Prairie land.

This period also saw some 2,000 Icelanders arrive in Canada after volcanic eruptions in 1872 spread pumice over a large farming area in their impoverished country. They established short-lived settlements in the Muskoka and Ottawa areas of Ontario and then in Markland, Nova Scotia, before heading west to Manitoba, where, in 1875, they founded the community of Gimli (meaning paradise) on the south-west shore of Lake Winnipeg.

From the very beginning they were beset by hardships, including floods, brutal cold, poor accommodation, and a scarcity of food. In addition to these initial setbacks, the colony was devastated by an outbreak of smallpox in 1877, which killed 100 people out of a population of approximately 1,500.

The end of the smallpox epidemic did not signal the end of adversity for the colony, however, because a series of unusually wet growing seasons and the resultant destruction of crops persuaded many to leave the settlement; by 1881, over half had departed for North Dakota. As devastating as these setbacks were, though, the original settlement soldiered on with the aid of an $80,000 loan from the Mackenzie government and even managed to prosper in the 1880s. By 1888, the colony was reported to boast a population of more than 5,000.

In fact, by this time, other parts of Manitoba and the north-west were home to several other Icelandic settlements as well. Between 1872, when the influx began, and the outbreak of the First World War in 1914, an estimated 10,000 to 12,000 Icelanders left their wind-swept, volcanic island for Canada.

The frugality, honesty, and industriousness of the Icelanders encouraged the Canadian government to do its best to attract ther Scandinavian settlers. And in the 1870s the government did try valiantly to persuade Scandinavians to immigrate to this country, but few responded to Ottawa's overtures, preferring instead to emigrate to the United States. Not until 1886 was a Scandinavian colony of any size founded in the West.

That year, a party of skilled Norwegian workers left Eau Claire, Wisconsin, for Calgary, where they established the Eau Claire Lumber Mill, which became one of the city's major industries. Other Norwegians, many from the American mid-west, made their way to British Columbia in the following decade. Their ranks included a group of newcomers who established a co-operative settlement at Bella Coola on the coast. According to the colony's constitution and bylaws, the settlement's purpose was to "induce moral, industrious and loyal Norwegian farmers, mechanics and business-men to come to Bella Coola and to make their home here under the laws of British Columbia."

Individual Jews and Jewish families from Britain and Europe had trickled into the west as far back as the 1850s as farmers, merchants, fur traders, and gold miners. They didn't begin to arrive in appreciable numbers in western Canada, however, until after until the assassination of Tsar Alexander II in 1881 unleashed pogroms in Kiev, Odessa, and other towns and villages in the Ukraine. Homeless, hungry, and penniless, they poured into Austria, not knowing where they would end up.

The west was slow at first to acknowl-dge the plight of these unfortunates, but then it responded in a frenzy. Among those Canadians determined to help the refugees was Alexander Galt, then Canada's high commissioner to Great Britain. Eager to find suitable immigrants for Canada and to interest the banker Lord Rothschild and his friends in investing in this country, Galt raised the issue of Jewish immigration with Sir John A. Macdonald. Jews, he informed the prime minister, were a superior people who had the necessary funds to get estab-shed in Canada and he wanted to see his country assist them.

Fortunately the cause had Macdonald's upport. With a view to bringing some Jews to Canada, he instructed government officials to make land available for them. Alluding to the stereotypical image of the Jew as an old

clothes peddler, he predicted that a sprin-kling of Jews would be good for the north-west as they would involve themselves in peddling and politicking.

In April 1882, therefore, some 240 refugees left for the north-west, the first of several such parties sponsored by the Mansion House Committee in London or by relief committees in Berlin, Paris, and New York. The most celebrated of the agricultural settlements founded by the Russian Jews was New Jerusalem, established in 1884 on an inhospitable tract of land near Moosomin in present-day south-eastern Saskatchewan. Although this colony failed, several Jewish settlements later succeeded at Oxbow, Hirsch, Wapella, and Qu'Appelle in what would later become Saskatchewan.

Although the term "Hungarian" is today used to describe Magyar-speaking people, this was not the case before the First World War when the term was a political desig-nation that might also have included some Slovaks, Romanians, Croatians, and various other peoples.

The first organized "Hungarian" settle-ment in the Canadian west was founded in 1885 near the village of Minnedosa

in Manitoba. Composed of Magyar and Slovak families, who had immigrated from Pennsylvania, it was led by Géza de Döry. The following year, the colorful adventurer "Count" Paul Esterhazy established another group of newcomers near the site of present-day Esterhazy, Saskatchewan.

The Manitoba colony failed to thrive after the premature death of Döry and the decision of many Magyar settlers to leave. It was a different story with the Saskatchewan settle-ment. After overcoming such challenges as the brutally cold winter of 1886–87, prairie fires and discord among the colonists, it managed to survive thanks to the arrival of newcomers from Hungary and the United States in 1888. In the mid-1890s and at the turn of the century additional Hungarian settlements came into being south-west of Yorkton, and near Kipling in Saskatchewan.

The laissez-faire policy embodied in the Immigration Act of 1869 remained essen-tially intact to the 1890s. The one notable exception was the passage of an act in 1885 to "restrict and regulate Chinese immigra-tion." The federal government introduced this legislation in response to pressure from British Columbians, who deplored the large

Scottish immigrants waiting to go ashore at Quebec, P.Q.. Photo ca 1911

numbers of single Chinese men who had entered the province to work on the Canadian Pacific Railway.

Although the act did not ban Chinese immigration outright, it levied such a stiff head tax ($50) as to deny entry to the province of a significant number of Chinese. Still, this was not enough to satisfy British Columbia. Accordingly, the tax was subsequently raised to $100 and then $500, thereby helping to shape a unique, long-surviving bachelor community with its own distinctive cultural and organizational features.

The first known Chinese had arrived in Canada in 1858 after news had drifted down to San Francisco that gold had been discovered on the Fraser River, on the mainland of present-day British Columbia. Then, starting in 1859, more came directly from Hong Kong on chartered ships.

By far the largest number, however, began coming to Canada in the 1880s after Andrew Onderdonk, an American contractor, was awarded the contract for building the section of the Canadian Pacific Railway that runs from the Rocky Mountains to the Pacific Ocean. Between 1881 and 1884, an estimated 15,700 Chinese males entered British Columbia, most to work at cutting out hills, filling gullies, and ravines, and later handling explosives and tunnelling on that historic stretch of railway.

With the completion of the CPR's western link, most of the Chinese rail workers, who had survived the arduous and dangerous work assigned to them, had drifted back to the British Columbia coast, principally to Victoria, where Canada's first Chinatown had developed. Others, however, followed the railway east to such centres as Calgary, Moose Jaw, Winnipeg, and Toronto.

The First Wave of Immigrants

Canada's immigration prospects only began to look up in the 1890s. By 1896, the so-called "Great Depression" (1873–1896) had lifted and a general economic recovery in both Europe and North America was creating a demand for Canadian foodstuffs. Moreover, Europe was in the midst of a population explosion. This phenomenon was both relatively new and more severe in southern and eastern Europe, where high taxes and debt burdens, land clearances, and ethnic tensions would lead many to try their luck overseas: in Canada.

Interest in the west was aided and abetted by breakthrough developments in Canadian agricultural technology, such as the development of winter-resistant strains of wheat and the adoption of dry farming techniques. There was also the widespread belief after 1890 that the United States was finally running out of good free land and higher returns for farm products.

Poised to take full advantage of these new developments was the Liberal government of Prime Minister Wilfrid Laurier, which was swept into power in 1896. In the years preceding the First World War vigorous expansion would be the order of the day.

In fact, between 1896 and 1914 Canada would experience the first of two great waves of European immigration (the second occurred between 1946 and 1961). In the first wave, approximately 1,352,000 newcomers arrived in this country. Of this number, more than 750,000 came from the British Isles, 240,000 from the United States, and well over 350,000 from continental Europe.

In this first wave, single men clearly predominated. Usually a young man was the first to journey overseas, receiving financial aid from his father, his uncles, and his cousins. It was expected that once he had become established in Canada he would repay his passage money and contribute funds to family members who remained in his homeland. The far fewer women who immigrated were invariably the wives and fiancées of men who had already settled in Canada.

Unattached women did emigrate from Great Britain and the Continent, but they were few in number and usually they married soon after reaching their destination. Among these unattached women were some who came to work as domestics.

If there is one man who symbolizes the vigorous expansion of the Laurier years, it is Clifford Sifton, who was in charge of immigration between 1896 and 1905. As minister of the Interior and Superintendent of Indian Affairs, this Manitoba lawyer, politician, and newspaper publisher exploited his restless drive and celebrated energy to the full to fill the empty prairies with suitable farmers and agriculturalists. He was even prepared to admit agriculturalists from places other than Great Britain, the United States, and northern Europe, observing that "a stalwart peasant in a sheepskin coat, born on the soil, whose forefathers have been farmers for ten generations, with a stout wife and a half-dozen children, is good quality."

Clifford Sifton became an aggressive salesman for his pet project. "In my judgment," he observed in 1899, "the immigration work has to be carried on in the same manner as the sale of any commodity; just as long as you stop advertising and missionary work the movement is going to stop."

The Macdonald government had relied chiefly on its offer of free homesteading land; the completion of the Canadian Pacific Railway (1885); the efforts of colonization companies; and the perceived lack of free or cheap land in the United States to ensure a steady influx of newcomers to Canada. As a result, it had neglected promotion. Sifton, by contrast, launched an aggressive advertising campaign.

A Ukrainian settler's family in Canada. Ukrainians started immigrating to the Canadian west in the 1890s

To attract settlers, the minister hired agents who went overseas to deliver stirring lectures on Canada's many advantages. Canadian exhibits were mounted at fairs, public displays, and exhibitions in Britain, the United States, and Europe. Sifton also had foreign journalists wined and dined on guided tours across the west and encouraged successful homesteaders to visit their homelands. And to crown his efforts, his department flooded Great Britain, the United States, and Europe with immigration pamphlets and underwrote the production of "editorial articles" for insertion in foreign newspapers.

However, since urban immigrants were not desired, the department of the Interior instructed its agents to discourage "laboring men and mechanics" although it did not always pursue this policy when it clashed with the requirements of the Canadian labor market.

Sifton also stressed new fields for soliciting immigrants. One of these was the United States. The Conservatives had generally regarded it as merely a competitor for immigrants whereas he saw the republic as a vast reservoir of potential new settlers. Previously the Canadian government had concentrated on repatriating former Canadians south of the border.

Under Sifton's direction, his department rapidly expanded its network of American offices and agents and pulled out all stops in its attempts to attract experienced American farmers with capital. It is estimated that between 1901 and 1914 nearly a million immigrants entered Canada from the States. Many of them were returning Canadians while about one-third were newcomers from Europe – Germans, Hungarians, and Scandinavians who had originally settled in the American west but who now sought better land for their children.

Some of the Americans who entered Canada were members of groups founded on a religious basis. Notable among these pioneers were Mormons who headed north from Utah to join the small colony started in 1887 by Charles Ord in present-day southern Alberta. With them came a knowledge of irrigation techniques that would prove invaluable in developing the dry lands of the Palliser Triangle, an area encompassing the valleys of the Souris and South Saskatchewan Rivers.

Pioneer log house of an early family located in the first Hungarian settlement in Alberta. Photo 1906

Sifton's second field of recruitment was eastern and central Europe. And it was here that the minister tilled a field rife with controversy and difficulty. To attract stalwart peasants who could push back the frontiers of western settlement and supply seasonal or casual labor when needed required exceptional measures. This was because most European governments were hostile to emigration; some actually prohibited it. To meet this challenge, Sifton's department established a clandestine organization, the North Atlantic Trading Company, a network of European shipping agents who agreed, whenever possible, to direct agricultural settlers to Canada in return for a larger bonus.

In a further attempt to draw the desired type of immigrant to the Prairies, the government did everything possible to establish bloc settlements of the different ethnic groups. These colonies often had a powerful magnetic effect, especially in the case of groups like the Doukhobors, a Russian peasant sect whose pacifism and simple lifestyle invited persecution and harassment from the tsarist authorities. In January 1899, the first of over 7,500 Doukhobors headed west to settle in what is now Saskatchewan. Here, they occupied three large areas in the east-central part of

the province after being promised freedom from military service and the right to live in communal villages.

The Ukrainians

By far the largest group from central and eastern Europe to emigrate to Canada in these years were the Ukrainians, the collective name applied to Slavs from regions of the Austro-Hungarian and Russian empires in eastern and southern Europe. It is clear that some Ukrainians (or Galicians, as they were commonly called) settled in Canada before the closing years of the 19th century, but the arrival of the symbolic first Ukrainians in 1891 heralded the beginning of a massive Ukrainian immigration to this country.

Ukrainian immigration to Canada occurred in four waves, the largest being the one that occurred between 1896 and 1914. Spurred to emigrate by poverty, land congestion following the abolition of serfdom, and oppression, approximately 170,000 Ukrainians made their way to Canada in this period.

For the most part these were small farmers and laborers from Galicia and Bukovina (both provinces of the Austro-Hungarian Empire) who headed for the West. Here, many of them settled in the aspen parkland of the Prairie provinces because they wanted wood for fuel and building purposes and because the prime land had already been taken up by British, American, German, and Scandinavian settlers. In this wide parkland belt that extends in an arc from south-eastern Manitoba through central Saskatchewan to the Rocky Mountain foothills the Ukrainians would change forever the social fabric of the Prairies.

Among the thousands of Prairie pioneers in these years were settlers of German origin, many from the Russian Empire, Austria-Hungary, and the Balkan countries, where Germans had founded colonies in the eighteenth century. When a shortage of land and a growing class of landless workers developed in these settlements, many Germans were spurred to emigrate. In other areas increasing nationalism and the resulting abrogation of original rights and privileges provided the necessary stimulus.

The German pioneers in the west followed in the wake of some 7,000 Mennonite trailblazers, who had left Russia between 1874 and 1879 to settle in Manitoba, where they occupied the east Reserve, east of Ninerville and west of Steinbach, and the west Reserve, east of Morden and west of Rosenfeld.

By the time the First World War erupted, in 1914, approximately 35,000 German-speaking immigrants had settled in Manitoba, representing 7.5% of the province's total population. The newly created provinces of Alberta and Saskatchewan (1905) also experienced a dramatic growth in German immigration, Saskatchewan's German population increasing from less than 5,000 in 1901 to over 100,000 in 1911.

The government continued to promote immigration from Great Britain to Canada during the Sifton years, and this despite the fact there were relatively few good agriculturalists left to court. This promotion was deemed politically necessary because English Canadians believed Ottawa should do everything possible to retain the British character of the country.

Prior to 1903, Canada's immigration service in Britain was under the control of the Canadian High Commission, but that year Sifton decided to establish an immigration office that was effectively

Russian-Orthodox Church at Smoky Lake. The onion-shaped domes are characteristic landmarks throughout central and northern Alberta. The Russian-Orthodox, Ukrainian Catholic, and Ukrainian Greek-Orthodox churches competed for support among Ukrainian immigrants

independent of the High Commission. This move heralded a significant increase in British immigration. In 1900, fewer than 1,200 Britons entered Canada. Five years later the annual number had soared to above 65,000, exceeding the number of newcomers arriving from the United States.

Most of these newcomers were individuals who immigrated to Canada on their own in search of a higher standard of living and freedom from the rigidities of the British class system. The ranks of these unsponsored

immigrants included not only people modest means but also well-heeled individuals who often invested their money in large scale ranching or farming ventures in western Canada. Many of these well-off middle and upper-class Britons struck out for Canad because employment was difficult to obtain in the overcrowded and highly competitive professions in Britain and emigration seemed the only answer to maintaining their and their children's lifestyle.

The great influx from Great Britain also comprised poor newcomers who had bee assisted by charitable organizations eager to rid the United Kingdom of paupers and help them get a fresh start in the colonies. One of the many philanthropic organizations involved in the immigration boom was the Salvation Army. Established in Canada in 1882, it opened a recruiting office in London, England in 1902, and before long it was dispatching chartered shiploads of the "deserving" poor of Great Britain to Canada.

The Home Children and the Barr Colony

Conspicuous in the ranks of the newcomers from Britain were thousands of slum children, sent to this country by well-meaning philanthropists, philanthropic rescue homes, and parish workhouses. Dispatching them to Canada appeared to be the ideal solution to a two-pronged problem: what to do with thousands of children from families of the urban working poor and how to meet the soaring demand for cheap labor on Canadian farms.

After their arrival in this country, most of the boys – many of whom were eight, nine, and ten years of age – were located on farms, where they apprenticed as agricultural laborers. Girls were sent to smaller towns or rural homes to work as domestic servants.

Although British children had been dispatched to farms in Lower and Upper Canada in the 1830s, the movement really traces its beginnings to 1869 when two women, Maria Susan Rye and Annie Macpherson, brought parties of children to Ontario in the wake of the last great London cholera outbreak. None of the "home children" who sailed to Canada in this and subsequent years were accompanied by their parents, and this despite the fact that only one-third of them were orphans. And during the Sifton era they came in unprecedented numbers.

Many of these youngsters were wards of the well-known Barnardo homes, established by the Irish-born authoritarian trailblazer, Thomas John Barnardo, known everywhere that he went as "Dr. Barnardo," although he had never completed his medical studies. All told, approximately 30,000 Barnardo children were sent to Canada over the years.

This program of uprooting British slum children and packing them off to rural Canada for their own good had its critics, even in its early days. Harriet Beecher Stowe, the celebrated American author, roundly condemned the shipping of little girls like so much cattle. A member of the Canadian parliament, James Somerville, lashed out at the program for depriving Canadian children of employment. And decades later, Charlotte Whitton, when serving as director of the Canadian Welfare Council (1920–1941), described the program as inhumane.

Nevertheless, despite the ill treatment meted out to many of the children, the movement continued. Canadian governments and the public supported it, furnishing grants-in-aid, transportation subsidies, and a continuous supply of applicants for the children's services. In all, between 80,000 and 100,000 children were packed off to this country before the program ended in 1939.

Although the movement of the "home children" in the closing years of the Sifton era failed to capture the attention of Canadians, the same cannot be said of the remarkable saga of the Barr colonists. It was closely watched by not only Canadians but also by the international press.

The Barr colonists were the central players in the one attempt made to establish a British colony in western Canada during this period – the Barr Colony, named after the Reverend Isaac Barr, an impractical but charismatic visionary. In 1903, he joined forces with another Anglican cleric, the Reverend George Lloyd, to found a settlement of 2,000 British townsfolk, most lacking any farming experience, in a remote part of present-day Saskatchewan.

Barr, who handled nearly all the administrative arrangements, proved so inept at the task that the newcomers underwent more than their fair share of trials. In fact, halfway through the 300-kilometre wagon trip that took them from the railhead at Saskatoon to their destination west of Battleford, the surviving colonists deposed Barr and replaced him as leader with the Reverend George Lloyd.

The colonists spent a ghastly first winter in poorly constructed sod huts on the open prairie. Nevertheless, those that persevered succeeded in establishing a flourishing settlement, which they named Lloydminster after the man who had won their confidence. With the arrival of the railway in 1905, the settlement's success was assured.

A group of Jewish orphans who immigrated to Canada. Photo 1927

Immigration to British Columbia

The Prairies were not alone in attracting a large influx of immigrants during the Sifton years. British Columbia was also a magnet for newcomers, although the volume of immigration to it was not nearly as large as that to the Prairies. Nevertheless, it was impressive.

Since the province faced the Pacific, many of its non-British immigrants were Asians. Japanese, for example, began settling in south-western British Columbia in 1900, while newcomers from India began arriving in 1904. Of this latter group, the largest number were Sikhs (members of the reformist religion that originated about 1500 in the Punjab in northern India). Between 1904 and 1908, some 5,000 Sikhs arrived in the province, where most found work in the lumber mills or in the logging camps.

Among the British immigrants who headed for Canada's most westerly province were farmers, retired businessmen, and the younger sons of aristocratic families. Their attention was initially aroused by advertising material that described the joys of farming in interior valleys speckled with pristine pure lakes filled with trout. Inspired further by the enthusiastic reports of Lord Aberdeen, Canada's governor general, well-off British immigrants purchased fruit farms and ranches in the Okanagan Valley, where the Scottish aristocrat had extensive properties.

Clifford Sifton's policies did succeed in attracting large numbers of agriculturalists to Canada. Nevertheless, approximately 70% of the newcomers obtained work in industry and transportation – and not entirely by accident – for railway and business interests actively promoted the importation of unskilled immigrant labor. As a result, immigrants from south-eastern and central Europe became either part-time or full-time industrial workers.

Among these immigrants were many who went to work for the railway companies, then engaged in a frenzy of construction. In 1904 alone, some 3,000 Italians arrived in Montreal. When construction of the Grand Trunk Pacific, Canadian northern, and National Transcontinental main lines began in earnest two years later, their numbers increased dramatically.

Growing Discord on the Prairies

Unfortunately, even good agricultural immigrants from Europe posed problems for Sifton and his policies because in western Canada newcomers from south-eastern and central Europe raised a groundswell of hostility. It did not matter that less than half the total number of immigrants to Canada in

Japanese picture bride. A predominantly male immigrant society tried to recruit women by means of advertisements in the old country. Without knowing their future husbands, these picture brides decided to go to an unknown country. In this case, the marriage wa prearranged by the families. Tsuki Hironaka arrived at Vancouver on April 9th, 1913 and married her husband Yoichi one day later

most years (and usually far less than half were other than British in origin. What di matter was that many Anglo-Canadians especially those living in the West, saw sizeable pockets of unassimilable ethni groups that, in their opinion, threatene the very fabric of the dominant Protestar Anglo-Saxon society.

Anglo-Canadians were not alone i resenting this immigration. There were als French-Canadians who were alarmed abou the transformation that Canada's popula tion was undergoing. As immigration figure rose dramatically, these observers wondere what the future held for them in a Canad where the overall relative size of the French Canadian population was decreasing, an in the West, where the numbers of French Canadians were being exceeded by those c several other ethnic groups.

One of these observers was Henri Bourass the barometer for many of the concerns c these French-Canadians. The celebrate journalist and Member of Parliament initiall supported Sifton's immigration policy, bu

Japanese sugar beet workers, Raymond, 1911. Since 1908 Japanese workers had been recruited by the Knight Sugar Company to work on sugar beet farms

when he realized that immigration was shifting the balance of Canada's population he lashed out at the Laurier government and the newcomers to the West.

Organized labor also opposed the government's immigration policy. In 1900, James Wilks, a Trade and Labor Congress vice-president, wrote to Laurier deploring the impact an influx of Finns and other Scandinavians from Minnesota was having on the Canadian labor market. He beseeched the prime minister to enforce the Alien Labor Act, for only rigorous enforcement of this law would prevent Canada from being inundated with "ignorant, unfortunate…non-English-speaking aliens," who would do irreparable damage to the community.

Canadians who had grave misgivings about the direction being taken by immigration demanded a more selective immigration policy. To their delight, Frank Oliver, who succeeded Sifton as minister of the Interior and Superintendent of Indian Affairs in 1905, was prepared to meet this demand.

Like Sifton, Oliver was a politician, newspaper publisher, and transplanted easterner who had migrated west when a young man, in his case to Edmonton. Unlike Sifton, however, Oliver believed that the ethnic and cultural origins of prospective immigrants should take precedence over occupation. In this minister's hierarchy of desirable settlers for the West, newcomers from eastern Canada occupied the top rung. British immigrants, who arrived as "ready-made citizens," were ranked next, closely followed by American settlers. Whether British immigrants hailed from the countryside or from Britain's teeming cities and towns mattered little to Oliver, who did not share Sifton's distaste for immigrants from urban cities. In fact, Oliver preferred urban Britons to agriculturalists from southeastern and central Europe.

In his determined effort to lay the free-entry policy officially to rest, Frank Oliver introduced more restrictive immigration acts (the Immigration Act of 1906 and the Immigration Act of 1910). To supplement these, he levied landing taxes on all immigrants, concluded a bilateral agreement with Japan (1907) to curb Japanese emigration to Canada, and implemented the Continuous Journey Regulation (1908) in an attempt to choke off east Indian immigration. He also instituted an immigration inspection service

on the Canada-United States border and cancelled Sifton's system of bonuses for agriculturalists from designated countries (the North Atlantic Trading Company Agreement).

The same year that he cancelled the North Atlantic Trading Company Agreement (1906), Oliver took steps to increase British immigration, convinced that Canada had to reinforce her British heritage if it was to become one of the world's great civilizations. To this end, he raised the bonus paid to British booking agents who sold tickets to British agriculturalists and domestics, and had new immigration offices opened in England and Scotland. The following year, the Immigration Branch appointed 100 government agents and paid each one a bonus for every British agricultural laborer recruited and placed in Quebec or Ontario. Thanks partly to these initiatives, immigration from the British Isles soared from 86,796 in the fiscal year ended March 31, 1906 to 142,622 in the fiscal year ended March 31, 1914.

The able and energetic superintendent of immigration during this period, William Duncan Scott, shared Frank Oliver's enthusiasm for British and American immigration. Since he was a cultural nationalist like Oliver, Scott set great store by the ability

of prospective newcomers to conform to the values and institutions of Protestant Anglo-Canadian society. Because they adapted most readily to Canadian conditions and were by and large agriculturists, Scott assigned top billing to American immigrants.

The Immigration Branch under Scott, however, courted only White American farmers. As was the case during the Sifton regime, no attempt was made to solicit Black agriculturalists. Not only did the Immigration Branch not encourage Black immigration, it effectively throttled it by instructing its agents in the United States to withhold assistance to individual Blacks who wanted to emigrate to Canada. In 1911, when anti-Black sentiment in Oklahoma threatened to promote a large migration of Blacks to the Edmonton area, Ottawa even took steps to have Canada acquire the first racial exclusion ordinance in the western Hemisphere. It was never implemented, however, because in the general election of that year the Liberals were thrown out of office.

Despite Frank Oliver's and the Liberals attempts to implement a more selective immigration policy, Canadians believed that their country's prosperity required a large dose of immigration. So, despite the introduction of restrictive legislation, newcomers continued to pour into Canada. In 1906, the

Greek immigrant family in Sudbury. Photo ca.1920

influx exceeded 200,000; in 1911, the year the Liberals were toppled from office by the Conservatives, over 300,000. Two years later, in 1913, one year before the First World War erupted, immigration rocketed to 400,810.

The Liberal and Conservative governments succeeded in dramatically reducing immigration from Asia, but they failed to staunch the flow from central and eastern Europe. Moreover, although both governments declared that their goal was to attract agriculturalists to western Canada, the fact remained that Canadian manufacturers, railway companies, and resource extraction industries clamored for a large pool of labor to supply the goods and services needed by the new settlers. In response to the demands of this powerful business lobby, the Conservatives under Robert Borden opened the floodgates still wider, admitting growing numbers of unskilled and semi-skilled laborers in the period 1911–1913.

Some three million newcomers settled in Canada between 1896 and 1911. In the ten-year period, 1901 to 1911, the country's population increased by 43% and the percentage of foreign-born exceeded 22%. Almost overnight, it seemed, immigration from Europe, Great Britain, the United States, and Asia had transformed the country, particularly western Canada, into a multicultural society.

The most exuberant years in Canadian immigration history occurred in the years immediately preceding the First World War. They were then followed by the most inglorious period, the three decades between 1915 and 1945. War, recession, uneven prosperity, the Great Depression of the 1930s, and then another world war, each in its turn helped to create antipathy to immigration and to throttle the movement of newcomers to Canada.

The Great Depression had by far the greatest impact on immigration to Canada in this period. Indeed, no single development other than World War II did more to choke off immigration to this country than the devastating depression of the 1930s. In its wake, the federal government passed a series of measures designed to dramatically curtail the entry of prospective settlers from Europe, the United Kingdom, and the United States. As a result, immigration plummeted from 1,16,000 in the decade 1921 to 1931 to only 140,000 between 1931 and 1941.

Among those barred from entering Canada during the 1930s were thousands

Wedding of Tot Yeng Lee and Peter Quan. Photo 1921

of desperate refugees, many of them Jews fleeing persecution at the hands of the Nazis. Thousands of Jews who managed to escape the Nazi tide sought refuge in Canada, but by and large their appeals were ignored. There were many Canadians who opposed the government's policy. Nevertheless, their efforts on behalf of a more liberal immigration policy were in vain.

Canadian immigration policy continued to be highly restrictive in the first year or two after World War II. Eventually, however, the requirements of the country's booming economy, mounting pressure from assorted organizations, and returning diplomats who had seen first-hand conditions in Europe forced the government's hand. In reaction to all these pressures Ottawa began to slowly open the doors to European newcomers. Among those who arrived in the ensuing era of mass immigration were 100,000 displaced persons from the Second World War, who started to arrive in the late 1940s. Large-scale European immigration continued in the 1950s, although with the onset of the Cold War immigration from eastern Europe came to a halt. By contrast, large numbers of newcomers began arriving from southern Europe, particularly Italy, Greece, and Portugal.

A long-awaited Immigration Act was finally implemented in 1952. While simplifying the administration of immigration, it placed a heavy emphasis on which prospective immigrants should be excluded. It also retained the hierarchy of desirable immigrants. Occupying the top rung were newcomers from the United Kingdom, the white Commonwealth, the United States, and France. They were followed by other western

Europeans, and immigrants from southern and eastern Europe. A restricted category of Asians was at the bottom of the hierarchy.

In addition, the Act vested a large degree of discretionary power in the immigration minister and his officials. When used creatively and responsibly this could be an invaluable tool in assisting desirable and/or humanitarian immigration. For example, in 1956–57, after the crushing of the Hungarian revolt, Canada admitted some 37,000 Hungarian refugees on ministerial permit.

Major new initiatives took place in Canadian immigration policy in the 1960s and 1970s. One of these occurred in 1962 when the federal government implemented regulations that virtually eliminated racial discrimination as a major feature of Canada's immigration policy. This was followed five years later by the government's implementation of the so-called "points system," an objective, fair method for selecting unsponsored immigrants.

Another bold development took place in 1978, when the government implemented the Immigration Act, 1976, the cornerstone of immigration policy from 1978 until 2002. The Act, which was more liberal than its predecessors, broke new ground by spelling out the fundamental principles and objectives of Canadian immigration policy and by providing for an identifiable class for refugees, selected and admitted separately from immigrants.

No sooner did the new legislation come into force than Canada began admitting some 60,000 refugees who had fled Communist regimes in Indochina (1979–80). Although this was not the largest single refugee group to enter Canada since World War II, it represented the highest number of "boat people" admitted per capita by any country during this period.

In the 1980s, Canada sought to forestall the entry of ballooning numbers of "asylum seekers," i.e., people who arrived on its doorstep claiming refugee status, but who all too frequently did not qualify as refugees under the United Nations Convention of 1951 and its 1967 Protocol. Even as it did this, however, Canada opened new avenues for immigrants to enter it, especially those with desirable skills or significant resources to invest in Canadian enterprises.

The rising unemployment rate for first year immigrants, a continuing backlog in

he refugee determination system, and the
failure to implement more stringent controls
on individuals claiming refugee status led to
mounting criticism of the country's immigration system in the 1990s. In the wake of this
criticism, the federal government appointed
an independent advisory panel to examine
Canada's immigration policy. Its report,
released in January 1998, recommended a
massive overhaul of the country's immigration policy to restore public confidence in
what was perceived to be a flawed and highly
bureaucratic system.

With a view to adopting a simpler but
tougher immigration system, the government introduced Bill C–11 in February
2001. Its amended version came into law
as the Immigration and Refugee Protection
Act on June 28, 2002. The new act outlined
several basic economic, social, and cultural
goals for Canada's immigration program, set
out humanitarian goals for refugee protection, and provided for the establishment of
an independent, quasi-judicial body, the
Immigration and Refugee Protection Board
of Canada. As recently as March 2008, the
government proposed changes to this act,
changes that would reduce wait times so
that families could be reunited more quickly
and skilled workers could arrive in Canada
sooner.

Because of its aging population, low birth
rate, and increasingly knowledge-based
economy, Canada desperately needs skilled,
educated immigrants. And they are arriving on this country's doorstep, but not from
the principal source countries of a bygone
era. In 2006, recent immigrants born in Asia
(including the Middle East) made up the
largest proportion (58.3%) of newcomers to
Canada. This was virtually unchanged from
59.4% in 2001, but in 1971, only 12.1%
of recent immigrants were born in Asia.
In 2006, European newcomers comprised
the second largest group (16.1%) of recent
immigrants. By contrast, they made up
61.6% of newcomers to Canada. in 1971.

Much has changed in Canadian
immigration since 1830. But one thing has
not. Historically, Canada has never had a
clearly articulated consensus about what
role immigration should play in its future.
Only rarely have Canadian governments
found it necessary to proclaim clearly
defined long-range immigration goals,
whether economic, social or demographic,

and, with one exception, Canadians
themselves have never shared a common
view about immigration. The one point on
which they can agree is that they do not
want to see too many immigrants admitted
to this country.

Sources

Citizenship and Immigration Canada.
Citizenship and Immigration Statistics
1993. Ottawa: Supply and Services
Canada, 1996.

Cowan, Helen I. British Immigration Before
Confederation. The Canadian Historical
Association Booklets, No. 22. Ottawa:
Canadian Historical Association, 1978.

Craig, Gerald M. "The 1830s." In: Colonists
and Canadians, 1760–1867, edited by
J.M.S. Careless. Toronto: Macmillan
Canada, 1971.

Dreiszinger, N.F., M.L. Kovacs, Paul Body and
Bennett Kovrig. Struggle and Hope: The
Hungarian Experience in Canada. Toronto:
McClelland & Stewart Ltd. in association
with the Multiculturalism Directorate,
Dept. of Secretary of State and Canadian
Government Publishing Centre, Supply
and Services Canada, 1982.

Hallowell, Gerald, editor. The Oxford
Companion to Canadian History. Don
Mills: Oxford University Press, 2004.

Knowles, Valerie. "Canada's Changing Ethnic
Mix from 1860 to the Present." In Canada,
Confederation to the Present. Edmonton:
Chinook Multimedia, 2001.

Knowles, Valerie. Strangers At Our Gates:
Canadian Immigration and Immigration
Policy, 1540–2006. Toronto: Dundurn
Press, 2007.

Roberts, John A., editor. The Canadian
Family Tree: Canada's Peoples. Don Mills,
Ontario: Corpus, 1979.

Story, Norah. The Oxford Companion to
Canadian History and Literature. Toronto:
Oxford University Press, 1967.

Weaver, John C., James De Jonge and Darrell
Norris. "Trans-Atlantic Migrations,
1831–1851." In Historical Atlas of Canada
11: The Land Transformed, 1800–1891.
Toronto: University of Toronto Press, 1993.

Estonians, fleeing from the Communists who had taken over their country, arrived at the port of Saint John, New Brunswik aboard an 80-foot sailboat after a 61-day, 6,000-mile voyage from Sweden, August 19, 1948

This set of cards from the Liebig company's picture series (printed in chromolithography) shows the departure of Columbus from Palos, his arrival in the New World and his return to Barcelona in 1492. As early as 1840 the German chemist Justus Liebig had developed a method of producing meat extract which was then taken up by the British firm Liebig Extract of Meat Company (Lemco). For many people meat was too expensive, but Lemco owned big cattle farms in Uruguay and it was cheaper to ship meat in the form of extract from South America to Europe where it could then be sold at reasonable prices. In order for meat extract to gain acceptance on the domestic market a new marketing strategy was developed: colorful sets of cards came as a supplement free of charge with Liebig's products. These cards date from 1895

Diethelm Knauf

To Govern is to Populate! Migration to Latin America

When in 1492 Spanish boots were first planted in the sand of the island of Guanahani in the Bahamas, later called San Salvador by the new arrivals, immigration to Latin America had begun. After the discoverers came the conquerors, lured across the Atlantic by gold, silver, and storied treasures to fill the empty coffers of the government in Madrid, and soon also in Lisbon. The power politics of the European countries, constant warfare, and extravagant court life required new sources of income.

Early European Expansion

The treaty of Tordesillas in 1494, arbitrated by the Pope, divided the newly discovered and even the not yet discovered lands of the New World, by Apostolic Grace, between Spain and Portugal: a line of demarcation was drawn from north to south 370 miles west of the Cape Verde Islands; it separated the Spanish possessions and sphere of influence to the west from the Portuguese areas to the east. Africa and the north-eastern corner of what is now Brazil was granted to the Portuguese Crown, while the rest of America was granted to the Spanish. The Conquistadors encountered many different native peoples, Indians as they called them, who were living at widely varying levels of cultural and technological development. Practically anything was possible among the Native Americans: astronomers and engineers, but also people living under stone-age conditions. The conquest was first directed against the great empires, the Aztecs and Mayas in Central America and the Incas in northwestern South America. These areas were linked to the legend of El Dorado and did indeed possess vast treasures, undreamed-of riches, gold and silver mines. All too soon it became clear that plans for economic exploitation here could be realized only by force, against the resistance of the native population.

A campaign of genocide began, with the weapons and instruments of torture blessed by the Catholic church, which had no understanding for the native cultures and regarded the Indians only as the targets of their missionary work, as mere heathens, despite the obvious achievements of the native civilizations. There were also critical voices, like that of the monk Bartholome de Las Casas, who wrote a description of the criminal behavior of the Whites toward the Indians in order to preach against it. But these reports had practically no effect on the colonial policy of the state.

It is estimated that North and South America had 40–60 million inhabitants at the time Columbus arrived, although estimates as low as 10 million and as high as 90–110 million (with 60 million in Mexico and Peru alone) have been put forward as well. A population of 25 million seems reliable for the present-day territory of Mexico, nor is there any doubt that large numbers were systematically wiped out as a result of wars, epidemics, and slavery. In Mexico between 1519 and 1532 more than 8 million people lost their lives. Thirty years later only 3 million of the original population of 25 million remained, and by the beginning of the 17th century the population had been reduced to 4% of its original size. Brazil had about 22 million native inhabitants; today the number is 220,000. When Columbus landed on Hispaniola, the island holding the present-day countries of Haiti and the Dominican Republic, about 1 million Indians lived there, but by 1520 the number had shrunk to 25,000.

The white man's appropriation of the Americas was characterized by the plunder of advanced civilizations, the exploitation of gold and silver deposits, and the decimation and enslavement of the native population. In fact a significant and continuous stream of immigrants from Europe (as soldiers and military officials, bureaucrats, monks and missionaries, merchants and tradesmen,

craftsmen, or farmers) was necessary in order to take possession of the large land area; build the economy, government, and bureaucracy; and establish functioning colonies.

From the beginning migration from Spain to the new colonies was strictly regulated by the state. Emigration matters were handled by the Casa de contracion de las Indias (House of Trade) in Seville and later by the Consejo de Indias (Council of the Indies), in Madrid. These offices evaluated applications to emigrate and enforced a strictly exclusive emigration policy which kept non-Spaniards and non-Catholics out of the colonies.

Brazil was claimed for Portugal by Pedro Alvares Cabral in 1550, but the first settlers there were mainly degredados, exiled criminals. There were no Indian cultures there with gold and other riches to be plundered, nor even any known deposits of valuable minerals. For

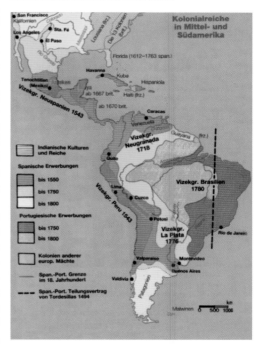

Colonial empires in Central and South America

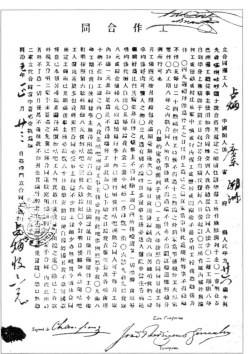

工 合 作

Work contract in Chinese script from Peru, 1866. In 1854 slavery and Indian tributes were abolished which, on account of the rapidly spreading shortage of labor, led to a severe crisis in agriculture. Chinese coolies took over the role of the slaves. Between 1860 and 1874 around 75,000 Chinese arrived in Peru; almost 8,000 died during the voyage because of the appalling conditions. As a rule, the coolies were given work contracts for eight years. It was in effect a kind of bondage which was often extended because of mounting debts. "In Lima one finds Chinese working as servants, cooks, carriers, etc., in a word: in all possible occupations", according to a contemporary source

this reason Portuguese colonial policy was less restrictive, and Dutch and French merchants established trading posts on the north-east coast. This situation changed when gold was discovered in the province of Minas Gerais around 1700: new regulations prohibited the immigration of foreigners. Even Portuguese subjects were forbidden to travel to Brazil in 1720, in an effort to stop the depopulation of the northern provinces of Portugal, a region where emigration had become a tradition.

In 1550 there were about 220,000 Spanish colonists in Latin America, concentrated mainly in Mexico, and about 30,000 Portuguese on the coast of Brazil. Over the following 200 years the Spanish population rose, to about 500,000 by the year 1700. This increase was due primarily to a high birth rate, especially in mixed marriages linking a Spanish husband and an Indian wife, and a low mortality rate (relative to that among the native population). On the other

hand, immigration also played a certain role. Using records of ship traffic between Spain and America it can be estimated that about 450,000 colonists left Europe for the Spanish colonies between 1500 and 1650, a sizeable number considering that the total population of Spain in 1600 was only about 8 million. Purely theoretical estimates put emigration from Portugal during the same period even higher, at 580,000, followed by 600,000 more during the Minas Gerais gold rush between 1700 and 1762.

During the period of conquest the proportion of women among the immigrants was only about 8%, but by the middle of the sixteenth century it was 25% and later rose to 33%. These figures serve to correct the erroneous assumption that the early emigration was a purely masculine enterprise.

There was also return migration, although this is only documented for the conquistadors and their troops. Since these were soldiers rather than colonists, return migration for this group is really to be expected.

With the consolidation and development of a new society the immigrants, both Spanish and Portuguese, became the ruling class in the American colonies, the source of the military, administrative, economic, and political elite. The majority of the population still consisted of Native Americans, although these continued to be decimated, and an increasing number of African slaves. The deportation of slaves by force from Africa constituted a second inglorious chapter in the white history of the Americas. Even the most conservative estimates indicate that 500,000 slaves were imported between 1500 and 1650, and the trade reached a high point in the period 1760–1810, when over 1.3 million people were shipped as freight to Latin America. A total of 4 million Blacks were taken to Brazil alone, where they constituted over half the population by the beginning of the 19th century. In 1816 there were 1.9 million slaves in an overall population of 3.5 million, and Whites made up only 23% of the total. Around the same time Spain's weakened position in Europe (as a result of the Napoleonic expansion) and a feeling of common identity among the colonists led to independence for most of Central and South America: Argentina in 1816, Chile in 1818, Mexico and Peru in 1821, and Brazil in 1822. These new states abolished first the slave trade and later slavery itself; nevertheless, by 1860 almost 1.7 million black slaves

had reached Brazil, Cuba, and Puerto Rico alone.

Slaves were used as laborers in the mines and also on the large farm estates, for the private acquisition of vast areas of land and their agricultural exploitation in the form of single-crop plantation farming played just as important a role as the hunt for gold, silver and jewels. Plantation agriculture began around the middle of the sixteenth century, only a few decades after Columbus made his discovery, and involved mainly sugar cane, cattle, and natural resources such as lumber. Alongside the large plantations (similar to the latifundia of ancient Rome) and the extensive cattle ranches there were also small peasant holdings granted to colonists or resident soldiers. The urban settlements were dominated by the offices of trading companies and factories for processing raw materials and agricultural products; e.g., sugar refineries and tanneries.

Colonization Programs and Labor Recruiting

In the 1840s the liberal Argentine writer Juan Alberti characterized the Latin American governments' new thinking in immigration policy with the slogan, "In South America to govern is to populate". The progressive approach seemed to be to recruit immigrants from all the developed countries of Europe. There were vast land areas to be explored and made ready for cultivation, and immigration also seemed to be a way to alleviate the chronic labor shortage on the plantations.

In the first half of the 19th century migration to Latin America was quite heterogeneous. Large numbers of merchants, artisans, and sailors established themselves in the coastal towns and port cities to seek their fortunes. British and Irish soldiers fought in Simon Bolivar's armies of liberation, and many political refugees and exiles found new homes in Latin America – including Giuseppe Garibaldi, who arrived in South America in 1820 with his band of Italian revolutionaries.

The characteristic activities for this period, however, were colonization projects and the foundation of agricultural settlements, frequently initiated for economic reasons by European entrepreneurs and travel agents who hoped to use the pro-immigration policies

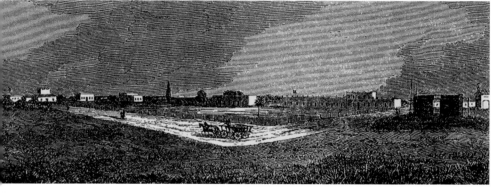

ove: the German colony "Blumenau" in the south of Brazil. Newspaper illustration from around 1870
elow: the Swiss colony "Esperanza" in the province of Santa Fé, Argentina. About 200 families arrived between the end of January
d the beginning of June 1856. Each colonist family received around 33 hectares of land

f the Latin American governments for their
wn purposes.

Most of the countries made great efforts
o recruit European emigrants to found
ettlements. The prospective immigrants
ere promised free land, exemptions from
axes and military service, and sometimes
ven free equipment to start up – tools,
attle, a place to live – and other advan-
ges. Settlers from Germany, Ireland, and
orthern Europe were especially attracted
y these offers, but they were joined mainly
y Spanish, Italian, and French immigrants.
wo popular destinations were the Rio de la
lata region and southern Brazil. One of the
ost spectacular settlement projects was
tarted in 1819 by 2,000 Swiss, mainly in
mily groups, who founded the colony Nova

Friburgo in the highlands of Brazil's Rio
de Janeiro province. Many were willing to
emigrate because of failed harvests, famine,
and unemployment in Switzerland, explaining the relatively large number of colonists
and the positive stance taken by the Swiss
authorities. This enterprise ended tragical-
ly: almost 19 % of the settlers died during
the voyage, mostly from malaria, which
they had contracted during an unnecessari-
ly long layover in a swampy area of the
Netherlands. The site chosen for the settlement turned out to be very poorly suited,
and the hard work, many deprivations,
poor food, and unaccustomed climate and
geological conditions kept the death rate
very high at the beginning. Nova Friburgo
was a catastrophic failure, and most of the

colonists left to try their luck at establishing
a new home elsewhere.

Baja Verapaz, in the north-eastern part of
Guatemala, was another ambitious European
colonization project. It was initiated by
President Mariano Galvez, but its implementation was in the hands of English and Belgian
entrepreneurs who had little understanding
of how to organize travel or set up a colony.
Like Nova Friburgo, Baja Verapaz demonstrated how hard it is to practice European-
style agriculture in a tropical or subtropical
climate.

The colonization projects in the temperate zone had better initial conditions for
success; the German settlements in southern Brazil, for example, relatively quickly
enjoyed a certain degree of prosperity. So
São Leopoldo, founded in 1824, was the
first of numerous German settlements in Rio
Grande del Sul. In the following years over
5,000 Germans migrated to this area, most
of them signed up by the notorious adventurer
Georg Anton von Schäffer and his unscrupulous recruiters. São Leopoldo was a colony of
small farmers, sharing the land in equal plots
of 24 hectares per family.

There were also successfully functioning
German settlements in Chile, in the forests of
Valdivia and Llanquihue; by 1850 there were
about 3,000 pioneers living there. Swiss and
French colonists settled in Argentina, and in
Uruguay a native entrepreneur was able to
recruit 850 Spanish settlers from the Canary
Islands.

All Latin American governments tried
to establish colonies of this type. Despite
the successes mentioned above the overall
results of these colonization projects, however,
were disappointing. All too often the natural
obstacles proved insurmountable, the settlers
were poorly organized, or the governments
broke their recruiting promises. The land that
was granted the colonists was unsuitable for
farming; the promised housing, tools, or bank
credit were unavailable; there were no means
of transportation to the site; etc. When the
projects failed, the settlers were in dire straits;
many paid with their lives.

Despite the repeated failures of immigrant
colonies, the Latin American governments
maintained a policy of opening their borders
to new settlers. In the course of the 19th
century the global economy and world politics
played an increasingly important role. The
progress of industrialization in Europe and

Above: A delegation from the Katharinengymnasium, a secondary school in Florianópolis in the German speaking region in Brazil, taking part in a military parade. In the left foreground the "Sargento" teacher. Photo about 1905
Below: The "Club de Ciclistas", the cyclists' club of pupils attending the German school in front of the "Escola Alema" in Joinville, Brazil. Photo between 1906 and 1910

abolished in Brazil in 1888 and in Cuba i 1886. But even earlier there were signs tha the institution of slavery had become economi cally obsolete, primarily due to the low birt rate among the slaves and their low life expec tancy – in British Guiana, for example, it wa about 28 years in 1830.

A potential solution for this problem wa to recruit technically free contract laborers. worker was loaned the price of a passage ticke by the owner of the plantation or business o by a professional emigration agent; to pay back, these poorest immigrants contracte to serve their creditor for little or no pay fo a certain number of years. Contract labor ers were recruited mainly among Chines coolies, 142,000 of whom migrated to Cub alone between 1847 and 1874, mainly to wor on the sugar plantations. Peru recruited abou 75,000 Chinese during the same period, fo plantation work and also for railroad construc tion. Chinese laborers also had a significar role in building the Panama Canal. Contrac laborers for the British colonies in Lati America were recruited mainly from Indi however 239,000 Chinese indentured labor ers were registered between 1838 and 191 in British Guiana, and 140,000 in Trinida during the same period.

Living conditions for contract labor ers scarcely differed from those for slave Over 10% died during the sea voyage as a Cuban merchant cynically explainec "Supposing that 600 men were shipped from China, and that only 300 arrived in Cuba these would cover all the losses and still leav a brilliant profit". At their workplaces the were subjected to inhumane treatment, house in isolated camps without their wives an families, abused, cheated of their wages, an often forced to sign oppressive new contract Only a few were able to return to China or lea an independent life after their contracts ra out.

The Period of the World Wars

Until the second third of the 19th centur immigration to Latin America was a constan phenomenon but involved only a few thousan people; in general the ambitious plans of th Latin American governments could not b realized. This was due primarily to condi tions in the different countries, to climate an

North America drew Latin America into world trade as a source of raw materials, an exporter of agricultural products, and a market for industrial products. Many workers were needed to build up the infrastructure, settle the land, and operate the plantations. Because the population had grown only gradually over the preceding decades, these needs could not be met with native resources alone. Policies favorable to immigration were designed to

bring in not only workers and know-how but also capital.

The labor shortage was even more intensely felt when the Latin American states which were still practicing slavery came under international pressure to abolish it in the 1830s. Cuba (still under Spanish rule) and Brazil, two major slave importers, had to close the slave trade in 1855 and 1865, respectively, although slavery per se was only completely

eography and to a lack of economic development and political stability. From the time the atin American countries became independent it took until the last decades of the 19th entury for their border squabbles and internal political conflicts to be resolved, for the rocess of state formation to be completed and the political and economic structure consolidated. In southern Brazil and the Rio de la Plata basin the climate and soil were such that European colonists could live, grow crops, and raise farm animals using the methods they had brought from home. In these areas it was also possible to produce goods that were in demand in Europe: meat, grain, leather, coffee, and certain wood and fiber products. After slavery was abolished there was no satisfactory answer to the labor shortage, and as living conditions in Europe worsened and the cost of a transatlantic passage grew cheaper, all the necessary conditions for a wave of mass migration to Latin America were in place.

It is well known that the greatest number of transatlantic migrants went to North America. Nevertheless, about 11 million people, about one fifth of the total number of migrants, chose Latin America. It is surprising, for example, that 68 % of the Italian transatlantic migrants, 0 % of the Portuguese migrants, and a great majority of the Spanish emigrants between 375 and 1898 came to Latin America.

By 1880, 440,000 migrants from Europe one had settled in Argentina and in 1914 the proportion of the population born abroad was 30 %, of which 12 % had Italian roots. In razil, 73 % of the immigrants who arrived between 1887 and 1900 were of Italian escent. At the end of the 19th century three quarters of the foreign-born population in uba were Spanish in origin.

In the case of the emigrants from Spain and Portugal, linguistic and cultural affinities

An Alemannic village in Tovar, Venezuela. The rural settlement pattern and half-timbered buildings clearly point to a European origin. Photo around 1975

may have played a role, although at this time the former colonial powers and their one-time colonies were not on the best of terms politically; other factors must be taken into consideration. For the individual migrant, the choice of destination was based on a number of criteria: the need to avoid a financial or social step downward in times of economic or political crisis; the desire to maintain one's standard of living or earn a small step upward in the social hierarchy; travel subsidies from the country of immigration; chance occurrences (like which emigration agent or shipowner one happened to meet); the sources of information one had access to; and where friends and relatives had gone previously. In terms of expense it was significant that Argentina, Uruguay, and Brazil subsidized the travel and transportation costs. In São Paulo around 1890, when the need for workers on the coffee plantations was especially high, the proportion of immigrants arriving on subsidized tickets varied between 82 and 99 %. The living costs in Latin America were also relatively low: around 1900 they were only 25 % of wages in Argentina, compared with 33 % in the U.S. and 60 % in Spain and Italy.

The shipping lines and most of the emigration agents used all available means to lure potential emigrants to the country they represented. Priests were sometimes agents, taking advantage of their positions to convince the emigrants, and agents would take young men out of the country illegally in order to avoid military conscription. In the 1890s an agent from Udine, northwest of Venice, was able to stir up a "Brazil-fever" among the very poor and economically exploited peasants of western Galicia. Workers were needed to build the railroad line from Madeira to Marmor and

thousands signed up. Many became ill in the jungle – for them "fever" became terrifying reality. Emigration agents had a significant influence on which country people decided to migrate to; as one Italian historian discovered, many Italians simply left the choice of destination to the shipping-company agent.

The more personal reasons given for emigration sometimes seem less than serious. A Catalan woodworker left for America because he could not endure constant arguments with his mother-in-law. A Syrian living in Chile claimed he had been sent away by his family because he had a passion for raising pigeons. Two Swedish engineers selected their destination by sticking a pin into a globe, ending up in Peru.

Intercontinental migration between 1824 and 1924 involved 52 million men and women, of whom 72 % went to the U.S., 21 % went to Latin America, and 7 % went to Australia. Of 11 million emigrants who went to Latin America, about half (5.5 million or 10 % of the global migration) went to Argentina; 36 % went to Brazil (mainly to the temperate south); 5 % went to Uruguay; and the remaining 9 % were divided among the other countries.

Toward the end of the 1860s the number of immigrants attained significant numbers, surpassing 50,000 per year. The peak immigration period, with over 250,000 per year, began after about 1850 and continued until World War I. After the war immigration reached almost the same level, but dropped sharply during the worldwide depression of the 1930s.

The immigrant population was concentrated in the areas of production for export, as wheat-growing tenant farmers in Argentina, for example, or as wage workers on the coffee plantations in São Paulo. With time many of the rural migrants returned home to Europe

Italian immigrant family in Argentina around 1920

e Italian immigrant Fernando Maria Perone in Argentina 1890

Escola do „Schulverein zu Joinville"

BOLETINS
(Schulzeugnisse)

para
(für)

Theresa Hromatka

5.° Anno

Significação das notas:
(Bedeutung der Noten)

1 = **optima** (sehr gut).

2 = **boa** (gut).

3 = **soffrivel** (genügend).

4 = **má** (schlecht).

5 = **pessima** (sehr schlecht).

1° SEMESTRE
(Erstes Halbjahr)

Comportamento: (Betragen)	1	Portuguez: (Portugiesisch)	2
Applicação: (Fleiss)	2	Geographia do Brasil: (Landeskunde von Brasilien)	2
Attenção: (Aufmerksamkeit)	2	Historia do Brasil: (Geschichte Brasiliens)	2
Faltas: — dias. (Versäumnisse: Tage)		Educação civica: (Staatsbürgerliche Erziehung)	2
		Allemão: (Deutsch)	2
Marcas tardes — (Zu spät)		Inglez: (Englisch)	—
Observações: (Bemerkungen)		Arithmetica: (Rechnen)	2
		Algebra:	—
		Geometria:	—
		Historia universal: (Weltgeschichte)	2
		Geographia universal: (Länderkunde)	2
		Physica: (Physik)	—
		Chimica: (Chemie)	—
		Historia natural: (Naturgeschichte)	2
		Historia sagrada: (Bibl. Geschichte)	2
		Calligraphia: (Schreiben)	2
		Desenho: (Zeichnen)	2
		Canto: (Singen)	2
		Gymnastica: (Turnen)	3

Joinville, 19 de Julho de 1924

O Director:
(Der Direktor)
N. L. Petschke

O Professor:
(Der Klassenlehrer)
Wanda Brier

Assignatura do responsavel:
(Unterschrift des Vaters oder dessen Stellvertreters)
Emma Hromatka

Joinville was one of the centers of German colonization in the southern Brazilian state of Santa Catarina. German language and culture were fostered particularly in schools. School report from 1924

or moved on to the cities. By 1895 only 16 % of immigrants to Argentina were employed in agriculture, with 17 % craftsmen and skilled workers, and 14 % in business, trade, and transportation.

Naturally the agricultural workers and tenant farmers settled in the more fertile regions; in the later phases of the migration their numbers were far surpassed by those of unskilled workers, who tended to go to the urban centers, hoping to find work in the industries being established there. An especially characteristic example of urbanization is Montevideo, which grew from a small provincial town to the fourth-largest city in Spanish-speaking America during the 19th century.

São Paulo also experienced rapid urbanization. At the end of the 19th century it developed into a center of agricultural industry for coffee production, and then a powerful and comprehensive industrialization process made it the second-largest city and most important industrial region of Latin America. Overall immigration to Latin America had an urban character. The census of Argentina in 1914 showed that 68 % of the foreign-born population lived in cities, with only 10 % in the interior or southern provinces.

Along with Brazil, Argentina was the primary country of immigration in Latin America. Between 1881 and 1935 about 3.4 million people settled there, while about 3.3 million chose Brazil between 1872 and 1940 and Uruguay definitely had fewer immigrants, about 600,000 for the same period. The high point of immigration was between 1880 and 1900, but the rate of return migration was also very high. In the 1880s about three-quarters of the immigrants remained, which was considered the best percentage attainable – in the previous decade the proportions were reversed, and three-quarters emigrated again. In years of crises (1890 and during World War I) the number of emigrants was greater than that of immigrants. Between 1857 and 1926 5.7 million immigrants came to Argentina, and 2.3 million left; the proportion of returners was thus almost 50 %. In the period immediately before World War I Argentina became known as the land of "swallows" or "birds of passage". The farming regions had fallen into the hands of a few great landowners, by direct seizure and through legal machinations tolerated by the government, and thus there was little usable land available and few opportunities for immigrant settlers. Many had to take jobs as agricultural laborers. As soon as the

harvest season was over, the workers travele back to Spain or Italy, where they arrived ju in time for the European harvest. This cyc was interrupted by World War I; when th war was over and the U.S. tightened immigra tion restrictions, it seemed as if immigratic to South America might reach pre-war leve again, but the Depression ended this tren and with it mass migration to South America

The largest fraction of immigrants to Sou America came from the Iberian Peninsu and Italy. Between 1857 and 1924 about 1. million Italians and 900,000 Spanish cam to Argentina, along with 200,000 Frenc including some refugees from the Par Commune of 1871. The following figure show how important this immigration was f Argentina: according to the 1914 census 30 of the population of the country was foreig born. In the period 1840–1940 about 29 % the population growth in Argentina was fro direct immigration, and another 29 % wa second-generation immigrants. These figure are twice as high as the corresponding value for the land of immigration par excellenc the U.S., where the maximum was reached i 1910 with 14.7 % foreign-born. Without ma migration the population of Argentina in 194 would have been 6 million, instead of th actual value, 13 million.

In Cuba the situation was determine by the lateness and long duration of the wa of independence, which ended only in 189 with the defeat of the Spanish colonial powe Before that time population growth stagnate and even decreased (because of the war) in th

Pie chart from Walter Willcox/Imre Ferenci, International Migrations 1929, the pioneering sociological study of migration history

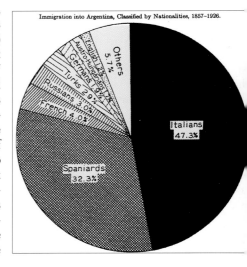

Immigration into Argentina, Classified by Nationalities, 1857–1926.

Italians 47.3%
Spaniards 32.3%
French 4.0%
Russians 3.0%
Turks 2.9%
Germans 2.1%
Austro-Hungarians 1.7%
English 1.2%
Others 5.7%

ecade before independence. The new republican government had an open-door policy, eeding immigrants in order to stabilize the economy, especially the sugar industry. Large umbers now immigrated, especially from pain (about 800,000 between 1902 and 930), securing Spanish dominance in Cuban ociety. However, the immigrants were now ore likely to be employed in the productive ctor than in administration or the military bs typical of the colonial period. Another ajor source of immigrants to Cuba was the Vest Indies, especially Haiti and Jamaica; bout 300,000 came to Cuba, most of them fter World War I. The return migration rate as probably relatively high for this group, ith only a fuzzy distinction between immigraon and the migration of harvest workers mong the sugar plantations of Cuba and the eighboring islands.

he Example of Brazil

ext to Argentina Brazil was the most imporant country of immigration in Latin America, ncluding – in contrast to the other destinaons – a significant German component. The riginal inhabitants of Brazil were stone-age ndians, and the Portuguese were the pioneers nd dominant force in colonizing the land and stablishing a nation and a state. The main roups represented in the mass migration f the 19th century were Italians, Spanish, ermans, and Japanese. In addition, Brazil as a major importer of black slaves well into e second half of the century.

The different raw materials and agricul-ural products of Brazil reveal the relation-ips between colonial exploitation, export ade, settlement of the land, and immigra-on. Brazilwood, which gave the country its ame and was used to produce a sought-after ye in Europe, attracted the first Europeans, ho established military and trading posts. he introduction of sugar cane led to the first ermanent settlements, where an agricultural ristocracy grew rich on the plantations, and illions of slaves were shipped in to provide bor. The sugar industry also drove territorial xpansion, as more and more land came under ultivation. With single-crop agriculture there as also a market for cattle, and the leather ade fueled expansion of the settlement area the south, down to the Rio de la Plata. The iscovery of gold brought the first wave of

mass migration from Europe and the permanent settlement of the interior. A new generation of planters profited from rubber, and new areas were cleared to grow cotton and coffee. Coffee was the primary basis for the industrialization of the important São Paulo region and provided jobs for millions of European labor migrants.

The coffee plantations were very labor-intensive, which led the state of São Paulo to encourage immigration through aid programs. Between 1889 and 1924, 2.5 million immigrants came to Brazil, 58% of them with financial support from the state.

After Pedro Alvares Cabral claimed Brazil as a domain of the Portuguese Crown in 1500, the land was divided into 15 inheritable fiefs (capitanias) to ensure the economic exploitation of the colony and promote settlement of the coast of the Amazon region, the south down to the Rio Grande do Sul, and some of the interior; the holders of the fiefs (donatários) were granted complete authority. Once the Portuguese had fended off Dutch and French attempts at conquest and solidified their power in Brazil, they could expand the borders of the territory to the west, southwest, and north-west, far beyond the line agreed to in the treaty of Tordesillas. An especially strong reason for expansion and the establishment of Brazil as a colony of the Portuguese Empire was the discovery of gold in Minas Gerais province, which motivated the government to close the colony, limiting trade and transport and prohibiting immigration – or even internal migration – to make sure the gold went exclusively to the state treasury. The result of this policy was that the original Portuguese immigrants were the dominant force in colonization, settlement, and the establishment of a government. In 1816 there were about 850,000 Portuguese immigrants and their descendants living in Brazil, making up the economic, political, military, and administrative elite.

When Napoleonic troops invaded Portugal, Prince Regent João VI fled to Brazil, and in 1815 he transformed the Kingdom of Portugal into the United Kingdom of Portugal, Brazil, and Algarve, giving Brazil a status equal to that of the motherland. When the Portuguese parliament tried to declare it a colony again, Brazil broke its ties to Portugal and declared independence with Dom Pedro I as its Emperor.

The "Capitanias" of the 16th century. The federal states of today developed from these "Capitanias"

The increasing need for raw materials and agricultural products in Europe had forced Portugal to give up its exclusive and protectionist colonial policies and open the Brazilian ports in 1808. The government's new recruitment policy was supposed to lure European immigrants to Brazil, with promises of a right to grants of free land (sesmarias). In addition, settlers were exempted from fees and taxes for ten years and supplied with money, cattle, and equipment to get started.

According to calculations using data from the Brazilian Institute for Geography and Statistics, about 5 million immigrants came to Brazil between 1800 and about 1950, the main phase of immigration. Among these were 2 million Portuguese, 1.5 million Italians, 600,000 Spanish, 300,000 Germans, and 190,000 Japanese. The Portuguese and Spanish immigration came in spurts over the entire 150-year period; the first Germans came in 1818, while the Italians began coming in 1870 and the Japanese started in 1908. The European and Japanese immigrants preferred the southern areas because of the climate. The proportion of return migrants was about 20%. The dominance of the Portuguese in economy, politics, and society is explained

Illustrations of Indians from Brazil in the late 17th century. On the one hand Europeans were fascinated by their "naturalness" and "unspoiled wildness", that is, the Indians' "natural state", in a romantic-idealistic sense, and on the other hand they were repulsed by their "uncivilized" and "barbarous" way of life.
When the Portuguese arrived in the Amazon region it is thought that in fact between 3 and 30 million Indians were living on the coast and along the rivers in the south-west. Direct evidence or written records do not exist

by the colonial ties between Portugal and Brazil, which guaranteed this group linguistic, economic, and cultural advantages and thus a better starting position for integration into Brazilian society and improvement of their status.

German emigration to Brazil seems insignificant compared with that to the U.S. (about 6 million), but it is different in that settlements there were more closely knit than was possible in the U.S. Settlement colonies like São Leopoldo or Blumenau were typical, and between 1820 and 1830 about 50 % of the German emigrants chose Brazil. Most came from south-western Germany, especially the Saar-Hunsrück area. Only after 1830 did German emigration settle into a general pattern with over 90 % heading for the U.S.

Over the years Brazil's economy, culture, and politics were influenced by immigrant groups of varying ethnic background. They explored and settled the land, cleared the jungle, built railroad lines and formed the working class of the cities, were responsible for economic and technological progress, won riches as industrialists and attracted foreign capital for Brazil. Although substantial immigration was advantageous for the Brazilian government, it did not pursue a policy of integration but instead acted to secure the dominance of Portuguese-Brazilian culture. Because of the close ties between church and state belonging to the Catholic religion was necessary to achieve advancement in government and society during the early centuries, when Protestant faiths were tolerated but not really treated fairly. Later, after the global depression of the 1930s, a quota system was introduced, mainly to keep working-class people from immigrating but also to favor certain ethnic groups (from southern Europe) over others (Japanese and Jewish immigrants). Laws were also passed to regulate the way the members of different ethnic groups lived together. For example, these laws could prohibit the sale of land in existing colonies to immigrants if one ethnic group would become dominant as a result; a 1940 law prescribed a proportion of 50 % Brazilians and no more than 25 % of any other nationality. All schools had to be headed by Brazilians; the language of instruction was exclusively Portuguese; and pupils under 14 were not to be taught foreign languages. Companies and clubs were not allowed to have foreign names, and foreign-language publications required special government approval. Eighty percent of the immigrants admitted under the quota system had to be farmers. These restrictions of the rights of immigrants were loosened somewhat in 1957, but they were not completely abolished.

Migration and the Receiving Culture

An unfriendly attitude toward immigrants o the part of officials and the general popula tion is well known from other countries an during earlier periods. In Argentina, fo example, there was already a tendency t see immigration as a threat to material wel being and progress in the years after Worl War I. These ideas came mainly from certai members of the political and intellectual eli and from their opponents in the same socia groups. Especially successful "Turkish" an Jewish merchants were the targets of attack in 1919 a pogrom was stirred up in Bueno Aires, and 150 Jews were injured. Asian were also the victims of hostility: during th revolutionary upheaval in Mexico in 191 Chinese immigrants were brutally persecute their property was confiscated, and they wer expelled from the country.

Discrimination and persecution were pa of the immigrants' history just as they influ enced the history of all the Latin America countries. Immigrants were responsible for th growth of agriculture in Argentina, Urugua Cuba, and southern Brazil; they made poss ble the expansion of industrial production i Buenos Aires, São Paulo, Santiago de Chil and other economic centers; they were th driving force behind the development of trad culture, science, and general education; the brought about the professionalization of th armed forces. Immigrants introduced barbe wire, more effective farming methods, diffe ent kinds of food and clothing, new custom and a new work ethic. As poor tenant farmer and capitalist wage workers immigrant produced the wealth of the great landowne and barons of industry; they also organize the labor movement and fought for a better wa of life.

The history of immigration recalls suc men as Francesco Matarazzo, who came fro near Naples and arrived almost penniless i Brazil in 1892. He worked hard as a stevedor and street peddler and lived frugally. Soon h had saved enough to buy a small grocery stor where he put his entire family to work, and few years later he was the head of a blossom ing business that continued to expand rapidl Today the Matarazzo organization is one of th largest businesses in all of South America controlling over 300 smaller companies wit a total of 35,000 employees. It is said tha

Weihnachtsabende in Brasilien.

———

Deutsch-brasilianisches Leben und Treiben.

Für die reifere deutsche Jugend

von

Julia Engell-Günther.

Mit 4 Zeichnungen von Sam.
CINCINNATI
UNIVERSITY
LIBRARY

Berlin.
Verlag von Julius Springer.
1862.

German-Brazilian publication, 1862

The Matarazzo factories used more electrical power than all of Peru.

There are even fairytales about immigrants. In 1849 a young Irishman named Patrick Mullins, soon changed to Patricio Milmo, came to Nuevo Leon in northern Mexico. He married the daughter of the governor and founded an economic empire based on cattle, trade, and banking; his daughter even married a Polish prince. The happy ending was missing, however, because the family had to flee during the Mexican revolution.

Most immigrants, of course, had no such success stories to tell – as reflected by the high rate of return migration, about 50% for Latin America as a whole. This number includes the so-called Indianos of the Mediterranean countries, who made their fortunes in the New World but returned to spend their retirement years in their homelands; it also encompasses temporary labor migrants such as the "swallows" of Argentina, who had never intended to remain abroad. But it is also clear that many who returned had not intended to do so but rather gave up in the face of difficult conditions in the new homeland. Above all, land ownership in Latin America was already clearly established: if immigrants had come from a rural area dreaming of owning their own farms, they were disappointed when they found an agricultural economy dominated by large estates. For a worker on one of São Paulo's coffee plantations, for example, it was much easier to save up the 300 milreis needed to transport the entire family back to Europe than to get 6,000 milreis together to buy a small farm. Sometimes the Latin American governments were disturbed by the high rate of return migration: in 1911 Argentina forced the shipping companies to double the price of a return steamship ticket.

The stream of transatlantic immigrants almost completely dried up during World War II, but in the period 1947–1950 about 12% of the world's "displaced persons", refugees and former forced laborers, found their way to Latin America, especially to Argentina, Brazil, and Venezuela. Many Nazi war criminals found hiding places in South America as well. In the 1950s the immigration rate rose again, and again Argentina and Brazil were the most popular destinations (with 600,000 and 450,000 immigrants, respectively, between 1946 and 1957). After 1960, however, the rate dropped off; for 1970, for example, Brazil reported only 6,900 immigrants. Many potential emigrants from southern Europe were now being recruited to work in European industrial countries such as Germany.

The oil boom in Venezuela spurred immigration in the 1960s, luring laborers from the rural areas and from Colombia and skilled workers, engineers, managers, businessmen, and bankers from Europe. This example shows how most transatlantic migration today has become the labor migration of an intellectual or technological elite: people come for a limited time to perform tasks such as building up a new branch of industry.

After the 1960s, the historical direction of migration was reversed, as Latin America became a land of emigration. First of all, the oppressive conditions in many countries forced people to seek out the more prosperous lands of North America, legally or illegally. While the U.S. census of 1920 already registered 500,000 Mexicans living in the southwestern states, today about 750,000 people are arrested for illegally crossing the border each year, and the numbers continue to grow rapidly. Spanish is becoming the second language of U.S. business in the border states. During the 1980s and 1990s, 750,000 illegal immigrants were arrested annually along the southern US border, a rapidly growing trend. Spanish has become the second language in the USA.

Second, the so-called "brain drain" takes the same general direction, representing a further loss to the poor countries of Latin America. Well educated and highly skilled people leave for the industrial nations of North America and Europe, where the jobs and pay

Girls of German origin in the Brazilian state of Santa Catarina, a federal state with a high proportion of German immigrants. Under the dictatorship of President Getúlio, the German language and German cultural practices were forbidden. These girls are dancing and singing. What could they be singing? Maybe a well-known folksong: "Where have you been, you billy-goat, you billy-goat? In the mill, in the mill, my master. What did you do in the mill, you billy-goat, you billy-goat? Grinding, grinding, my master. Grinding, grinding, my master!" Photo 1942

are better; the costs for educating them, on the other hand, are still paid by their impoverished Latin American homelands. The term brain drain was coined to show how the skills and potential sorely needed by the poor nations are drained away by the rich nations.

The third component of this migration stream is made up of political refugees who have sought and continue to seek asylum from the brutal dictatorial regimes of Latin America.

In addition to this continental movement there is a complementary interregional migration, from sparsely populated, underdeveloped rural areas to the large cities and developed industrial areas. Between 1960 and 1980 the population of Mexico City shot up from 5 million to 15 million, and every sizeable city of Latin America has its barrios, conventillos, or favelas – miserable strips of temporary huts made of earth, corrugated metal, and cardboard, without water or sanitary facilities, without schools or any infrastructure at all, and without a future.

Migration to the cities is not new, of course. Even in 1900 the poor development status of the rural regions forced European immigrants to settle in the cities. But there are significant differences. At the beginning of the 20th century the cities seemed to offer unlimited possibilities. The expansion of industry was underway, so there was work; social advancement, even if limited, was still possible; immigrants seldom lived in the slums for more than one generation – no such hopes exist for the residents of today's villas miserias.

Considering the overall demographic trends in Latin America over the last 200 years, we find three main tendencies. First, the population doubled between 1850 and 1900, from 30.5 million to 51 million. There was rapid population growth, especially in the temperate regions and later in Cuba, and mainly due to immigration from Europe. These immigrants favored a moderate climate. In Argentina and Brazil first-generation immigrants accounted for 30 % of the population increase, and their children made up another 30 %. Mass immigration from Europe is thus responsible for the rapid population growth around 1900.

Second, there was only relatively slo natural population growth in the area settled the earliest, such as Mexico and Peru Immigration to these countries during the 19th and 20th centuries was negligible. The population in the tropical areas rose onl about one-third as fast as that in Brazil, an there, too, there was no rapid jump aroun 1900. Mexico had especially slow growth due to the Mexican revolution and to severa epidemics, which hit harder there than i other countries. The population actuall decreased by about 885,000 between 191 and 1921. When internal stability wa restored toward the end of the decade, th population began to rise again.

Third, there was a significant if ne spectacular population increase in Centra America and the Caribbean which was du less to immigration than to natural factor such as higher birth rates and lower mortalit rates. The countries to the west of the Ande which had been important in earlier centurie lost out to those on the Atlantic coast.

Mass immigration from Europe left perma nent economic, social, and cultural marks o

German language newspaper in Buenos Aires 1953

Deutsche Nachrichten

NOTICIAS ALEMÃS — EINZIGE BRASILIANISCHE TAGESZEITUNG IN DEUTSCHER SPRACHE

7. Jahrgang   São Paulo, Freitag, den 13. März 1953   Nr. 1646

Wo *kaufen wir jetzt am günstigsten ein?*

CAMISARIA

TANNHAUSER

Führend in Herrenartikeln

AV. SÃO JOÃO, 259
Gegenüber der Post

RUA 24 DE MAIO, 215
Gegenüber der Casa Lemcke

The "Deutsche Nachrichten" (German News) in São Paulo 1952

the receiving countries. It also speeded up the demographic development of the most popular destinations and had a decisive influence on the growth and political formation processes.

Recent Migration Trends in Latin America

More recent trends in migration in Latin America and the Caribbean cannot be seen in isolation from a chain of far-reaching global connections, namely: the recurrent long-term, cyclical and structural crises in the monetary, financial and economic sectors in all the Latin American countries; the unequal and unfair distribution of societal wealth – both within the individual countries and between the so-called emerging markets and the economically less developed countries; and huge disparities in the standard of living between individual countries and regions, between urban and rural areas and between the different levels of the social class structure. In addition to these factors are the issues of material need, political instability, social unrest, the militarisation of conflicts, disengagement of the populace and the lack of future prospects for the majority of the population.

Against this background three general migration patterns can be identified.

Immigration from overseas has decreased dramatically since the 1960s. The classical receiving countries of Latin America have lost their appeal. While it is likely that the

economic boom in most of the European countries following World War II contributed to the minimal increase in the emigration rate during the 1950s, a high proportion of returning migrants, demographic change (higher mortality rate, also among the aging immigrant population) and the lack of new immigrants arriving led to a continual decline in the proportion of immigrants in the total population. Whereas, in 1970, the Latin American countries registered nearly 4 million overseas immigrants, by 1990 this figure had fallen to less than 2.5 million and to as little as 2 million in 2,000. The proportion of immigrants in the overall population decreased accordingly, from more than three quarters (1970) to approximately half (1990) and 41 % (2,000), respectively.

Argentina is a particularly good example of the way in which a traditional immigrant country has changed. Between 1870 and 1930, Argentina took in more than 7 million Europeans. Since the 1990s, unpromising job prospects in Argentina and the high demand on the international labor market (which was manipulated in part by the granting of favorable visa conditions in the countries seeking qualified workers) caused many Argentineans, primarily the young and well-qualified, to emigrate. An estimated 300,000 people (many of European origin) left following the economic collapse of 2001/02. The main destinations were the USA, Spain, Italy and Israel. Around 185,000 Argentinians emigrated between 1960 and 1970 and a

further 200,000 left in the following decade. In addition to the countries named above, western Europe and Venezuela also played a role. During the military dictatorship (1976–1983) 300,000 people, first and foremost the intellectual elite, left the country. Most of them never returned, not even after the downfall of the dictatorship. In 2004 almost 158,000 people who were born in Argentina were living in Spain; in 1999 the figure had been just over 70,000. In Italy the proportion of citizens of Argentinian origin doubled between 1999 and 2003, from just under 6,000 to just short of 12,000. Straightforward naturalization formalities, which facilitated access to the job market throughout the European Union for those able to prove that they had Spanish or Italian ancestry, further increased the attractiveness of these countries.

In 2005, around 1.05 million Argentinians were living outside the country's borders – twice as many as in 1985.

Economic problems in the 1990s had also caused many Brazilians of Japanese origin to leave for the land of their ancestors. In 1991 the authorities assumed that 150,000 Brazilians (whose ancestors had emigrated to São Paulo in the 1930s, when the Japanese economy had hit rock bottom) were employed in Japanese industry as temporary employees, where they took on the jobs that the local workers did not want because they were too difficult, too poorly paid or too dangerous. In just five months, 46,000 Japanese Brazilians came to Tokyo and other industrial centers; in 1988 the overall figure had been only 15,000. In Oizumi, 70 miles north of Tokyo, 1,000 of the 40,000 inhabitants of the town are Japanese-Brazilians, who have set up the typical immigrant structures there: ethnic neighborhoods with their own Portuguese language, their own cultural focal points (temples, shops and restaurants) and their own cultural coherence. The Japanese-Brazilians are viewed with disdain by the locals, who presume that the government wanted to import these people, who look so similar and yet are so very different, as cheap labor. For its part, the government had assumed that the issue of ethnic diversity and conflicts would be avoided because of the common origins. Unfortunately, this was not the case, since the Japanese did not understand any Portuguese and the Japanese-Brazilians did not understand Japanese. In 2000, 300,000 of the foreign-born Japanese

Hamburg-Südamerikanische Dampfschifffahrts-Gesellschaft

EGGERT & AMSINCK
HAMBURG 11 · HOLZBRÜCKE 8
Telephon: 34 17 11 bis 19 · Telegramme: Columbus · Fernschreiber 021 2146

4 neue „SANTA"-SCHIFFE der HAMBURG-SÜD

im Passagier- und Frachtverkehr zwischen HAMBURG, BREMEN *und* AMSTERDAM *und der*

OSTKÜSTE SÜDAMERIKAS

BAHIA · RIO DE JANEIRO · SANTOS · (SÃO FRANCISCO DO SUL) · MONTEVIDEO · BUENOS AIRES

The "Hamburg-South American Steamship Company" announces the commissioning of four new "Santa" class ships on the occasion of the maiden voyage of the first one in 1952

population came from Latin American states, 80 % from Brazil.

According to 1994 figures issued by the United Nations Population Division, the proportion of the "foreign population" (which should be understood both as "foreign born", i.e. not born there, and those with a different nationality) in the traditional immigration countries of Argentina and Brazil sank in the 1965–1990 period by 31 %, and 14 % respectively. In other countries it increased during the same period – by 84 % in Venezuela, for example, and by 235 % in Mexico. This suggests a significant increase in immigration.

However, given the absence of immigration from Europe, we can assume that this is a case of intra-regional migration. As early as 1980, intra-regional migration had doubled to over 2 million. In 2000, as a consequence of the great economic instability and social problems of the 1990s, more than 3 million people in Latin America had traveled across national borders, attracted by better job prospects, higher salaries and better standards of living elsewhere. Deep-rooted historic structures, the absence of language barriers and a generally

limited cultural distance encouraged such intra-regional migration.

Around the millennium, two thirds of "internal" Latin American migrants, who were not living in their home country, were concentrated in Argentina and Venezuela. Higher salaries in agriculture, in the manufacturing industry, in structural and civil engineering and in the service sector in Argentina attracted workers from the neighboring countries of Bolivia, Chile, Paraguay and Uruguay in particular, as well as from Peru. Colombians especially saw the oil boom in Venezuela as their ticket to employment and food.

At the same time, however, countries that had traditionally been source areas for emigration were growing in attractiveness for immigrants. Thus, the construction in the 1970s of massive hydro-electric power stations in Paraguay and intensive settlement programs in the rural areas triggered an economic upswing, leading many Paraguayans and their relatives in the surrounding states to return to Paraguay. In the 1990s, Chile not only registered considerable numbers of returning migrants but also an unprecedented share of immigrants from the surrounding countries,

even though the immigrants accounted for less than 1 % of the overall population.

Despite peace agreements, an increasingly stable democratic situation and repatriation in Central America, migration patterns have remained essentially unaltered. Belize and Costa Rica continue to be the focus of various migration movements. In Belize, immigrants, mainly from El Salvador and Guatemala, account for 15 % of the population, not including seasonal workers and transmigrants. Costa Rica is the destination for many Nicaraguan migrants, who are drawn by the demand for workers in the agricultural and service sectors and in 2000 accounted for 83 % of the regional immigration to Costa Rica. Mexico also took in many migrants from Guatemala and El Salvador. In absolute figures, however, Colombians accounted for the greatest proportion of intra-regional migration in the 1990s (just over 600,000) and after the millennium (approx. 700,000). Almost 90 % were registered in Venezuela.

Since the 1980s a striking trend has been developing in the gender make-up of the migrants: the proportion of women involved in intra-regional migration is increasing. In 2000, for every 100 female Colombians in Ecuador and Venezuela there were only 91.4 and 89.2 men respectively; the ratio among Chileans and Paraguayans living in Argentina was 73.3 and 91.9 % respectively, and of the

Colonial house in the German colony in Valdivia, Chile. Undated newspaper illustration, probably 1890s

Peruvians in Chile it was 66.5%. It can, however, be assumed that in addition to job prospects, personal migration motives, such as reuniting families, also played a role for these women.

Apart from the downturn in overseas immigration to Latin America and the various aspects of intra-regional migration, the third most prominent characteristic of current migratory movements in Latin America is emigration. Although Canada, the European states and Japan play their part, three quarters of emigrants choose to go to the USA. In 2000, 14.5 million emigrants from Latin America and the Caribbean were counted; by 2004 the number had already increased to 18 million. Of the other countries, Spain is worthy of note: 840,000 immigrants from South America were counted there in 2001, the majority of them women. Female immigrants play a major role in the healthcare sector in Spain, where their high level of qualification, their ability to speak Spanish and the cultural affinity provide good chances of promotion. In Canada and Great Britain the majority of the Latin American immigrants come from the Caribbean and here, too, there is a large proportion of women. In Canada the numbers of immigrants increased from 320,000 (1986) to 555,000 (1996), while in Great Britain they fell from 625,000 (1980) to less than 500,000 (1991).

Money transfers arranged by the migrants for their families at home now play a major role in the economy of the source countries. In 2004, 724 million dollars were remitted back to Argentina, three times as much as in 2001. This money was used to finance the living costs of the families, as well as being used to repay debts and for lucrative investments. Money transfers from the USA to Latin America in 2006 amounted to a total of 45 billion dollars, 51% more than two years previously. "If you don't send money to your mother, you are a bad son" was the slogan used by money transfer companies and banks.

Large amounts of money also flow to Latin America from Louisiana, more than 200 million dollars in 2006 – an increase of 240% compared with 2004. This is due to Hurricane Katrina, or, to be precise, the repair of the damage it wreaked in New

A postcard entitled "La Carreta – Montevedo" with Christmas and New Year's greetings written in 1952

Orleans. More than 50% of the workers involved in the rebuilding work were Latinos – word had got out that workers were needed in the Mississippi Delta.

Further south, in São Paolo, the 2008 carnival celebrated 100 years of Japanese immigration. Brazil is home to the largest Japanese community outside of Japan. The Brazilian Reuters website reported that the Samba Parade included floats with Japanese shrines and an enormous Buddha statue with a red and gold kimono, surrounded by drumming bands from Bahia, the home of samba. Although the Japanese immigrants in the country of the Sugar Loaf Mountain are already in the third or even fourth generation, it would appear that samba is not yet entirely in their blood; dancers from Bahia had dressed in kimonos and made themselves up to look Japanese. This goes to show how complex and far-reaching the process of cultural assimilation can be.

Migration has become a multi-faceted and complex issue. Countries that traditionally were immigrant countries have turned into simultaneously immigrant and emigrant countries. In addition, these countries are also home to many transit migrants, temporary working migrants (both highly-paid specialists and managers and untrained ancillary workers in low-paid sectors) as well as asylum seekers and displaced persons wishing to return to their homes.

References

Fouquet, Carlos: Der deutsche Einwanderer und seine Nachkommen in Brasilien 1808–1824–1974. São Paulo, 1974.

Galeano, Eduardo: Die offenen Adern Lateinamerikas. Die Geschichte eines Kontinents. Wuppertal 1971, repr. 1988.

Mörner, Magnus: Adventurers and Proletarians. The Story of Migrants in Latin America. Paris, University of Pittsburgh Press, 1985.

Sanchez-Albornoz, Nicholas: The Population of Latin America. A History. Berkeley/Los Angeles, California University Press, 1974.

Mala Jachimowicz, Argentina: "A New Era of Migration and Migration Policy", Migration Information Source, Feb. 2006, www.migrationinformation.org

United Nations, International Migration in Latin America and the Caribbean: A Summary View of Trends and Patterns, by Jorge Martinez Pizarro and Miguel Villa, New York, July 2005.

A. Pellegrino, Migrantes latinoamericanos: sintesids historica y tendencias recients, Montevideo, Universidad de la Republica-CEPAL-CELADE, 2000.

S. also website Comisión Económica para América Latina y el Caribe: www.eclac.org; and IMILA – Investigacion de la Migracion International en Latinoamerica.

IN CELEBRATION OF THE OPENING

PARLIAMENT of the COMMONWEALTH of AUSTRALIA

To meet Their Royal Highnesses
The DUKE and DUCHESS of CORNWALL &
YORK

His Majesty's
MINISTERS of STATE for AUSTRALIA
have the honor to invite
The Consul for the German Empire for Queensland.
Mr. Wm. Von Ploennies and Mrs. Von Ploennies

to an Evening Reception at the
Exhibition Building MELBOURNE,
on the 9TH of May 1901, at 8 o'clock.

Invitation issued to the German Consul in Brisbane, Wilhelm von
Ploennies and his wife to attend a reception in Melbourne to mark
the Federation of the six Australian colonies to form the Common
wealth of Australia in 1901

Diethelm Knauf/James Bade

The Legendary Southern Continent: Australia

From Discovery to the Founding of the Colony

The history of human presence in Australia began with migration, although it came relatively late because of the continent's geographical isolation.

It was probably during the last ice age, about 40,000 years ago, that dark-skinned people from Asia settled the land, at a time when the level of the sea was much lower and land bridges joined many of the islands of the present Indonesian archipelago. Nevertheless, the voyagers did have to cross many deep and dangerous straits. It is assumed that they were not very experienced sailors and did not possess any sophisticated navigation skills; thus it was probably more by chance than by carefully steered courses that small groups of them reached Australia on rafts.

These first migrants, the Aborigines, were nomadic hunters, fishermen, and gatherers, and they spread gradually over the entire Australian continent, including the southern island of Tasmania, which was joined to the mainland at the time. As the great ice masses of the northern Hemisphere melted about 16,000 years ago, the level of the seas rose and many of the land bridges disappeared. Now any migration through the Indonesian archipelago required seafaring skills, and only peoples with substantial knowledge of navigation dared to venture out onto the unknown open sea. Until the eighteenth century the culture and economy of the Aborigines developed without contact to other peoples, although ships from Papua-New Guinea and other nearby islands sometimes landed on the Australian coast. Australia was colonized not from the adjacent Asiatic culture area but from white Europe.

The ancient Greek legends of a fantastically rich southern continent had survived through the Middle Ages, and with the discovery of America and the opening of new sea routes to the Far east these legends experienced new growth. Magellan's circumnavigation of the world (1519–1521) established its spherical shape and the connection between the Pacific and Indian Oceans; people now assumed that, somewhere in these seas, there must be a southern continent, a terra australis, to balance the great land masses of the northern Hemisphere. In the sixteenth century Spanish and Portuguese explorers tried to find the mysterious terra australis by sailing west from South America, but unfavorable winds and ocean currents drove them too far to the northwest, to the Spice Islands. The Spanish navigator Luis Váez de Torres discovered the strait between Australia and New Guinea which was named after him, but without sighting the Australian coast. The Netherlands, having established their dominance over the Spice Islands with the founding of the Dutch East India Company in 1602, also joined the search for terra australis. The Dutchman Willem Jansz landed in 1606 on the west coast of Cape York, the first European to set foot on Australian soil; others followed to sail along and map the coast of Australia, which they named New Holland. But since they saw none of the expected wealth and riches, since they found the coasts barren and deserted, and since they considered the natives brutish, menacing, and completely uncivilized, the Dutch rather quickly lost interest in Australia.

Tasmanian Aborigines, 1858. By the mid-19th century the indigenous population had been decimated from about 7,000 at the beginning of the century to just 47

A convict supervisor (in the company of two ladies) observes prisoners at a government farm in Tasmania (known until 1855 as Van Diemen's Land); colored ink drawing from about 1840. After about eighteen months' work clearing land and constructing bridges and roads most convicts were set free. To the free settlers they then represented a threat to their livelihood. In 1866 the transportation of British convicts to Australia ceased

Great Britain began to show interest in the Pacific area only in the second half of the eighteenth century, when the discovery of Tahiti by the Englishman Samuel Wallis (1767) again fueled hopes of finding the legendary southern continent with its riches. In 1768 the British government equipped an expedition under the leadership of Captain James Cook; the secret aim of the mission was to find terra australis. After months of fruitless searching Cook gave up on this plan and sailed to New Zealand, which had been discovered by the Dutchman Abel Tasman in 1642. From here he intended to explore the unknown eastern coast of New Holland. This decision led to the discovery of the attractive, fertile, thickly forested, and well watered coastal areas of eastern Australia, which Cook claimed as British territory and named New South Wales. Cook did not find terra australis on any of his following voyages across the Pacific, from South America to New Zealand, from North America to China, and from the Bering Strait to Antarctica – apparently there was no such continent.

The history of white Australia begins with the American War of Independence, for at first the areas discovered by Cook had little interest for the British. People only remembered the far-off land of New South Wales after Britain had lost its American possessions (and with them both profitable trade relations and penal colonies), when the prisons of English cities and even the prison ships in the Thames were completely overfilled, and when prison revolts and protests in the liberal press led to a politically dangerous situation. In 1787 the King declared that from then on convicts were to be deported to Australia, where a penal colony was to be established. Arthur Phillipp, the future governor of New South Wales, became Commandant of the first fleet of ships, which in January 1788 brought over 1,000 men and women, over three-fourths of whom were convicts, to Australia. The settlement they founded lay somewhat north of Botany Bay – which soon became a synonym for convict deportation – and was called "Sydney Cove".

Convicts and Free Settlers

Australia, too, has its myths: one persisted well into the 1950s and claimed that the convict-settlers were actually innocent and courageous men who fought for freedom and against social injustice and political oppression. Many of them were supposedly small farmers and poor rural workers, driven to poaching and other criminal acts by the poverty which resulted from the capitalistic enclosures, consolidations of tenant farms and pasture lands to form large estates. This myth was a way to hide that the history of white settlement in Australia did not begin with the intrepid free pioneer, forcing nature to his will by honest hard work, but with the convict, a criminal who only came to Australia to pay his debt to society – a flaw in the self-understanding and self-image of the country.

This nationalistic interpretation of history was called into question in the 1950s and replaced with a new view, that the deported convicts were neither workers forced to steal by economic necessity nor victims of cruel British society, but rather members of a criminal class which included thieves, pickpockets, robbers, and prostitutes and which was different from the working class, the source of most of its members. This group was described as a criminal subculture distinguished by particular types of upbringing and psychological characteristics. In this view, those who were deported were the scum of humanity and raised from birth to be criminals.

But this view is one-sided as well. Studies of the ships' documents, which recorded up to 18 pieces of information (age, sex, education, marital status, height, occupation, place of birth etc.) for each convict, show that the majority of deportees were young, strong, healthy men, and that about 16 percent were women. Before deportation they were highly mobile, and thus had migration experience. The occupational distribution corresponded roughly to the general figures for the British urban working class and included brass founders from Warwickshire, stocking weavers from Nottingham, potters from Staffordshire

prospective emigrants, because Australia had no real advantages over North America; it was thousands of miles farther away, and the passage cost three or four times as much. Australia did have attractions for businessmen with capital to invest however: free land and the cheap labor of the convicts. At first the convicts worked on state-owned farms or in other state operations, felling trees, clearing pasture land, building roads, slaving in stone quarries, or firing bricks and lime. As the number of free settlers increased, more and more convicts were assigned to private employers, who had to provide food and shelter in exchange for their forced labor. Wages were not permitted and seldom paid. This system was very economical for the government, which was no longer financially responsible for keeping and housing the convicts, their supervision, and administrative handling.

However, since most of the convicts came from the working-class neighborhoods and slums of the British cities, their knowledge of farming, cattle-raising, and agriculture in general was very limited. For this reason there was still a great demand for free settlers who would clear the land and build up the economy on their own initiative, with energy and motivation. In order to arouse interest for agriculture among the convicts as well, Governor Phillipp quite early on issued a proclamation which pardoned deportees with good behavior and granted free farmland to "those convicts so emancipated", known as "Emancipists" because of this formulation. The settlers in the early colonial period were thus free immigrants, military or administrative personnel who had decided to stay in Australia, and convicts who had been pardoned or completed

Printed letter to Lord Ashley M.P. (later the famous social benefactor Lord Shaftesbury), from Mrs. Caroline Chisholm, South Australia, August 1849. Caroline Chisholm was known as the "emigrant's friend". In Sydney she ran a home for emigrants. In this open letter she proposed a scheme for lending money on reasonable terms to the worthy poor so as to enable them to emigrate.

Title page from booklet entitled "Practical Hints for Emigrants to our Australian Colonies", Liverpool 1858. It outlines the pitfalls and problems the emigrant will find on his journey to the gold diggings of Australia or sheep ranches of New Zealand.

Emigrants eager to join the Australian gold rush board the Eagle at anchor in the Mersey; Lithograph by W.J. Hammond, Liverpool, after original painting by Thomas Dove

and cotton-mill and factory workers from Lancashire, as well as watch-chain makers, mule spinners, and button polishers. The learned professions and agricultural workers were underrepresented, but the majority of the convicts had some training, specific job skills, or qualifications to offer. The ability to read and write was also surprisingly common: only 65 % of the population in England could read and/or write in the second quarter of the 19th century, but among the convicts the number was 75 %. Those who were sent out to establish a penal colony on the other side of the world were well equipped for the task of transforming an open prison into a capitalist economy.

A total of about 160,000 convicts were shipped to Australia, 80,000 to New South Wales and almost 70,000 to Van Diemens Land, which because of its miserable

reputation as a penal colony was later renamed Tasmania. New South Wales also had a bad reputation: Peter Cunningham, a medical doctor on the convict ships and a landowner in Australia, complained in 1827 that even a very friendly conversation partner in a British coach moved farther away on learning that he was from New South Wales, pretending to look for a toothpick in order to check that nothing had been stolen from his bags.

According to the census of 1828, New South Wales had a population of 36,598, of whom only 5,000 had come voluntarily – and these free settlers included members of the military organization, supervisors, and administrative officials stationed there. In the decade 1830–1840 the ratio began to change, with 65,000 free settlers as well as 50,000 deportees. The British government had to offer considerable subsidies to

Advertisement for the "Gulf of Siam", 1892

Above: Bullock drivers on the way to remote sheep farms to collect bales of wool. By the second half of the 19th century the arable land had extended much further inland, resulting in greater distances between farms and coastal ports
Below: German family in Rosewood, Queensland. Photo about 1890

their sentences; all of these were given land by the British government.

This procedure was discontinued by the government in 1831, and land was now sold for not less than 5 shillings per acre. The money collected was to be used to pay for an Assisted Immigration Scheme, in which the government paid for the passage tickets of immigrants who could not afford it themselves. The aim was to release population pressure in Great Britain and at the same ease the chronic labor shortage in Australia.

Australia now became a country for emigrants as well as for convicts. Many of the emancipated convicts viewed the free immigrants as intruders. When a group of Scottish craftsmen docked in Sydney in 1831, they were greeted with angry cursing: "There are these bloody emigrants come to take the country from us". In 1825 the free immigrant Alexander Harris was told, "One of the free objects – bad luck to 'em. What business have they here in the prisoners' country?".

Toward the end of the 1830s there was increasing pressure on the deportation system

and forced convict labor. Many cattle ranchers still saw the deportees as a source of cheap labor, which could be replaced by Indian and Chinese coolies if the number of subsidized free workers ("bounty migrants") was insufficient. Others saw the deportations as an obstacle to eventual political independence and/or as a depressive force in the free labor market. Probably the strongest protests were heard at home in England, especially from those who believed that deportation was too mild a punishment to deter crime. There was dissatisfaction with the amount of freedom convicts enjoyed in Australia, displeasure with the economic success emancipated convicts often achieved, and shocked surprise that deported criminals seemed to have a much higher standard of living than poor workers in English cities.

In fact, many Emancipists were able to earn a decent living or even achieve a degree of prosperity. George Howe, sentenced for shoplifting, was immediately given the task of publishing the only newspaper, the Sydney Gazette and New South Wales Advertiser, and Edward Wills, deported as a highwayman in 1799, was a rich merchant and dock owner at his death in 1811, and his widow married George Howe. Daniel Cooper, deported for theft and pardoned in 1821, entered a partnership with Solomon Levy and made a fortune in trade; they were the most famous example of a rapid rise from disgrace to prosperity. Women were successful as well: Mary Haydock, deported for horse-stealing in 1790, married Thomas Reibey, a free settler and partner of Edward Wills. After his death Mary Reibey further expanded his business and became one of the richest people in New South Wales. As the deportation system grew more and more discredited in the 1840s and 1850s, the number of convicts transported to Australia dropped; the system was abandoned in 1868.

The Myth of the Bush

The second important Australian myth is the bush myth. The bush is the vast hinterland which began where the fertile strip of coastal land ended and contained the frontier, the borderline between the settled land and the wilderness. The bush was the stage for many

mber workers in the Blackall Range, north of Brisbane, ca. 1890. ìe prized red cedar (Cedrela Australis) was much sought after for rniture and building. The tree reaches a height of about 150 feet. ; wood is light, soft, easy to work, cuts firmly, bends well, dresses eanly and polishes well

f the heroic deeds and tragedies of Australian ioneer history, a hard land for hard men. Part f the myth was the mythical Australian or working bushman", whose ethic was based n independence, egalitarian collectivism, nd the concept of "mateship", loyalty to his ompanions through thick and thin, complemented by dislike for authority and sympathy or the underdog. Especially the elements of galitarianism and solidarity show that this ıyth has its origins in the penal colonies and ıe working-class milieu.

Around 1900 the Australian cities lost ıeir image as examples of British business ense and material prosperity. Among the ıtellectuals in particular there was heated ociopolitical discussion of the Australian ational character. In the outside world many onsidered the city a place of decadence; the igh degree of urbanization and the fact that ıe majority of the population lived in cities ere surprising for such a young nation. The ity no longer demonstrated the vitality of the olony but rather stood for racial degeneracy, nd its apparently uncontrolled growth was ıken as an indication that Australia had lost s pioneer spirit. The vision of the parasitic ity absorbing the valuable energy of the ation was contrasted with the fascinating icture of rural Australia and its inhabitants, specially the bush workers.

Industrial-scale agriculture and cattle-ıising were and still are the most importınt branches of the Australian economy. 'he agricultural sector produced a special ind of rural proletariat characterized by very igh mobility. The extreme conditions in the ustralian hinterland, the "outback", and the chronic shortage of women produced the mythical bushman with the traits described above. After the "squatting rush" for land which began in the 1820s and led to occupation of the continent over the following decades, there was an army of unemployed cattle drivers, riders, shepherds, shearers, oxcart drivers, cowboys, and farm hands constantly on the move. The extent and intensity of internal migration movements can be seen in the following examples: a convict might have spent months or years working on road construction in the cities before being assigned to a landowner as a farm worker, and the opposite path from years "up the country" to the city was also possible. Small farmers and hands often looked for work as shearers in the west to improve their incomes, and many urban wage-earners did the same, especially when there were economic crises on the coast. Teamsters, driving their oxen back and forth on a regular basis from the colonial centers and port cities to the interior of the continent, were important before the railroads were built, reaching into the interior by the 1870s. Along with their loads of wool and hides they brought news, gossip, songs, fashions, customs, and attitudes. Cattle drivers not only delivered the sheep and cattle to the city markets; they also spread curious clothing, a special language, and unusual behavior. The myth traveled with the men.

In reality, however, the typical Australian is more a city-dweller than a wild, sunburned bushman. Australia is one of the most urbanized nations in the world, and this is not a new phenomenon, but has been typical of the country since the first convict settlements. The 1921 census found that the urban population outweighed the rural by 61 to 39 %; among immigrants, 70 % lived in cities. Today the urban population is much greater, with the two cities of Sydney and Melbourne taking up half of the total population of Australia. Only 4 % of the working population is engaged in agricultural, forestry or fishing occupations.

The Gold Rush

By the middle of the 19th century about 220,000 free settlers had immigrated to Australia, so that they already outnumbered the convicts by 60,000. When gold was discovered in New South Wales in 1851 and a few months later in Victoria, there was a dramatic increase in the number of free immigrants. Within ten years the population almost tripled, from 400,000 to almost 1.2 million. The influx of immigrants was of great significance for the economic development of Australia, because it included people with job skills in the crafts, business, and commerce, thus closing some gaps in the occupational structure. Among the gold-diggers were not only Britons but also members of other ethnic groups such as Germans and especially Americans (who came to try their luck in Australia after failing to find gold in California). Their numbers were not great, but they did bring new cultural practices and political ideas. Some later played a big part in conflicts with the police and government officials. In 1854 there were armed confrontations in Ballarat, the so-called Eureka Stockade. The gold prospectors were dissatisfied, because the deposits were not as rich as they had expected; big corporations and wealthy entrepreneurs had already taken out large amounts; and the government also tried to get its share by imposing high license fees

Menu for adult passengers on the ships of the Golden Australian Line, which plied the route from Liverpool to Melbourne. Advertising poster, 1855

The **PROVISIONS** supplied the Vessels of this Line are all personally inspected by the Owners and H. M. Government Emigration Agent, and are purchased of the best quality, regardless of cost.

ALL PASSENGERS AND THEIR LUGGAGE ARE LANDED AT MELBOURNE WHARF, FREE OF EXPENSE.

The CABINS of these Vessels are fitted in the most luxurious manner.

The **INTERMEDIATE** will be found to be ventilated and lighted on a most superior principle, and the Berths and Fittings are in a style that cannot be surpassed. All **PROVISIONS** are served to the Passengers cooked, and an ample number of Stewards are provided to wait on the different classes of Passengers.

Dietary Scale for each Adult Passenger per Week.

ARTICLES.	SECOND CABIN	INTERMEDIATE.	ARTICLES.	SECOND CABIN	INTERMEDIATE.
Biscuits	3½ Lbs.	3 Lbs.	Rice	12 Oz.	1 Lb.
Beef	1 "	1¼ "	Potatoes { Raw	2 Lbs.	....
Pork	1 "	¾ "	Potatoes { or Preserved	½ "	¾ Lb.
Preserved Meats & Soups	2 "	½ "	Pickles or Vinegar	1½ Gill.	1 Gill.
Flour	3 "	2½ "	Butter	12 Oz.	4 Oz.
Raisins	½ "	2 Oz.	Oatmeal	1 Lb.	1 Lb.
Suet	12 Oz.	4 "	Salt	2 Oz.	2 Oz.
Peas	1 Pint.	¾ Pint.	Mustard	½ "	¼ "
Tea	2 Oz.	2 Oz.	Pepper	½ "	....
Coffee or Cocoa	2 "	2 "	Treacle	½ Lb.	¾ Lb.
Sugar	1 Lb.	¾ Lb.	Salt Fish	½ "	¼ "
Cheese	8 Oz.	....	Water	21 Qts.	21 Qts.

Left: In the middle of the 19th century the gold rush brought countless gold seekers to Australia. Gold was first discovered on the east coast, from 1851 in Victoria (Ballarat, Bendigo). Illustrated London News, January 1853
Right: Camp of traveling cattle herders and sheep-shearers, Photo about 1900

for prospecting. When the police were too vigorous in collecting taxes and license fees, the gold miners armed themselves, set up barricades, and traded shots with the police, but their resistance was broken after two days. A Reform League founded by the miners also made radical political demands for things such as general elections with a secret ballot.

The gold fever had a strong negative effect on the traditional Australian economy, because the farmers were suddenly left with no workers. Workers, businessmen, salaried employees, and even policemen left their jobs and hurried to the gold fields. On closed shop doors in the cities hung signs saying, "Gone to look for gold".

In 1891 gold was found in western Australia, but despite this discovery immigration did not increase significantly. In the previous decade about 175,000 new immigrants had come, the highest number thus far. The proportions of European and Asian immigrants began to shift in favor of Asia, mainly because Australia was not attracting enough to immigrants from countries with relatively high standards of living. The worldwide depression at this time probably had an effect as well, since poorer potential migrants could not afford the trip. The most important component of the gold rush to western Australia was internal migration from the east coast. Another factor was the fact that claims

were staked and ownership rights to the gold mines transferred more quickly than had been the case in New South Wales and Victoria. By the time gold was discovered in Coolgardie and Kalgoorlie, the lonesome prospector patiently working his small claim was the exception, and most gold-seekers had to take jobs working as miners for large companies. In this situation the police had their hands full keeping gold theft under control: it wasn't enough to watch the miners, and gold was smuggled out of the mines in blankets, candles, and water bottles, and sometimes transported out of town in coffins. In 1970 Australia was still the world's fifth largest gold producer, with about 70 % coming from the fields of western Australia; more recently the cost-intensive operation of the mines and a fall in the price of gold on the world market have made things more difficult. The former eldorados on the edge of the Great Australian Desert threaten to become ghost towns.

Gold fields and gold-mining camps have traditionally attracted Chinese immigrants; they came in great numbers to Victoria in 1855–1857, as the amount being mined was already noticeably decreasing. In 1857 there were 24,000 Chinese working in the gold fields of Victoria, or about 12 % of the population there. From the very beginning Whites viewed their arrival with distance and skepticism. The Chinese kept to themselves and

spoke no English, and there was hardly any contact between them and the other miners. Many of them were contract laborers tied to wealthy Chinese employers, who had paid their passage, or to white farmers and entrepreneurs. They worked for extremely low wages and were seen by white miners as a threat to their standard of living. Although they were hardly ever in direct competition with Whites, working mainly on the slag heaps and tailings piled up by other miners, in abandoned mines, or at poorly paid jobs in laundries and kitchens, they were blamed for the economic decline of the gold fields.

As early as 1843 skilled workers in Sydney fearing depression of wages had voiced opposition to bringing in Indian coolies. The

Wedding party in Hatton Vale, Queensland. Photo around 1900

ere vehemently opposed to the resumption of convict deportation and the subsidization of free immigration. Anti-Chinese feelings culminated in pogroms, the worst in Buckland, Victoria (1857) and Lambing, New South Wales (1861); Chinese workers were the victims of violent attacks, robbery, looting, and arson. Some were murdered, others scalped, and still others died as a result of their injuries. "Patriots" told their children to stone the Chinese, who were mocked in countless stories, songs, and newspaper articles. Their persecutors were seldom arrested by the police or convicted by the courts, and the racist feelings and pogroms gained official state sanction in the "White Australia Policy", as embodied by the "Commonwealth Immigration Restriction Act" of 1901, a law passed by the Australian government to prohibit the immigration of non-Europeans. This law was not replaced by non-discriminatory legislation until 1973.

After the various spells of gold fever subsided, the immigration rate sank significantly, and the population born in Australia soon surpassed that of immigrants. At the beginning of World War I only one in ten was born outside Australia, and the 1921 census found 85% natives, even though another 86,000 immigrants had arrived between 1911 and 1920 – the highest number ever attained in a decade. Of the foreign-born, 80% came from the British Isles, 8% from the rest of Europe (2.7% from Germany), 4.5% from New Zealand, and 3.5% from Asia. These figures also show that Australia, unlike North America, never became a destination for mass European emigration; instead it remained, at least until after World War II, a country with a predominantly British population and strong cultural, economic, and political links to the motherland. The social and political environment encountered by the new arrivals was familiar to most of them, whereas the natural environment was new. Unlike typical immigrants to North or South America, who were strangers at first, had to learn a new language and come to terms with a new cultural milieu, immigrants from Great Britain, setting foot for the first time on Australian soil after a long sea voyage, remained subjects of the same monarch and settled among people who spoke their own language. Here, as in New Zealand, colonists seldom had to share the land with people from other European countries, and the resistance of the native population was also

weaker than in North America or New Zealand. Although the journey was longer, people came to areas that were familiar to them, because they could easily consider them provinces of Great Britain.

The Irish formed one easily distinguishable group that did not share the pro-English sentiments of the Australian majority. Irish immigrants were not only ethnically different, they were also Roman Catholics and mostly members of the lower classes. Their numbers among the convicts were disproportionately high, and among the free Irish immigrants were many poor agricultural workers who came as contract laborers with long terms of service to serve before their passage money was paid off. For this reason the Irish element was always strong in the working class, and it is not surprising that the labor and trade-union movement had strong links to Ireland and the Catholic church.

The marks left in Australia's history and present-day culture by German immigrants are also notable. Individual migrants took part in the settlement of Australia from the very beginning – for example, the German-born navigator of the first English fleet or Ludwig Leichhardt, who led one of the expeditions to explore the interior, successfully charting the land between Darling Downs and Arnhem Land in 1844–1845. When Leichhardt set out to cross the continent from east to west, he never returned, and no trace of him was ever

found. The Lutherans from Silesia, however, who arrived in Adelaide in 1838 were emigrants rather than adventurers, having defied the order of King Friedrich Wilhelm III of Prussia to worship together with their Reformed religious opponents in a unified state church at home in Germany. Although they settled near the town at first, most of them moved on into the Barossa Valley and planted vineyards; Barossa today is synonymous with good wines and German traditions. German villages were also founded in Queensland in the middle of the 19th century; the emigration movement was preceded by the work of five missionaries, who had come to preach Christianity to the native population near present-day Brisbane. A few years later a German merchant sailed from Brisbane to recruit new settlers in his homeland, promising free passage to farm workers, vintners, mechanics, and domestic servants, or a free piece of land on arrival in Australia to emigrants who could pay their own way. German family names in the sugar-cane-growing areas and country towns with names like Minden and Marburg recall this early settlement period, although not much more is left. No German settlements remain in Victoria or New South Wales, either: although there were about 10,000 Germans living in Victoria in 1861, only a few small groups founded new villages. About 6,000 of the immigrants lived in the gold-mining camps, and many

Postcard of Sydney, early 1920s

2033. Central Square. Sydney.

Multicultural leaflets about the Australian health system as part of the National Ethnic Information Campaign which was launched in Sydney and Melbourne in 1990. Radio and newspaper information was given in 18 different languages

Team-teaching avoids isolation

Flemington High School has developed a 'team teaching' approach which attends to the needs of its 67 per cent majority of NESB students.

A significant proportion of these are girls, and have been in Australia for less than three years, making English an important component for all subjects.

Team-teaching involves ESL teachers working with mainstream teachers (or vice versa) in science, maths, information technology and the humanities to ensure the needs of NESB students are catered for.

ESL teacher, Irene Iliadis explained how the team-teaching program works in a Year 11 information technology class:

"There are 25 students in the class, and 14 have been in Australia less than three years. People might say that information technology is just typing and computer knowledge, but there is a lot of language involved.

"I'm in here as an ESL teacher. I don't know the course, but in terms of planning and giving assistance to students, I become fairly crucial for them to be able to understand the content, and use it effectively.

According to Anna Venuto, "Co-operative cross-curriculum education is essential. The level of ESL support varies from just having an ESL teacher to prop up the NESB kids, to a quality team-teaching program like this one where the teachers are sitting down together planning curriculum and teaching together on an equal status in the classroom. All students ultimately benefit".

Flemington High's language program has provided a strong base for building a work experience program, an extensive careers program which heavily involves parents, and a School- TAFE Integration Program with Footscray TAFE college.

Hong Limngeun, Buonyong Phothitay, Xiouming Chen, Yolanda Hernandez and Nalan Ulukan at Flemington High School, Victoria.

From a brochure brought out by the Office of Multicultural Affairs, National Agenda for a Multicultural Australia, 1990. Note the different ethnic origins of the children of Flemington High School in Victoria

moved on to New South Wales when gold was discovered there. Two Germans, Bernhard Otto Holermann and Ludwig Beyers, found the largest known single piece of gold ore at Hill End, near Sydney, in 1872. It was almost 5 feet high and 26 inches wide and weighed 570 pounds. Beyers retired on the money he got for the ore, whereas the Hamburg native Holtermann built shops and hotels, set up factories, and invested in a railroad line.

The settlements of Germans in New South Wales, Queensland, and Victoria adapted to their Anglo-Saxon environment in only a few years; only in the Barossa Valley did German customs and traditions remain unchanged for over a century. Most of the Lutherans there had brought their families with them to South Australia, and Adelaide, the nearest city, was 40 miles away: the settlers lived in voluntary isolation. Only a few applied for Australian citizenship. The unifying element for this community was the Lutheran religious faith, and the Lutheran bible was the most popular book. In 1891 there were 25,000 first- and second-generation Germans living in South Australia, and at the turn of the century there were 46 Lutheran schools in that province alone. Members of the Lutheran community in Adelaide also founded the Hermansburg mission station on the Finke River in central Australia. For them basic aid for the Aborigines was more important than religious conversion. In 1875, only thirteen years after the John McDouall Stuart expedition crossed the continent in the north-south direction for the first time, a small group set out on an overland journey which almost cost many of them their lives. Their destination was the area around the present-day city of Alice Springs, and the trek through the desert lasted eighteen months. The members of the expedition suffered from scurvy, and many of their animals died of thirst befor the group reached its destination in Jun 1877. Today about 600 Aborigines live a the station, near the border of the Arund tribal reservation. There is a school an hospital to help the sick. A cattle ranch provides jobs, so that the Aborigines are not solely dependent on welfare.

Populate or Perish – Immigration after 1945

By the end of World War II the population of Australia had reached 7.5 million. The war and the threat of invasion by Japanese troops not only caused Australia to change its political orientation from Great Britain to the U.S., but also led to a new attitude toward immigration. The belief was, at least until the end of the 1960s, that only a continually growing population could discourage Australia's northern neighbors from making territorial claims. In addition, the country needed a strong labor force to fulfill its economic potential. As at the end of the 19th century, it was considered important to populate the vast empty continent and strengthen its economy, and thus to take permanent possession of it. In 1946 the government announced plans for promoting and financially subsidizing immigration from Europe at unprecedented levels. Immigration would be open to all Europeans and not just to British subjects. At first the recruitment strategies and immigration programs were aimed at the many refugees and displaced persons in post-war Europe, but soon they were extended to all countries. Since 1946, 6 million immigrants have come to Australia. The 2001 census shows that by far the greatest number of Australian residents born in Europe were Britons (25%), followed by Italians (5.3%), Greeks (2.8%), Germans (2.6%), Dutch (2%), and Poles (1.4%). However the increasing diversity of the Australian population is shown by the fact that 5.3% were from Korea, 3.8% from Vietnam, 3.5% from China, and 1.6% from Hong Kong.

Today every fifth Australian is of non-British ancestry in the first or second generation, and almost half of the population is a direct or indirect descendant of post-war immigrants. But one-eighth of present-day immigrants remain only a few years in Australia before returning to their homelands.

After 1971 immigration policy took a new turn. Series of full-page advertisements in European newspapers were canceled, and a rest was ordered for the embassy recruiters, who had been traveling across Europe, using film presentations to interest hundreds of thousands in Australia. The immigration quotas were lowered, so that in 1971–1972 only 140,000 instead of 170,000 migrants were granted visas. The Assisted Immigration Scheme had put a big hole in the budget – according to the estimates of government critics, the state hired two employees and spent almost 8,000 dollars for every immigrant who came. Most of the new arrivals traveled free, with the Australian taxpayers paying the fare. In 1971 it was said that Australia spent almost twice as much for the immigration program as the budgeted amount, 74 million dollars. Today Australia is still very much a migrant country, actively recruiting young immigrants with good English ability and recent work experience whose skills and qualifications match Australia's Skilled Occupation List, in order to compensate for emigration and declining fertility. Thanks to a policy of welcoming migrants from non-English speaking Europe since the 1940s and non-Europeans since the 1960s there is markedly more cultural diversity in present-day Australia. The 2001 census shows that 54% of Australians trace their ancestry to north-western Europe; 11.5% to southern and eastern Europe; and 7% to Asia. Of those recording north-western Europe as their ancestral region, 742,212 (4%) wrote they were of German origin. The historically significant German immigration to Australia has continued unabated in recent years. The 2001 census shows that there were 21,794 Germans living in Melbourne and 19,711 in Sydney, and that Australia had a total of 108,220 German-born residents.

Ethnic origin	1787	1846	1891	1947	1988	2001
Aboriginal	100	41.5	3.4	0.8	1.0	2.2
Anglo-Celt	-	57.2	86.8	89.7	74.6	76.3
Other European	-	1.1	7.2	8.6	19.3	13.6
Asian	-	0.2	2.3	0.8	4.5	6.3
Other	-	-	0.3	0.1	0.6*	1.6
Total	100	100	100	100	100	100
Nos (000s)	500	484	3,275	7,640	163,000	18,769

* Includes black African and West Indians, Pacific Islanders and American Indians. More than half this total are Pacific Islanders

Ethnic composition of the Australian population, 1787–2001

References

Clark, C. M. H.: "The Origins of the Convicts Transported to eastern Australia, 1787–1852", in: Historical Studies of Australia and New Zealand. Vol. 7, No.26 und 27, 1956.

Günthner, Ulrich: Australien heute. Wien/Düsseldorf, 1973.

Inglis, K. S.: The Australian Colonists: An Exploration of Social History 1788–1870. Melbourne, 1974.

Löffler, Ernst; Rose, A. J.; Warner, Denis: Australia. London/Melbourne, 1977.

Mc. Phee, E. T.: "Australia – Its Immigrant Population", in: Willcox; Ferenzci: International Migrations. Vol. 2, New York, 1929/1931, p. 173ff.

Nicolas, Stephen; Shergold, Peter R.: "Sträflinge als Migranten", in: Gulliver. Bd. 23, Hamburg, 1988, p. 13ff.

Walker, David: "National Identity: Aspects of its History in Australia", in: Gulliver. Vol. 23, p. 27ff.

Ward, Russel: The Australian Legend. Melbourne, 1958.

Australian Bureau of Statistics website: www.abs.gov.au

Australian Government Department of Immigration and Multicultural Affairs website: www.immi.gov.au

Calligan, B. Roberts, W.: Australian Citizenship. Melbourne 2004.

MacLeod, C. L.: Multiethnic Australia: Its History and Future. Jefferson (NC), London 2006.

HOMELAND NEWS

FOR MEMBERS OF THE NZ EGHALANDA ASSOCIATION ORIGINATING IN PUHOI AND OHAUPO

VOL. III No. 3   June 1986

Mies

Pilsen

Staab

This year, 1986, will be the 123rd celebration of the arrival of the first large group of the Puhoi pioneers in 1863. There had been a small earlier group – in March of 1860 – arrived under the leadership of Captain Martin Krippner but the 1863 arrival was the

In 1863 a group of Egerländer from the Bohemian districts of Mies, Pilsen and Staab emigrated to New Zealand and founded the settlement of Puhoi. The "New Zealand Eghalanda Association", now called the Bohemian Association, keeps the Egerländer cultural traditions of the founders of Puhoi and Ohaupo alive. In 1963, to commemorate the centenary of the arrival of Egerländer in New Zealand, a book appeared with historical photos: a coach in front of the Puhoi general store; Farmer John with his cattle; Egerländer musicians in their new homeland; the church school

Diethelm Knauf/James Bade

New Zealand – "The Land of the Long White Cloud"

"The land of the long white cloud" is what the two islands now known as New Zealand were called by the first Polynesian migrants, whose descendants were the Maori found by the white explorers in the 17th and eighteenth centuries. Little is known for sure about the first settlement of New Zealand. The first migrants came from eastern Polynesia and probably had the Society Islands as their home base. About 1,000 years ago they landed on the coast of New Zealand, either by chance, as a result of violent expulsion from their homeland, or as voluntary exiles fleeing economic or political troubles at home. Maori legend tells of the original immigrants who arrived in a fleet of long outriggers with their leader Kupe, who is credited with having discovered the North Island. Many Maori trace their origin to this first settlement, and scholars have learned that the early settlers even brought dogs and a supply of food, which suggests planned migration rather than a chance landing.

Polynesian settlement sites from the eleventh and twelfth centuries have been found all over New Zealand, especially near protected natural harbors on the north-east coast of the North Island, but also at river mouths and in bays on the South Island. The settlers were a peaceful people at first, living in open villages and basing their economy on locally available foods. By the time the Europeans arrived, however, tribal warfare was part of the Maori way of life; territorial rivalries had led to violent conflict. Fortified villages were the typical settlement form at this time.

In 1642 about 260,000 Maori were probably living in Aotearoa, the "land of the long white cloud", when the Dutch explorer Abel Tasman touched the western coast on his search for gold and spices – neither of which he found there. The islands of New Zealand were soon forgotten in Europe and remained so until James Cook claimed them for Great Britain in 1769. Settlement by white colonists began only sporadically: in the late eighteenth and early 19th centuries there were only short visits by official representatives of the penal settlements in Australia, and from time to time ships stopped to take on food and water.

This painting is entitled "An incident in the New Zealand Wars" (Major Gustavus Ferdinand von Tempsky; watercolor and pencil sketch) and is said to represent a scene from the land wars between the British and some Maori tribes. In 1840 some 540 Maori chiefs had recognized British sovereignty in the Treaty of Waitangi; in return the British promised to protect the right of the Maori to their land. But after a series of misunderstandings on both sides, bitter fighting broke out in the 1860s. The resulting confiscation of Maori land added to grievances against the British Crown which are now being settled by the New Zealand Government in compensation agreements with individual Maori tribes. The painting shows a wounded British soldier being carried from the battlefield after British troops stormed a North Island Maori pa (fortified village) in 1866

The Otago gold rush (1861–1863) was New Zealand's largest and had a marked influence on the development of the South Island province of Otago and its capital city, Dunedin. Most of the first miners came from Australia, Europe and the USA; they were joined from 1866 by Chinese, both respected and resented by the others because of their devotion to the task, which led to some unpleasant confrontations. The gold rush finished when mining companies took over operations in 1869. Some gold-diggers tried their luck elsewhere; others stayed and took up employment with the mining companies. The two illustrations show goldmine excavations and the tent camps of the gold-seekers

Then the first small settlements were founded, and missionary stations soon followed. Gradually the continuing search for new trade goods and a certain amount of population pressure in New South Wales made New Zealand a permanent part of British businessmen's financial calculations. Several whaling bases, financed by merchants from Sydney, were set up on the south coast of the South Island; lumber camps were established in the

forests of kauri trees, related to European firs; and the Bay of Islands developed into a provisioning center for trading ships, whalers, and seal hunters in the South Pacific. The mission stations grew, but by 1839 there were still only about 2,000 Europeans living in New Zealand.

The first significant immigration of European settlers began in the 1840s, after Great Britain had formally declared its

sovereignty over New Zealand in the Treaty of Waitangi, concluded with 500 Maori chiefs. A long time had already passed since the first colonization companies had been established to acquire land, to recruit and settle colonists, and to open up the interior of the islands economically and make it usable. The New Zealand Company of Edward Gibbon Wakefield had several divisions and was supported by the Scottish and Anglican churches. The New Zealand Company brought nearly 9,000 British immigrants into the settlements of Wellington, Nelson, Wanganui and New Plymouth between 1840 and 1843. Christchurch and Dunedin followed, while Auckland, as the nation's capital between 1841 and 1865, attracted many settlers in its own right.

At first the goal of the companies was to interest people of all British social classes in their project, including investors and rich landowners. In reality, however, it was mostly artisans, farm hands, unskilled factory workers, and domestic servants who joined the companies. After some early disappointments, most of the colonists were able to establish themselves as farmers or sheep ranchers, or more likely practicing the trade they brought with them in the growing cities.

Among the New Zealand Company settlers there were also two German groups. They were Lutherans from the Rhineland, Hamburg, Bremen, and Mecklenburg. They settled in the Moutere and Waimea valleys. They are commemorated in the present-day Ranzau and Upper Moutere Lutheran churches and the settlement of Neudorf. German settlements followed in Wellington, Canterbury, Otago and Southland provinces. Up to 1914, the Germans formed New Zealand's second largest immigrant group after the British.

The Native Land Acts of 1862 and 1865 did away with the royal monopoly on land ownership, and settlers could now buy land from the Maori without restriction. After the New Zealand Land Wars, in which the settler government used armed force to put down resistance among some Maori, both the colonization companies and the provincial government made new efforts at recruiting settlers. In the South Island there were fertile farms and vast pasture lands, and therefore a need for many agricultural workers, who were to be recruited overseas. They, like domestic servants and artisans

New Zealand immigration map, 1976

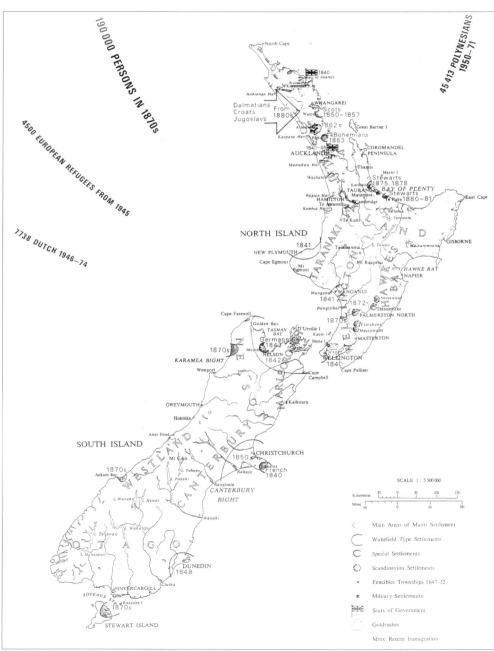

Sarau School about 1899. Upper Moutere (known as Sarau till 1915) is a village in the Moutere Hills of Tasman Bay near Nelson, in the north of the South Island. The first German immigrants to New Zealand settled in this area in 1843

were given financial aid to pay for the passage, and there were also grants of free land to those who could pay their own way, as in Australia. The Bohemian Germans who settled at Puhoi, near Auckland, are an example of the latter type of migrant. They arrived in 1859 and had to fight for survival for several years because of the poor soil.

These migrations were insignificant in terms of absolute numbers, compared with the major influx to the South Island which began in 1861, when gold was discovered in the river beds and valleys of Otago. At the beginning of the gold rush the population of Otago was 12,000, but by September 1863 it was already about 50,000. From the gold fields of California, from Victoria in Australia, and from other areas of New Zealand miners, shopkeepers, clerks, innkeepers, and businessmen joined the search for gold. In a single month, March 1863, over 14,000 people arrived at Dunedin. Most of the new arrivals were men – the ratio of women to men in the gold fields was 1:100 in 1863 and still only 18:100 in 1864. The majority of the prospectors came from Australia and moved on when they heard about new finds farther north, but a fair number remained. At the end of the 1860s Otago province was the most populous and prosperous in New Zealand. In total 132,000 people came to New Zealand during the gold rush between 1860 and 1864.

Westland province profited from gold as well. Beginning in 1864, thousands streamed into the almost uninhabited province, mainly from Australia and Otago. As in Australia, Chinese immigrants arrived when the gold deposits were beginning to dry up, and here, too, they encountered prejudice, discrimination, and efforts to limit their immigration through taxation, language tests, special permission forms, and after 1881 with quotas. The government of New Zealand passed the Undesirable Immigrants Exclusion Act, discriminating against Chinese, Indians, and other Asians, in 1919.

In 1870 the gold rush was over, and immigration came to an almost complete stop in all the provinces; the central government now decided on an ambitious program to support immigration, construction, and settlement. These measures helped the population double during the 1870s. Of the over 190,000 immigrants, most received government financial support, while the others were attracted by well-paid jobs in government-sponsored construction projects and by favorable economic factors, such as the availability of government and private loans.

By far the most immigrants came from England, Scotland, and Ireland and thus assimilated easily into the existing ethnic and cultural structure of New Zealand. There were also small groups of Germans (about 2,000), Scandinavians (about 2,500), and Italians. Otago and Canterbury had the most immigrants, with 27,000 and 27,000 respectively. The largest occupational groups were agricultural workers and domestic servants.

The year with the greatest number of immigrants was 1874, when 44,000 entered New Zealand. After that the figures decreased, although in 1879 there were still 24,000 immigrants. In the early 1880s the Long Depression began, a severe economic crisis brought on by excessive dependence on exports, speculation, and high public and private debt. The Depression lasted almost 20 years, and New Zealand became a land of emigration: between 1886 and 1890, for example, the number of emigrants was about 9,000 higher than that of immigrants. A comparison of immigration and emigration figures for 1900 shows that many arriving in New Zealand were not settlers who planned to remain for a long time; similarly, in the period 1921–1924 only 36% of new immigrants indicated a desire to settle permanently. These data suggest that many emigration decisions were not definitive. New Zealand had significant emigration beginning in the 1870s, about 121,000 between 1870 and 1880 alone. In the following decade the number was 172,000, or 90% of the immigration rate, and for the period 1900–1910 it was 250,000, or 75% of the immigration. The main destination of these emigrants was Australia.

In the period from 1870 to 1924, the net immigration to New Zealand, with emigration subtracted, was 357,000. In 1879 the population included 450,000 Europeans, of whom 42% were born in New Zealand; after 1875, however, only 25% of New Zealand's population growth was due to immigration. For the period 1869–1919, the total immigration was 1.36 million, 30% from Great Britain and Ireland, 66% from British possessions, especially Australia, and only 4% from other countries.

After 1880 natural causes of population growth outweighed immigration, and settlement patterns were determined by internal migration. There was a rapid jump in economic development in the farming and agricultural processing industries of the North Island as the bush was cleared for new pasture land, and as new refrigeration technology made it feasible to export meat and milk products as well as wool to distant markets, mainly Great Britain; this was naturally accompanied by a northward movement of the population. A number of small towns were founded to service the agricultural areas, and these attracted migrants as well. Today more than 2 million people live on the North Island, while only about 800,000 live on the South Island.

Immigration in the 20th century depended for the most part on the economic situation. The government promoted limited immigration from 1906 to 1927, and in 1947 subsidized passages for immigrants were reintroduced to fill labor shortages in certain occupational and age groups. This program was limited to immigrants from Great Britain until 1950, but then it was extended to other countries; the principal beneficiaries were about 7,000 Dutch migrants. Another group of over 4,500 came under an agreement with the International Refugee Organisation after World War II, mainly from Poland and Rumania.

Most of the new immigrants settled in the cities, although urbanization in New Zealand had already begun decades earlier and continued at an increasing rate. In 1874 two-thirds of the population still lived on the land, but by the census of

Above: A view of Auckland as it would have been seen by European immigrants in the late 19th century
Below left: The Egerländer immigrants brought musical instruments with them such as the Dudelsack, the Bohemian version of bagpipes, which meant that melodies from the homeland were heard at dances and family celebrations.
Below right: Huge logs were brought down from the hills by way of driving dams and barged to Auckland

1926 the ratio had virtually reversed itself, with 63 % living in cities, and by 1966 the number was over 77 %. The urban population grew from 740,000 in 1926 to 1.4 million in 1961, an increase of 95 %, and in 1965 43 % of the total population lived in the five largest urban centers. In 2006, the population of the South Island exceeded one million for the first time, but the North Island had three times that total, with 1.3 million living in the Auckland region alone, followed by 451,400 in Wellington.

New Zealand's economy in the first half of the 20th century was heavily dependent on exports to Great Britain, and protection of its trading routes was the main strategic reason for its participation in both world wars, quite apart from questions of patriotism and solidarity with the British Empire and Commonwealth. From the 1960s onwards particularly as Britain's priorities changed as it moved to become part of the European Common Market and later the European Union, New Zealand diversified its export markets to such an extent that exports to Britain now form an almost insignificant part of its total exports. In 2002, New Zealand's major trading partner was Australia accounting for 19 % of all merchandise exports, followed by the United States and the European Union (15 % each), and Japan (12 %). Market reforms introduced by successive governments in the 1980s, which abolished import substitution and opened up New Zealand to cheaper imported goods, led to high unemployment in the early 1990s, but under the careful stewardship of Labor-led administrations since 1999 the unemployment rate dropped substantially to 3.6 % in June 2006. Maori and Pacific Islanders were hardest hit by the unemployment of the

1990s. In 1991 the unemployment rate among Maori was 21.8 %; by the end of 2005 it had dropped by two thirds to 7.6 %. Similarly, the unemployment rate among the Pacific Island population had dropped from 25.3 % in 1991 to 6.2 % in 2005.

Unlike Australia, New Zealand has a large Polynesian population, partly due to the strong presence of the indigenous Maori, and partly due to ties that developed between New Zealand and the Pacific Islands in the course of the 20th century. The Maori population was 609,700 in 2003, 17 % of the New Zealand total. The Pacific Island population in 2001 was 231,800, 6.5 % of the total; this included 115,000 Samoans, 51,500 Cook Islanders, and 40,700 Tongans. Changes in New Zealand's immigration policy in 1991, which broke with a long-standing tradition of preference for English-speaking immigrants, saw a large increase in immigration from Asian countries, particularly China, which more than doubled to 237,459 within the ten years to 2001, and now represents over 6 % of the population.

The New Zealand Government made a number of substantial changes to New Zealand's immigration policies in 2002–03, partly in response to concerns expressed by New Zealand parliamentarians about unemployment among recent migrants. The points system for immigration introduced in 1991 had created an entitlement to residence so long as points were met, which turned out to be particularly problematic in the General Skills Category, as the points system granted residence to those who had acquired the requisite number of points whether or not there were jobs available that matched their skills and experience. In November 2003 the General Skills Category was replaced with a Skilled Migrant Category, under which applicants register expressions of interest which are pooled and ranked according to points, those gaining the highest tally being invited to apply for residence only if it is shown that they have the ability to settle successfully and contribute to New Zealand's social and economic development. In addition, stricter English language requirements were introduced. These new policies have led to increased employment among new migrants: in the 2004/5 year, 96 % of those who had entered in the skilled migrant category had jobs.

The largest non-English speaking European immigrant group in New Zealand is the Dutch, with 27,400 in 2001. The Germans, with 8,700, represent the second largest group, and German, because it is, like French, taught in schools, is the sixth most widely spoken language in New Zealand, after English, Maori, Samoan, French, and Cantonese. New Zealand, with its scenic grandeur and its relaxed life-style, enjoys a high profile in Germany both as a desirable place to live and as a tourist destination. German visitors to New Zealand, averaging over 50,000 a year, outnumber those from all other European countries apart from Britain. Like their predecessors they have found the fascination of the "land of the long white cloud" irresistible.

References

Osborne, Charles, (ed.) Australia, New Zealand and the South Pacific. A Handbook. Belfast, 1970.

Cruickshank, D.J. "New Zealand – External Migration." Pp. 179 ff in International Migrations, ed. Walter Willcox and Imre Ferenczi, Vol. II (1929).

Dalziel, Raewyn. "Patterns of Settlement," Pp. 53 ff in New Zealand. Atlas, ed. Ian Ward (Wellington, 1976).

Foster, John. "The Structure of New Zealand Society." Pp. 418 ff in: Australia, New Zealand and the South Pacific. A Handbook, ed. Charles Osborne (Belfast, 1970).

Johnston, R.J. The New Zealanders. How They Live and Work. New York, 1976.

Bade, J. (ed.) The German Connection. Auckland, Oxford University Press, 1993.

Bade, J. (ed.) Out of the Shadow of War. Melbourne, Oxford University Press 1998.

McKinnon, M. (ed.) New Zealand Historical Atlas. Wellington, 1997.

Statistics New Zealand website: www.stats.govt.nz

New Zealand Government web site: www.beehive.govt.nz

Left: Maori chief, 1820
Right: This facial gesture, designed to repel the enemy, belongs to the detailed repertoire of sophisticated Maori rituals and symbols to be found in intricate carvings on Maori marae (meeting houses), which give the history and traditions of the Maori iwi (tribe)

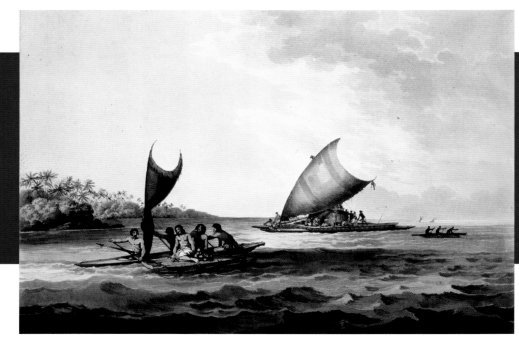

Boats of the Friendly Islands. John Webber, 1809

James Bade

Tonga – The Friendly Isles

The Kingdom of Tonga covers 150 islands, about 30 of which are inhabited, in the south-west Pacific ocean. The three main areas of settlement are the largest island, Tongatapu, which has the capital Nuku'alofa, the Ha'apai group of islands, and the northern group Vava'u, 200 kilometres north of Tongatapu. Its closest neighbors are Fiji to the north-west and Samoa to the north-east. The first contact with Europeans came when a Dutch expedition under Willem Schouten and Jacob Lemaire sighted the northern islands in 1616. They were followed by Tasman (1643) and Cook (1773, 1774, 1777), who named the Ha'apai Islands the "Friendly Isles" after the hospitality extended to him and his crew by the inhabitants; later the name "Friendly Islands" was used by Europeans to cover the whole of the Tongan Group. In 1781, the Spanish frigate Nuestra Señora del Rosario under the command of Captain Francisico Antonio Mourelle visited Vava'u. A number of British and French expeditions followed between 1787 and 1793. Tonga continued to exert a fascination over Europeans well into the 19th century. Visitors to Tonga were impressed not just by the friendliness of the Tongans but also by their fine stature. George Angas's comments on the Tongans in his 1866 study of the Polynesian islands are typical: "They are a fine-looking race, tall, well made, with fully-developed muscles; and the women as well as the men are equally remarkable for their personal beauty."

The earliest sustained contact with Europeans was with missionaries. The Wesleyan missionaries John Thomas and John Hutchinson, who arrived in 1826, were particularly successful. The baptism of Taufa'ahau, the ruler of Ha'apai, in 1831, started a new chapter of Tongan history. Taufa'ahau, who named himself King George Tupou after King George of England and Hanover, about whom he had heard so much from the missionaries, established his authority over Vava'u in 1833, and, after a series of wars, added Tongatapu to his conquests in 1852. Everywhere King George Tupou went, the people converted to Christianity and were baptized. The unity that resulted helped Tonga to retain its independence during the period of European colonisation of the Pacific. Another factor that helped in this regard was the promulgation, with the help of the missionaries, of the first written code of law for Tonga in 1839. The code limited the power of the chiefs and consolidated the King's position.

In the 1850s and the 1860s, European settlers began to establish themselves in Tonga. King George Tupou became closely associated with them. One of the Wesleyan missionaries, Shirley Waldemar Baker, who arrived in Tonga in 1860, assisted him in drawing up a new Code of Laws, which came into force in1862. This Code changed Tongan life radically. It meant an end to serfdom, by abolishing forced labor and compulsory contributions to the Chiefs, made all Tongans, including the Chiefs, subject to the law, and set up a parliament, consisting of Chiefs and representatives of the people. The Code also made it possible for the first time for foreigners to lease land. Such arrangements were confirmed in the Constitution of 1875, which provided for equality between Tongans and Europeans, permitted 21-year leases of town allotments to Europeans and, with the prior approval of Cabinet, the lease to Europeans of bush or plantation lands. The laws of 1862 and 1875 attracted European traders. With the high prices for coconut oil which prevailed at the time, traders came from Great Britain, Germany, Sweden, France, Russia and the United States to set up coconut plantations and establish trading stations. In 1867 the German firm J. C. Godeffroy & Sohn set up business in Tonga, trading in copra, and within a few years it had 24 stations on the Tongan islands. Because of the Godeffroy interest, German private traders set up businesses throughout Tonga, but particularly in Vava'u. In 1875 Captain Schleinitz of the German frigate Gazelle reported that in all three ports of Tonga all ships he met were almost without exception German, and that of seven or eight business houses in Vava'u six were German. Shirley Baker noted in 1875 that "more than three-fourths of the commerce of these islands is in the hands, directly or indirectly, of the German merchants, and especially that of the world-wide-known firm of J. C. Godeffroy & Son." At the turn of the 20th century, half the European population in Tonga was German. In Vava'u alone there were reportedly over a thousand Germans.

One of the European pioneers in Tonga was August Sanft, from Pyritz in Pomerania, who, in 1848, at the age of 28, left his homeland for the New World, arriving first in Boston. Hearing of the gold rush in California, he spent some time in California prospecting and panning for gold, before trying his luck at the gold fields in Queensland, Australia. It was while he was in Australia that he heard of the Pacific Islands and the lucrative coconut oil trade.

Coconut Palms, Tongatapu, 22 April 1889. Watercolor, Lister Family

Above: This 1777 engraving by J. K. Shirwin, after a painting by William Hodges, entitled "The Landing at Middleburgh, one of the Friendly Isles", is an idealistic portrayal of the hospitality extended by the Tongans to Captain Cook and his crew

Below: Europeans of German, British, and Norwegian nationality. Prominent members of the Riechelmann and Whitcomb families attend a picnic on Fafa Island, Tongatapu, put on by the German trading company Vine, Utting and Perston, in 1893

He arrived in Nuki'alofa in 1855, and, after a few years there, leased some land fronting the harbour in Neiafu, Vava'u, where he established a business importing goods from Germany and exporting copra, bananas, vanilla and cotton to Hamburg. His most important partner in this enterprise was Godeffroy & Sohn. He invited Sophie Dörner, from Freiburg im Breisgau, to come to Vava'u, and they were married on her arrival in 1864. They had six children. In the early 1870s they were joined by eight of his nephews: four Sanfts and four Wolfgramms, and Hermann Guttenbeil. Together, they continued the business that August Sanft

had set up and branched out into their own businesses, many of them marrying Tongans. Sanft, Wolfgramm and Guttenbeil are some of the best known European surnames in Tonga today, with many descendants also in Samoa, New Zealand, and Australia. Other names of early German settlers in Tonga which are well known throughout the region are Brähne, Hansen, Hoeft, Riechelmann, Schober, and Schulz.

There was no doubt also that Germans were highly regarded by Tongan royalty. The British Consul in Tonga wrote to the High Commissioner in Suva at the end of 1916, more than two years into World War I, of his

concern for the "German sympathies" of the Tongan King. He commented that the King wore ceremonial decorations supplied by the Germans, and bemoaned the fact that in the King's Palace there were large portraits of the German Emperor, Bismarck, and von Moltke but no portrait of the British King. One could add to this list the fact that the Royal Palace was built in 1867 by the German firm Godeffroy. As far as the Tongan royal family was concerned, however, the most indelible memory concerning the Germans would have been the fact that the body of King George Tupou's son, the Tongan Crown Prince Tevita 'Unga, had been brought back from New Zealand in May 1880 on the German naval frigate Nautilus, and that the ship had stayed for the funeral, adding greatly to the pomp and ceremony of the occasion, including a gun salute fired once a minute and ceremonial marching by forty-five German marines who acted as pallbearers.

Colonial expansion had had drastic effects on the very existence of a number of Pacific nations in the 19th century. Fiji was annexed by Britain in 1874; Germany took large portions of New Guinea and New Britain in the 1880s, and administered Samoa from 1900; France had New Caledonia and part of the New Hebrides. The reason for intervention seemed to be divided government or little government to speak of. The Tongan Code of Law, however, protected Tonga in this respect because it meant that an orderly form of government had been established quite early on. The Constitution of 1875 meant that by that year Tonga had effective code of law, a constitutional monarch, a functioning parliament, and a free and united people. As Charles St Julian told the King in 1855, "With your Kingdom thus governed there can be no pretext whatever for any other power to attack its independence." Because of this unity, suggestions that Spain should annex Vava'u or that Prussia should annex Tongatapu came to nothing.

The main thrust of King George Tupou's foreign policy was to maintain Tonga's independence by endeavouring to gain its recognition by the major European powers. With the continued advice and assistance of Shirley Baker, who became Prime Minister in 1880 (after the death of his predecessor, the King's son, Tevita'Unga), King George Tupou gained treaties of friendship with the three main Pacific powers, starting with Germany in 1876. The German treaty was regarded by Baker as the pivotal one: "Should the German Empire make such a treaty with Tonga," he wrote, "it will be a stepping stone of the acknowledgement of Tonga by other great Powers." The King's words at the 1877 ratification ceremony for the German treaty showed just how much importance he attached to it: "in consequence of the ratification of the Treaty Tonga has become a nation amongst the family of nations […] So it is a full country today and later on we will discuss the many good things that Germany has done for Tonga, of which the most important is that it has lifted up Tonga to the standard of the other countries."

The treaty with Germany led, as had been hoped, to a treaty of friendship with Great Britain (1879). Great Britain had been reluctant to recognise Tonga as this would severely restrict plans for a western Pacific High Commissioner's jurisdiction over "uncivilised" territories. The German treaty forced Britain to recognise Tonga as a "civilised" state, and had another beneficial effect as far as Tonga was concerned, as it led to Bismarck's seeking an assurance that Britain will guarantee the independence of Tonga so long as Germany does so. A treaty of friendship with the United States followed in 1886, which also served to protect Tonga's independence, as it led to American insistence on a neutral zone for Tonga.

While Tonga became, under an agreement with Britain, Germany, and the United States, officially a British protectorate from 1900, King George Tupou II, who succeeded King George Tupou in 1893, refused to sign the clause which gave Britain the power to determine Tongan foreign policy. Tonga remained a self-governing state. Tonga regarded herself as technically "neutral" during World War I, but in 1916, under pressure from the British, declared all German citizens in Tonga as "enemy aliens", and some were interned in New Zealand. During World War II, German "evacuees" from Tonga were similarly interned in New Zealand, but only from 1942 onwards. The treaty of friendship with Britain was revised in 1958, after which the British Consul's approval of Tongan revenue and expenditure was no longer necessary, and in 1970, after which the British purview of Tongan external relations ceased. Tonga was now once again free to pursue its own political alliances,

and, while remaining a member of the Commonwealth, resumed friendly relations with Germany. Great festivities accompanied the commemoration of the one hundredth anniversary of the ratification of the German Treaty of Friendship with Tonga in 1977, and a new treaty of friendship was signed. When the King of Tonga made an official visit to Germany in 1979, the German government donated two vessels to Tonga: the Olovaha, for inter-island travel, and the Fua Kavenga, for Pacific trade. Tonga also ratified the Treaty of Friendship with the United States at its centenary in 1986.

The European presence is still strong in Tonga. Quite apart from the many descendants with European surnames, a considerable number of recent immigrants from Europe are to be found mixing with the local population. Immigrants from Austria, Britain, Germany, Italy, the Netherlands, and Spain, many of them involved in education, tourism, or the hospitality industry, have discovered in Tonga, the Friendly Isles, the South Seas paradise that they were seeking.

References

Angas, George French: Polynesia. London, 1866.

Campbell, Ian C.: Island Kingdom: Tonga Ancient and Modern. Christchurch, Canterbury University Press, 2001.

Cummins, H.G.: Sources of Tongan History. Nuku'alofa, 1972.

Düring, Kurt: Pathways to the Tongan Present. Nuku'alofa, 1990.

Latukefu, Sione: "The Treaty of Friendship and Tongan Sovereignty", in: Renwick, Sovereignty and Indigenous Rights, Wellington, New Zealand, Victoria University Press, 1991.

Rutherford, Noel: Shirley Baker and the King of Tonga. Auckland, 1996.

Voigt, Johannes H: "Tonga und die Deutschen oder: Imperialistische Geburtshilfe für eine Nation im Pazifik", in: Hiery, Die deutsche Südsee 1884–1914: ein Handbuch. Paderborn, 2001.

Wood, A. H: History and Geography of Tonga. Kingston, 1978.

Wood-Ellem, Elizabeth: Queen Salote of Tonga. Auckland, Auckland University Press 2001.

Neiafu, Vava'u Harbour, 1875; showing the German trading station in the foreground and Hermann Guttenbeil's pub in the background

Early photo of the Royal Palace at Nuku'alofa, built in 1867 by the German firm J. C. Godeffroy & Sohn, from New Zealand kauri timber

The main trading station of the German firm Deutsche Handels- und Plantagen-Gesellschaft at the Tongan capital Nuku'alofa, c. 1880, showing the railway built by the company which ran from the wharf to the main building

Germans from Tonga interned on Somes Island, Wellington, New Zealand, from 1942

Kaiser Wilhelm II in Hagenbeck's animal park, Hamburg 1909. As early as 1875 Carl Hagenbeck had opened his first "Völkerschau" (ethnographic show). With the help of animal catchers throughout the world he had brought three Nubians to Europe in 1876, immediately followed by an Eskimo family from Greenland. In 1883 and 1884 he organized a Kalmuck show and a Singhalese, or Ceylon, show. In 1908 Carl Hagenbeck opened an animal park in Stellingen on the outskirts of Hamburg on his own exhibition site, where Somalis, Ethiopians and Bedouins appeared. In order to give the ethnographic shows an air of respectability and attract a more sophisticated audience he had to rise above the fairground atmosphere. The great success of these "Exhibitions of Exotic Peoples" from foreign cultures has to be seen in the context of the expanding exploitation of the colonies and it illustrates the racist spirit of the epoch

Helga Rathjen

... and Divided up the Loot: Africa

Prior to the colonial era, Europeans saw Africa as the dark, wild continent, too inhospitable a place to stay. It was only adventurers who traveled there – businessmen like Adolf Lüderitz, researchers like Heinrich Barth or Gerhard Rohlfs, who sought to satisfy their scientific curiosity and their appetite for conquest in the great expeditions of the 19th century. Their forerunners were the Portuguese explorers of the 15th and 16th centuries. Their search for the sea route to India took them ever further south, along the coast of Africa, until, in 1498, Vasco da Gama finally succeeded in rounding the southern point, the Cape of Good Hope, and sailed around it to be the first European to reach India.

Initially, gold was the most important commodity; following the discovery of America, it was replaced by trade in "ebony" – the transatlantic slave trade in people from Africa. The New World held great treasures for its conquerors, but these had first to be unearthed. Many Native Americans had been wiped out; there were no laborers for the silver mines and sugar cane plantations, and, from the 17th century, for cotton plantations in North America. It made sense to use the apparently infinite reserves of black people in Africa. Over several centuries, African slaves satisfied the insatiable demand for workers needed to exploit and plunder the American continent.

It was the Portuguese who began trading in slaves. In conflict with Spain (their rivals in the apportionment of the world of the 16th century) the Church had granted Portugal the right to take Africa for itself. The slave trade was Portugal's way of compensating itself for the fact that Spain had been granted the entire West, that is, America. Soon, however, a race began between all of the major European trading nations for their share in the most profitable trade of that time. Holland's new status as the leading sea power enabled it to dominate the slave trade during the 16th century and into the beginning of the 17th century; France challenged its position and took the lead during the second half of the 17th century. Ultimately, however, it was Britain, as the ruling sea power of the 17th and 18th centuries, that controled the slave trade. Some Germans (e.g. the Electorate of Brandenburg) also attempted to enter the slave trade, though largely without success, and established several forts in what is now Ghana.

It was not necessary for the Europeans to occupy Africa in order to maintain the slave trade. It was enough to keep strongholds and trading posts on the coasts, manned with just a few European staff, which were protected by the warships that appeared from time to time. Places like Goré, Elmina or São Tomé became synonymous with horror: the slave hunters and traders met there to sell off the "negroes" en masse; the shackled captives then waited for the dreadful slave ships to deport them to America, to a new and wretched life in slavery.

On the African continent, the slave trade triggered a massive, violent wave of migration. The number of Africans deported between the 15th and the 19th century is estimated somewhere between 50 and 200 million. Over a period of four hundred years, the African peoples were robbed of their most productive working population, since they were the most desirable and profitable booty.

The pressure of the hunt for slaves left the continent in a constant state of war. Those living at the coast became slave hunters and traders. Entire tribes fled inland, displacing the tribes that lived there. The less powerful retreated to remote areas or from that point onward made their homes in caves, on marshland, or in the desert; farmers who once had been settled were forced to live as nomads. The national economic and cultural development, such as had existed in the flourishing black African realms until the 16th century, was brought to its knees.

Africa – The Colonial Era

The industrial revolution altered Europe's interest in Africa. British warships enforced the abolition of slavery and replaced the slave

Fortress and slave prison in Keta (Ghana). The fortress, built in 1784, later became an important center for the transatlantic slave trade

Rail and road construction in Cameroon; the left and right photos below show rail tracks, a locomotive and a station, while above right a road is being built. Such measures to develop the infrastructure were an important prerequisite for the colonial exploitation of Africa, as only then was it possible to transport raw materials and agricultural products. Photo undated, probably around 1900

trade with trade in tropical goods for the domestic market.

At the end of the 19th century the European race for raw materials and export markets heralded the age of imperialism. The phase of free trade on the world's oceans came to an end and the European powers set up colonial rule by force. A European infrastructure of settlements, transport routes and economic enterprises was created under colonial administration. The continent was "developed" and "civilized" – what this meant in reality was that Africa was subjugated, made habitable for Europeans and exploited.

Britain
Until the end of the 19th century, Britain controlled the oceans and overseas trade. By the 17th century at the latest it had ousted Spain as the leading sea power and in the 18th century it had also asserted its dominance over its rivals Holland and France. Outposts and forts along the coasts of west and east Africa ensured their involvement in the slave trade. Strategic naval bases controlled all sea routes. Colonies in the New World, in southern Africa, in Oceania with Australia and New Zealand, in Malaysia and Singapore and the "jewel in the imperial crown", the crown colony India, were the foundations of

the incalculable wealth that Britain accumulated during this time and then invested with even greater success in the industrialization of the country. Until the end of the 19th century, there was no rival power that could have refused it unlimited access to every market in the world. Its economic empire reached every corner of the globe, beyond the boundaries of the Empire.

For this reason, Britain favored a free trade policy. The establishment of direct colonial power (India was a special case) was not in its economic and political interests.

The rise of imperialism, that is to say a policy of protectionism and colonial conquest, came at a very bad time for the British Empire: by the end of this development it had exchanged its informal control of the majority of overseas countries for formal control of just a quarter thereof. The competition between the rival states of Europe for commodities, markets, and worldwide recognition opened a race for colonial possession that forced all countries to take action, even Britain. The aim was to take possession of land before anyone else could.

In addition to the Ottoman Empire, which was in the throws of dissolution, it was first and foremost Africa that was up for distribution. Initially, interest focused on Egypt,

which Britain released from French influenc step by step, then took control of before finall annexing it in 1882.

The Anglo-Egyptian expansion polic in Sudan had opened up access to th south for Britain. British colonial player allowed themselves to be seduced by th "Cape to Cairo Dream", which envisione a colonial empire spanning eastern Africa German expansion interests and the estab lishment of a German protectorate, Germa east Africa (1885) in the area that is nov Tanzania, Rwanda and Burundi, disrupte these plans, but the conflict was resolve peaceably by means of a reconcilia tion of interests (Zanzibar in exchange fo Heligoland).

In the south of Africa, the British ha controlled the Cape of Good Hope since 179 and, since 1843, the Natal coast as the bas for trade with east Asia. In 1879, Britai crushed the resistance of the Zulu, and i 1880 the Boer uprising against British sover eignty. In the second Boer war (1899–1902) annexed the Boer republics, after the discov ery of diamonds and gold had phenomenall increased the value of this region. The advanc further northward served the expansion an security of the Cape Colony. In negotiation with Germany, which was claiming south west Africa, and Portugal, which dreamed c a southern African colonial empire stretchin from the west coast (Angola) to the east coas (Mozambique), Britain was able to secure it dominance in southern Africa. In the Cap

Colonies in Africa before World War I

Colony it held the largest and most profitable settlement colony on the African continent.

West Africa had been invaluable as part of the three-way trade with America. Following the end of the slave trade, however, it was less interesting economically for all of the trading powers, and they gradually withdrew. Britain, too, restricted its interest and presence to a small number of outposts along the endless western coast of the continent. Industrialization triggered new interest in west Africa as a supplier of raw materials. Thanks to the exploration of the Niger, trade with inland areas became lucrative for Britain and for its competitor France, because it allowed them to exclude African middlemen from inland trading. The fear that France was going to incorporate the Niger region into its colonial empire was the starting shot for a race for the west African coast, in which Germany also participated. At the Congo Conference in Berlin the British claim to the Niger and its interland was approved. Later, Britain and France agreed on their claims in both east Africa and west Africa.

Holland

In 1652 the United East India Company set up a permanent supply post at the southern tip of Africa for its ships sailing to the coveted spice lands of east Asia. Economic and strategic considerations meant that Calvinist settlers were permitted to immigrate. These first settlers developed into a colony of reformed protestants from Holland, Germany, and France, who, in a similar fashion to the North American pioneers, took native peoples" land from them in the name of God and providence.

Since Britain occupied the Cape in its own strategic trading interests, these Protestants moved as part of the legendary Great Trek (1835–1837) into "wild and dangerous territory"; into religious and political freedom. The trek shaped the founding myth of Apartheid south Africa, while the wars of conquest against the equally legendary Zulu King Chaka, the creation of the Boer republics and later the Boer wars against the British supremacy of the Cape served the ideological assertiveness of the Afrikaans, both against the black majority of the population and against the British upper class in the country.

The 17th century was Holland's golden age. Its wealth was founded on trade, primarily with "East India", but the slave trade with its west African outposts also contributed.

Two white supervisors oversee track laying in a banana plantation in Angola. Alongside the tracks on the left are Indian workers. 32,000 such Indian coolies were brought to Africa between 1896 and 1901 for rail construction work. Workers from Asia were brought in to expedite the export of colonial goods from Africa. Photo around 1890

Holland's downfall began in the 18th century when it had to defend itself first against British then against French attacks on its sea power, leading it ultimately to lose its power. It ceased entirely to play a role in Africa.

France

With the end of the Napoleonic reign the colonial empire of the former French superpower shrank. The economy stagnated in restoration France with the return of the monarchy and the aristocracy. Industrialization occurred in small businesses and family operations with little capital, emitting little impulse for growth. As a result, France was without the economic motor needed for imperialistic expansion.

Nevertheless it developed into the second-largest colonial power, particularly in Africa and Indochina.

In 1871, France lost the war against Germany and subsequently Alsace-Lorraine. This national shame called for "revenge – the recapture of the lost provinces". France had, in fact, lost its role as the continental superpower and the politicians put their faith in a policy of "overseas compensation for Alsace-Lorraine". France sought a new role as the Mediterranean power. The dissolution of the Ottoman Empire had left a power vacuum in the southern and eastern Mediterranean that France intended to fill – in fierce competition with Britain, whose ambitions were similar. This was why France relocated its power politics to North Africa. Maghreb was to form the center of its new overseas empire.

Ever since the Napoleonic campaign, France had seen itself as the protector of Egypt, which had by that time freed itself from the sovereignty of the Ottoman Empire. The Egyptian rulers were following their own policy of expansion and modernisation, which also included the construction of the Suez canal (1869). War, corruption, and public spending were financed using European government loans; national debt forced the country into dependency on France and Britain and finally resulted in the loss of its sovereignty.

France applied a similar policy in Tunisia. With the help of exorbitant government loans, the government became a dependent debtor and finally succumbed to colonial rule.

Algeria (that is, the Mediterranean coast of the country) had been under French occupation since 1830, not for any colonial purpose, but to divert attention from the domestic political issues thrown up by the July revolution. The colony initially served

"The blessing of emigration to the Cape of (lost) Good Hope. Half roasted and eaten by the Hottentots." Anti-emigration caricature, Germany, around 1819

The Congo Conference in Berlin (1884)

In the 15th and 16th centuries Portuga ruled the west coast of Africa. In th 19th century it barely played a role as colonial power, even though its rights i the Portuguese colonies by birthright wer recognized (Wesseling). The coast along th Congo delta had once been at the center of the slave trade; since then, every tradin power held outposts and interests there.

In 1876 King Leopold of Belgium, one of the richest men in the world, decided that h had to buy a colony somewhere in the worl one that was as profitable as the Dutch "Ea: India". It was by chance that his hungry eye fell on that huge area of no man's land. Fror then on, under the guise of philanthropy an science, he put all of his energy into acquir ing the Congo.

At the same time, the attention of al Europeans began to focus on the Conge due to the promising accounts of this are given by legendary explorers such as Davi Livingstone, Henry M. Stanley and Pierre I de Brazza. In colonial policy, the Congo repre sented a huge system of tributaries leadin into one of the greatest and most dangerou currents of the earth, which symbolized th colonial gateway to the inaccessible inlan areas of Central Africa.

To prevent an agreement between Portuga and Britain on the exploitation of the Cong region, the German Imperial Chancelle Bismarck convened a conference in 188⁄ which went down in history as the Berli Congo Conference. The configuration of th interests of the major powers at the conferenc meant that King Leopold was able to satisf his greed. After promising free trading right for all, he took possession of the Free State of Congo. He soon broke his promises, but th remained as of little consequence as did hi unilateral expansion of the colony to includ Katanga. Only later did it become clear tha Leopold was sitting on a goldmine: firs natural rubber promised riches, then mor and more mineral resources were discovered above all in east Congo. To the present da campaigns to pillage these riches and deva tating bloodbaths have ensued. The rapidl growing industrial demand for rubber brough Leopold massive profits. These were the frui of such merciless and cruel exploitation of th peoples of the Congo that there was a publi

the deportation of the revolutionaries of 1848. In 1871 it was expanded. 100,000 hectares of land were used to compensate those from the Alsace and Lorraine who were willing to emigrate for the loss of their homes. Algeria became an important settlement colony and was awarded the status of "département".

Intellectuals and the military supported this reorientation of French policy against the backdrop of worsening social tensions in France. As in Germany, the purpose of the colonies was to relieve domestic political pressure that France had come under as a result of the Paris Commune of 1871.

France's North African colonial empire was the outcome of a deal between the European superpowers. The deal concerned "the Orient issue", that is to say, the dissolution of the Ottoman Empire and the distribution of the inheritance of the "sick man of the Bosporus" among the European powers. The various interests and desires were discussed at the Berlin Congress of 1878; because Britain claimed Egypt as its own, and was in fact given it on account of its political power, France's sphere of interest in Tunisia and Maghreb (which was expanded in 1912 to include Morocco) was recognized in its entirety.

The French Africa policy developed from its ambitions regarding Maghreb. Black Africa

was originally seen as the hinterland of the North African empire, whose southern borders were undefined.

The colonial players in the parti colonial went further still, dreaming of the Trans-Sahara region and the Sudan, which at that time referred to the entire area between the Sahara and the Central African rainforest, from the west coast to the east coast (approximately the same as the Sahel region). Imperialism found its way into government policy. Sudan was seen as a new Canada, or a "French India" with infinite resources and millions of people, who were all potential customers for French products. Starting from the coastal colony of Senegal in 1880, western Sudan was put under military administration with the aim of linking together Algeria in North Africa, the French Congo in Central Africa and west Africa into a single colonial empire. Almost continuous war against the well-organized resistance of the peoples of the Sahara and the Sahel pushed expansion forward.

Rivalry with Britain and the desire for a colonial empire defined the direction of the development. Ultimately, France's military expansion policy was victorious over the British strategy of power through trade, and France became the leading colonial power in west Africa.

Poster of the "German East Africa Line" shipping company founded in 1890 in conjunction with the acquisition of the German East Africa colony

Contracts with African leaders that had been concluded under questionable conditions were pulled out of pockets and with a wink of the eye accepted as validation of the claims, while the European leaders were agreed that such "papers with Negro crosses on them" (Bismarck) were as unimportant as the people whose land and lives were being disposed of here. The contractual agreements regarding European territorial claims were of course accepted as valid confirmation of the formal division of Africa in the last few years of the 19th century.

Germany

Britain and France were the true colonial leaders in Africa. Germany played a subordinate role in the colonial concert. The colonial estates that it had been able to win as a late entry in the colonial race were unimportant in economic terms and short-lived, and between 1914 and 1918 the German colonial empire ceased to exist entirely. But it left deep scars, both in Germany and in the former colonies.

The idea of colonies had already come up during German mercantilism. During the pre-March era, before a German state had been established, the champions of the German Nation were enthusing about the expansion of German greatness – admittedly,

they were thinking not of Africa, but the Balkan states and the Levant. The revolutionaries of 1848 also included colonial ownership on their list of demands.

But concrete colonial efforts were hesitant, reluctant and late in coming. The upper middle-class merchants were open to free trade since they needed access to all markets and could not risk a protectionist German policy featuring protective duties that would provoke Britain, as the dominant economic power, to take protectionist countermeasures. Meanwhile, the dominant power elite in Germany of aristocratic large-scale farmers saw no use for foreign properties. The economic and strategic interests lay in central Europe. Under Prussia's leadership, the political and economic unification of Germany, the formation of the Reich in 1871, and the development of a new balance between the superpowers, which the new power block in the center of Europe had shifted, were now on the agenda.

The imperialistic claims of power which went on to take the form of the annexation of colonies in the 1880s, developed with the industrialization of Germany. Only since the 1840s, that is, relatively late on, did rapid industrial growth begin. This growth was, however, disrupted several times by economic

outcry even in Europe, which was accustomed to colonial brutality. As a result Leopold saw no option but to assign the colony to the state of Belgium.

Contrary to popular belief, the Congo Conference itself did not divide up all of Africa, but it became a symbol of and a prelude to an imperialistic policy of division. While the claims of the European powers to the various specific sections of coastal Africa were geographically defined and to some extent recognized, the claims to the hinterland in each led to massive conflicts of interest between the powers. The vague ideas regarding this unknown land made it even more difficult to define the interest zones; often it was not at all clear where, for example, the mountains that had been designated as the border actually lay or which way the river declared as the border actually flowed. This necessitated exploratory expeditions, which were intended not only to clarify the geography but primarily to further the occupation of unknown and remote areas, in order, through an on site presence, to add weight to territorial claims and to afford them an image of legality.

Cameroonian soldiers ("askaris") on exercise. The illustration shows the hierarchy: white officers in white dress (on horseback and on foot) march in front of the black auxiliaries. Undated photo, probably around 1890

downturns. The economic crises and a structural agricultural crisis sent shockwaves, causing fear and anxiety in the face of the powerful societal upheaval that people were experiencing. The number of industrial workers was growing at the same rate as the economy. Since the middle of the century a militant and class-aware proletariat with revolutionary potential had been taking shape.

Contrary to the new economic and societal conditions the pre-industrialized class of landowners with large estates, the "landed nobility from beyond the Elbe", held doggedly to the outdated power structures and were not prepared to share power, not even with the middle classes, as they made very clear in the restoration following the 1848 revolution.

The push for overseas expansion during the last decades of the century served as a "conservative distraction and domestication policy" (Hans-Ulrich Wehler) to deflect the reform efforts of the liberals or the social democrats, which were threatening the leadership. Among the middle classes there was also a need for a "safety vent" for the "overheated steam kettle" of social tension: the steam was to be let off in the form of emigration to the colonies.

Settlement colonies were at the center of the colonial idea in Germany from the outset.

German colonies were seen as the answer to mass emigration to America. German colonies were to flourish in "exchange and change" and increase Germany's wealth; they were to carry "German customs and culture" out into the world. The German essence was to cure the world.

Wo fern im Afrikanerland die deutsche Flagge weht,
Die Palme in der Sonnenglut so stolz und prangend steht,
Wo frei und wahr der deutsche Ahr
Die Flügel frei und kraftvoll schlägt,
Sind wir die Wehr,
Die deutsche Ehr,
Die deutsche Sitte trägt.

Far away in Africa the German flag flies,
where the palm trees stand tall and proud in the blazing heat of the sun,
where the German eagle
beats its wings strong and free,
we are the force,
the German glory,
carrying the German tradition.

(Friedrich Clark)

Division of the world. Zeus to Germania: "And where were you when the world was divided up?" Drawing from a German magazine

Harvesting bananas in Cameroon. Note the white plantation owner in boots and the barefooted black workers. The AFC (African Fruit Company) operated large banana plantations as for example near Tiko. In 1913 the AFC's banana harvest yielded 12,000 bushels. Undated photo, probably around 1900

The middle-class fear of the Socialists mixed with national enthusiasm and then with the nationalist superpower fantasies of the German Reich, and was finally expressed in calls for the proverbial "place in the sun" for Germany's worldwide recognition and glory.

With the economic crises, monetary motives joined the ideological interests for an active colonial policy. The protection of German industry (and the rural economy) against foreign competition was the objective of a new German economic policy; free trade policy was replaced with protectionism in the form of protective duties. The major economic crisis of 1873 in particular raised the issue of secure markets for industrial products and for access to raw materials. The acquisition of colonies thus became economically desirable.

Colonial associations were set up throughout the Reich and were later combined in the German Colonial Society. A broad base from the middle class helped the professional overseas interests of merchants, entrepreneurs and bankers develop a propaganda that fitted perfectly with the conservative-nationalist state ideology.

As an old-fashioned family and homeland idyll, "the colony" penetrated deep into the German psyche, which saw in the African bush the lost peasant world of pre-industrialized Europe, satisfying the middle class's romantic desires for a perfect world and nature. This was not seen as a contradiction to the aggressive vision of the "German nation, driven by the fight for survival, by the desire to expand the race, whose native soil is becoming too crowded", which bestowed upon the colonial efforts the blessing of a greater power. Despite heir lack of economic and strategic importance, far beyond the Empire, in the Weimar Republic and during National Socialist rule, "our colonies" became an evocative symbol and a flagship for chauvinistic fantasies of world domination.

The German Colonies in Africa

The imperialistic balance of power prevented German wishes from being satisfied with colonial property in east Asia or South America; not even Kiao-Chau in China fulfiled its colonial dreams. By the end of the colonial race, there were only a few, less desirable, territories left over in Africa and in the South Pacific.

In 1884/85 "Togoland" and Cameroon on the west Coast, German south-west Africa (now Namibia) and German east Africa (now Tanzania) were annexed as "German protectorates" in Africa.

Germany's defeat in the First World War also brought an end to German colonial rule. The German population in the colonies was interned by the victorious powers and deported to Germany. German south-west Africa was declared a League of Nations Mandate territory, with South Africa responsible for its administration. The country was not able to free itself of this until the 1980s. Parts of Togo

Voermann Line poster, 1927

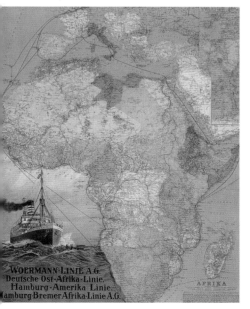

Cutting sisal agaves in German East Africa. Photo around 1900

and Cameroon came under French rule, while German east Africa and south-western Togo came under British rule.

In the 1920s missionaries and merchants were allowed to return to their work in the former German areas. In south-west Africa, the settlement colony of German descent was allowed to keep its trade and agriculture. In 1944 a large proportion of Germans were extradited for their open support of the Nazi regime; in 1948 they were allowed to return. South Africa assured them – like all white colonial settlers – superiority and privileges in the Apartheid system of Namibia, to which the Germans had made a significant contribution.

However, the colonial propagandists' hopes for flourishing German settlement colonies were dashed.

Economically, Togo was of interest primarily as a supplier of palm kernels; in industry, palm oil, which was cheaper, replaced fish oil for use as machine oil. Palm kernels were collected by African hunter-gatherers or were grown on tiny plantations. The colonial administration thus had an interest in maintaining the native small-scale farmers and its policy regarding Germans wishing to immigrate was decidedly restrictive: before they were allowed into the country, those who came from Europe had either to produce an employment contract or to pay a deposit for a return ticket. There were only a few, largely unsuccessful attempts to set up plantations

(cocoa, coffee, cotton). Only 2% of the Germans in Togo were identified as plantation owners.

The Togolese were employed in the colonial administration and in the colonial army. Catholic and Protestant missionary societies had set up a school system, where Africans learnt everything they needed to know to serve the Whites. The merchant's outposts made do with only a few German members of staff.

In addition to the merchants, the Whites who lived in the colony were missionaries and deacons, as well as some officers and administrative workers, most of whom did not have families and were there on a temporary basis. In total, in 1913 there were no more than 320 Germans living in Togo.

In contrast, in less than three years Cameroon became Germany's most important plantation colony, above all for rubber production. This did not, however, attract migrants.

The plantations, in which major investors with a large amount of capital held the shares, divided the large concessions of land granted by the colonial administration amongst themselves. The shareholders in Germany left the running of the plantations in the hands of a manager. Owners of small or medium-sized plantations, who managed their businesses themselves, were able to survive only in the less profitable niche markets, at best.

As was the case in Togo, the class of German colonial officials and the military remained small. In order to keep down the

Above: Hendrik Witboi, chief of the Nama, and his men, 1894, prior to the attack by German troops
Below: "Africa in chains" – survivors of the Herero uprising 1907. The colonial war between German troops and the Herero and Nama peoples in German South-West Africa (today Namibia) in the years from 1904 to 1908 is referred to as the Herero and Nama uprising

occupation costs, which regularly exceeded the income of the colonial administration, all lower positions in the military and the administrative offices were staffed by low-paid Africans. As a result the German colonial population also remained low until the outbreak of war in 1914.

Only in the areas in the south that could be used for agricultural purposes (German south-west Africa, now Namibia) and the east of the continent (German east Africa, later Tanganyika, now Tanzania) did real emigrant settlement colonies develop. Nonetheless, 5,300 Europeans were registered in German east Africa in 1913. The export of coffee, cotton, peanuts and sisal, grown on the fertile soil that once belonged to the native Moshi in the north of the country, was quite profitable for the plantation owners. But here, too, the major investors dominated – much to the chagrin of the lower middle classes and the middle-class members of the colonial societies, who had supported the settlement of middle-class owners and as a result had become embroiled in serious disputes with the large investors. The figures illustrate the outcome of the dispute: the companies divvied up the land among themselves; only a minority of 900 planters and plantation workers were registered amongst more than 5,000 white residents.

German South-West Africa

German south-west Africa became a colony after the explorer and merchant Adolf Lüderitz, from Bremen, had wangled by fraudulent means a number of landholdings on the west coast of southern Africa from Namibian tribal chiefs, for which, through sheer stubbornness he managed to get German protection from the Reich government in 1884.

Initially, "Lüderitz's sandpit" offered few prospects for economic exploitation or settlement. The adventurous diamond hunter's hopes of valuable mineral reserves had been dashed (diamonds were not found until 1907). Furthermore, at this point the resident African peoples were still in charge of their own land.

Settlers and the "protection force" had arrived in an area in which the Nama and Herero tribes ruled, battling out their own age-old rivalries. They had concluded the Treaties of Protection of 1884 with the Germans to achieve their own goals.

The German colonial policy attempted by way of a "divide and conquer" policy, and with the help of a small number of German soldiers from the protection force, to set up a German power between the rival tribes, which the latter recognized sometimes more and sometimes less. Between them, on "Crown land" claimed by the Reich, a handful of German emigrants attempted to settle. The dry soil was suitable only for livestock and, to a small degree, for horticulture. Tradesmen and traders joined the livestock farmers, and were followed by administrative officers, soldiers, and missionaries.

The small troop of German settlers (1,500 in 1896) had a difficult time making a living in the face of competition from the Herero shepherds in the market and for land. In many ways, including the provision of wage laborers they were dependent on the good will of their African neighbors, who, incidentally, were more than capable of defending themselves against abuses by the Whites.

Within just a few years the balance of power had been reversed. In 1896 a cattle plague devastated practically all of the Herero's cattle herds, robbing them of their livelihood. Worse still, their autonomy and cultural identity, which were based on their livestock, had been destroyed. They became dependent on the Whites for their wages.

An increasingly aggressive and racist "policy of mastery" replaced the indirect rule that had left the Africans with autonomy in their internal affairs, and the policy of negotiating, which the colonial administration had been forced to observe due to the balance of powers, was abandoned.

The colonial government's plans to set up reservations were taken by the Herero and the Nama as a signal for the forcible confiscation of their land.

And with good reason – the settlers took advantage of the crisis to steal land and for uninhibited exploitation. Their behavior became increasingly racist and violent. The African's disintegrating family groups were unable to prevent the mistreatment and assaults committed by the Germans, including sexual assaults, while the justice system protected only the Whites.

A Herero uprising against colonial rule began with an attack on settlers and soldiers in January 1904. The Nama joined the rebellion in October 1904. Both tribes were almost wiped out in a monstrously brutal and systematic war of extermination. Following this genocide the white settlers pursued a colonial policy aimed at the complete subjugation of the survivors.

The land and all of the native people's possessions were confiscated. Large tribal units were broken up, the clans were torn apart and individual families were forcibly resettled, in order to extinguish their cultural and social identity.

The central task of colonial policy is "wherever possible to disrobe the Herero of his folklore and national peculiarities and to gradually merge him with the other natives into a single colored working class" (Colonial Commissioner Paul Rohrbach).

At the same time, their livelihoods were destroyed. Africans were allowed to own only a restricted amount of land and livestock and had to have their property approved, forcing them to scrape a living as laborers.

"The inferior native culture must give way in power and ownership on every inch

On a German cattle farm in "Southwest" (Namibia), before World War II

of African soil in which German culture (which is, per se, better and more invaluable to the development of the world and mankind) can thrive; in this we must persist" (Paul Rohrbach).

In order to create the desired reservoir of cheap workers at one's disposal, each African was required to enter into an employment contract with a white settler. He was required at every turn to prove this working relationship by displaying a work log and identity card. These requirements were an early precursor to the pass laws of the Apartheid regime in South Africa. The colonial legislature created the legal and political framework for complete regulation, control and supervision of the black population – not only in German south-west Africa, but in all of the German colonies.

An aggressive and cruel form of racism formed the general ideological consensus; the settlers reclaimed their rule as members of the "master race". The African's complete lack of rights afforded every white man unlimited power: everyone had police power over the Blacks. The unrestricted and cruel rule over the African workers using the rhinoceros-hide whip was referred to cynically as "training the negro for work", thereby stylizing it into a civilizing mission.

Thanks to the appropriation of African land and African workers, the settlers were able to advance to rationalized extensive livestock rearing. From 1907 they operated successful breeding programmes for Karakul

sheep and ostriches; later came wine and fruit cultivation.... our new land shall be German, its residents shall be German, German its conventions and customs, German its thought and feelings ...(German Colonial Newspaper 1912).

Colonial society in German south-west Africa presented itself to the outside world as an idyllic community for all Germans; it was essential that the black population looked up to every white person as their master. By virtue of their nationality and skin color, even emigrants from the lower classes were able to graduate into the societal elite; even the poorest white man could act the lord over black subjects. In fact, the class barriers of Wilhelminian society had by no means been removed in the colonies, and many a settler complained of the "extreme caste spirit" of the upper classes.

The white supremacy, which was, of course, based on the racist consensus of all settlers, would have been threatened if individual white settlers were to withdraw from this understanding. Those who contravened the racist code of conduct and treated Africans like humans were deemed to be "verkaffert" (the German version of "going native" in Africa) and were expelled from white society. This affected mostly men who married African women (instead of just raping them). "Mixed marriages" posed a further problem for colonial society, since "the white minority must assert their rule over the colored by maintaining the purity of their race" (von Lindequist, Governor of German south-west Africa). From 1905 colonial legislation was passed which first prohibited "mixed marriages", then annulled marriages that had been entered into earlier. In reality, "mixed marriages" were unimportant in practical terms: in German south-west Africa a total of 47 German men were married to Africans. There were, however, a large number of "half-breed" offspring; many men kept up more or less forced sexual relationships with African women. "The hard-won land was in danger of going completely native... for a growing race of half-breeds was threatening to stifle German heritage from the outset" (Adda von Liliencron, Chair of the German Colonial Women's League, 1905).

Pursuant to the patriarchal family law that applied at that time, a child inherited the nationality of its father. It was unthinkable that "half-breed children" and "bastards" could be German. The prohibition of "mixed marriages" marked these children as "natives" without civil rights. It refused the mothers any claims against the fathers and those men that stayed in their marriages in spite of all this were excluded from the social life of the settlers. As long as the lineage from a member of a primitive people can be proven, the offspring is a native, by virtue of his blood", held the High Court in Windhoek in 1907.

Concerns about "keeping the race pure" led the Women's League to form a plan. The aristocratic middle-class association of colonial propagandists in the German Colonial Society saw it as their task to prevent "mixed marriages" and organized their own emigration campaigns. The men in the colonies, who, for the most part, were single, should be kept away from African women under the watchful eyes of wives and brides; this would also avert the risk of them "going native". "The man builds the house, the woman keeps it! This is even more true than ever today for our German colonies. If only we could attract you, you young German women and girls, to come to our nascent Germany overseas. ... It truly is a happy fate to be able to play a part in this triumphal procession of German culture." (Adda von Liliencron).

Fiancées and wives were sent over to join their men and brides were recruited for the unmarried men in the colonies from amongst those women in the Reich willing to marry and emigrate. These "Christmas hampers" (as they were called in German south-west Africa) were sent primarily to Namibia. The women were mostly servants, who jostled for a place on the waiting lists of the German Colonial Society. Africa offered them an opportunity to climb the social ladder that they could only dream of in their poorly-paid and dependent (in all senses of the word) employment in Germany.

The women who fought for the emigration of women in the Colonial Society did so "in the German national interest" of course, but also in their own interests: educated women in particular hoped that this would result in a move away from the middle-class patriarchal disregard for women. They envisioned an image of women that, despite being grounded in outdated gender roles, included demands for emancipation. They saw the female emigrant as a pioneer in the wilderness, who would confidently take her place at the side of her man as an equal partner, or even lead an independent life as a single woman.

Zambia 2008

Colonial Migrants

It is a little-known fact that since the 19th century some Africans from the colonies (albeit a very small number), most of them from Togo, lived in Germany. They were sent to be trained as craftsmen or missionaries or to work as servants for colonial officers who had returned to Germany. Some were used as "wild men" who had to act out the bush life of native Africans in ethnographic shows (Völkerschauen), which were put on by Hagenbeck and others. The majority of them returned or, like the people in the ethnographic shows, died in Germany, but a handful of them settled here and married German women. Until the beginning of the 20th century, the education of a culturally adapted African elite in the service of the colonial administration was desired. The intention certainly was not for these people to stay and even "mix" with German women. As colonial rule stabilized at the beginning of the 20th century, the authorities prohibited such relocation. The colonial migrants were excluded from German society. German women who were guilty of "Rassenschande" (racial defilement) were stigmatized. Spouses were not allowed to move to the home colony of their husbands – the "natives" were not to think that white women were an option.

At the end of the colonial age, probably around 500 Africans and their descendants were living in Germany. Following the loss of the colonies they served as "German negroes", that is, as loyal servants, to legitimize the colonial revisionist policy.

They and their descendants retained this function in Nazi Germany. While the Nuremberg race laws, which denied them citizenship and annuled their marriages, applied to them they were not persecuted but were instead integrated into the illusory colonial world as directed by the Ministry for Propaganda, and only some of them were able to avoid this. As the living reminder of past colonial glory people who had been away from Africa for a long time, or who were actually born in Germany, were removed from their surroundings and virtually interned in "mobile negro villages". They were still needed and were sent on tour with a "German Africa show" as propagandists for future German colonial power.

The history of the German colonies shows how colonial rule systematically and intentionally destroyed the autonomy and sovereignty of the colonized lands and undermined their economic and cultural livelihood, with the sole objective of appropriating any and all resources that could be profitably used. In this way the native peoples were forcibly incorporated into the capitalist global economy.

Even then they were the losers in globalization. The global economic structures, which unilaterally favor the developed countries, have not been overcome to this day. Poverty and instability rule those parts of the world that were once colonized and this affects Africa in particular. One of the many dramatic consequences is the uprooting of millions of people. More than 40 million people were forced to flee from their homes last year (UN High Commissioner of Refugees, 2008); over 70 million people emigrated from their home country, because it was unable to provide them with a livelihood (Global Commission on International Migration, 2008) – and the trend is growing. This is why the former colonial powers are now building up "Fortress Europe" and are raising the ramparts ever higher to fend off further uninvited and unwanted immigrants, who are standing at "our" doorstep. But today's emigrants, who risk their lives to get to Europe, teach us that the global links created during the colonial age cannot be undone. As long as the blatant inequality in the global distribution of chances of survival and security continues, people will rush to those areas that promise survival and safety. This, too, is our colonial heritage.

Literature

Gründer, Horst, Geschichte der deutschen Kolonien, Paderborn, 2004

Hinz, Manfred O.; Meier, Arnim; Patemann, Helgard (eds.): Weiß auf Schwarz. 100 Jahre Einmischung in Afrika. Deutscher Kolonialismus und afrikanischer Widerstand. Berlin, 1984

Hücking, Renate; Launer, Ekkehard: Aus Menschen Neger machen. Wie sich das Handelshaus Woermann an Afrika entwickelt hat. Hamburg, 1986

Ki-Zerbo, Joseph: Die Geschichte Schwarzafrikas, Frankfurt 1984

Kundrus Birthe, Phantasiereiche. Zur Kulturgeschichte des deutschen Kolonialismus, Frankfurt 2003

Mamozei, Martha, Herrenmenschen. Frauen im deutschen Kolonialismus, Reinbek 1982

Mayer, Hans; Weiss, Ruth (eds.): Africa den Europäern! Von der Berliner Kongokonferenz 1884 ins Afrika der neuen Kolonisation. Wuppertal, 1984

Walgenbach, Katharina, Die weiße Frau als Trägerin deutscher Kultur, Koloniale Diskurse über Geschlecht, "Rasse" und Klasse im Kaiserreich, Frankfurt 2005

Wesseling, Hendrik, Teile und herrsche. Die Aufteilung Afrikas 1880–1014, Stuttgart 1999

Impressions of Africa from a village in Zambia 2008

English actor Charlie Chaplin, starring in the film classic "The Immigrant" (1917). The film highlights the misery of the emigrants traveling steerage, the overwhelming joy when seeing the Statue of Liberty, but also the panic they felt because they still had to pass the immigration controls at Ellis Island. Ironically, Chaplin's own mother was detained at Ellis Island, the doctors certified her as mentally deficient and feeble-minded. She had failed the mental tests. She was released and allowed to enter the United States only after her son posted a bond guaranteeing that she would not become a public charge

Elliott R. Barkan

Crossing the Atlantic Rim: European Immigration to the United States after World War One

The Interwar Years: The Rise of Fascism and American Isolationism

Noon, January 30, 1933, the day that should truly live in infamy – the day that changed the history of Europe if not of much of the western world, the day Adolf Hitler was appointed chancellor of Germany. Of course, that transformative moment and its impact on European immigration to the United States did not occur in a vacuum, for the United States had radically altered its immigration laws nine years earlier, followed by the onset of the Great Depression in 1929 that took hold of Europe and the United States. During the next decade American public opinion would prove inhospitable to Europeans fleeing fascist governments, and Germany would initiate World War Two. Those events proved to be so cataclysmic that the ultimate consequences would not only be unimaginable upheavals in Europe but also, as their legacy, a series of revolutions in European and American immigration. The changes dramatically compelled both Europe and America to embark on paths marked by new policies and new migration patterns. Yet, no one could have foreseen the magnitude of the slide of Europe's migration to the United States over the next six-seven decades (Table 1)

The 20th century history of European immigration can best be appreciated as one that was refashioned by a half-dozen series of jolts and redirections that amounted to watershed, even revolutionary, developments. The first was the product of America's Immigration Act of May 1924 (Johnson Reed Act), which cemented a quota system that was intended to better screen who would be admitted from outside the Americas. It particularly reaffirmed the primacy of northern and western European immigration by severely curbing that from eastern and southern Europe and by leaving

Table 1 European migration to America, 1921–2006

Year*	Europeans admitted to the U.S.	Europe's portion of total U.S. immigration
1921	652,364	81.0 %
1926	155,562	51.1 %
1936	23,480	64.6 %
1946	64,877	59.7 %
1956	175,883	54.7 %
1966	125,023	38.7 %
1976	72,411	18.2 %
1986	62,512	10.4 %
1996	147,581	16.1 %
2006	164,285	13.0 %

* Figures for 1921 and 1931 are based on Country of Last Residence; all the rest are based on Country of Birth

few slots for those outside Europe. The formula was based on a total annual admission of 154,277 quota migrants (versus the several earlier years in the century when more than one million were admitted annually) and was based on 2 % of the distribution of the foreign-born population in 1890 – before the heavy influx of southern and east Europeans. Great Britain was given 65,721 visa slots, Germany 25,957, Ireland 17,853, France 3,086, Italy 5,677, Poland 6,524, Czechoslovakia 2,874, and the U.S.S.R. 2,798. (Only small changes were made to some figures in 1929, but the total to be admitted after that time was shaved to 153,774).

The results were immediately apparent. northern and western European immigration shot up from 17.4 % of all newcomers (1911–20) to 40 % (1925–30). At the same time the volume of southern and eastern European migration plummeted from 59 % to 13 %. However, the onset of the

Jewish emigration from Germany, February 1, 1933 to March 31, 1936: total 93,000 (to Palestine, Overseas, Europe, return migration to eastern Europe)

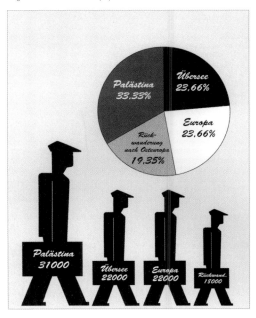

Depression in the early 1930s altered the situation considerably. Between 1930 and 1941 almost 822,000 persons were admitted to the United States but over 527,500 foreigners (64%) departed, mostly for European destinations (Table 2). For the only time since federal records have been kept (1820–21), four years passed (fiscal years 1932–35) with 138,900 more foreigners leaving than arriving, especially for the United Kingdom and Ireland.

The responses ranged from more leaving America than arriving (English and Irish) to departures equaling three-fourths the number of admitted Greeks, half the number of arriving Poles, and two-fifths of Italian immigrants. The Jewish figures, beginning most dramatically in fiscal year (f.y.) 1934, starkly illustrate the increasingly desperate efforts of the Jews to escape the Nazis. From a low of 2,372 admissions in 1933 their numbers steadily rose to 43,450 in f.y. 1939. Their minimal departures from the United States – some apparently to Europe, others to Palestine – began at 319 (1931) and slid to just 150 in 1940. These selected examples of the most severe economic years corroborate the overall pattern, for 1932–36 were the bleakest years, driving many to return to their homelands. Only the English and Irish continued to depart America in greater numbers after 1936. The increase in the number of those departing was most conspicuous among Germans, particularly among those who had come to America after World War I and who were drawn to Germany's revival. Alternatively, the combination of President Roosevelt's New Deal and growing concerns among Italians about Mussolini's fascist program and invasion of Ethiopia appears to have limited the appeal of abandoning America for Italy.

In fact, the German/Austrian data rather dramatically illustrated the probable split between leaving and staying (Austria having been occupied by Germans in the March 1938 Anschluss), as Hitler moved toward rearmament and more aggressive actions against Jews, Gypsies, political and cultural radicals, and neighboring countries. Many German Jews had not expected conditions to worsen much following the burning of the Reichstag in February 1933 and the boycotting of Jewish businesses that spring. However, the political climate did steadily deteriorate that year. Some 15,000

Table 2 European Immigration and Emigration, 1931-1940

Selected Countries of Last Residence	Admissions to the U.S.*	Admissions to Europe	Departures/ Admissions
England	31,573	60,296	191.0 %
Germans/Austrians	117,621	37,170	31.6 %
Irish	10,973	12,800	117.0 %
Italians	68,028	27,874	41.0 %
Greeks	9,119	6,854	75.0 %
Poles	17,026	9,105	53.5 %
Jews (»Hebrews«)**	137,525	2,925	2.0 %

*   Admissions were those with visas for lawful permanent residence. Data for departures provide country of intended residence, not the ethnicity of those departing; we assume most were returning to their homelands.

** Data on Jews drawn from table based on "race" of persons arriving and departing. The large numbers of arriving Jews and Germans/Austrians therefore considerably overlapped. Malcolm J. Proudfoot reported an estimate of Jewish refugees admitted by the United States, 1933–39, at 93,548 out of 319,800 who relocated from "Greater Germany" to countries outside German control (29%). About 101,100 more went to countries subsequently under Germany control. However, he also noted that, for 1933–39, there were an estimated 136,000 Jewish refugees going to America out of 1.152 million refugees from the larger sphere of Germany, Saarland, Austria, Danzig, Sudetenland, and Spain. The latter figure included 382,000 non-Jews and 350,000 Republican Spaniards.

Identity card for the Jewish merchant Moses Kirchheimer, born 1858, from Bremerhaven. Cards like these were mandatory from November 1938 on

During the Pogrom Night, often euphemistically called Night of Broken Glass, on November, 9 1938, Jewish Germans were killed, their synagogues and community centers devastated, and several thousand Jewish people were deported to prisons and concentration camps. The synagogue in Bremen after its destruction

Germans relocated to the Netherlands, and over 60,000 more, mostly Jews, also chose to leave, with 40 % going to France, nearly half to Palestine, and others to Switzerland. In late 1933–34 about 4,400 Germans sought American visas, yet thousands of others had a change of heart and returned to Germany from both France and the United States. But then conditions turned poisonous more rapidly; Jews were increasingly stripped of their civil rights (Nuremberg Laws, 1935), and some 80,000 fled Germany, with thousands embarking for Palestine. In 1935–36 about 6,300 German Jews gained admission to the United States, and the following fiscal year (1936–37) nearly 11,000 secured American visas. Before September 1939, within mainland Europe refugees went to Czechoslovakia, France, Poland, and the Netherlands; outside of it, they migrated to Palestine, Britain, Argentina, Brazil, China, South Africa, as well as the United States.

In massive public bonfires books by left wing and Jewish authors were burned; the German government supported (and displayed) an exhibit denouncing "degenerate art," much of it by Jewish artists; and the denial of minority rights climaxed with

Reichkristallnacht in November 1938, which was marked by the destruction of 191 synagogues, many Jewish cemeteries, and approximately 7,500 Jewish businesses throughout Germany. What soon followed was the arrest and confinement of Jews and dissidents in concentration camps (not yet death camps). Acute anxiety now intensified among Jews and other political and ethnic groups, and there was now a sheer desperation to flee. And that quest arose after about 135,000 were reported to have left Germany the year before, especially for destinations outside Europe. It is said that 190,000 Austrian Jews made their exodus following the Anschluss. Between 1932 and 1938, 80,693 Germans did acquire U.S. visas, but that figure was less than half the available German quota of 191,400 for those six years.

The Nazis made it more and more administratively difficult and costly for those wishing to emigrate from Germany. For example, the government levied a 25 %, the "Reichsfluchtsteuer", just for leaving, along with severe limits on the amount of currency one could remove from Germany and the prospect of losing one's property in Germany as part of the cost of departing. However, the factor complicating emigration lay not only with the Nazis but

also with the widespread anti-Semitism in America. Although over 125,500 persons born in Germany and Austria (mostly Jews) emigrated to the United States (1933–42), compared with only 29,300 persons who returned (for the most part) to Germany, the anti-Semitism in the U.S. State Department was provoked especially by Breckinridge Long (a long-time friend of Roosevelt whose official role was to supervise the immigrant admissions process) and Wilbur Carr, head of the Consular Division (who also referred to Jews as filthy and often dangerous, among other things). They helped prevent as many as 100,000 additional persons, principally Jews, from obtaining visas available within the quota provisions.

Yet, the fear, paranoia, and intentional inaction were not confined to the U.S. State Department. The international conference of 32 nations in Evian, France, in July 1938 yielded no concrete results — with Great Britain, for example, indicating it would admit no more refugees into Palestine (later adding they would not do so without Arab approval) and the United States declining to increase quota limits (whereas the Dominican Republic agreed to admit 100,000 refugees). Indeed, the word "refugee" did not yet exist in American

The shipping company Norddeutsche Lloyd's flagship, the "Bremen", on its way into New York harbor. After the Nazis had seized power in Germany, mandated Jewish-only quarters were instituted on board the "Bremen" and other ships of German companies, Jewish refugees from Hitler-Germany thus preferred non-German ports of embarkation. On foreign ships they were treated like all other passengers

immigration laws, and opinion polls in 1938–39 reported that 60 % and then 82 % of Americans opposed the presence of Jews in America and the further admission of any large numbers of them. While Roosevelt would not risk any political capital needed for his New Deal programs by confronting the anti-Semitism, he did authorize the automatic extension of six-month visas of between 12,000 and 15,000 Germans then in the United States – although hastening to add that they were "not all Jews by any means."

When Senator Robert Wagner and Congresswoman Edith Nourse Rogers introduced a bill to admit 20,000 German children, over four-fifths of those polled opposed any such measure, and Roosevelt let it die. Indeed, during that spring of 1939 the most heart rendering episode involved the SS. St. Louis, with 936 passengers, nearly all Jews. Arriving in Havana in May, only 28 were allowed to land, and the ship was forced to leave. It sailed up along the U.S. coast, and passengers could hear the music from land. And yet, the U.S. government would not permit the ship to dock, notwithstanding that over 700 passengers had received preliminary permission to enter but their monthly visa numbers had not yet come up. The government would make no allowances, and the captain was compelled to return to Europe – "the saddest ship afloat," declared the New York Times. Subsequently, American Jewish organizations did arrange and provide financial guarantees for several hundred to be admitted by Great Britain, France, Belgium, and the Netherlands, most of which countries would shortly be invaded by the Germans. They proved to be short-term havens, for many of those who had stood on the decks of the St. Louis, seeing and hearing the inviting sights and sounds of America, would perish at the hands of the German invaders.

Throughout these years some Jewish groups and others, most notably Varian Fry and the Emergency Rescue Committee in Marseilles, helped a remarkable roster of European intellectuals, scientists, and artists to escape to America along with those who had chosen not to wait until faced with the full scale of Nazi threats. Over the decade, those who left, those who fled, and those who were helped to escape included an astonishing array of gifted individuals: Salvatore Dali, Lion Feuchtwanger, Heinrich Mann, Franz Werfel, Alma Mahler-Werfel, Thomas Mann, Piet Mondrian, Bertholt Brecht, Bela Bartok, Andre Breton, Marc Chagall, Claude Lévi-Strauss, Vladimir Nabokov, Jacques Lipschultz, Ossip Zadkine, Albert Einstein, Enrico Fermi, Edward Teller, Eugene Wigner, Franz Alexander, John von Neumann, Paul Tillich, and Hannah Ahrendt as well as Arturo Toscannini, George Solti, Eugene Ormandy, and Eric Leinsdorf. It has been estimated that between one-half and two-thirds of the America-bound refugees were Jews, but, on another level, putting aside the two dozen persons who ultimately became Nobel laureates, 23,000–25,000 men and women refugees were in professions, an estimated 5,000 were physicians, and more than 1,500 were lawyers, among other professionals who brought their talents and education from Europe to America.

During the war years of 1940–45 over 103,500 more Europeans were admitted, but by December 1941 there were already 335,000 stateless Jewish refugees in Europe and rumors were circulating, not yet confirmed (or believed), that Hitler was already planning a Final Solution for the liquidation of Europe's Jews and other "deviants". When Secretary of the Treasury Henry Morgenthau, Jr., at the behest of a leading rabbi, Stephen Wise, finally confronted the president in January 1944 with irrefutable evidence regarding an impending genocide that Roosevelt could no longer ignore, the president issued Executive Order 9417 on January 22, establishing the War Refugee Board.

On December 1st 1934 German and Austrian emigrants founded the newspaper "Aufbau". It soon became the most important source of information for and about German Jewish culture in the U.S. At times such celebrities as Albert Einstein, Thomas Mann, and Stefan Zweig were among the contributors

AUFBAU

Festnummer.

NACHRICHTENBLATT DES
GERMAN-JEWISH CLUB INC., NEW YORK, N.Y.

I. Jahrgang—No. 1   NEW YORK, DEN 1. DEZEMBER 1934   Preis 5 Cents

ZEHN JAHRE!

In sturmbewegte Zeiten fällt das zehnjährige Gründungsjubiläum des German-Jewish Club, Inc.

Aus der Fülle freudiger und leidvoller Ereignisse einer über ein Dezennium sich erstreckenden Geschichte seien weder bestimmte Namen, noch einzelne Geschehnisse besonders hervorgehoben, denn es ist nicht leicht, davor bewahrt zu bleiben, einen Mitarbeiter auf Kosten der anderen zu überschätzen, oder den Wert irgend eines Vorfalles zu verkleinern. Der Erfolg ist vielmehr das Resultat des organischen Zusam-

der Eintracht und der Solidarität geführten Verhandlungen führten sehr bald zu einer völligen Verständigung und nach einem Uebergangsstadium von 4 Monaten wurde die Vereinigung tatsächlich und endgültig vollzogen.

In richtiger Auslegung und Anwendung der Satzungen suchte der Klub vornehmlich durch Vorträge, Referate und Diskussionen für die Verbreitung jüdischen Geisteslebens unter den Mitgliedern zu wirken. Daneben wurde auch allen anderen Gebieten wissenschaftlicher und künstlerischer Natur grosse

Leider ist dies nicht immer restlos in dem Masse gelungen, wie es wünschenswert gewesen wäre und wie die allgemeine Erwartung verdient hätte. Immerhin legt die enorme Anzahl der Vorträge und die stets aufs neue überraschende Steigerung der Besucherzahl ein lobenswertes Zeugnis dafür ab, dass die Mitglieder stets mit Ernst und Interesse an den Darbietungen teilgenommen haben.

Wenn wir so die Wirksamkeit unserer Organisation bis zum heutigen Tage überschauen, dann müssen wir und jeder, der es

1   During the war, it has been calculated, out of 230,343 Jews from German and Soviet controlled areas, 79,300 were admitted by the United States, whereas 58,300 went to Palestine.

War, Genocide, and America's New View of World Affairs

The shift in U.S. policy marked by E.O. 9417 was less in terms of government funding for the WRB and much more in its symbolic representation of growing official American concern about the fate of Europe's Jews. Although it was largely through private financing that the Board ultimately saved some 200,000 lives, especially in Hungary, it was the perceived U.S. government support for the WRB warnings given to officials in Europe that mattered. They were advised that if they refused to cooperate they might eventually be tried as war criminals or collaborating with the Nazis.

It has been estimated that between 1933 and 1945 some 1.6 million refugees fled from Germany and Occupied Europe (nearly one-third of them from Germany and Austria), and the United States admitted 318,000 Europeans, approximately one-quarter million of whom were Jews. Overall, some 278,000 German Jews did escape their homeland and scatter across the globe, concentrating especially on reaching Palestine or America. Nonetheless, while millions more were being annihilated, over 140,000 U.S. visa slots allotted just for Germany and Austria went unused between 1933 and 1942.

By and large Roosevelt limited himself to more or less symbolic gestures, even though a particular one in August 1944 can now be seen as a small step for American humanitarianism — and part of Roosevelt's strategy to transfer responsibility for processing refugees away from the State Department, dominated as it was by "a bureaucracy largely unaccustomed to humanitarian initiatives." The president authorized the special, unofficial, "temporary" admission of 982 "guests". These men, women, and children had been in camps and had been selected in Rome. It was announced that they would be placed in a "War Refugee Center" called the "Haven," in Fort Oswego (a decommissioned military facility in upstate New York). It was said that they would reside there until they could be sent home at the war's end. However, in response to public support, President Truman issued an executive order in January 1946 releasing the 982 persons and allowing them to remain in America under quota law provisions.

That action followed merely 18 days after Truman's December 22, 1945, Directive broke new ground in U.S. refugee policy. It initiated a profound redefinition of America's role and image in global refugee affairs — beginning with Europe.

During the prior summer the president had sent Earl Harrison, Dean of the University of Pennsylvania Law School, to investigate and evaluate the Displaced Persons camps in Europe. As he reported in August 1945, he was stunned by the number of refugees, the conditions in which they were living, and their ability to survive such trauma. In fact, a September 1945 analysis found that shortly after the war ended there had been over ten million displaced persons representing about 20 different nationalities and that between May and September of that year some 7 million persons were repatriated

America's tough immigration restriction law of 1924 remained in force for 41 years. It had an especially negative effect on the lives of thousands of refugees in the 1930s and 40s who fled the torments of Nazi Germany, as well as the wars in China and Europe. This 1946 cartoon from the Washington Post features Pres. Truman's questioning why American liberty is no longer available to immigrants. Congress finally agreed to let in Displaced Persons outside the normal quotas

"What Happened To The One We Used To Have?"

U.S. IMMIGRATION POLICY

HERBLOCK

to their homelands. (Other reports put that figure at 5 and even over 10 million.) Reports from September 30, 1945, range between about 1.77 and 1.89 million refugees remaining scattered in and around DP camps across Europe, including 210,000 in Austria (11%), over 1.2 million in Germany (64%), and 75,500 in Italy (4%). Among them were

1.055 million	Poles
178,900	Balts (those from Estonia, Latvia, and Lithuania)
124,600	Yugoslavs
122,000	Hungarians
68,100	Jews (also cited at 69,000)
58,600	Romanians
54,800	Soviet nationals
34,800	Italians
33,100	Greeks
25,500	Czechoslovaks

Truman's response to Harrison's report was the Directive in which he noted that only 5 to 10% of the quotas had been used each year between 1942 and 1945, that the unused did not accumulate (or roll over), and that only one-tenth of the 1946 quotas had been allocated. Truman recognized that the National Origins system was considered by Congress the core of U.S. immigration policy and that any relief measures would have to work through those provisions. The tactic he followed was to declare that, as an expression of "common decency and fundamental comradeship of all human beings," the State Department would be instructed to expedite quickly the admission of refugees within the existing quotas. By giving preference to them, between 41,400 and 44,000 persons were admitted by July 1947, three-fifths of them Jews. (In f.y. 1946, a total of 64,877 European-born persons were admitted and in f.y. 1947 96,865.) One indication of the upheavals and flight of the post-war refugees was that 35,400 of those nearly 162,000 admitted immigrants in 1946–47 (22%) had been born in Europe but were not living there at the time they were admitted to legal permanent residence in the United States. The flood of additional refugees into the camps would also continue for several more years, compounded by political events in southern and eastern Europe that compelled new categories of persons to seek asylum.

Six days after issuing the Directive Truman signed the War Brides Act (December 28, 1945), providing for the

Displaced Persons departing Germany for the United States with their luggage in the former Tirpitz Naval Yard in Bremen in 1947. Before it became a DP camp Tirpitz had been a forced labor camp. In the context of the UNRRA resettlement programs DPs were transported primarily to the United States, Canada and Australia via Bremerhaven

admission over the next three years of foreign-born spouses and children of military personnel as non-quota immigrants. By December 1948, 119,693 had been admitted under this legislation, including 102,662 wives, 333 husbands, and 4,669 children. Over 87,600 were Europeans, including:

35,469	British
14,931	Germans
9,728	Italians
8,744	French
2,741	Belgians
2,674	Poles
2,302	Austrians
1,469	northern Irish
1,469	Greeks
1,348	Czechoslovaks
1,245	Irish
808	Soviets

At the same time, the situation in Europe was complicated not only by the continuing arrival of Displaced Persons but also by the outbreak of anti-Semitic pogroms, especially in Poland, the Soviet Union's gradual consolidation of

control over eastern Europe, the refusal of many DPs to be repatriated to those Soviet controlled areas, the expulsion of German descent persons from eastern Europe and the Soviet Union (the Vertriebene[2]), and Britain's resistance to admitting more Jews into Palestine. By January 1946 the DP population in western zones peaked at 1,243,263 of whom over 628,600 were in U.S. zones. During 1946 the number of Jewish DPs increased from 75,000 to 207,800.

Although American public opinion in late 1945 and 1946 had generally favored fewer immigrant admissions, especially

---

2   This is a more commonly used term, particularly for those expelled from eastern Europe. Aussiedler became a more widely used term during the 1980s and 1990s, referring to those of German extraction entering the Federal Republic of Germany (West Germany/FRG) and then the reunited Germany (with the consolidation of the German Democratic Republic (East Germany/GDR) and the FRG)

ews, many private agencies were urging the government to take action and they offered o sponsor individual DPs. In his 1947 State of the Union address Truman called upon Congress to authorize the admission of DPs. The American Jewish Committee and other public service organizations established a multi-denominational organization to promote the legislation, the Citizens Committee for Displaced Persons (CCDP). Eventually, the CCDP came to represent 200 religious, welfare, and civic organizations. Moreover, for the first time in American history, a plan was developed whereby the government sanctioned "the idea that social agencies could accept responsibility for receiving and resettling newcomers" - VOLuntary AGencies, VOLAGs - so that he DPs would not become public charges.

After 18 months of lengthy negotiations in and between the House and Senate, Truman signed the unprecedented Displaced Persons Act of June 25, 1948. It provided for a Displaced Persons Commission to oversee he admission of 205,000 refugees. Rather han altering the quota system, the innovative idea of "mortgaging" – borrowing from – specific future annual national quotas would be employed to facilitate the admissions. 40% were to come from the three Baltic states (areas "annexed" by a foreign power),

and 30% had to be in occupations related to agriculture. Provisions for 3,000 orphans and 2,000 Czechoslovaks (following the Communist coup there in early 1948) were added, along with 15,000 DPs temporarily in the United States who would be allowed to adjust their status to Legal Permanent Resident.

Serving as sponsors would be major Jewish and Catholic agencies, the American Friends Service, the Hebrew Sheltering and Immigrant Aid Society (HIAS), the Joint Jewish Defense Council (JDC), the Armenian National Committee for Homeless Armenians, the United Ukrainian American Relief Committee, the American Fund for Czechoslovak Refugees, the American Conference on Soviet Jewry, the Order of A.H.E.P.A. – the American Hellenic Educational Progressive Association – and many others. Those Volags, in partnership with the government, became "an integral part" of the refugee resettlement program.

One unfortunate effect of the legislation was that it superceded Truman's 1945 Directive, and 23,000 persons with preliminary approval for visas lost their advanced status. On the other hand, so successful was the 1948 act that it was expanded and renewed for one year on June 16, 1950, and

for one more on June 28, 1951. The revised legislation provided for:

The deletion of the preference for those from the Baltic states and in agricultural occupations – The setting of total admissions at 415,744 persons via the following:

Raising the ceiling on DPs to 341,000
Including now the addition of

54,744	German expellees (Vertriebene),
10,000	Greeks fleeing civil disorders
15,000	Polish war veterans in Great Britain
5,000	Italians from Venezia Giula (which had been transferred to Yugoslavia)
4,000	refugees who had made their way to Shanghai
5,000	orphans, and
500	recent political refugees (mostly those fleeing Communist takeovers) – significantly revealing the evolving definition of refugees.

According to the official report of the DP Commission, 393,542 immigrants were admitted under the 1948 and 1950 legislation. They included:

337,244	DPs
2,000	Italians
3,312	Shanghai refugees
10,487	ex-Polish soldiers
8,977	Greeks
53,448	German expellees (Vertriebene)
2,838	Orphans

By country of birth/nationality these 393,542 refugees were made up of:

34.0%	Poles
15.0%	Germans
9.3%	Latvians
8.7%	Soviets
7.9%	Yugoslavians
6.4%	Lithuanians
4.0%	Hungarians
2.7%	Czechoslovaks
2.6%	Estonians
2.5%	Greeks
2.5%	Romanians
2.1%	Austrians
0.4%	Ukrainians
0.3%	Turks

Embarkation of Displaced Persons in Bremerhaven in 1947

From the beginning of 1945 until the end of World War II about 3 million refugees fled to the west from the eastern parts of Germany, escaping from the Soviet Army. Refugee trek in Upper Silesia, photo February 1945

Republican president signed the Refuge Relief Act, enacted by the Republican controlled Congress. The new law acceler ated the unraveling of the National Origin program. And that represented just one of the key developments during the 1950s and early 1960s that reflected how a combi nation of events in Europe, in European colonies, and in the United States had globa consequences for international migration These developments culminated in a revolu tion in American immigration law. At th same time, a revolution in European affair was materializing from the founding of NATO in 1949 and the European Economi Community [EEC] in 1957. They dramat ically altered the economic and militar (and eventually political) position of Europ and thereby the currents of migration to th United States.

Of additional interest is the fact that DPs were resettled in 113 different countries. Those DPs entering the United States made up 44 % of all Europeans admitted between 1946 and 1952. 16 % of the DPs were Jews, 47 % Catholic, and 35 % Protestant or Orthodox. It has also been calculated that between May 1945 and December 1952, 137,450 Jews were admitted into the United States, half of whom were DPs. In addition, 54 % of the DPs were males, about 17 % had high school or higher education, and 47 % came with white collar occupations. Finally, to accomplish this DP program the U.S. government mortgaged 356,000 visas, a situation that would compel Congress to act and, in the process, further weaken the entire system of quotas.

Paradoxically, congressional leaders remained wedded to the quota system, as was apparent in the major omnibus immigra tion law enacted in the same month that the DP legislation expired, June 1952. And yet, the United States was now the undisputed leader of the Free World and engaged in an increasingly high stakes Cold War with the Soviet Union. Consequently, immigration- related actions became necessary in order to respond to ever more complex global events. In so doing they would steadily undermine

the admissions quotas which had just been solidly reaffirmed. The fear of subver- sives and communist infiltration (replac- ing the old fear of ethnic invasion) had now to be weighed against pragmatic as well as humanitarian goals. The upshot was the passage of a series of a half-dozen (mostly refugee-related) laws between 1953 and 1961. All affected European immigration. At the same time, the beginnings of western Europe's recovery and the stark contrasts between data by immigrants' countries of birth versus their countries of last residence suggest that considerable internal migra- tion was taking place and that for many thousands of Europeans who had been uprooted their migration to America was actually a secondary step migration.

The irony of the 1950s is that Congress overrode President Truman's veto of the I&N Act in part because of its commitment to the existing National Origins system. His recommendation to adjust the visa allot- ments to the 1950 census data was rejected, as was his call for 300,000 additional visas for refugees over a three-year period. President Eisenhower took office and supported that proposal. On August 7, 1953, merely fourteen months after the I&N Act had become the law of the land, this new

On the Move: Turmoil Among Post-War Europeans

Clearly, the war had created severe economi dislocations. Even though the Marshall Pla would generate enormous recovery efforts i Europe, that recovery took time and som local economies and some nations did no recover equally fast. It appears, for example that in many nations post-war educationa institutions were beginning to produce far greater number of educators, profession als, and skilled workers (along with entre preneurs, business managers, etc.) tha those economies could yet absorb. Moreove seemingly unexpected but understandabl given the war time losses of men, Europea nations (West Germany – the Federa Republic of Germany – being one of the first began to sign agreements with Italy, Turke and others (especially countries borde ing the Mediterranean) to provide for th admission of temporary workers from thos nations, especially for construction, publi works, agriculture, service work, etc. B 1976, during the time of the major economi crisis of the 1970s, 1.63 million worker from within the EEC had been recruited b other EEC countries for work, along with 4. million others from outside the EEC, partic ularly Portugal, Turkey, and Yugoslavia.

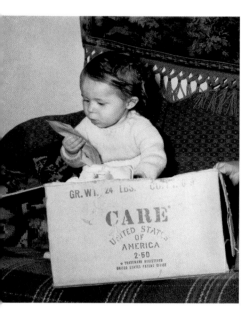

From August 1946 to October 1949 millions of CARE parcels were sent from the United States to Germany, worth more than 20 million dollars; photo from 1946

Meanwhile, the native-born middle class in many receiving countries (notably, Germany, France, and Great Britain) was disinclined to take such menial, dead end work. Many chose instead to emigrate in search of opportunities elsewhere (an increasingly common occurrence in late 20th century developed nations). It is also reported that many Germans, Austrians, Bulgarians, Hungarians, Romanians, Lithuanians, Serbs, Czechoslovaks, Poles, Belgians and Yugoslavs migrating to the United States during this post-war decades period were well-educated and skilled workers. Many were professionals seeking American jobs in universities, labs, and businesses, as was the case at this time with Belorusians, Lithuanians, and Latvians – if they could get out.

American perceptions underlying the quotas were that nations (that is their principal populations) remained immutable. However, the gradual disassembling of Europe's internal travel, trade, and labor migration barriers that began in the 1950s and the signing of those international temporary migrant labor agreements would gradually transform most northern and western European nations into multi-ethnic, immigrant-receiving countries and less and less migrant-sending ones. That heterogeneity would also undermine the rationale behind American law of using the quota system to preserve America's principal northern and western European ethno-cultural roots. It profoundly affected Europeans' perceived homogeneity of their respective countries; it set up still on-going struggles to integrate the growing numbers of persons from former colonies, southern and eastern Europe, the Middle East, and North Africa; and it significantly complicated the management of the incoming waves of workers – referred to as gastarbeiters by Germans (and then their families) – and out-going streams of native-born persons to Canada, Australia, parts of Latin America, and the United States.

In other words, post-war European migration was altered by the convergence of events and policy changes in both the sending and receiving nations. Another such prominent situation involved the Soviet Union's expansion westward and its imposition of controls on many east European nations – e.g., Poland, Czechoslovakia, Ukraine, Albania, Romania, Hungary, Bulgaria, Latvia, Lithuania, Estonia, and east Germany (German Democratic Republic) – which seriously impeded emigration from those countries as well as from the U.S.S.R. For example, merely 581 persons living in the Soviet Union were able to emigrate directly to the United States during the 1950s; in Czechoslovakia that number fell from 7,540 previously (1947–53) to 702 (1954–60), although during those latter seven years 17,730 persons who had been born in Czechoslovakia were admitted by the United States (meaning, some 17,000 Czechoslovaks had been living elsewhere when admitted to the United States). Poles and Yugoslavians evaded, or defied, Soviet pressures, but the Hungarian revolt in the autumn of 1956 was one of the more spectacular instances of resistance, for 200,000 fled to Austria and Yugoslavia when faced with Soviet tanks, and in 1959–60, 30,751 were admitted into the United States as permanent residents. They were "paroled" into the country in unique fashion by President Eisenhower and given a conditional status for two years. During the other comparable act of resistance, in Czechoslovakia during the spring of 1968, 42,000 Czechs who were abroad did not return. Over 7,800 were admitted into the United States in 1969–70. Thus, in addition to the economic changes underway, political dislocations in Europe would interfere with, or narrow, and even redirect migration streams.

While many parts of Europe were going through the recovery efforts, England was experiencing stagnation until the late 1950s, prompting many Irish to turn to America for employment opportunities. In fact, the number of English-born persons migrating to the United States jumped beginning in 1952 (from to 8,300 to 12,050) and that continued for much of the rest of the decade. Similar trends were apparent among the Welsh and Scots, too.

More distant environmental and colonial events likewise came into play, notably unrest in Portugal's Macao and, in the wake of Indian and Pakistani independence in 1947, the breakaway of Indonesia from the Netherlands, generating a substantial outflow of Dutch nationals. At roughly the same time, Portugal's Azores was struck by both an earthquake and a volcanic eruption on Fayal island (September 1957), prompting

Advertisement for the European Recovery Program, named after American Foreign Secretary George Marshall, 1947. The program aimed at supporting the recovery of European economies and promoting the idea of a free market

American intervention to assist refugees who, in this instance, were not fleeing communism. (Under the September 1958 legislation [see below] 22,213 Portuguese and Dutch Indonesians were admitted by the United States.) In addition, given the considerable war time upheavals that generated millions of displaced persons across Europe, in many places, such as Bosnia and Croatia, accusations of collaboration with the Nazis forced people to flee. Along with that, ethnic discord, such as Greek opposition to Slavic-speaking Macedonians, eventually compelled some 70,000 of them to emigrate to North America and elsewhere in Europe. Meanwhile, several million Germans (Vertriebene)[3] scattered across central and eastern Europe were also being forced to relocate, in their case "back" to Germany.

Finally, one aspect of the European data suggests that there were significant variations among the European groups because of the often overlooked differences in U.S. immigration reports between admission figures based on country of birth and those linked to country of last residence prior to admission. Although records are unavailable in the United States for years prior to 1972 that match individuals' birth and residence information, the two annual tables, going back to World War Two, provide further evidence of initial migration patterns within (most likely) Europe.[4] In some countries the two figures are relatively similar during the 1950s, such as for Hungarians – where country of birth totals rose 29,500 and those for last residence by 33,500 (1954– 60 vs 1947–53) – and Portugal with totals of 10,000 and 9,500, respectively. From these two cases one could infer that they

Postcard of the Bremer Überseeheim 1952. These accommodation facilities were the last abode on European soil for emigrants on their way to the U.S., to Canada or Australia

were not heavily sought out as initial destinations[5] nor did great numbers born there depart for other countries before gaining admission to the United States. In the case of Ireland both figures rose. For the United Kingdom the movement of peoples into and out of that country can be seen in the 25,000 increase of those born there (and admitted to the United States), whereas there was hardly any change among those last residing there but born elsewhere (1947–53 vs 1954–60). The fact that 14,400 more persons born in the United Kingdom left for America than among those last living in Great Britain indicates that many of the former had gone elsewhere first, or were even in the United States as non-immigrants now having their status adjusted to permanent residents. At the same time, with those 14,400 probably having emigrated, the roughly stable figures for last residence in Britain would indicate that other non-British persons

had gone there before acquiring American visas. On the other hand, in France the total for last residence persons was 9,400 greater than the number born in France, revealing that many non-French had settled in that country before receiving American visas.

The steep increase among Greek (14,500 in both categories) reflected the unrest and recent civil war there and, most likely, that it was also not yet an immigrant receiving destination. In contrast, some 4,800 more Yugoslavian-born persons departed for America during this period (1954–60), yet the figure for persons last residing there fell even more, by 8,000. Together they indicate that not only were more Yugoslavs emigrating but also an even greater number of them had left that homeland (most likely for other locations in Europe) before being granted U. S. visas. Such instances of political and economic unrest and the fact that many involved persons who had been sent (or had made their way) to another host society before relocating once again (to America) are revealing details of this turbulent decade of recovery and political realignments. Additional evidence of this is the fact that the communist coup in Czechoslovakia in 1948 had almost certainly been responsible

---

3 Vertriebene usually referred to expellees and Flüchtlinge to refugees.

4 The table for country of last residence in Europe is self-explanatory. The table for country of birth can conceivably include individuals born in a specific country but living elsewhere in Europe, or some other location, or even within the United States prior to admission. Based on the post-war displaced persons and other refugee data and legislation, it is likely that most of the initial migration by Europeans occurred within Europe.

---

5 Were that the case there would have been, among those admitted to the United States, a larger number of persons last residing there than the number of those who had been born in those countries.

for the subsequent drop of 10,700 in the number of persons born there who were able to migrate directly from that country.

What cannot be determined from these various illustrations but is hypothesized here is that people who relocated and lived elsewhere before a secondary migration to America may well have acquired skills of adaptation (and education) and networks of friends and family (invaluable human and social capital) that subsequently eased their integration there, especially among those with more education and more skilled or professional occupations.

U.S. Policy Responses to Migration Pressures

The other half of the situation during the 1950s lay with American legislation that concretely represented the emerging awareness among U.S. leaders of the responsibilities that come with being the first super power and that it could no longer embrace isolationism. Six laws enacted between 1953 and 1961 built on some of the acts and actions of the prior eight years. They would, unwittingly, set the stage for the legislative revolution of 1965.

The Refugee Relief Act of August 7, 1953, was remarkable. It defined "refugee" as one fleeing a non-Communist country to escape persecution and an "escapee" as one specifically fleeing from a Communist-dominated country or the Soviet Union out of fear of persecution. Essentially, the act ignored the quota system and authorized 205,000 "special nonquota immigrant visas" as follows:

50,000	German expellees in West Germany (GFR) (Vertriebene)
35,000	German escapees in West Germany (GFR) (Flüchtlinge)
10,000	escapees in NATO countries
2,000	refugees in the British Isles who were Polish war veterans
45,000	refugees of Italian origin in Italy or Trieste
15,000	Italians who were parents, siblings, or married children of U.S. citizens or spouse and unmarried child of a resident alien
15,000	Greek refugees in Greece
2,000	Greek relatives (see Italians above)
15,000	Dutch refugees in the Netherlands
2,000	Dutch relatives (see Italians above)
2,000	Refugees in the Far East
3,000	Refugees born in the Far East
2,000	Chinese with ties to Nationalist China
2,000	Refugees in Palestine
4,000	Orphans, aged 10 or younger

The Refugee-Escapee Act of September 11, 1957, focused on orphans, raising the ceiling to age 14. It also provided that several classes of individuals related to those in America could receive visas, regardless of quotas – if "extreme hardship" could be established, or the person has misrepresented himself/herself due to a fear of persecution. Most crucially, the act declared that those admitted by prior refugee laws were now nonquota immigrants and the earlier mortgaging of future quota visas was entirely canceled. As an instance where the existing immigration quota requirements were waived in order to address the priority of reducing the immigrant backlog, this act classified as non-quota (immediately admissible) those foreigners initially approved for admission before July 1, 1957. Finally, and also indicative of the changing diplomatic conditions, the act now more specifically defined a refugee-escapee as one fleeing from a communist controlled area OR someone from the Middle east who could not return "on account of race, religion, or political opinion."

The Act of July 25, 1958, provided that anyone paroled into the United States

New York Harbor 1956, seen from Liberty Island

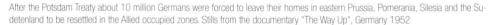

After the Potsdam Treaty about 10 million Germans were forced to leave their homes in eastern Prussia, Pomerania, Silesia and the Sudetenland to be resettled in the Allied occupied zones. Stills from the documentary "The Way Up", Germany 1952

(mostly Hungarians at this point) and present for two years could be admitted nonquota. The Act of September 2, 1958, originally authorized 1,500 special nonquota immigrant visas for Portuguese affected by the volcanic eruption and earthquake in the Azores and also authorized 6,256 visas for Dutch citizens displaced from Indonesia after January 1, 1949. Neither section dealt with political refugees or communism or were limited by quota ceilings. The National Origins program was once more just set aside.

The Fair Share Refugee Act of July 14, 1960, provided for paroling 500 additional refugees and extended parole provisions for Hungarians until June 1962 and the orphan provisions of the 1957 act to June 1961. Finally, the Act of September 26, 1961, of great significance as a stepping stone to 1965, eliminated the requirement in visa applications requesting the race and ethnic origin of immigrant applicants. American immigration was on its way to becoming colorblind.

The 15 post-war years had dramatic consequences for Europe because they marked the overlapping of major migration developments. Ironically, to the east the Soviet Union sharply restricted European out-migration; to the west, the United States controlled and screened European in-migration. Still, in terms of net migration during the 1950s, more persons left Europe than entered, a trend that would continue until the 1970s. And, whereas there were startling examples of net out-migration during the 1950s (to various destinations in and out of Europe) – e.g., 1.09 million from Italy, 540,000 from the United Kingdom, 395,000 from Ireland, 1.33 million from the Soviet Union, and even the 136,000 from Austria – Germany experienced a sharply different pattern due to all the refugees and expellees (Vertriebene) repatriated there. west Germany experienced a net in-migration of 996,000 persons during the 1950s.

The United States was but one destination for Europeans, and the evidence, based on country of last residence and country of birth data, suggests, as noted, that many of them left Europe before gaining admission to the United States. The overall figures for the various sending countries based on birth place exceed the totals for last residence in Europe by 8 to 11 percentage points, such as the nearly 77,300 more persons born in Europe and admitted to the United States between 1947 and 1953 (being 77,300 more than the number of those admitted and last residing there) and the total of 134,900 more between 1954 and 1960. In other words, between 1947 and 1960, it appears that over 212,200 European-born persons were not residing in Europe at the time they were accepted for admission by the United States.

But, given Europe's recovery, the other available emigrant destinations, and the constraints of non-refugee aspects of U.S. immigration law, one other vital trend in retrospect also proved of great significance. Between 1947 and 1953 almost 73 % of total U.S. admissions were persons born in Europe however, between 1954 and 1960 that figure fell to somewhat over 55 %. Over the next seven years (1961–67) it would sink to 41 %, and the bottom was yet to be reached.

Fundamentally, western Europe was experiencing a remarkable renaissance, and the European Economic Community would literally open new doors and lower barriers, profoundly impacting the region's migration history. At the same time, the United States was eroding its National Origins immigration system, for after taking a hard nose stance defending it in 1952, Congress and the president promptly accelerated the dismantling of it. The Immigration Act of 1965 would indeed be revolutionary, particularly for its concentration on family reunification. But it was especially with respect to Europeans that that law was a culmination of legislative exceptions and piecemeal changes and not entirely a reform out of whole cloth. By the time it was enacted much of Europe would for decades either not be politically free to take advantage of the changes and opportunities in the new American law, or did not wish to do so given the diverse options within Europe, or they could not meet the new array of preferences concerning immediate family ties and/or employment skills.

Farewell ceremony for the 15,000th emigrant after 1945 from Bremen, Grandma Aukzemas on board of the Beaverbrae. Photo 1952

American Policy Reforms and a Changing Europe

A key principle of international migration is the interaction of conditions in the sending country and those in the new host society. European migration to the United States did not steeply drop solely because American laws were changed, especially in 1965. Indeed, on the one side, the point had been made here that the various American refugee laws enabled many Europeans to escape untenable political, economic, environmental, and military conditions. They were enacted without a narrow and inflexible adherence to quotas that characterized the pre-war years and which were reaffirmed in the omnibus codification of immigration and nationality laws in 1952.

However, at the same time, by the 1960s within the European Economic Community (EEC) many parts of Europe were experiencing a new era of peace and prosperity to such an extent that, as mentioned, the countries along the Mediterranean had completed agreements to permit temporary labor migration by their nationals to central and western European countries. Some of the latter nations went farther and were executing agreements to admit temporary workers from outside Europe proper, too, or they were witnessing the arrival of former colonials, such as from Algeria into France, from India, Pakistan, and the West Indies into Great Britain, and from Indonesia into the Netherlands. In most cases these workers occupied lower status, menial jobs that, we observed, many among the native western European populations no longer wished to do. In other cases a full economic recovery was slowed either by political events – as with the military junta in Greece (1967–1974); the [Antonio] Salazar regime in Portugal (1926–74) and the left wing revolt that ousted him; Soviet controls over much of eastern Europe (notably east Germany); and the Soviet invasion of Hungary in 1956 and Czechoslovakia in 1968 – or by the prolonged consequences of the war and/or natural disasters, as beset the Netherlands, which had experienced the war time bombings of a key seaport, the removal, forced labor and execution of many middle class Jews and others, and major flooding of its delta countryside in 1953.

It was also becoming apparent that the population was aging and birth rates were beginning to slide below replacement levels, such as in Italy and then Germany, and that put pressure on governments to promote larger families and in-migration. The catch, we have seen, was the scant experience in many places across Europe with respect to integrating large numbers of temporary migrants who chose to remain and bring or to begin families and whose cultures and religions often varied considerably from that of the principal native populations. Concurrently, there was the struggle to hold on to native workers who were being drawn to job prospects and opportunities in North America, New Zealand, Australia, and parts of Latin America or elsewhere in the broader EEC.

Of course, the U.S. quota system still lopsidedly favored Europeans – specifically northern and western Europeans – until the more neutral provisions of the Immigration and Nationality Act of October 3, 1965, altered the ground rules, particularly affecting those who had been previously most favored. Within the 1952 I&N Act parameters the country quotas came first (determining the maximum admissible number) and second were the preferences emphasizing skilled workers and family members of both citizens and legal resident foreigners. Nevertheless, and notwithstanding the northern European bias in the quotas prior to 1965, European immigration to the United States still fell by over 15 % between 1954–60 and 1961–67, that is before the 1965 provisions became fully effective (1968). Migration patterns, it appears, had been changing more in response to the economic and

Postcard of North German Lloyd steamship "Berlin", 1957

Around 1950 housing conditions in many German cities were still bad. Housing shortages were prevalent. Photo: Bremen 1951

political conditions within Europe than to American legislative changes. The latter would, however, rather quickly become an even more critical variable than they had been during the 1950s.

To the extent that they wished to migrate, many Europeans sought to take advantage of certain provisions of the revised 1965 U.S. immigration law, such as applying for non-preference visas. Between 1966 and 1970, for example, 85% of all such visas went to Europeans – principally the British and then Germans, Greeks, Poles, and Portuguese. As the number of Asian immigrants steadily increased, they, too, learned of this option and applied for the non-preference visas. At that point, the European share fell to one-third. Another alternative was to go to the United States as a nonimmigrant and afterwards apply to "adjust" one's status to Legal Permanent Resident (LPR) (frequently by securing employment or marriage). Between 1968 and 1974 one in five Europeans did just that. Then that figure declined to 15% (1975–81). Nonetheless, these alternatives could not suppress the effects of other telling changes. Between 1961–67 and

1968–74 – with the 1965 law now assigning three-fourths of the preferences to family reunification with citizens and LPRs and only one in five for occupation – European immigration quite promptly again dropped by another 16%, to 27% of all U.S. admissions.

At that point (1973–74), global events forcefully intervened in the form of the international oil embargo, which severely impacted Europe and the United States, worsening a recession already under way and compelling European nations to end temporary worker programs. The economic uncertainties and recession plagued both sides of the Atlantic, and many Europeans opted to pursue opportunities in Europe. Spiraling further downward, European immigration to the United States between 1968–74 and 1975–81 plunged by more than 31%. By the late 1970s the number of European-born immigrants was less than half (48.9%) of what it had been two decades earlier. The European portion of all U.S. immigrants now stood at 14.3% and would soon fall to 9% during the latter half of the 1980s.

Of course, one major variable was now receding as a factor influencing the volume of European migration to the United States. Between 1946 and 1965, 739,532 refugees had been admitted to the United States and only a few thousand of them were not European. As the focus of attention shifted

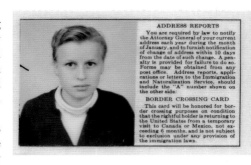

A German immigrant's green card, 1956

to Cuba and Southeast Asia, the one significant exception involved the U.S.S.R. Congress in 1974 approved a law denying a most favored nation trading status to the U.S.S.R. unless it relaxed its policies and permitted more persons, principally Soviet Jews and other minorities (notably Russian Evangelicals and Pentecostals), to emigrate. The Soviet Union acceded to the [Henry] Jackson – [Charles] Vanik provision, which enabled 16,750 refugees to leave the U.S.S.R. and enter the United States just in 1980–81. (Overall, some 130,000 left the Soviet Union during this period, with most going to Israel.) In fact, between 1948 and 1970, only 59,600 persons had been permitted to emigrate from the Soviet Union, but 347,300 were allowed to leave during the 1970s, including nearly one-quarter million Jews.

German emigrant with the family's road cruiser in Minnesota. Photo 1956

34,100 Armenians, and 64,300 Germans (Aussiedler).[6]

On the other hand, changes within Europe were altering the profile of European emigration. For example, between 1960 and 1975 about 948,000 more migrants left Italy than entered (principally workers bound for diverse destinations). Between 1975 and 1980 that reversed (for a time) and net 37,000 more entered Italy. Coinciding with the overthrow of Portugal's Salazar regime in the spring of 1974 and the end of the military junta in Greece a few months later, emigration from both countries partially declined and some citizens began returning. Even in the Soviet Union a switch occurred in 1975–80 that reversed 25 years of out-migration. About 625,000 more persons were reported entering than left (mostly non-Europeans). In Poland, by contrast, the negative migration pattern (net more emigrating) since the war's end continued and between 1975 and 1981 another 141,700 emigrated, with 31,900 of them going to the United States – 50 % more than in 1968–74. Many were well-educated and skilled workers.

Thus, despite the fact that not all western European nations equally shared in the prosperity of more open regional trade and less rigid borders, and eastern Europe was not yet free from Soviet Union domination – although cracks in the Cold War walls were appearing – the combination of European, American, and global circumstances certainly affected European migration. Most of the nations studied here saw a dramatic decline in emigration between the early 1960s and the late 1970s, with

the chief exceptions being the politically volatile Yugoslavia, the economically lagging Portugal, the political roller coaster that was Greece, and an increasingly troubled Soviet Union. However, it is not that European emigration dried up under America's new immigration law, for almost one and a quarter million did emigrate to the United States in the 14 years between 1968 and 1981 and over 1.63 million more would be admitted during the next 16 years (1982–97). Rather, following the oil embargo and recession, the renewed prosperity in Europe, along with the continued reduction of trade barriers and the on-going arrival of non-West Europeans, generated attractive opportunities there (Table 3).

The collapse of the Soviet Union and the disruption of its domination of eastern Europe plus the establishment of the European Union, with its Schengen Plan for open borders, dramatically impacted the last quarter century (1980–2005).

America's lure, we have just noted, did not disappear, which the renewed debates over "brain drain" would also reveal, but the new realities in Europe could not but play a role in reshaping migration to America.

Accelerating Changes Overtake Migration Patterns

The years following 1981 were filled with a major series of dramatic events that undoubtedly affected European immigration and emigration and American immigration policies. These developments reinforced even more the earlier observation regarding the interaction of circumstances in sending and receiving nations within the context of global conditions. A calendar of largely unanticipated events altering U.S.-European

Table 3 Changes in selected European immigration flows to the United States by country/region of birth, between 1961–67 and 1975–81

Origin	1961-67	1975-81	PCT Change*
Europe	875.310	507,412	-42.0 %
Soviet Union	12.724	48,406	+280.0 %
Portugal	37,387	67,455	+80.4 %
Greece	43,000	49,568	+15.3 %
Ireland	35,840	8,066	-77.5 %
Germany	165,087	45,257	-72,6 %
Italy	134,467	53,195	-60.4 %
Czechoslovakia	11,943	5,130	-57.0 %
France	26,397	1,256	-54.3 %
Hungary	11,655	603	-48.5 %
United Kingdom	172,694	96,30	-44.2 %
Yugoslavia	21,929	18,78	-14.4 %

The "+" sign represents greater net migration into the U.S. The "-" sign represents a decline of net immigration into the U.S. Most of the latter Soviet figure was made up of refugees under the Jackson-Vanik agreement.

---

6 These are exit figures, those departing from the U.S.S.R. American refugee data can be confusing because many cite this number who departed from the homelands or last countries of residence, or those interviewed who said they planned to go to America (or elsewhere), or persons admitted conditionally into the United States (at that time for a two year probationary period). Actually, the final number is of those adjusted to Lawful Permanent Residents. Unless otherwise noted, the specific refugee data here represent the numbers actually admitted to permanent resident status and based on their country of birth.

relations included U.S. recessions in the early 1980s and early 1990s; the imposition of martial law in Poland in 1981 aimed at stifling the Solidarity Movement; the enactment of America's Immigration and Reform Control Act in 1986 (IRCA) and the Immigration Act in 1990[7]; the Soviet Union's tightening of emigration policies between 1982 and 1986 (only 44,000 were permitted to migrate), followed by further deterioration of the Soviet Union and a relaxation of those policies, enabling 308,200 to emigrate between 1987 and 1989 (almost one-third were Jews[8]); the destruction of the Berlin Wall in 1989 and the collapse of the U.S.S.R. in 1991; and the impact of 9/11 on the screening and admission of immigrants – particularly from certain regions.

These changes were paralleled by massive outpourings of refugees and workers from eastern to western Europe, Israel, and the Americas (along with places within the British Commonwealth – especially Australia); then the breakup of Yugoslavia in 1991, precipitating near genocidal civil wars during the ensuing decade and, with

The last step before receiving the immigrant visa: Prospective American immigrants taking the oath in front of the vice-consul in Bremen

them, the extensive exodus and dispersal of (mostly) Bosnians and Herzegovinians; and the Maastricht Treaty of 1992 and Schengen Agreement of 1995, launching the European Union and then various measures to reinforce uniform tariffs with a uniform currency and to commence the removal of border stations and inspections between EU member nations (as America has between states in the U.S.). With the radical changes in eastern Europe, the EU moved to expand and include most east European countries – including most of the former partners of the pro-Soviet Warsaw Pact (enlarging the E.U. by 2004 to 27 nations). Its progress did increase economic competition between Europe, the United States, and Japan; prompted American institutions and corporations to heighten efforts to attract students, engineers, scientists, information technology experts, and other professionals; and regenerated the debate over "brain drain circulation" and "brain exchanges."

These events were accompanied by the easing of regulations by the EU on the inflows of workers and students from east European countries (although several receiving countries in the EU were permitted to establish limited moratoriums to slow these population movements across their borders). Along with that came a further accelerated in-migration – legal and undocumented – from Turkey, Africa, South America, and the West Indies plus, as seen earlier too, a reverse migration of native-born emigrants returning because of improved political and economic conditions in their homelands and

pensioners retiring – on their American savings and Social Security. The convergence of these many developments from the 1980s to the early 2000s continued to foster struggles within the EU aimed at devising policies and programs to better integrate regionally the new member nations. And, internally many western European nations were exploring ways to hold on to their professional and skilled workers and to better incorporate (not always effectively) the expanding – and frequently quite diverse – foreign-born populations. Since 9/11 they have also faced an additional dimension of devising effective responses to scattered cells of radicalized Muslims – both native and foreign born.

All these overlapping movements and trends in part siphoned off some European workers from those bound for America – professionals and skilled workers most notably – who were now pursuing job opportunities within Europe. The trend also contributed to a shift in the origins of many "Europeans" still migrating from Europe to the United States. To illustrate, let us pick up on the issue introduced above. For 28 years following the end of World War Two more persons admitted into the United States from Europe had been born in Europe – largely in the countries from which they departed and in which they last resided (leaving aside refugees and asylees) – than the total number last residing there before acquiring admission into the United States. In fact, at that time some 354,800 more

---

7   IRCA provided an avenue to legalization for undocumented migrants and "Special Agricultural Workers." They had to register and take courses in English and American civilization within a two-year period. At the same time IRCA included sanctions against employers who "knowingly hired" illegal aliens. While over 2.9 million migrants did receive lawful permanent residence, IRCA's enforcement provisions were scarcely implemented.
    The 1990 legislation significantly raised the ceiling on the total number who could be admitted each year to 675,000 persons: 480,000 for those with immediate family ties in the United States; 140,000 with employment or business related qualifications; and 55,000 "diversity" visas awarded by a lottery system to persons in underrepresented countries. Many other changes were included, particularly with respect to naturalization procedures, which were now removed from the courts and made an administrative function of the Immigration and Naturalization Service (INS).

8   Nearly 55% [168,900] were Germans (Aussiedler) and Greeks returning to their countries of origin; 39,100 were Armenians, Evangelicals, and Pentecostals, most of whom were bound for America.

ndividuals reported that they were born n Europe than indicated they last resided here (1946–1974), not too surprising in light of the many refugees resettled outside Europe together with relocation efforts by some European governments.

However, in a shift during the next thirty years (1975–2005) more persons indicated they last resided in Europe than were born here (129,800 did so[9]). Thus, in a reversal paralleling the many other upheavals discussed, a not insignificant number of non-Europeans have been migrating into Europe and residing there before gaining admittance to the United States. In this case, therefore, the secondary settlement into America followed a prior initial European residence, whereas in the earlier scenario (1946–74) a large number of Country of Birth Europeans had relocated outside Europe before gaining admission to the United States.[10] The new pattern was still evident in 2005.

Several dimensions of the European-American situation during the latest period specifically and dramatically influenced these migration trends. The number of Europeans settling in America had remained rather level during the decade prior to 1990, when three profound developments altered conditions in Europe, substantially redefining the dynamics of European life and reshaping links to America. First, the one already noted was anticipated, the establishment of the EU in 1993 and the subsequent Schengen Agreement two years later. Labor flows

9   There are no data distinguishing Country of Birth from Country of Last Permanent Residence for 1980–83 (the tables are the same), but I would estimate the difference at 20,000 more over country of birth, bringing the total of excess European country of last residence to about 150,000.

10   For example, Europeans who had come to America as temporary nonimmigrants and were having their status adjusted to Legal Permanent Resident would not have listed their last residence in Europe. Unfortunately, we do not have available the data on what birth places were provided by those 150,000 listing a European last residence.

Above: In the 1950s and 60s European industrial countries increasingly became destinations of international migration flows. People came as an unskilled labor force from North Africa to France, from the West Indies to Great Britain, from Italy, Yugoslavia and Turkey to Germany. Turkish so-called guest workers in Essen (Ruhr area), 1990
Below: After the Schengen Treaty the term "Fortress Europe" came into use, meaning that greater freedom of movement within the European Union was juxtaposed by a rigid closing of the door against non-European migrants. Refugee organizations and human rights activists pleaded for a generous, tolerant and humane policy of immigration to EU countries

Above: Demonstration in Rostock, German Democratic Republic, October 1989, in favor of democratic rights and freedom to travel.
Below: November 1989: The Neue Forum, a movement of GDR-critical forces, called for a human chain

to cope with the termination of its control over Warsaw Pact members. As the Pact came apart and east Europeans were learning about the market economy, the barriers between eastern and western Europe rather quickly began to drop (most powerfully seen in the reunification of the two Germanies). Millions of east Europeans sought jobs in the west and were now free to seek admission to the United States. For its part, America was only too willing to relish victory by recognizing the huge number of persons in the former Soviet satellite states and in the former Soviet Union [FSU] itself who were applying for asylum or refugee status. With new waves of Europeans making their way to America after 1989, residents from eastern Europe and the FSU vastly outnumbered western Europeans.

Third, as mentioned, overlapping the dismantling of the FSU were events in a very unstable Yugoslavia. It had long pursued its somewhat more independent and more open ties to the West, but its internal relations (especially between Muslims and Orthodox and other non-Muslims) were too frayed to maintain for long the political balance which President Josip Broz Tito had managed to do until his death in 1980. In 1991 the federation split apart, torn open by Slovenia's desire for independence and then by several civil wars that powerfully affected many western European countries and the United States, where Bosnians and Herzegovinians Croats and others sought refuge. The slaughter rent their country for a decade, and NATO and the UN had to intervene militarily to halt the carnage.

Spurred by these events, the U.S government ment reassessed who would get priority among the new waves of refugees. Total European migration to America jumped considerably between 1984–90 and 1991–97, from nearly 510,900 to 995,200. Over the next eight years (1998–2005) over 1.07 million more Europeans were admitted. According to the 2000 U.S. census 32.9% of the 4.9 million Europeans counted that year had arrived during the 1990s, and 13.9% during the 1980s. A key variable, as observed, was the leap in refugees admitted from Europe, beginning with a 150% jump from the FSU in 1990 (9,264 [1989] to 23,186 [1990]) and a doubling of that figure in 1991 (to 51,551). However, once the FSU imploded and

within the region were certainly opened further, and the percent of "foreign-born" populations in many member countries moved steadily upward, adding complexity to the issue of who resided in Europe and where.

Second, for all the anticipated drama that unfolded with the EU, the tearing down of the Berlin Wall in 1989 stunned everyone. Berliners acknowledged to this writer that they never thought they would witness that in their life time. In 1990, near dissolution, the Soviet Union allowed a remarkable 377,200 persons to emigrate (over 53% were Jews

[201,300][11]). The following year the U.S.S.R. collapsed, not only forcing Russia to devise a new confederation and new policies to deal with former members of the Soviet Union who were now "foreigners" but also

---

11 Almost two-fifths were Germans [148,000] – Aussiedler; 11,000 were Armenians, Evangelicals, and Pentecostals, almost all bound for America; like the Germans bound for the two Germanies, the 14,300 Greeks were planning to return to Greece.

A young Russian woman, willing to emigrate, scrutinizing her passport in front of the German embassy in Moscow, 1998

borders to the west were opened, there was for some east Europeans a loss of incentive to seek (or need) refuge outside Europe, although there were modest increases after 1990 in the number of migrants going to America from most of the east European countries, including Albania, Armenia, Bulgaria, Lithuania, and especially Romania and the Ukraine. At the same time the United States also began to shift refugee priorities, beginning in 1991–92, to the former Soviet Union. The modest volume of many other east European immigrants reported in U.S. data reflected not just attractive job opportunities opening up in western Europe but also a weakening in the specific number of refugees admitted by the United States from Czechoslovakia, Hungary, Poland, Rumania, Bulgaria, and even Albania.[12] The strongest example, undoubtedly, was Poland, for in 1984–89,

43 % of the 59,500 Poles admitted were refugees, but, in 1990–99, merely 6 % of the 180,000 admitted were refugees or asylees.

Further illustrating the turn of events, while 318,253 refugees were admitted from the FSU between 1990 and 1997 (with over 50,000 in both 1991 and 1994) – representing 82.5 % of all European refugees during that period – Czech refugee numbers declined from 883 to zero (1991–97); Hungary's dropped from 868 to 24 (1990–97); and Poland's fell from 4,200 to 143 (1991–97).

The refugee flow from the FSU subsequently declined to about 135,900 (1998–2005), but by now the Yugoslav flood had begun – with almost 32,200 (1994–99) jumping to over 113,700 (2000–05), almost three-fourths of whom were from Bosnia and Herzegovina. In other words, between 1990 and 2005 Europeans comprised 14.3 % of all immigrants admitted to the United States but 41.3 % of all refugees and asylees admitted as LPRs. The numbers bear out both the magnitude of events in Europe and the scale of America's response.

Given these major developments influencing migration patterns, there surfaced controversies over exactly who

were entering the United States (legally, illegally, or by overstaying their visas) and who were departing. Significant numbers of Europeans in the United States had begun overstaying tourist, student and other visas, particularly since the early 1980s recession. Others, especially in Ireland, benefited from new provisions in American law beginning in 1986 that were in part designed to help countries which had been complaining about restrictions in American immigration laws since 1965. The new changes opened doors for "diversity visas" (see footnote 7, above) that Europeans eagerly seized upon to gain admission. And yet, despite opening the gates to refugees, asylees, lottery winners, students and professionals seeking adjustments of status to remain in the United States, Americans were still accused by some European critics of using these policy options to take advantage of Europeans. What some Europeans labeled a brain drain Americans saw as a circulation of brains across the Atlantic World – a "brain exchange," or "brain export," or simply "brain globalization." Indeed, in a number of countries a significant number of professionals, academics, engineers, physicians, etc., had migrated to America following the war; now, during the late 20th century such persons were once again prominent, particularly from Great Britain and Poland. Moreover, the huge flow of remittances from migrants to their home communities and families was most welcomed.

In addition, it appears that there had been a steady return migration to Europe that may have equaled one-fifth of arriving immigrants. Indeed, three of the top ten emigrant destinations from the United States in the 1980s were the United Kingdom (31,000 estimated), Germany (29,000), and Italy (4,000). The fact that overall estimates of return migration for 1991–2005 range from 252,000 to 311,000 annually suggest that the pattern from the 1980s (and before) has most likely persisted since then.

The United States sought to come to terms with the gaps between its immigration laws and immigration realities and with those persistent issues of undocumented migrants and those groups whose criticisms of the 1965 law ultimately

---

12 Between 1990 and 1999 the following number of immigrants were admitted from these east European countries: Albania, 21,513; Armenia, 25,346; Belarus [1992–99], 22,894; Bulgaria, 18,654; Hungary, 11,003; Latvia, 4,796; Lithuania, 6,768; Romania, 55,303; Ukraine, 125,487; and Poland, 180,026.

YOUR CARD shows you have an insurance account with the U. S. Government, under the old-age and survivors insurance system provided for in the Social Security Act.

YOUR ACCOUNT is a record of the pay you receive which counts toward old-age and survivors insurance benefits.   The size of benefits will depend upon the amount of wages credited to your account.

MONTHLY BENEFITS MAY BE PAID:

When Man is Insured	When Woman is Insured
If living,	If living,
to man and wife, 65 and over, children under 18, wife (any age) with children under 18.	to woman 65 or over and dependent husband 65 and over.
If deceased, to widow 65 or over, widow (any age) with children under 18, dependent parents 65 or over.	If deceased, to children under 18, dependent widower 65 and over, dependent parents 65 and over.

In addition, when an insured worker dies a lump-sum payment may be made to the widow (or widower) or, if there is no widow or widower, to the person who paid the funeral expenses.

YOUR CARD shows the number of your social security account.   The number is necessary to identify the account as belonging to you.

For more information . . .

ASK ANY social security district office. If you don't know where to find a district office, ask your post office or look in the telephone directory.   Any district office will —

1.—help you to check up on your social security account.

2.—explain your rights and duties, and the insurance benefits you and your family may receive.

3.—help you or your survivors to file claim for benefits when the time comes.

Do not notify the Social Security Administration when you change your address unless you are receiving old-age and survivors insurance benefits.

SOCIAL SECURITY IS FAMILY PROTECTION

Form OAAN-7006 (9-54) U. S. GOVERNMENT PRINTING OFFICE: 1954 O—318766

Social security card of a German immigrant woman, 1956

sparked legislative changes. The legalization program implemented in 1986 with IRCA was an effort to bring undocumented persons into the open and to establish sanctions against employers who knowingly hired such persons. Between 1989 and 2000, 2,688,824 persons were legalized. Undocumented Europeans were known to be present in the United States and some 100,000 to 150,000 Irish, for example, were widely reported to have overstayed visas, particularly during the severe recession that struck Ireland in the early 1980s. During that decade Poles fleeing the crackdown on the Solidarity Movement came to America for a "vacation" – in fact, 374,622 did – and many appear not to have returned home. A 1996 study of twenty countries contributing most to this undocumented population included Poland, Ireland, and Portugal. Yet, only 34,900 Europeans acquired legalization. They did include

16,100 Poles, nearly 1,400 Irish, and over 2,500 Portuguese. Other cited European countries included Great Britain (4,800), the former Yugoslavia (over 1,700), Greece (nearly 1,500), Italy (1,230), and Germany (1,030). Apparently, however, most undocumented Europeans chose not to come forward, especially among the Irish.

Far more avidly pursued was the diversity visa provision included in IRCA in 1986. Introduced by Congressman Brian Donnelly (Massachusetts) in response to efforts by the Irish Immigration Reform Movement to publicize the perceived inequalities and narrow qualifications in the 1965 legislation, the initial "diversity" effort involved 10,000 "Donnelly visas" to be distributed by lottery in 1988–89. The Irish, forewarned, sent in some 1.5 million requests and got 4,161 of these new visas – the first "unsponsored" ones. In 1988 the program was extended and another 20,000 were

approved for 1990–91.[13] This diversity visa program was then incorporated into the 1990 Immigration Act. It allocated 120,000 for three years (1992–94), once again by lottery in countries that had low immigration numbers for the prior five years. Through Sen. Ted Kennedy's efforts, 40 % were set aside for the Irish and, indeed, between 1992 and 1994 over 38,600 (out of 108,435) were awarded to the Irish. In fact, during those three

13 The number of Irish admitted jumped in 1989 to 6,961 and then to 10,333 in 1990 but none were clearly identified with this novel program. The Immigration and Naturalization Service (INS) reported that in 1991 9,802 "diversity transition visas" were awarded but gave no further details. However, in 1992, 33,911 were given out, and 25,401 went to Europeans.

transition years, 87 % of the total went to Europeans (nearly 94,100).

The 1990 law stipulated that, beginning in 1995, 55,000 diversity visas would be given out annually to lottery winners, with a maximum of 3,850 for any one country. That diversity ceiling was reduced in 1999 to 50,000 visas (maximum 7 % for any one country). Over the years between 1992 and 2005 almost 323,000 Europeans received such visas, 41 % of the overall total. Significantly, over 70 % of those visas for Europeans were awarded to east Europeans with some astonishing results (Table 4).

Finally, we observed that during the 1970s fewer Europeans were adjusting their status in America to Legal Permanent Resident, but that was a hiatus largely in terms of refugees, and the situation changed immensely with the transformation of eastern Europe beginning in 1990. Refugees were the largest category to adjust, for most were already admitted and present when their new status was conferred on them, as was true of asylees and parolees. The annual reports reveal that, besides this class of newcomers, numerous Europeans apparently learned about coming as visitors and then applying for a change of status or getting temporary employment and, with that, assistance in applying for a permanent status. The Poles in particular made good use of this strategy, as did a steadily growing number from the FSU and other east European nations (especially Romanians). As Table 5 illustrates, well over one million

Europeans between 1991 and 2002 (no data available beyond that year) adjusted their status – nearly 63 % of all the Europeans admitted. While some of the older groups might appear to have the lower percentages, such as the Irish and Portuguese – implying less need for this avenue – the Poles in fact had the lowest. Many nationalities from across the European region made use of these options, including the French, Italians, and British, as well as Czechs, Ukrainians and others from the FSU. Along with visitors and refugees, many students, temporary workers, and even those who were EWI – had Entered Without Inspection – made good use of adjustment procedures. In fact, as recently as 2001 and 2002 70 % of all Europeans admitted did so.

The 2000 U.S. Census: A Brief Profile of Europeans

Between 1930 and 2006 over 7.95 million Europeans were admitted into the United States as Legal Permanent Residents, and the top dozen nationalities followed in this essay (1930–2004) represented all sections of Europe (Table 6 below). A brief snapshot of the 2000 U.S. census will summarize where the European foreign born stood at the turn of the century as a consequence of the many shifts and recent dramatic developments we have described.

The almost 4.92 million Europeans in the census represented 15.8 % of all foreign born (31.1 million), a decisively lower figure than the 75 % share in 1960, or

Table 5 European use of adjustment-of-status for legal permanent residency in the United States 1991–2002

Nationality	Number	in %
All Admissions	6,078,179	54.2 %
All Europeans	1,040,654	62.8 %
Former Soviet Union	505,747	83.8 %
Former Yugoslavians	110,272	73.9 %
Hungarians	8,302	64.4 %
French	12,036	63.8 %
Czechs/Slovaks	8,298	62.8 %
British	104,218	61.2 %
Italians	16,624	59.1 %
Greeks	8,797	55.6 %
Germans	44,177	51.2 %
Swedes	8,173	49.6 %
Portuguese	11,549	45.1 %
Poles	57,491	29.6 %
Irish	10,189	16.5 %

even the 61.7 % in 1970. As a result of the huge recent influxes from the FSU and especially the Ukraine, almost 39 % of the Europeans were east European (Table 7 below). Not surprisingly, the most recent, or newest, groups were from Bosnia and Herzegovina, Moldova, and Albania. Equally unsurprising is that the populations with the greater proportions who arrived prior to 1980 were also those with the largest number naturalized: for example, over three-fourths of Greeks, Hungarians, and Italians.

In general, Europeans were older than other foreigners, with a median age of 50 versus 37, and they included decidedly more women, with a sex ratio of 83:100. Giving some credence to those concerned about whom America was attracting among Europeans, three-fourths had a high school diploma or more (with Bulgarians, Swiss, and Irish above 90 %), and 29 % held college degrees. (Three-fifths of all foreigners had diplomas and less than one-fourth had B.A.s or more.) While labor force participation was lower because of the generally more advanced age of the European population (and retirees), among

Table 4 European recipients of diversity visas, 1992–2005

All Europeans	322,964	(50.8 % of all *Diversity Visa*)
East Europeans	227,568	(70.5 % of all Europeans)
Former Soviet Union	70,100	
Poles	65,100	
Irish	45,900	
Albanians	29,300	
Bulgarians	26,000	
Rumanians	20,900	
British	12,250	
Germans	10,150	
Lithuanians	9,900	
Former Yugoslavians	6,200	
Italians	2,400	

those who were working, 40 % were in management, professional, and related fields (versus 28.5 % for all foreignborn) – the strongest difference occupationally between Europeans and other foreigners in America. As expected, incomes for both European men and women well exceeded those of all foreign born.

Table 6 Total European immigration to the United States, 1930–2006, and total immigrant population of selected European nationalities, f.y. 1947–2004

Total European Immigration (1930–2006)	7,953,854
Total U.S. Immigration (1947–2004*)	31,299,056
Total European Immigration (1947–2004*)	6,704,611
British	984,375
Former Soviet Union	894,764
Germans	877,397
Poles	653,802
Italians	641,165
Former Yugoslavians	355,921
Greeks	285,819
Portuguese	275,609
Irish	243,320
Hungarians	128,211
Czechs/Slovaks	105,925
Swedes	78,785

* The principal statistical analyses in this essay cover from July 1946 (fiscal year 1947) to September 2004 (end of fiscal year 2004), during which time the data were most consistent. All the country and regional data here are derived from Country of Birth tables, except for 1982-83, when an INS reporting problem omitted separate tables for birth and last residence.

Europeans' Persisting Presence in the U.S.

The post-war era made Americans acutely aware of the reality that immigration policy was not only a domestic policy; it had become global. While America was pursuing strategic anti-Communist policies that dominated, for example, the new refugee legislation of the 1950s, western Europe was experiencing a remarkable economic recovery, benefiting from U.S. Secretary of State George C. Marshall's support and his belief that "the task of war does not end when the

Table 7 Leading foreign-born European nationalities in the United States, census 2000

All Europeans	4,915,557
Germans	706,704
British	677,751
Italians	473,338
Poles	466,742
Russians	340,177
Ukrainians	275,133
Portuguese	203,119
Greeks	165,750
Irish	156,471
French	151,154
Romanians	135,966
Bosnians-Herzegovinians	98,766
Dutch	94,570
Hungarians	92,017
Czechs/Slovaks	83,081
Spanish	82,858
Austrians	63,648
Swedes	49,724
Belarusians	38,503

shooting ends." In fact, by the late 1950s several European nations were making agreements with countries along the northern Mediterranean coast to provide increasingly needed low skilled and service workers. As European nations drew closer together this economic competition with the United States became more of a reality, adding to a weakening of the flow of immigrants to America until the huge refugee surge beginning in 1990. Nonetheless, a large number of those who did go to America went as nonimmigrants – as students or as temporary, short term skilled, technical, and professional workers – many of whom subsequently applied for an adjustment of status so that they could remain.

Although the evidence is not clear how many eventually chose to settle in the United States, Europeans began raising the specter of brain drain by the United States, but the growing globalization of trade, travel, communications, corporate enterprises, military operations, education, and technology exchanges led some to reconfigure the "drain" as more of an "exchange," a "circulation" of human capital in which both host and home countries benefited. Moreover, the billions of dollars in remittances being sent to home countries have been a vital part of the exchanges and have certainly

counterbalanced some of the concerns about home country losses.

If the formation of the European community and, by the early 1990s, a European Union was an event of great drama in terms of the region becoming an immigrant-receiving one – and a more racially and ethnically diverse one at that – the new prosperity undoubtedly affected the volume of immigration to the United States. However, far more revolutionary in their impact was the collapse of the FSU and its domination over eastern Europe, followed by the near genocidal Yugoslav civil wars. Immigration from east to west accelerated, especially as a dozen of those countries joined the European community. The various U.S. immigration measures – especially its refugee policies – strongly demonstrated that those cataclysmic events profoundly impacted immigration to America.

It has not been so much a matter of Europeans not going to America as that the volume of newcomers from Asia and the Americas has so greatly overshadowed the Europeans. Nonetheless, a united Europe at peace has had its own grandeur, and migration into and out of it has played a key role in the transatlantic population movements. Indeed, even if we assume a 22% return rate among the 7.95 million Europeans who migrated to America between 1930 and 2006, that still leaves over 6.2 million Europeans resettling in America. The fact that 1,051,400 persons born in Europe were admitted as Legal Permanent Residents between 2000 and 2006 and 1.29 million during the prior decade (1990–99) should remind us that the bonds between Europe and the United States are likely to remain strong in this 21st century.

Turbine steamer "Imperator" of Hamburg shipping company HAPAG, paintig around 1913

Polizeidirektion Würzburg
9 6 2 0
11. 10. 1935

Photograph of Karl Rosenthal taken by the Bavarian Political Police a day after his arrest on 10 October 1935

Manfred Wichmann

Nothing Saved but His Own Life –
The Banishment and Flight of the Jewish Lawyer
Karl Rosenthal from Nazi Germany

"If you grant me my request it would mean that my emigration could be speeded up by almost 4 months. You will understand that under the tragic circumstances I have outlined to you this would constitute an act of humanity; no other applicant will be disadvantaged by this. In any case, only one person instead of the anticipated 4 will be emigrating." With these words Dr. Karl Rosenthal, in December 1938, pleaded with the US Consulate in Stuttgart to be given the opportunity to emigrate from Nazi Germany. His long-planned departure had turned into a desperate attempt to escape after three members of his family had fallen victim to the pogrom of November 9, 1938. The quickest possible means of leaving the German Reich had become a matter of life and death, not only for Rosenthal but for tens of thousands of German Jews, yet efforts to obtain a life-saving visa for foreign countries were confronted by bureaucratic hurdles and beset with harassments and uncertainties extending over several months. Although each escape story followed a different course, the emigration of the Jewish lawyer Karl Rosenthal can serve as an example of the difficult conditions which prevailed when German Jews fled from the NS regime, if they succeeded in doing so at all.

Karl Samuel Rosenthal was born in Nuremberg on July 7, 1879, the second child of Jewish parents, Heinrich and Babette Rosenthal. Following his secondary school education the merchant's son commenced his one-year of military service as a volunteer in October 1898 after which he went on to study law. For the next four years he took courses at the universities of Erlangen, Würzburg, Munich, and Berlin. After his doctorate and law degrees he was called to the bar in 1906 in Würzburg and there joined the chambers of his uncle, Ignaz Freudenthal.

On March 12, 1910 Karl Rosenthal married Clara ("Claire") Buschhoff, a merchant's daughter from Worms, with whom he had three children. During World War I he served in the German infantry and was at the front from the spring of 1915 until the end of 1918. He received several promotions and was awarded the Iron Cross Class I and Class II. He was demobilized with the rank of First Lieutenant on December 7, 1918, following which he became an active member of the anti-communist "Einwohnerwehr" in Würzburg, a civil defence corps dedicated to the fight against the revolutionary soviet movement.

From 1919 onward Rosenthal again practised as a lawyer and took on numerous honorary positions which earned him high regard in his adopted home of Würzburg. As a politician and member of the liberal German Democratic Party (DDP) he supported the Republic and joined the so-called "Reichsbanner Schwarz-Rot-Gold", a republican paramilitary force, as well as the "Deutsche Friedensgesellschaft" (German Peace Society). In 1928 this highly respected lawyer was awarded the title of "Justizrat"

(Queen's Council). Karl Rosenthal saw himself as a Jew with liberal religious views and as such led reform movements within the Jewish community itself. As a self-assured representative of the Jewish bourgeoisie he established a local branch of the "Reichsbund jüdischer Frontsoldaten" (RjF) (Association of Jewish Front-line Soldiers) and was appointed its chairman. Karl Rosenthal became one of Lower Franconia's most important exponents in the fight against the defamation of Jews by right-wing parties, national associations and the anti-Semitic press and he took over the local chairmanship of the Würzburg C.V. (Centralverein deutscher Staatsbürger jüdischen Glaubens – Central Association of German citizens of the Jewish faith). As early as the 1920s Rosenthal had thus become one of the main opponents of the strongly anti-Semitic NSDAP in Franconia. In response to anti-Jewish propaganda in connection with a child-murder, re-interpreted as the "Ritual Murder of Manau" in Julius Streicher's weekly

Karl Rosenthal with his wife Claire and their children Anni, Fritz, and Paul in 1924 on the island of Norderney

Ideological brain-washing of children and militarization of school instruction: from "The Roland Primer, The First Reading Book for the Children of Bremen", 1935

newspaper "Der Stürmer", Karl Rosenthal organized a large-scale counter event in 1929 with 1500 participants, supported by the city council, which was severely disrupted by around 300 mobilized National Socialists. Rosenthal was persecuted not only on account of his permanent and partly effective fight against NS propaganda but also because of his long-standing membership of several Masonic Lodges: for a while he chaired the "Zu den zwei Säulen am Stein" Lodge in Würzburg and when Rosenthal was stationed in Belgium in 1915 he co-founded the "Zum Eisernen Kreuz" Field Lodge in Liège. All this led to a constantly recurring propaganda campaign against Rosenthal by the national NSDAP and in the anti-Semitic press.

Soon after the National Socialists had come to power Karl Rosenthal became the victim of state repression and despotism. In the spring of 1933, the Bavarian "Politische Polizei" (Political Police) – a precursor of the Gestapo under the leadership of Reinhard Heydrich – carried out several raids at the premises of the RjF and the C.V. In the summer of that year Rosenthal himself became a target: on July 15, officials of the Political Police broke into his home confiscating numerous documents and four days later his legal offices were searched. Extensive material relating to local opposition thereby fell into the hands of the NS. As a highly decorated front-line officer, Rosenthal was still able to retain his position as a lawyer; however, the secret police intercepted his mail and tapped his telephone calls.

In spite of the ever increasing exclusion and defamation of the Jewish community, Karl Rosenthal remained a staunch patriot and put

his trust in the legal system in force at the time and the protection which, for the time being, continued to be given to front-line soldiers.

Thus, in 1935, in a widely publicized trial Rosenthal agreed to take on the defence of a lawyer who had been portrayed as a Jewish child abuser by NS propaganda. The newspaper "Der Stürmer" took this opportunity to again publicly disparage Rosenthal who was accused of being not only a member of the Freemasons and the "Reichsbanner" (as well as, falsely, an SPD member) but also of fomenting resistance: "When National Socialism also took root in the Mainfranken region it was the Jew Rosenthal of all people who declared war on it in the most bitter and

malicious manner." In an attempt to break his resistance, the Political Police once again resorted to action and Rosenthal was arrested on October 10, 1935. In consideration of his position as a public figure he was not incarcerated in a concentration camp but in the Würzburg district court prison. During his three-month internment, Rosenthal was harassed and warned that he should no longer practise as a lawyer or stay in Germany.

It became increasingly evident that in the final analysis emigration was the only option available to him in order to escape once and for all the persecution and mortal danger which threatened him. His family urged him to emigrate. The pressure to leave became

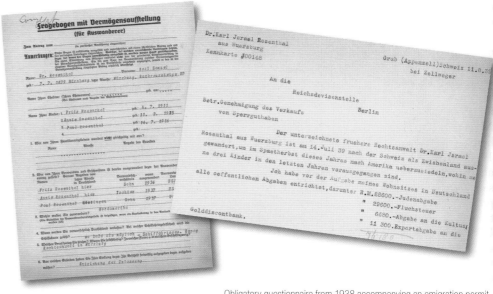

Obligatory questionnaire from 1938 accompanying an emigration permit application in which all assets had to be itemized

ever more acute and yet there were numerous reasons not to flee abroad. First of all, emigration for Jews was made significantly more difficult because of the huge economic and legal restrictions imposed upon the Jewish minority. If one succeeded at all it entailed not only the loss of one's entire social environment, that is, relatives, friends, neighbors, and colleagues, but also the loss of one's home, one's home town and the fatherland. An important factor was that the Jewish bourgeoisie saw themselves as an inseparable part of German culture and tradition. Also, from an economic point of view, emigration incurred immense losses, because from 1938 onwards Jewish emigrants had to forego at least 95 % of their assets on account of special taxes, limitations on foreign exchange, and export bans. In addition, there were the uncertainties associated with building a completely new existence in an unknown country and the efforts required to do so, and for those with a university education it also meant a loss of social status and unpredictable employment prospects. All this – and, in many cases, the hope or belief that the NS regime could not last and its persecution policy could not worsen – made it unimaginable for many German Jews, amongst them the almost 60-year-old Karl Rosenthal, to leave Germany at this time.

On the other hand, Rosenthal's children no longer saw a future for themselves in Germany and they emigrated. The eldest son Fritz, born in 1911, had studied chemistry on completion of his secondary education and by the end of 1933 had already moved to Bern to do his doctorate. In September 1936 he emigrated to the USA and worked as a chemist in a number of large companies. Rosenthal's daughter Anni, born in 1915, was able to complete her secondary education in 1934 and trained as a gym teacher. She then worked in London for one year before emigrating to the USA in November 1937. His son Paul, born in 1916, had to leave secondary school prematurely, in 1934, in accordance with NS laws and started an apprenticeship in Göttingen as a precision engineer. Since there was practically no prospect of him getting a job in Germany he too decided to emigrate and arrived in the USA in April 1937. All three children made great efforts to convince their parents to take the same decision as they had and to facilitate their immigration into the USA.

The year 1938 proved to be a reversal of fortune for Karl and Claire Rosenthal as well

A suitcase of this kind, produced from around 1900 onwards, was found during a house clearance in 1995. It has not been possible to establish how the Star of David, which obviously had been added at a later stage to the suitcase, came to be there

as for many thousands of German Jews. Ever stricter constraints, loss of material livelihood through occupational bans and "Aryanisation", and the pressure of persecution, using force and deportation, led to a surge in Jewish emigration. This was compounded by the expulsion policy in Austria following the "Anschluss", in the wake of which the Center for Jewish Emigration in Vienna, established by Adolf Eichmann, enforced the uncompromising and virtually complete disfranchisement of Jews and expropriation of their assets within the space of a few months. In the summer of 1938, Karl and Claire Rosenthal, who had stayed behind in Würzburg, decided to follow their children to the USA. Claire was presumably the driving force behind this decision, as she was the one who initiated emigration procedures. At the end of July she traveled to Stuttgart and visited the US Consulate to submit an affidavit from their son Fritz in America in support of his parents. Such a guarantee with a statement of income, certified by a notary public, was intended to ensure the private financial support of new immigrants and was indispensable for obtaining a permanent residents permit. The USA had tightened up on its immigration policy during the world economic crisis and as a result many refugees

without an affidavit were denied a visa on the strength of the so-called LPC clause ("Likely to become a Public Charge"). It was only at the Consulate that Claire Rosenthal became aware of the fact that entry on the immigration lists was equally important in order to receive a number on the waiting list for the quota of German immigrants permitted into the USA. She immediately applied for a place as any kind of delay of entry on the list would have meant a higher number and a longer waiting period. On August 1, 1938 the Rosenthals received waiting number 7922 and it was anticipated that this would entitle them to a visa in September of the following year. The Consulate confirmed in writing that their livelihood in America was secured by the affidavit; however, there were restrictions: "There is no guarantee that on the day of summons you will receive your visa and final travel arrangements should only be made when the visa is actually in your hands."

In fact, precisely the opposite was the case. Timely and long-term planning with regard to emigration was essential if one wanted to make immediate use of the long-awaited entry permit on the due date of one's waiting number. By now it had become ever more difficult for Jewish emigrants to receive an exit

In 1939 the HAPAG steamer "St. Louis" aroused considerable publicity. Although most of the more than 900 Jewish passengers had valid visas for Cuba, the authorities in Havana refused to allow them ashore. In the end, the ship returned to Antwerp and the refugees were accepted into France, Belgium, and Holland only to be threatened again a year later by persecution and deportation by the Nazis

permit to leave Germany, not only because of the escalating numbers of people wanting to flee but also on account of NS policies which, on the one hand, forced emigration yet, at the same time, made it ever more difficult by constantly introducing new restrictions and by ever greater harassment. In the first instance, the Rosenthals were required to submit further documentation to the US Consulate such as a valid passport, several copies of birth and marriage certificates, certificates of good conduct as well as passport photographs. At the same time, arrangements for leaving the country had to be made which also required a number of official certificates and authorizations, attempts to transfer some assets abroad and, last but not least, planning the actual removal and the travel route.

During the second half of 1938, right in the middle of making all these preparations, the situation deteriorated dramatically. At the end of September the NS regime decreed that Jewish lawyers were no longer allowed to practise and their accreditation would expire automatically on November 30. For Karl Rosenthal this meant that his professional career would be finished once and for all and that there would no longer be a secure income. Not long afterward, the pogrom night of November 9/10, with its violent and unchecked anti-Semitism, did not stop at Würzburg and both the Rosenthals became direct victims. Karl Rosenthal was arrested by Gestapo officials during the night without any reason given and against the protestations of his wife. After she had been left behind on her own, a group of men ransacked their home. On enquiry at the police station Claire Rosenthal learnt that her husband had been taken to the Buchenwald concentration camp. In desperation she swallowed an overdose of Veronal and left a farewell letter in which she requested the release of her husband. Having been taken to hospital by friends, Claire Rosenthal died on 17 November 1938. As a result, Karl Rosenthal was released from the concentration camp the same day. He returned to Würzburg unaware of the fate of his wife.

In these tragic circumstances Karl Rosenthal now had to press ahead with his emigration in order to save his own life. Emigration plans turned into a desperate search for the quickest possible way to flee from Germany. Rosenthal's letter, quoted above, left no doubt that it was a cry for help. In order to expedite his entry permit, he asked the US Consulate on 1 December 1938 to grant him the waiting number 6162 as "heir", so to speak, to his sister Karoline ("Nelly") Schloß, a merchant's widow, who had taken her own life in Munich two days previously because her only son Hans, with whom she had planned to emigrate, had been arrested during the pogrom night and had died on November 13 at Dachau concentration camp. Nonetheless, the US Foreign Office rejected his plea, drawing attention to the allocation practice in force which did not allow for an exchange of waiting numbers. He was told that his visa was still not due for consideration until September 1939.

Until then the hardships of overcoming official chicanery and fulfilling the numerous preconditions inevitably associated with an exit permit would remain. Several Jewish organizations – in Germany, mainly the Aid Association of German Jews – offered manifold and often indispensable help. They distributed general information and gave advice in individual cases, they offered support with official applications, endeavoured to obtain financial aid for the destitute, organized occupational retraining, and arranged vital contacts in emigration countries. However, the main burden and responsibility of fleeing in each individual case lay with the person concerned. As a priority Karl Rosenthal had to obtain a passport, but this was only issued on submission of several official statements. These included proof that all taxes and outstanding debts had been paid, and that all dues, insurances and membership fees had been settled. This was in line with the economic plundering of German Jews which stopped at nothing, even when they planned to emigrate. The capital levy imposed on Jews following the pogrom night in November, combined with taxes to avoid the flight of capital, the so-called "Reichsfluchtsteuer", amounted to about half one's total assets and in the case of most refugees, Rosenthal included, exceeded the cash readily available to them. A further aggravating fact was that since April 1938 Jewish assets had been accurately recorded and frozen by the NS regime. Insofar as there were any assets left worth mentioning, when all required payments had been made, these were initially blocked by currency regulations and later confiscated. Karl Rosenthal was forced to make his own house and land, his mother-in-law's mortgages, the inheritance from his sister and part of his share portfolio over to the state as security, at appreciably reduced valuations, in order to come up with the required payments. Rosenthal made several requests to decrease the stipulated amount of taxes, but all were rejected and not even the so-called Jewish Wealth Levy for his deceased wife was waived. In this way the state took virtually all of Rosenthal's assets, amounting to about 110,000 Reichsmarks (RM), and when he left the country he was not allowed to take more than 10 RM in cash.

In addition, great efforts were made by the NS regime to reduce the amount of personal belongings taken abroad to an absolute minimum and to withhold all valuables. Detailed lists of all items, with exact valuations, had to be presented before permission to export these was given. The comprehensive account submitted by Karl Rosenthal for assessment in January 1939 included individual items ranging from pieces of furniture to a sugar bowl, a hair dryer, kitchen towels, and socks. During the following months he tried to gain special permission from the tax authorities to take part of his furniture and household effects to the USA, in addition to clothes and other personal items. He pleaded for an exception to be made because he had no other assets left and would be dependent on the support of his children, who had not themselves taken any household items with them when they emigrated. Therefore, it would only be "right and proper that children would receive a modest endowment of necessary furnishings from their parents' home". However, his request was rejected, and in February of that year his entire household effects, including furniture, office equipment and furnishings as well as his specialist library, were put up for private sale and auction. The proceeds went straight to the tax authorities and were held in blocked accounts. In a letter to friends Rosenthal remarked with cynicism upon this form of expropriation: "The less one has in the bank the more one becomes unconcerned about material assets." At the beginning of May 1939 he eventually sold his house to pay the final claims. On 13 May he was at last issued by the tax authorities with the "Unbedenklichkeitsbescheinigung", a document essential for emigration certifying that he had no taxes, loans, etc. outstanding. Meanwhile, in order to get his father out of Germany as quickly as possible, Fritz

Refusal of an entry permit into Switzerland: "Emigration to America is not sufficiently secured"

Hilfsverein der Juden in Deutschland e. V.

Vom Herrn Reichsminister des Innern durch Verfügung vom 31. 10. 1924 Nr. II 7781 als gemeinnützige Auswandererberatungsstelle für die Beratung jüdischer Auswanderer anerkannt.

Betrifft: Dr.S/Wch.

Bei Beantwortung unbedingt anzugeben

Jetzt: N4, Artilleriestr.31
Berlin W 35, den Sammel-Nr. 41 67 21
Ludendorffstr. 20   26.Juni 1939

Ihr Schrb.v.20.6.1939

Herrn
Justizrat Dr. Karl Rosenthal
W ü r z b u r g
Hindenburgstr.14.

Sehr geehrter Herr Justizrat,

Ihr Schreiben vom 2o.6. an Herrn Dr.Hirsch ist uns zu-
ständigkeitshalber zugestellt worden. Es ist nicht da-
mit zu rechnen, dass das Aufsuchen eines Zwischenlandes
eine Verlängerung der Wartezeit von nahezu einem Jahr
zur Folge hat. Vielmehr ist davon auszugehen, dass da-
durch nur eine Verschiebung um etwa 2 Monate eintritt.
Eine vernünftige Zwischenwanderung braucht also nicht
im Hinblick auf die Verschiebung dieser Wartezeit unter-
lassen zu werden.

Mit vorzüglicher Hochachtung
REICHSVEREINIGUNG DER JUDEN IN DEUTSCHLAND
Abt. Wanderung (Hilfsverein)

(Dr.J.L.Israel Seligsohn)

Letter by the Aid Association of German Jews concerning Rosenthal's wish to stay in Switzerland

Rosenthal had asked his Swiss wife's family in Grub (Appenzell) to take in his father until such time as his US visa had been issued. This required an entry permit for Switzerland but, in spite of the country's neutrality, it maintained a dismissive attitude toward Jewish refugees. At the beginning of December 1938 Karl Rosenthal submitted an application for entry to Switzerland making reference to his incarceration in a concentration camp and his wife's suicide. He explicitly pointed out that this would be a temporary measure until September 1939 at the latest, when he expected to emigrate to the USA. Parish priest Zellweger and his family confirmed to the cantonal police that they would guarantee Rosenthal's stay in Grub and pay for his keep. Nevertheless, the Swiss Confederation's aliens' police rejected the application in January on the ground that: "The outward voyage to America is not sufficiently secured."

Like most other German Jews desperately looking for an opportunity to flee Germany after November 1938, Karl Rosenthal left no stone unturned and in the course of December of that year applied to several countries for a

temporary residence permit. His application for a visitors' visa to the USA until such time as his waiting number would come up was immediately rejected by the US Consulate, as also was the bringing forward of his quota number. An attempt to spend his waiting time in the Netherlands failed because he had no relatives who could secure a transit visa for him. At the end of the month Rosenthal contacted acquaintances of his daughter in London asking them to look into the possibility of a limited residence permit. His emigration to the USA in September 1939 was secured but, he emphasized: "In my own experience and in accord with the general opinion in Jewish circles it is regarded as highly risky to wait patiently for so long in Germany." With the help of the German Jewish Aid Committee Rosenthal was able to apply for a residence permit in Great Britain, but the processing of his application dragged on for several months.

To his relief news of an entry permit finally came from Switzerland. It was lucky that he had personal contacts there as this proved to be the decisive factor. The Zellwegers had asked for the help of the Jewish Community in

Bern and were able to present their case to the Federal Vice-President Johannes Baumann. He succeeded in having the visa application reconsidered and, following a security payment of SFr 2,000 by Fritz Rosenthal, the Swiss Justice and Police Ministry approved a temporary residence permit for his father Karl until September 30, 1939. Rosenthal was now in possession of all the necessary documents and yet he delayed his exit for almost another two months. The reason for this was his concern – fed by rumours spread by emigrants – that residence in a transit country might delay entry to America for another year. Under no circumstances did he want to risk this happening. He made renewed enquiries at consulates as well as to the Aid Committee and asked for his entry date into Switzerland to be extended until mid-July. Also, he was still waiting for an answer from Great Britain which would have been his preferred option for an interim solution, since it would have given him an opportunity to learn the language. When, after six months, there was still no positive reply from Great Britain, he was strongly urged by the Aid Committee to leave the country. Hence, he left his home town on July 14, 1939 and traveled to Switzerland.

During his stay with the Zellwegers in Grub he had to organize the transfer of his visa documentation from Stuttgart to the US Consulate in Zurich. This proved problematic and clarification as to who would bear the postage costs alone dragged on for weeks. When at the beginning of September 1939 World War II broke out, Rosenthal again feared for his emigration overseas. He pleaded with the Consulate in Stuttgart to despatch his documents while it was still possible to make the journey by ship from Italy. Finally, on September 26, he received his visa for the USA and immediately booked the next possible passage. He left Europe on October 6, 1939 from Genoa as a third-class passenger on the Italian ship "Rex" bound for America.

Initially he lived with his son Paul in Chicago for a year. In March 1940 he described his situation in a letter as follows: "I reached Chicago at the end of October '39 and have settled in quite well, thanks to the care of my children; however, I miss having work to do which would fill the day, and I find it very difficult learning conversational English. I hear little from Würzburg and then only sad cases of fatalities." During the following years, Karl Rosenthal worked in

Karl Rosenthal in the rubble of his former residence in Würzburg after his return in 1952

New York as a salesman, factory worker, and department store assistant; he did not want to be a financial burden to his children. In 1949 he returned to Würzburg as a US citizen with the aim of again practicing as a lawyer. Following his readmission to legal practice in 1952 he mainly attended to restitution procedures. However, he was not able to settle down again in his former home town which had changed so much. Five years later he left Germany and returned to the USA where he remained with his children until his death in 1970. He never lost his bond with his native country which had banished him, and he was not able to come to terms with his new home: thus, in 1963 he described himself as merely "a spectator of American life".

Sources

Jüdisches Museum Berlin: Karl Rosenthal Collection

Staatsarchiv Würzburg: Files of the Gestapo offices and the Police Headquarters in Würzburg

Bayerisches Hauptstaatsarchiv: Officers' personal files, files relating to Compensation Law

Bayerisches Staatsministerium der Justiz: Personal file

Stadtarchiv Würzburg: List of registered inhabitants, "Grundliste" and "Trümmerräumakte"

Jüdisches Dokumentationszentrum Würzburg: Letter by Paul Rosenthal

Benz, Wolfgang: Flucht aus Deutschland. Zum Exil im 20. Jahrhundert, München 2001

Flade, Roland: Die Würzburger Juden. Ihre Geschichte vom Mittelalter bis zur Gegenwart, Würzburg 1996

Handbuch der deutschsprachigen Emigration 1933–1945, hrsg. von Claus-Dieter Krohn u.a. in Zusammenarbeit mit der Gesellschaft für Exilforschung, Darmstadt 1998

Heimat und Exil. Emigration der deutschen Juden nach 1933, Ausstellungskatalog, hrsg. von der Stiftung Haus der Geschichte der Bundesrepublik Deutschland und der Stiftung Jüdisches Museum Berlin

Strätz, Rainer: Biographisches Handbuch Würzburger Juden, hrsg. vom Stadtarchiv, 2 Bände, Würzburg 1989

Vogel, Rolf: Ein Stempel hat gefehlt. Dokumente zur Emigration deutscher Juden, München 1977

Weber, Reinhard: Das Schicksal der jüdischen Rechtsanwälte in Bayern, München 2006

Wetzel, Juliane: Auswanderung aus Deutschland, in: Benz, Wolfgang (Hrsg.): Die Juden in Deutschland. Leben unter nationalsozialistischer Herrschaft, 2. Auflage München 1989, p. 413–498

Wyman, David S.: Paper walls. America and the refugee crisis 1938–1941, Amherst 1968

A DP's way to U.S.A.

Des DP's Weg nach den U.S.A.

A political cartoon illustrating the obstacles impeding the emigration of Displaced Persons to the United States, date 1945/46. Stefan Czyzewski, portrait photo

Henriette von Holleuffer

Between Nowhere and Somewhere: One Displaced Person's Odyssey to Freedom

This DP story is an example of the odysseys of millions of men, women and children. Thousands of Displaced Persons left Europe in the aftermath of World War II. For these people, the port of Bremerhaven was one stop on their long journey to freedom. Displaced Persons were no typical emigrants. They left no home behind, they abandoned no home country, and few made orphans of their families. In fact, most of them did not even plan to go to a specific country. Nor did their lives as Displaced Persons start in the camps which the United Nations Relief and Rehabilitation Administration (UNRRA) established in the western zones of Germany. From here, in the years 1947 until 1951, thousands could be resettled with the help of the International Refugee Organization (IRO). The DP story is a history of many chapters. Millions of men, women, and children had been uprooted in their existence long before World War II started. They had been deprived of their rights, their relatives, their belongings, their identity and their future. Countless numbers had been expelled from their homes against their will. Millions were deported and driven into lives as forced laborers, as partisans or illegals who had to hide in the underground for years. In the end, those who had survived were either liberated by the Allied armies, or they simply remained stateless people in a new peace order, stranded in the turmoil of post-war Europe. Many of them lived in camps for nearly two decades. They were survivors without home and family, provided only with the legal status: Displaced Persons.

The IRO tried to find a proper definition for the heterogeneous group of homeless people. According to this definition, the term Displaced Person applied to a individual who, as a result of the actions of the authorities of the Nazi and Fascist regimes, "had been deported from, or had been obliged to leave, his country of nationality or of former habitual residence, such as persons who were compelled to undertake forced labor or who were deported for racial, religious or political reasons". This definition was only a general description which did not cover the complex stories of millions of Displaced Persons. It did not specify that people of Polish nationality were the largest single group among the Displaced Persons. Moreover, the document did not ensure any lasting protection for those 6 to 7 million people who were shipped back to eastern Europe immediately after the war. Furthermore, it did not specify that the Holocaust survivors were only one group among different groups of Cold War refugees who left eastern Europe after 1945, and who also applied for resettlement overseas.

The signers of the IRO constitution dealt with a complex resettlement program. When the governments of the United States, Canada, and Australia finally decided to start their resettlement schemes, this also was seen as an opportunity to choose from a pool of potential new citizens who were anxious to live and work overseas. For example, the United States took a "fair share" of nearly 400,000 Displaced Persons. About 37% of all Displaced Persons who went to the United States were of Polish nationality and more than 50% of those who were accepted by the Americans were singles without family, mainly at an age of between 25 and 44. This showed that the resettlement program was a carefully planned immigration project. However, plans were made by governments. In contrast to this, the Displaced Persons had learnt to live from day to day. When the Displaced Persons finally dispersed across the globe in search of a safe future, memories were all they carried as luggage.

Today, these memories are relevant for the reconstruction of the DP story, a phenomenon of the 20th century. Names, dates, places and incidents recollected by former Displaced Persons can document how individuals, families or ethnic communities were extinguished if not, in rare cases, resettled elsewhere. Now, one carefully chosen life story will illustrate the historical, social and psychological dimensions of the DP existence. Obviously, this single account of the life of a Polish farmer's son cannot tell the whole DP experience. Biographies are fragments which barely refer to all aspects of a DP life. One account may tell about expulsion and torture during the pre-war years, another may focus on resettlement and assimilation after the war. The following, however, exemplifies the odyssey of more than one million Displaced Persons who lived for many years in the British or American zones of post-war Germany and who desperately tried to find new homes in the years to come.

Childhood and Youth in Poland

Stefan Czyzewski was born on August 12, 1922 in the little village of Leśnogóra in Poland, located about 45 kilometres east of Warsaw. The son of Polish Catholics, he was born into a farm community where Polish peasants and Jewish merchants lived as neighbors. His parents had experienced the upheaval of years of war and the uncertainty of short periods of peace which characterized Europe's history at the turn of the century. As Polish patriots they witnessed their nation's fight for independence from foreign control. This ambitious struggle for self-government was successful and, during the years 1916 until 1918, Poland was re-established.

Stefan's father was a veteran who had fought on different battlefields. Jan Czyzewski had served more than 12 years in the Russian Imperial Army. As a young man, he was conscripted to serve in the Imperial Army of the Czar because he lived in a part of Poland occupied by Russia. Later on, Stefan's father was called again to fight against the Germans

Postcard of a lodge used as a state hospital after liberation where Stefan Czyzewski was a patient from 1945 to 1946, date 1945/46

during the First World War. He deserted and crossed enemy lines. The Germans imprisoned him, and then brought him to the front line between France and Germany, where he worked to build fortifications for the Germans at Verdun. He changed sides again, intending to serve in the Polish Legion which was fighting on the French side. He fought bravely and returned home a highly decorated veteran. By the beginning of the 1920s, Poland was an independent country. There was promise of a good life for Jan Czyzewski as a farmer and his young wife, Bogumila, who was a schoolteacher. Soon she gave birth to the first of three children: Stefan, who grew up on his father's farm.

It was the era of Józef Pitsudski, who had a decisive influence on Poland's domestic and foreign policy. The government led the country through difficult times and put up with political and social conflicts in her efforts to become a powerful nation. Stefan was an intelligent boy who was taught by his mother how to read at the age of three. For three years, he went to primary school in the village of Leśnogóra. During this time he developed a special interest in literature and was fascinated by French authors of the Romantic period. However, his parents were anxious to balance his interests, he had to read the Bible aloud every night after dinner by the light of a kerosene lamp amid of a crowd of children from the neighborhood who listened to the stories of the Old

Testament. By the age of 14 he had read the Bible twice. Later on, Stefan went to a public school in the town of Grębków. It was a seven-grade school where priests and nuns taught religion and prepared the children for first communion.

In these days, the social life of Poland's rural communities was very active. Farm markets, church activities and political

gatherings determined daily life. Catholics and Jews lived their lives and tolerated each other although both groups were strict in their respective religious practices. Many Jews were professionals, such as attorneys, doctors, and merchants, but also tailors or shoemakers. Although business contacts made it easy to come into contact with one another, both groups kept apart socially. Jewish children usually spent little time in public schools. They spoke Yiddish and sometimes learnt Hebrew in their own schools. Polish was their second language.

Stefan continued his education with a grant he received from the government. At the age of fifteen, he moved to the city of Węgrów where, two years later, his education came to a stop. He was seventeen when World War II began. The German Army invaded Poland in September 1939. The war started with the Gliwice incident. It soon became known that German soldiers had dressed up in Polish uniforms in order to feign a Polish attack on a German radio station in Silesia. Polish intelligence spread the news shortly after the incident. Stefan Czyzewski heard of this attack when he listened to the radio during his vacation at home. The family realized that Poland's national leaders had miscalculated the arrangements between the Nazi government and Stalin which eliminated the State of Poland. There had been fears that Germany

Deportees board a deportation train for labor camps in Siberia. Photo ca. 1939–1941

would extend her influence in the east. However, no one had planned to deal with the Soviet Union as a future enemy, and few had expected to fight at two front lines.

Stefan Czyzewski experienced the beginning of the war on his father's farm. Within three weeks, his village became a battle field where Polish cavalry and artillery fought the Germans. Finally, the Polish artillery escaped into the woods, and the Germans came in. Anxiety was great because the casualties among the German soldiers were high. However, nobody in the village was molested by the German patrols. Later on, Stefan watched the refugees arriving from Warsaw and seeking shelter on the farms. It was the first time that he had seen people who were displaced from their homes.

Deportation to Siberia

After the German attack on Poland, Stefan joined a Polish underground organization. He became a member of the Defenders of Poland (Obroncy Polski), who had sworn that they would "fight to the end for the freedom" of their country. The organization recruited young people who would execute secret orders such as collecting arms or attacking German patrols. Stefan was part of a local group of twelve boys, most of whom were dead by 1943.

Stefan's life changed dramatically when he left the German sector of occupation to visit relatives who lived among the Soviets. His parents wanted him to bring documents they had asked for. Consequently, Stefan went to the eastern Polish town of Szczuczyn in November 1939. On the day after his arrival, the Soviet Secret Police NKWD came to Szczuczyn with lists of names and arrested anyone who had served in the Polish local administration: Stefan's relatives were among nearly 1,800 people who the Soviets charged with high treason. Teachers, priests, policemen and their families were put on trial the same night. The trial lasted for four and a half hours. This meant that each sentence was determined in only a few seconds. The NKWD sent all persons sentenced to labor camps in Siberia, Outer Mongolia or Kazakhstan. They were condemned to periods of five, twelve, fifteen or twenty years of forced labor. Stefan could not escape although he declared that he had actually lived under German rule. The officers

Members of the Tehran children's transport are gathered in front of tents at a refugee camp in Tehran. Photo 1942. The Tehran Children were a group of about 1,000 Jewish children who had fled eastward from Poland with their families at the outbreak of World War II. Many of them had lost their parents during their flight. These orphans were allowed to emigrate from the USSR along with 23,000 Polish soldiers and refugees, under an agreement signed by the Polish Government-in-exile and the Soviet Government allowing for the enlistment of Polish refugees in the Soviet Union in the (Polish) Anders Army. In the spring and summer of 1942, the children were taken to Tehran along with the other refugees and soldiers. After immigration permits were obtained from the British, the children were brought to Palestine via Karachi and Suez on February 18, 1943

of the NKWD sentenced him to twelve years and six months in the Gulag. The farmer's son disappeared without being able to leave a note for his parents. He was put on a cattle train for deportation. The journey took more than five weeks. The trains crossed the Ural Mountains and finally reached the River Lena. Here, the deportees were loaded into boats and brought to a camp in the woods near the Arctic Circle. There was no chance to escape.

The deportees had to cut trees in the wilderness of Siberia. Every morning they walked several miles from their barracks to their place of work and back at night, during hot summers and icy winters when the snow was so deep that the front man of the gang had to be changed every hundred feet. Each prisoner had to cut a cubic yard of wood per day, regardless of their age. Some Soviet guards developed sympathy for the Polish prisoners. They told them to go and steal the wood which they had cut the day before in order to fill the target amount of the day. Then after six months, Stefan was given a course of political instruction in Soviet Communism. The course took about eight to twelve weeks and was strictly organized. Hard punishment was common. Finally, Stefan managed to get

a job as translator in the camp as he spoke Russian fluently, and he understood German. This job may have saved his life. He was sometimes allowed to leave the forced labor camp alone. So it happened that Stefan made friends with some of the locals who tended their reindeer herds outside of the prisoner camp. They went fishing with him and gave him warm clothes. These rare contacts with the Siberian people helped Stefan to survive the Gulag.

Odyssey from Siberia to Iran

Nazi Germany's attack on the Soviet Union in the summer of 1941 changed Moscow's military strategy. The Polish Government-in-exile worked out an agreement with Stalin. As a result, Polish deportees who had received less than fifty years of forced labor were released for the purpose of forming a Polish National Army which, together with the Soviet Army, would fight against the Germans. Soon political officers came and told the prisoners that the Soviets and the Poles were now

Prisoners at forced labor in the Wiener Graben quarry at the Mauthausen concentration camp. Photo 1941

allies. Stefan left the Soviet Gulag after eleven months together with his little cousin whose parents and brother had not survived bad treatment, hunger and hard labor. The Soviets transported the former prisoners from Siberia to the southern territories of the USSR. Stefan's journey ended at the Iranian border where the Soviets assembled thousands of Poles: men, women and children. Along with other children and women, his cousin was sent to India, where many Displaced Persons stayed until the end of the war.

For some Poles, Iran appeared to be the more attractive location because the British Army administered part of the country. Therefore, Stefan joined a group of Poles who sneaked into the British part of Iran. They got help from some local shepherds who guided them through the desert areas west of Tehran to a refugee camp in the British sector of Iran. After an odyssey of six months he had finally arrived at his destination, which was a tent city out in the desert. British officers checked his camp in order to recruit Polish refugees for underground work at home. It was late summer of 1941 when Stefan accepted an offer for training. He wanted to fight for an independent Poland. Again, he received political instruction. This time, the ideological instruction was given by the British, who emphasized their plans to bring the Nazis' supremacy to an end, and by the Poles who were trying to form a National Army under the control of the

Polish Government-in-exile. Military training followed, and the group was taught how to carry out sabotage and underground work. They learned how to blow up trains, bridges and buildings. Many of his comrades later formed the Polish Second Corps, which fought under General Anders in North Africa. Stefan left the British camp with six young men who set out on a long journey to Poland. They walked, jumped on trains and rode donkeys. The small group went through the western part of Iran, followed the path into northern Iraq and passed through Kurdistan. Then they crossed parts of Turkey and diverted to Syria before returning to Anatolia. When the men had come to the Bosporus Strait they realized that German intelligence in Turkey was following them. With the help of an old Turkish fisherman they succeeded to get to the north side of Bosporus Strait. From there the group found its way through Bulgaria and Romania to Nazi-occupied Poland, where the group joined the Polish underground forces.

A Partisan in the Polish Resistance Movement

Stefan was provided with arms and ammunition and sent to fight the Germans. It did not take long until Stefan was in charge of nineteen fighters who organized sabotage

in eastern Poland and behind the Soviet border. He usually made attacks on German trains which were transporting soldiers to the eastern front, sometimes on banks, but mostly on military buildings or squads of the German Special Forces. Then the fighters disappeared in the woods.

The daily life of an underground fighter was a constant move. The men slept on distant farms, in fox holes, and in forests. They never stayed more than two nights at any place. A backpack was all Stefan carried during these years: several books, soap, a razor, a towel, underwear, socks, a German and a Russian gun. They lived an existence between terror and shame. Stefan soon had experience in many roles: as a patriotic saboteur, as a religious Catholic, as a comrade of those who were caught by German intelligence, or as an ear witness to reports about the Holocaust crimes which the German Special Forces committed on Polish territory. While Stefan's life, ever since 1941, was in constant danger, it took a dramatic turn in early spring of 1944: he was caught in a raid by German police while he was traveling on a train from Warsaw, but left a suitcase of dynamite on the train. The Germans brought him to a forced labor camp in the forests of Silesia. There, the laborers had to collect resin, which was used to produce synthetic rubber. Stefan escaped after four weeks. He returned to occupied Poland and joined a group of the Polish National Armed Forces, which was the right wing of the Polish underground. He participated in a secret action in which a Gestapo man was executed. Soon after this, in April of 1944, he was caught by the Germans while he was staying on a farm in Blachownia. He was transported to Lubliniec, where he underwent brutal interrogation by the Gestapo. The interrogation took five days and five nights, during which he was not allowed to sleep, to eat and to drink. The young Pole was beaten and tortured because he did not want to reveal names or plans. Finally, the Gestapo put Stefan on trial. After pseudo-legal proceedings a German court condemned him to two death sentences. In addition, he was categorized for "N & N" ("Nacht und Nebel"), which meant that he would be put to death at the dead of night. He learnt later that this treatment was typical for political prisoners at the time. The Gestapo kept him in prison for some weeks before he was transferred to Gross Rosen in May of 1944. Gross Rosen concentration camp was close to the town of Breslau, and Stefan stayed here for transit. It was a place where Stefan learnt the hardest rules of survival in less than ten days: he had to witness the murder of a bishop from his archdiocese. He experienced the ambivalent behavior of the block elders, who gave help before they killed to survive. Stefan heard about Prince Radziwill, who had died in the quarries of Gross Rosen because he had refused to form a Polish Government under German control. Another transit stay followed in June of 1944, this time in Mauthausen concentration camp, where he saw how the death machinery of the Nazi system worked.

As an "N & N" prisoner, he lived in Block 22. It was the barrack from which the Nazis selected people for special actions behind the front. Apparently, he was on the death roll although he remained a special case; the Nazis usually sent the others to the gas chamber. Stefan was put into a punishment group. He was given the number 104222. Together with other inmates, he had to carry big rocks from the quarry to the camp. To Stefan, it appeared as a miracle when his number was called one day. He left Mauthausen with a group of 500 prisoners. From September 1944 on, he had to work twelve hours a day in a factory of Ostermann Sauer Company near Vienna. The factory was a sub-camp of Mauthausen which produced military equipment. Stefan worked there during the winter of 1944/45.

For the Gestapo, he was an important case: He was taken to a Gestapo office in Mauthausen every four weeks. Again and again he underwent the tortures of interrogation because he did not cooperate by revealing secrets of his underground work. Finally, they put him in a bomb squad which had to clear the area from unexploded bombs. He returned to Mauthausen concentration camp one more time, in January 1945, before he was put on a train with several other prisoners. They were to be executed in a "night and fog action" not far away from Opole (Silesia). However, when the Soviet Army approached, the Germans decided to break off the operation. Stefan finally returned to Mauthausen. There, he got a new prisoner number. This number ended his prominent status as a "N & N" victim. At this time Stefan realized that he was one of only 13 prisoners who were still alive after six months in the concentration camp. He had previously arrived

in Mauthausen in a group of 600. The tortures of daily life did not end. When the Soviet Army made its way to the west, thousands of forced laborers were transported to Mauthausen which, by this time, was already overcrowded. Stefan was transfered to forced labor in Camp Gusen Zwei. This was another annex of Mauthausen, where the Nazis had placed armament factories in tunnels. They used this shelter to build tanks and Messerschmitt planes. During the winter of 1945, Stefan arrived with about 5,000 other prisoners in the concentration camp. There was little hope that Stefan would survive this transfer to Gusen Zwei. After their arrival, the newcomers had to stay outside in the winter cold without clothes until the morning. Hundreds of prisoners did not survive the first night. In Gusen Zwei, Stefan was one among 40,000 or 50,000 forced laborers who built tunnels into the mountains. He worked in the tunnels from February until May of 1945. It was work in the darkness of the night. The mortality rate was unbelievably high, and even the strongest among the prisoners did not last more than a couple of days. Others were killed by the guards.

Hundreds of sick laborers were murdered. Hunger and thirst were added to these daily tortures.

Survival and Liberation

The number of 5,000 newcomers was the weekly supply of forced laborers who had to step in for the loss of about the same amount of people who died during one week. However, Stefan survived the agony with the help of a Russian inmate who was a pickpocket. Together, they got hold of some extra food and shared it with other prisoners. Then, during the winter months of 1945, there were rumors that the Soviet Army was nearby. News was spread about the landing of Polish parachute units in Holland. But it was not until spring of 1945 that help would reach the tortured men. Someone from the Swedish Red Cross informed General George Smith Patton's headquarters about plans to kill about 42,000 survivors in the tunnels of Gusen Zwei. But before the death project could be executed, Stefan was liberated by Patton's army, which arrived shortly before the action was to take

Two emaciated survivors lie in a single bed in the newly liberated Gusen concentration camp. Photo May 1945

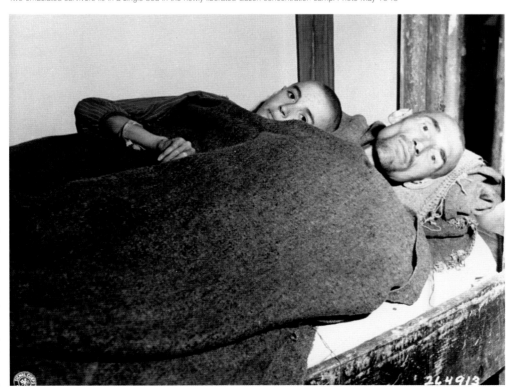

place. It was early May of 1945. He survived the last days of Gusen Zwei, where the Germans had tried to starve the rest of the prisoners to death.

In the end, only a few tanks and a couple of American soldiers were necessary to convince nearly 800 SS men to surrender. By this time, Stefan was not able to move or to sit. He watched how the Americans came into the camp. They walked around and took photos. Then the commanders gave the order that all Germans from the neighborhood outside the camp were to bury the bodies of nearly 18,000 inmates who had died during the last days before the liberation. When the American soldiers entered Stefan's barrack, he could not leave his bunk. They put him on a stretcher and washed him. He was taken to a field hospital and was fed a mixture of milk and water. During this period of recovery, he slept for many days.

A week later, the Americans took the sick to a city hospital in Bamberg (Bavaria), where nuns cared for the Holocaust survivors. Stefan stayed from June until October 1945. He had lost an enormous amount of weight. His lungs were full of liquid, and he was suffering from tuberculosis. The doctors gave him calcium shots, punctured his lungs and treated the starvation symptoms. He learnt to walk again. However, Stefan still had not fully recovered after five months, so the doctors decided to transfer him to a TB sanatorium in Forchheim, where the Swiss Cross and the American military provided help for the victims of genocide. For the first time since 1939, Stefan experienced normal life again. He stayed there from November 1945 until April 1946, when he was taken to a sanatorium in Lohr. After Stefan had finally recovered in summer 1946 he was transfered to the Displaced Persons Assembly Centre in Aschaffenburg in the American sector. At this time, he had the first contact with his family in Poland. With the help of the Swedish Red Cross, it was possible for Stefan to send a message to his family. Stefan was still alive, but he found out that his mother had died. His father remained alive although he had risked his life by hiding Jews, wounded underground fighters and Polish Communists on his farm.

Life in the DP Camp

The Assembly Centre in Aschaffenburg was a former German Army camp. Stefan shared his room with two families. He was able to get a full-time job in the camp. At the beginning, he worked in the camp kitchen. Later on he became a courier and delivered messages between the Polish, Russian, and Ukrainian DP camps of Aschaffenburg. The Americans gave him a motorized bicycle which he used for his trips. Stefan remained in Aschaffenburg until early 1948, when the DP camp was closed. He was sent to Camp Wildflecken near Schweinfurt (Bavaria), where he stayed until his emigration to America in 1949.

At that time, Wildflecken was temporary home to about 15,000 or 20,000 displaced men, women, and children, mainly Polish Displaced Persons. Many of them lived in constant fear of being shipped back to Communist Poland. This happened to a great number of Displaced Persons. The Soviet Gulag remained a threat for many repatriated Displaced Persons. Others learnt soon not to trust a future under Soviet rule. In fact, Stefan found out that some of his former comrades with whom he had battled Nazis and Communists were being victimized by the new system which governed post-war Poland. When the Communist Party took over Poland's government, they compiled a list of all who had fought for an independent Poland. Soon, the surviving men in Stefan's resistance group were arrested by the Soviet military and sent to Siberia and the Gulag, even though they were highly decorated fighters who had even received the Stalin medal. Two of them were Jews who had survived the Nazi system. They, too, were arrested by the Soviets and deported to Siberia, from where they never returned. Among those who were arrested in Communist Poland were two nieces of Stefan's who had disappeared for

Survivors in the "quarantine camp" section of Mauthausen after liberation. Photo May 1945

years. Both suffered in prison from 1947 until 1960.

News like this made the rounds in the DP camps of western Europe. Fears of new arrets contrasted with feelings of being "completely intoxicated with freedom" after years of torture and slave labor. Therefore, many talked of emigration. Only a few thought that they would be able to go to the United States: "America was regarded as a kind of heaven. Everybody wanted to come to this heaven, which was America." From 1948 on, a growing number of Displaced Persons went to Belgium or to Britain. The offer to work in the coal mines of Belgium or England was seen as a ready chance to leave the DP camps. Finally, Australia, Canada, and the United States joined the list of resettlement countries after long debates in Parliament. The Truman Government in Washington started a resettlement program as part of specific DP legislation in June 1948.

Stefan hoped to be one of the hundreds of thousands of refugees from other parts of eastern Europe, who shared his dream of a new life overseas, to be admitted to the U.S. The quota of Polish settlers was given preference over other nationalities. Therefore, many Displaced Persons of Russian, White Russian and Ukrainian origin falsified their documents to show Polish nationality. In this

Displaced Persons in Dillenburg after the liberation of the area by U.S. troops. Photo spring 1945

way, they joined the large Polish quota for the United States. In some cases, Stefan helped falsify papers for refugees who had no appropriate documentation. This almost kept him from getting a job in the camp administration. However, Stefan was lucky to get a paid job as a stenographer for the police force. He

had applied for it during his time in Camp Aschaffenburg. Displaced Persons were usually not allowed to apply for civilian jobs outside the camp. They volunteered for work such as chopping trees or sweeping streets in the camp.

The majority of the homeless had no training or occupation. This was a severe problem for many Displaced Persons, as they only waited passively for things to happen. Stefan soon found employment as a detective for the camp authority. For years he investigated crimes of all kinds. He dealt with cases of robbery, rape, incest, suicide, murder and gang conflicts between black market operators. Displaced Persons who were convicted by an appointed judge were usually sent to a camp jail. Another part-time occupation opened the way to resettlement. Stefan agreed to work for the Counter Intelligence Corps (CIC) of the U.S. Army in Aschaffenburg. The young man searched out war criminals; he conducted interrogations of Polish Nazi collaborators, German Nazis, Polish ethnic Germans who were hiding in the east, and Polish Communists who had sneaked into the west to act as spies. Sometimes the CIC team crossed the green border into the east trying to catch a suspect. Later on, Stefan learnt that many convicted war criminals left prison after a very short period of time.

View of the former Von Tirpitz Naval Yard. In the 1940s the yard was used as a forced labor camp for about 5,000 forced laborers. The Tirpitz Naval Yard was later used as a staging area for emigrants leaving Europe through the port of Bremerhaven. From here the Displaced Persons were transported to Bremerhaven

The Dream of America

Stefan was still in Camp Wildflecken in 1948 when he came across his former commander from the British Army who had trained him as a resistance fighter for underground work in Poland. They had last met in the training camps of Iran. As a result of this encounter with the British officer, Stefan was given a form to fill out which came from the Polish authorities in Britain. Stefan was to receive special honor. But Stefan refused to accept the decoration because he remembered times when not much support was given to his resistance group by the Government-in-exile. However, Stefan was able to contact people who paved his way to America. Part of this network was the wife of a close friend who worked for the U.S. Emigration Office. She managed to put Stefan on a list of emigrants who wanted to be sponsored by an American organization. Finally, he found his name on the list of the U.S. Catholic Conference. This organization helped to find sponsors who were willing to give someone from the DP camps in Europe a start in America. Many came with the help of the U.S. Catholic Conference. Stefan was one of them. Before leaving the camp, he took lessons in English. The essential part in the resettlement procedure, which was known as pipeline, was an interview conducted by the DP Commission. But the Displaced Persons had to pass several interviews, checks and approvals before a candidate was finally accepted for resettlement. Only healthy applicants were accepted. Those had the best chances of being admitted who were young and without family.

At the beginning of the U.S. immigration scheme, mainly Displaced Persons with an agricultural background were chosen for resettlement. And people with an agenda of anti-Communist activities enjoyed preference. The CIC played an important role in the work of the DP Commission which conducted the interviews. Stefan passed the interview successfully. He also had the essential documents although he did not do well in the medical check-up. His lungs showed scars of TBC. This time, Stefan's contact to the CIC proved to be an asset when his contact officer decided to settle the case for him. He got the American doctor's O.K. and passed the medical check. Stefan left Wildflecken in September of 1949.

A Ticket to New York

Displaced Persons who were accepted for resettlement in North America or Australia left Europe from different ports, usually from Bremerhaven or Naples. Stefan was on a list for Bremerhaven. He was transferred by train from his Assembly Centre in Bavaria to Hamburg. Countless groups of Displaced Persons arrived in Hamburg-Altona train station and went on from there to Bremerhaven, the port of embarkation. Here, the passenger groups stayed for a short period of time on the grounds of a former German Naval Yard before they were ready to board. Their passages to New York were paid for by the U.S. Government. The vessel Stefan boarded in September 1949 had previously been a troop transport ship. The General Hersey had a legal carrying capacity for 400 passengers; however, on this transport approximately 1,700 Displaced Persons were taken on board. On the Atlantic, many got seasick, while Stefan enjoyed the food. During the passage, he had a job as a typist. Together with some other passengers, he published a two-page newspaper for the Polish language group on board.

After several days at sea, the ship arrived in New York. It was about four in the morning when the Statue of Liberty appeared in the hazy light of daybreak. Stefan, like most people on board, was watching how the statue came near and nearer. Many called out: "Oh how tall it is, how big it is." Several passengers tried to take photos of people with the Statue of Liberty in the background. Finally the General Hersey docked within sight of the Statue of Liberty. The newcomers were checked immediately after the ship's arrival

Displaced Persons departing Germany for the United States wait with their luggage in the former Tirpitz Naval Yard. In May 1946, the Marine Flasher transported 867 European Displaced Persons to the United States, the first contingent to be admitted under President Truman's December 1945 Directive expediting the immigration of Displaced Persons to the United States. 450 of these new immigrants were assisted by the American Joint Distribution Committee

Farewell scenes at the Columbus Quay in Bremerhaven in 1948. Especially from the American Zone of Occupation and Berlin DPs were transported by train to Bremerhaven, from where they left the continent which had brought them such pain and sufferings. Screenshots from the moving image "DPs Departing from Bremerhaven", 1948

at the dock. Later, they were welcomed by a local Polish Committee, whose delegates assisted them on their way to the train station. Stefan got train tickets for his trip to the Twin Cities of St. Paul and Minneapolis. He also received five dollars and a tag which said that this person did not speak English so that help was appreciated. An old lady from the local Polish Committee helped him and two others find their way to the train station through the bustling traffic of Manhattan. People and cars everywhere, hectic speeds, traffic noises and tall buildings were first impressions when Stefan left the dockyards. On his first day in America, he asked himself: "Oh my God, what I'm going to do in this busy country?" His dream had become a reality. However, he wondered how he would master English and

where he would stay. Within a few hours he boarded a train to Chicago. His train ticket was paid for by the U.S. Catholic Conference. Many years later, Stefan repaid this expense.

On the way to Chicago, a young lady started to talk with Stefan. She spoke a little German. When the train arrived in Chicago she invited him for lunch and put him on a short sightseeing tour of Chicago before she helped him get to St. Paul. In the Twin Cities, Stefan was welcomed by delegates of the Polish American Club. One of them took him to a barber shop downtown where his sponsor worked. The man was an old Polish-American who had just recently responded to a call from the U.S. Catholic Conference to sponsor a Displaced Person. The barber and his wife had signed up to provide a

young man with room and board until he found a job. Both welcomed him with a big dinner in their house.

Start into a New Life

That evening, Stefan received good advice from the old Polish-American couple. Stefan was warned not to pay attention to people who would call him "greenhorn" or "Polack". "Most of them are quite stupid people", they told him. "The people who know better won't bother you." During the first week, Stefan did repair work in the home of his sponsor. He cleaned the house and fixed the old car. Then he earned his first money in America by cleaning the house of a neighbor. When he got his first half dollar he learnt that his neighbor, who was a postman, earned 50 dollars a week. "Oh my God, if I ever make 50 dollars a week in America, I will never want any more."

A week later, Stefan went to the Polish American Club, where he got an appointment to show up at a casket company. The manager was a German-American and a wealthy man. He owned a farm in Wisconsin and a big home in St. Paul. In his factory, he employed people of all ages, even men who were seventy or eighty years old. He loved to speak German with Stefan. The manager gave him a job as an unskilled worker. Stefan stayed until the factory closed a year later. Meanwhile, he could afford to rent a room on his own. He left his sponsors and moved to another place, where he had a small room overlooking the city of St. Paul which he liked very much.

It did not take long for the young immigrant to find new employment. He became a railroad worker in the maintenance sector and worked in a gang of so-called gandy dancers. These workers fixed the railroad tracks after new ties were put under the rail. It was hard work, especially during winter time. Stefan, who stayed in this job for a year, found out that Minnesota winters were longer than those in Poland. When he first came to the Midwest, he had actually thought that the climate in his new home would be as mild as the city of Metz in France. Metz has the same degree of latitude as St. Paul in Minnesota.

Stefan tried hard to get used to American English. It took him about six months to understand the new language. However, the young man of twenty-eight had no problem with social contacts. Most immigrants in his neighborhood went to the International Institute once a week, where teachers gave English lessons and social workers provided help for those who intended to apply for U.S. citizenship. Here, he met Polish, Ukrainian, and Russian boys and girls who had come to America as Displaced Persons. They enjoyed their evenings and weekends together, playing tennis, driving cars and flirting with the girls. At the beginning, contacts with Americans were limited to daily work. It took a long time for Stefan to converse in English. As a result, he sometimes felt intimidated at work, but no one ever offended him when he did not understand instructions right away. Most American colleagues were anxious to help him. Stefan never had a situation where he felt unwanted as an immigrant. By 1952 his English had improved, and he applied for a job in a church goods company in St. Paul.

The New American

Stefan also applied for U.S. citizenship. Immediately after his arrival in Minnesota, in 1949, he had signed a Declaration of Intent. He then passed a special citizenship course at the International Institute. Three years later, he became an American citizen. About 120 people attended the naturalization ceremony, at which Stefan was chosen to give a short speech. Soon after his naturalization, Stefan met his American wife Sylvia. Both were interested in literature and music. They got married in 1954, and in a short time had a boy. Both decided to bring up their son as an American, and so their son never learnt to speak Polish.

Although Stefan's job at the church goods Company was not well-paid, he stayed on for more than 45 years. For most of the time, he earned his living as a warehouse worker in the company, filling orders from churches all over the country. A dream of his became a reality when he was finally promoted to manager of the book department at the end of his professional career, at the age of 73. Stefan never became a wealthy man. He never wanted to get rich, although he worked hard: "I did not come here to make a fortune. I came here to gain freedom." Stefan spoke of a "most exhilarating experience" when he talked about his perception of feeling free in America. He remembered what freedom had meant for him when the American soldiers opened the gates of the concentration camp in May of 1945. Moreover, he regarded his early resistance in Nazi-occupied Poland against suppression and slave labor as a prolog to a life in a free and independent country. For him, his immigration to the United States was a logical outcome. The country's historic mission that guaranteed freedom and opportunity and declared both of them as constitutional rights appealed to Stefan. America's way of life made it easy for him to apply for U.S. citizenship. Moreover, Stefan had reasons not to return to Poland for a visit while it was under Communist rule. His two sisters, who had survived the war in Poland, had warned him early on not to come back. They feared that their brother would be imprisoned in post-war Poland.

Stefan had remained sceptical about Poland's political development because the fight for freedom was a dogma for him. This trust in the power of freedom remained an inspiration for his social commitment in the United States, especially to other refugees who had escaped from oppression and terror. His experience as a Displaced Person and an immigrant to the United States was an incentive for him to help other immigrants. For many years, Stefan and his

DP registration card in the former Bergen-Belsen concentration camp, 1945

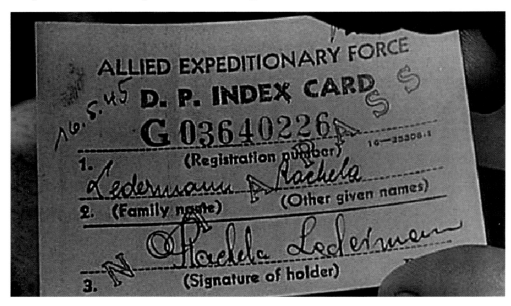

Displaced Persons of various nationalities seeking to immigrate to the United States line the decks of the General Black as it leaves the port of Bremerhaven. Photo October 1948. The USS General Black, dubbed the "Ship to Freedom" by its passengers, brought 813 European Displaced Persons from eleven nations to the United States under the provisions of the newly enacted Displaced Persons' Act. These were the first Displaced Persons allowed to enter the United States under the new quota. The ship's departure from Bremerhaven was marked by speeches by U.S. military and civilian leaders and by an Army Band concert

wife were active members of the Catholic community in St. Paul. When, in the late 1970s, their parish put out an appeal to sponsor the resettlement of two Vietnamese boat people, both stepped up to help. The Polish-American couple gave two boys a home for many years until the young men had found a job. Later on, Stefan and Sylvia assisted several other refugees from Asia to get settled in America. Stefan also worked in a church team that helped refugees from Vietnam and Laos to collect clothes and furniture, and to find work as well as a place to live.

In his last years, Stefan started to give interviews about his life as a Polish survivor of the German concentration camp system. The naturalized citizen Stefan Czyzewski talked at schools and colleges all over Minnesota, teaching young Americans that he was grateful to have come to "a good and free country". "I wake up in the morning and I think about it. I say: Man, I feel so free." Stefan Czyzewski died in August of 2000, more than 50 years after he, as a Displaced Person, had first seen the Statue of Liberty in the hazy light of New York's daybreak, at the end of a long odyssey.

Literature

Interview with Stefan Czyzewski, April 8, 1998, United States Holocaust Memorial Museum (USHMM), RG–50.030*0387

IRO Statute, Annex I, Definitions – General Principles, Part I, Section B, 15. December 1946.

U.S. Displaced Persons Commission, Memo to America: The DP Story – The Final Report of the U.S. Displaced Persons Commission, Washington, D.C. 1952.

The American flag is a mosaic of faces of over 750 Americans from all ethnic backgrounds. It signifies America's claim of being "A Nation of Immigrants" (display on Ellis Island). The little picture shows the borderline between the U.S. and Mexico. A small fence separates densely populated Tijuana, Mexico, right, from the UnitedStates in the Border Patrol's San Diego Sector. Construction is underway to extend a secondary fence over the top of this hill

Dennis Wepman

The Swinging Door – Changing Patterns in Contemporary American Immigration

Immigration to the United States has fluctuated widely, in both numbers and sources, throughout its history, reflecting changes in its economy and political conditions and in those of the sending countries. In 1820, the first year in which formal records were kept, 8,385 people obtained legal resident status in the young country; in 1907 the number had grown to 1,285,349. In 1933, during the Great Depression, it sank to 23,068, but by 1991 it had swollen to a record high of 1,826,595. From the year 2,000, immigration remained level at about one million a year, but, according to a U.S. Census Bureau report on September 23, 2008, as a result of the economic downturn in the country, the

Counselling of recent African and Latin American immigrants at the Center for Immigrant Rights in New York, 1995

number of immigrants arriving in 2007 was down to just 511,000.

A more striking contrast, however, appears in the range of countries from which these new arrivals have come. During the decade 1820–1829, a total of 99,272 immigrants entered the United States from Europe; the Americas (including Canada) sent 9,655, and the vast continent of Asia accounted for a grand total of 34. In the last decade of the 20th century, 1990–1999, the figures are very different: Europe sent 1,348,612, Asia 2,859,899, and the Americas 5,137,743. Of the latter region, Mexico accounts for more than half, with 2,757,418, not including illegal aliens. The number of immigrants arriving from Africa was so small that figures do not even appear in the government statistics until recently, although no area has shown a more dramatic increase among recent sources of new arrivals.

African Immigration to the United States

The most recent and least voluminous of the three major new sources of arrivals in the United States is Africa. Though that continent accounts for a considerably smaller number than either Asia or Latin America, it has generated no less intense a response among Americans. This is true in part because of the racial tensions that already exist between Whites and African-American descendents of slaves in the United States, leading to assimilation problems that do not exist for Latin-American and Asian newcomers, but African immigrants also encounter difficulties because of the sudden acceleration of their arrival. According to the United States Census Bureau, there

were approximately 364,000 African-born immigrants in the United States in 1990; by 2,000 the number had more than doubled, reaching 881,000, and it passed 1.25 million in 2005. According to a 2005 report by Sam Roberts in the New York Times, "Since 1990… more [African immigrants] have arrived voluntarily than the total who disembarked in chains before the United States outlawed international slave trafficking in 1807. More have been coming annually – about 50,000 legal immigrants – than in any of the peak years of the middle passage across the Atlantic, and more have migrated here from Africa since 1990 than in nearly the entire preceding two centuries."

Although some of the newcomers are from remote rural areas in their native countries and encounter special cultural and linguistic problems in adapting to their new homes, a large percentage are educated professionals, including doctors, lawyers, engineers, architects, accountants, and academics. U.S. census data from 2000 show that 43.8 % of African-born immigrants in the United States have college degrees, compared with 42.5 % of Asian-Americans, 28.9 % of immigrants from Europe and Canada, and 23.1 % of the U.S. population as a whole. Compared to the descendants of slaves in the United States, the contemporary African immigrants' average income is higher and their jobless rate is lower. This fact has two negative consequences: first, it has occasioned some hostility between the two communities, bringing about an elite of African-born Blacks isolated from the larger, but diminishing, majority of those whose ancestors suffered slavery and subsequent racial discrimination. And it is not only the higher-status African immigrant that encounters problems with American blacks; there has also been friction between less acculturated Africans and American-born Blacks in cities with large, long-established

Cape Verdean dockworkers who outfitted whaling vessels, New Bedford, Massachusetts, 1904. As early as that immigrants from the Cape Verde Islands established communities in Rhode Island and south-eastern Massachusetts

The lively African communities seen throughout the nation contain a microcosm of American life; like most immigrants, Africans have taken the menial jobs traditionally accepted by newcomers – taxi-drivers, domestic servants, factory workers – but most are also engaged in further schooling at night. Even the most conservative Americans have conceded that the talent and initiative of the African immigrant have made a positive contribution to the nation. As Mojubaolu Okome observed in 2005, "[T]he work ethic, the religious ethos, the characteristic virtues of the population make them especially suited for characterization as the ideal immigrants who relive yet again the Horatio Alger myth of fulfilling the American dream by creating something out of nothing."

Asian Immigration to the United States

Asian Immigration to America has a very different history from that of Africa. Of the 34 arrivals from the entire continent of Asia recorded during the first decade of U.S. immigration records, 1820 to 1829, three came from China, nine from India, and 19 from Turkey. Following the discovery of gold in California, the number of Asians reported as arriving from 1850 to 1859 was 36,080, of which 35,933 were from China. The flood of Asian immigrants so alarmed the native population, who saw it as "the Yellow Peril," that restrictive laws were demanded and passed. Chinese and other Asians were excluded from citizenship, ownership of property, and participation in many professions. Most of this legislation lasted until after World War II (the Chinese Exclusion Act of 1882, the first restrictive federal immigration statute in American history, was officially repealed in 1943 because China was a U.S. ally in the war, but an annual quota was set for the country at 105). Chinese workers were welcome but brutally exploited in the construction of the Central Pacific Railroad, and when the numbers proved overwhelming many cities passed laws against the residence of all Asians, often referred to generically as "Mongolians."

black communities, like Washington, D.C., and New York, both of which have reported African-born populations of more than 130,000.

A second negative aspect of the high level of education of the new arrivals is that it represents a serious brain drain for Africa. The decision by professionals to abandon their native lands is not surprising considering the disparity of income for the same work on the two continents. The salary levels for university professors in Africa, for example, averages about 10% of that in the United States; except for South Africa and Zimbabwe, where the starting annual wage for a university lecturer in 1997 was equivalent to $10,000 in American money, the salary in other African countries is below $4,000. However, the loss of educated workers to the home countries in Africa is compensated for to some extent by a significant gain in remittance revenue; David Crary reports in AfricaResource in 2007, that African-born residents of the United States are sending more than $3 billion annually to their families and friends in Africa. This has had a significant impact on the economies of several countries on that continent.

African immigrants can be found in all parts of the United States. Although such major metropolitan areas as New York City, Washington, Atlanta, Chicago, and Los Angeles have been the most powerful magnets for Africans, as they have for other immigrants, there has been an enormous increase in the spread of newly arrived Africans to small towns far distant from these centers. The sparsely populated state of South Dakota, for instance, saw the number of African immigrants grow from 210 in the 1990s to 1,560 in 2000, and Tacoma, Washington, reported an increase of more than 800%, from 202 in the 1990s to 1,802 in 2002. More significantly, the aspirations of the new wave of African immigrants have changed. While the few who arrived in the 1960s and 1970s generally reported the intention to return to their newly liberated countries with an American education and help their homelands in nation building, most African immigrants now clearly intend to remain in the United States and raise families.

And it is increasingly clear that this swelling tide of African immigrants is settling into their new homes successfully.

In the heart of New York's Chinatown, at Mott and Pell Streets, 2008

Although the law was to loosen considerably over the years – the McCarran-Walter Act of 1952 eliminated race as a barrier to immigration – it was not until the Immigration and Nationality Act of 1965 abolished national origins as a basis for admission that migration from Asia began to increase significantly. The Immigration Act of 1990 raised the total quota and reorganized the system of criteria for admissions, greatly facilitating Asian immigration. In 1960, people born in Asia represented only 5 % of the immigrant population of the United States; in 2000, they constituted more than a quarter of those born outside of the country. According to David Dixon, writing in Migration Information Source (March 1, 2006), the Asian-born are the country's second largest foreign-born population by world region of birth, behind those from Latin America. The number of Asian-born increased 65.2 % between 1990 and 2000.

Although the Chinese have dominated Asian immigration to the United States, as they have to most countries to which they have moved – it is estimated that more than 33 million ethnic Chinese live outside of China, Hong Kong, and Taiwan, up from 12.7 million in the early 1960s – new arrivals from Asia have come from other countries as well. India and Pakistan represent significant sources of Asian immigration to the United States, and in 1975, following the Vietnamese War, more than 130,000 found refuge from the Communist governments of Vietnam, Cambodia, and Laos in the United States. According to the U.S. Census Bureau, the total Asian-born population in the United States in 1990 was 6,908,638. In 2000 the number was up to 10,242,998. The Asian country providing the largest group in both years was China, followed by the Philippines, Japan, India, and Korea. As a result of political oppression, military conflict, and economic hardship, many countries have joined the stream crossing the Pacific. According to a report in the New York Times in 1991, the fastest-growing subgroups under the Asian-American umbrella in the 1980s were the Vietnamese (134.8 % growth), the Indians (125.6 %), and the Koreans (125.3 %). But for all their linguistic and cultural diversity, the experience of the Asian community in the United States has many common features. Nearly four in five Asian-born Americans have high school or higher degrees, and more than two in five have a college education. The median earnings of Asian-born men are 34.9 % higher than those of foreign-born men in general, and those of Asian-born women 21.1 % higher than those of all foreign-born women. More than half of Asian-born householders own their own homes.

One explanation for the generally higher educational and economic levels of Asian immigrants is the changes in U.S. immigration law, which has tended to favor skilled workers or investors. As John S. Park and Edward J.W. Park noted in the 2005 book Probationary Americans: Contemporary Immigration Policies and the Shaping of Asian American Communities, "Since 1990, as many as 300,000 Asian migrants have arrived in the United States every year under employment categories. Asian migrants have also invested in America's major urban regions. During the same period, admissions for family reunification, which had once been the most prominent route for migration from Asia, declined by about a third. Poorer immigrants are generally less likely to arrive in the United States today, largely because immigration rules have discouraged their migration."

Since Asians are now much more likely to have college degrees and professional backgrounds, they are better placed in the American social and professional hierarchy. As the Parks observe, this has strengthened Americans' perception that Asian immigrants are affluent. However, many scholars have challenged this perception.

Japanese picture brides detained on Angel Island, 1916. In addition to the Chinese, who made up the bulk of arrivals, the station near San Francisco also processed other Asians (including over 600 Japanese picture brides a year, until the practice was halted in 1921) and a small number of Koreans and East Indians

Sweatshop in New York City. These often employ Chinese women, who came to the U.S. illegally, for three to five dollars an hour, Third-World conditions in a capitalist metropolis. Filmed with a hidden camera, 1994

A study from the University of Maryland's Asian American Studies Program, reported in that University's ScienceDaily November 12, 2008, notes that "Chinese American professionals in the legal and medical fields earn as much as 44 % less than their White counterparts." The study concludes that Chinese, due to language barriers "or simply the difficulties that go along with being identified as an 'outsider,'" are confronted by a glass ceiling, even though they are seen by Americans as a "model minority." And of course the Chinese are not alone in this. As the economy of the United States has suffered reversals, aliens whatever their legal status are among the first to suffer from it, and immigration, from Asia and other continents, has slowed down accordingly. In fact, as in the Great Depression, some emigration from the United States has been noted, especially at the upper end of the socio-economic scale. A recent study in the Philippines notes, "As the American dream became a nightmare, a third of some one million skilled [Filipino] migrants in the U.S. are thinking of returning to their homeland and not just because of the country's economic meltdown but also because of its skewed immigration policies" (Alito L. Malinao, "US financial meltdown and reverse migration," The Manila Times, 14 October 2008).

Latin-American Immigration to the United States

"Latin America," a region comprising South and Central America, Mexico, and the Caribbean, has shown the world's highest rate of migration since long before the middle of the last century, but the direction of its migratory flow changed dramatically in the early 1960s, when the rate of its emigration began to exceed that of its immigration. As in the cases of Africa and Asia, the principal target of Latin-American migration has been the United States, because of both the proximity and the relative prosperity of its neighbor to the north. Latin America is by far the largest source of immigrants to the United States, and whatever racist and xenophobic sentiments Americans feel toward Africans and Asians, it is Latin-American immigration, legal and illegal, that generates the country's deepest fear and resentment.

Intra-regional migration within Central and South America, Mexico, and the Caribbean has never been extensive, but cross-border movement has increased appreciably since the middle of the 20th century, the two decades between 1970 and 1990 marking the highest rates of migration within Latin America in the history of the region. This internal movement was propelled by political conflicts and by socioeconomic factors. In the Andean region, workers from Colombia, Ecuador, and Peru have migrated into Venezuela for work in the sugar and coffee plantations and into Ecuador for jobs on the banana and flower plantations, while Bolivians and Peruvians have found jobs in agriculture and the textile industry in Argentina. Women from Colombia have migrated to Venezuela as domestic workers. The Colombian population in Venezuela was estimated at 177,000 in 1971 and swelled to 494,000 in the next ten years. The number of Chileans resident in Venezuela grew from 3,000 to 25,000 during the same decade. When the Latin American economy went into a slump in the 1980s, however, the receiving nations were no longer able to support the influx of migrants, and the flow was reversed. By the 1990s, the pattern had shifted from movements between countries in the same region to emigration to the

Mexican laborers picking cotton on a Texas border plantation in 1919. Already that early south-eastern agriculture depended on Mexican immigrant labor. 41 % of them worked in agriculture by 1930

Estimates of illegal immigration into the U.S. range from 12 to 20 million; no wonder the public debate about how to deal with illegal immigrants and continuing illegal immigration via the American-Mexican border is anything but harmonious

flight from economic hardship and political pressure have put a great strain on Mexican resources, especially during times of economic crisis. One survey showed an unemployment rate among Salvadorans in Mexico City of 72% in the 1980s, even though in the Salvadoran community in Mexico 42% are reported to have completed high school, and 22% to have received some college education. For most of these migrants, Mexico is seen as a point of transit, the ultimate destination being the United States. Those unable to obtain visas but able to afford the trip most often fly to Mexico City, and then either find their way to the border on their own or use the services of a smuggler to try to cross it.

The history of migration in Latin America for the first four hundred years since colonization began in the middle of

United States and Europe. In the southern Cone, the same shift occurred. Movement of Brazilians, Paraguayans, and Uruguayans to Argentina, and of Peruvians and Bolivians to Chile, ended when the southern region of South America suffered a recession in the mid-1980s. Argentines who had fled the Perón dictatorship were unable to find work when they returned after democracy was restored, and the population began to diminish as more people left the country than entered it.

Migration from Central America to Mexico has been especially high, because that country borders the United States. Neighboring Guatemala has, understandably, been the largest source of entrants, especially from the politically troubled northwest highlands. When the Guatemalan army began its counterinsurgency drive in 1981, thousands of Indians fled northward. In 1982, there were a reported 20,000 Guatemalan refugees in southern Mexico; two years later the number had more than doubled. El Salvador has also provided large numbers of emigrants, to Mexico and elsewhere. As Lars Schultz noted in 1992, "While the poorest rural Salvadorans tend to flee across the border into Honduras or southern Guatemala, urban dwellers and those above the lowest socioeconomic groups generally go elsewhere, especially to Costa Rica and Mexico" ("Central America and the Politicization of U.S. Immigration Policy," in Mitchell, p. 182). In 1982 there were 120,000 Salvadorans living in Mexico; in 1984 the Salvadoran embassy in Mexico reported an estimate of 500,000. These large numbers of Central Americans in

Women from Guadeloupe, French West Indies, at Ellis Island, 1911, after arrival on the S.S. Korona

Deportados
Deportees

Voy a con-tar-les, se-ño-res, voy a con-to
I'm going to tell you, good peo-ple, I'm going to

tar-les, se-ño-res, to-do lo que _____ yo su-frí,
tell you, good peo-ple, of all that I _____ had to bear,

Cuan-do de-je yo a mi pa-tria, cuan-do de-
When I de-part-ed my coun-try, When I de-

je yo a mi pa-tria, Por ve-nir a e-se pa-ís. _____
part-ed my coun-try, To come all the way up here. _____

This song dates from the early 1900s and describes the woes and sorrows of illegal migrant day laborers, constantly under the threat of being deported. It is still being sung, and not merely for historical reasons. The conditions that created the song still exist

the 16th century was essentially the story of European (and coerced African) immigration and movement across national and regional borders within the area. Since the middle of the 20th century, however, it has been largely a history of emigration. The reasons for international migration within and away from Latin America have been primarily economic, drawing workers from low-income regions to their more prosperous neighbors, but other variables have played a part. Conflicts within the sending countries, racial or cultural discrimination, and political persecution within the countries of origin have been important factors as well. The choice of destination is based on several factors; first among them is the difference in availability of work and per-capita income between the sending and the receiving countries, but other considerations include the availability of social services, such as health care and education, in the receiving countries; social or family networks in the countries chosen; the cost of travel to the receiving country; and, increasingly, the difficulty of gaining entry to the country chosen for immigration.

While the United States has been the main destination for all Latin American migrants since the beginning of the current wave of emigration, there has been an increasing movement toward Europe, with Spain the primary choice. There are several reasons for this, the most obvious being a shared language. Other reasons, however, are equally important. Spain has been especially hospitable, politically, economically, and culturally, to immigrants from all countries. It has facilitated welfare for the foreign-born, provided easier credit options for them than the United States does, and established a system by which its immigrants can help support their families in their home countries. Immigration to Spain from all countries is relatively easy, and Latin Americans from many countries have found a welcome there, with Ecuadorians representing the largest group. Since 2001, Spain's foreign-born population has more than quadrupled, to nearly 4 million people. According to Jerome Socolovsky, "The Spanish government's attempts to help immigrants make the most of the money they earn – and ease the process of sending funds and material back home – are leading many Latin American immigrants to Spain instead of the United States." In 2007, Socolovsky reports, "Latin Americans in Spain sent $5 billion in remittances to their home countries. That is almost as much as Latin America as a whole received in aid from the International Monetary Fund, World Bank and the Inter-American Development Bank combined."

The most important reason for the increase of emigration from Latin America to Europe rather than to the United States has been the tightening of visa restrictions in their neighbor to the north. Adela Pelligrino, of the University of the Republic

Protest demonstration of undocumented Latin American immigrants demanding "Legalización para todos"

Immigrants taking the oath as new U.S. citizens

one half of them from Mexico. And the number is growing: the Los Angeles Times recently reported, "The number of Mexican-born immigrants who became U.S. citizens swelled by nearly 50 % last year thanks to an aggressive citizenship campaign by Spanish-language media and advocacy groups. Some 122,000 Mexicans attained citizenship in 2007, up from 84,000 the previous year" (quoted in The Week, July 25 2008, p. 18). The United States census in 1990 reported 22,354,059 people of Hispanic origin, including Mexicans, South and Central Americans, and people from the Caribbean area. This number represented 9 % of the total population of the country and a 53 % increase since 1980. That year was the first time the census questionnaire was distributed nationally in both Spanish and English. The next census count, in 2000, showed an increase in Hispanic residents to more than 32 million, a 3 % increase over the previous decade, representing 12 % of the total population.

The flood of legal and illegal arrivals to the United States across the Mexican border, including both Mexican-born and other Latin-American immigrants using Mexico as a crossing point, has had a

of Uruguay, has noted that Spain is not alone in becoming a major receiving nation for Latin American immigration in Europe. "Most flows are directed toward southern European countries," she wrote in 2008, "although other European countries have also seen significant increases" ("Migration from Latin America to Europe: Trends and Policy Changes," IOM [International Organization for Migration] Research Series No. 16, 2008). The demographic profile of migrants from Latin America to Spain and Italy, Pelligrino reports, reveals a high percentage of young, relatively educated immigrants, with women representing more than half of the total number.

But though recent studies show an increase in Latin American migration to Europe, the vast majority of South and Central American and Mexican emigrants, as well as those from Cuba, Haiti, and the West Indies, have continued to choose the difficult path northward. According to Pelligrino (2002, p. 27), "Of all immigrants from Latin America and the Caribbean countries, the share going to the U.S. was 56 % in 1960 and 1970, 65 % in 1980 and 75 % in 1990." The population of the United States has recently passed 300 million, an increase of 100 million since 1970. It is the only industrialized country with a rapidly growing population, and according to a 2008 Pew Research Center report 82 % of its population growth is due to immigration. In 2000, more than 55 % of all legal immigrants resident in the country were from Latin America, about

Latin American immigrants demonstrating their loyalty to the U.S.

significant social, political, and economic impact on both the receiving and the sending countries. In the United States, still by far the largest recipient of migrants from Latin America, a resurgence of nativism – the anti-immigrant sentiment based on the fear that the culture and economy of the country is weakened by the presence of foreigners – has resulted from the large influx of "Latinos." To critics of a liberal immigration policy, Hispanics have replaced the Irish, the Italians, and the Chinese in the minds of many as threats to the cultural identity of the country. Organized labor has felt threatened by Latin American workers willing to work for barely subsistence wages (although management has welcomed them with equal ardor). A large literature has emerged in the United States warning of the danger of a disproportionate demand on the country's welfare system from Latin American immigrants. Another perceived source of danger from Hispanic immigrants, especially the undocumented, is the idea that they elevate the crime rate, although statistics clearly refute that belief. So extensive has the Hispanic presence become in the United States south-west that the region has assumed the character of a separate country, bitterly known as "Amexica" and described ironically by Time magazine (June 11 2001, p. 46) as "a country of 24 million." Similarly, the state of California, which is home to the largest Hispanic population in the country, has been referred to as "Mexifornia", a coinage that provided the title for a popular 2003 book by Victor Davis Hanson.

As with Africa and Asia, the impact of Latin American emigration on the home countries has been more complex, with both negative and positive consequences. On the one hand, as both Europe and the United States are more open to, and even actively recruit, highly skilled and educated migrants, there is the problem for the home country of a brain drain when its emigrants represent an important source of skilled labor or professional service. In 1966 Fidel Castro terminated all registration for emigration from Cuba partly to prevent the alarming brain drain that the island was suffering. But, as Clark, Hatton, and Williamson point out, if migrants send home substantial sums from their earnings in their new countries, or return to their native lands better qualified than when they left, or create business links with their home countries, "a current brain drain might well turn into a future brain gain… Individuals migrate to the U.S. for at least two reasons, to exploit the wage gain given skills, and to accumulate more skills in a host country labor market where those skills may be rewarded more generously than is true back home."

The most unequivocally positive consequence to the sending countries of the migration of Africans, Asians, and Latin Americans, whether their status is legal or illegal, is the remittance of a part of their increased income to their families and friends at home. Such remittances constitute a significant infusion of revenue to the home countries. According to IFAD (International Fund for Agricultural Development), a special agency of the United Nations, as reported in "Remittance Forum," October 15 2007, Latin America and the Caribbean received $68.062 billion in remittances in 2006, of which $24.3 billion went to Mexico, $24,298 billion to South America, $11,031 billion to Central America, and $8,379 billion to the Caribbean countries. These remittances averaged 20% of the per-capita income of the immigrants sending them and represented an average of 13% of the gross domestic products of the Latin American and Caribbean countries to which they were sent.

Since colonial times the United States has recurrently passed legislation restricting immigration to protect itself from various perceived threats to its economy or its racial and cultural integrity. But

whatever the consequences, positive or negative, of immigration for either the sending countries or the United States, there seems little reason to doubt that the flow will continue, whether the general public, the labor unions, or the governments on either side of the borders like it or not. And America's response to the flow of newcomers will undoubtedly continue to reverse itself as it has since colonial times. In 1753 Benjamin Franklin warned that if Germans were permitted to continue to come in such numbers as were entering Pennsylvania, "Americans" – that is, the English stock that had colonized the country – would not be able to maintain their language and government. At other times, immigrants have been actively invited into the country to fight in its wars, work in its mills, or develop its farmland. Immigration law has changed with such bewildering frequency that it was a standing joke among employees of the Immigration and Naturalization Service that the bureau's initials INS really stood for "I'm not sure."

The last major immigration reform was the Immigration Act of 1990, which created many new categories of immigrant, refugee, and asylee. It allowed for example, the entry of 1,000 displaced Tibetans living in exile in India and Nepal and granted "Temporary Protected Status" to entrants from Somalia, Liberia, Rwanda, Kuwait, Lebanon, El Salvador, and other troubled countries. But IMMACT 90, as the law was called, was so complex and unwieldy, and required such continuous amendment, that the need for a complete revision became increasingly apparent. The vast increase of illegal immigration from south of the border – or at any rate America's increasing awareness of it – was one of the factors that prompted the national demand for immigration reform. Another and more urgent one was the terrorist attack of September 11, 2001, in New York, which initiated a wave of hysteria aimed at all foreigners. Immigration reform was a major issue in the 2008 presidential election until the collapse of the economy became the focus of national attention.

Even though it was seldom mentioned by the end of the campaign, immigration remained a significant concern in America throughout it, and immigration rights groups had considerable influence

on its outcome. Clarissa Martínez, a senior director of the National Council of La Raza, a Latin American advocacy group, has written that immigration was "the driving push factor" influencing the Latino vote in the presidential election. "We've seen this trend since the election in 2006," she stated, "when Latinos started walking away from the Republican Party because of their embrace of anti-immigrant political strategies" (quoted in Rupa Dev, "Obama, New Congress Offer Hope for Pragmatic Immigration Reform," New American Media, November 15, 2008). The Democratic victory in this election was felt by many to promise a more liberal position for the country on admission of newcomers from all nations. As Angela Kelley, director of the Immigration Policy Center, has written, "Immigration is not just a Latino or Asian-American issue. This is an issue of America."

References

Clark, Ximena, Timothy J. Hatton, and Jeffrey G. Williamson. "What Explains Cross-Border Migration in Latin America?" HIER Discussion Paper No. 2012, Cambridge, Mass.: Harvard Institute of Economic Research, 2003.

Ibidem, "What Explains Emigration Out of Latin America?" Amsterdam, the Netherlands: World Development Vol 32, 2004, pp. 1871–1890.

Ibidem, "Where Do U.S. Immigrants Come From and Why?" NBER Working Paper #8998, Cambridge, Mass.: National Bureau of Economic Research, 2002.

Crary, David. "Africans Are Changing the Landscape of American Cities," AfricaResource, 26 July 2007.

Grieco, Elizabeth. "The African Foreign Born in the United States," Migration Information Source, 1 September 2004.

Hatton, Timothy J. and Jeffrey G. Williamson. The Age of Mass Migration Causes and Economic Impact. New York: Oxford University Press, 1998.

Hing, Bill Ong. Making and Remaking Asian America Through Immigration Policy, 1850–1950. Stanford, Cal.: Stanford University Press, 1993.

Mitchell, Christopher. western Hemisphere Immigration and United States Foreign

Policy. University Park, Pa. Pennsylvania State University Press, 1992.

Ocome, Mojubaolu Olufunke. "African Immigration to the United States: Dimensions of Migration, Immigration, and Exile," AfricaResource, 12 November 2005.

Park, John S.W. and Edward J.W. Park. Probationary Americans: Contemporary Immigration Policies and the Shaping of Asian American Communities. Florence, Ky.: Routledge, 2005.

Pelligrino, Andrea. "Skilled Labor Migration from Developing Countries: Study on Argentina and Uruguay," International Migration Papers No. 58. Geneva, Switzerland: International Labor Office, 2002.

Roberts, Sam. "More Africans Enter U.S. Than in Days of Slavery," New York Times, 21 February 2005.

Segal, Uma Anand. A Framework for Immigration: Asians in the United States. New York: Columbia University Press, 1992.

Socolovsky, Jerome, "Many Latin American Immigrants Opting for Spain," National Public Radio. http://www.npr.org, August 7, 2007.

Protest banner in New Orleans' Lower 9th Ward (July 2007) and a house demolished by hurricane Katrina. Migration experts agree: Climatic disasters will increasingly trigger migration movements. The German Emigration Center in Bremerhaven devotes itself not only to the presentation of "old" migration patterns, but also to new phenomena of international migration, e.g. the special exhibition "The Flight after the Flood. New Orleans – the city left behind" (2009)

For centuries Germany was both: a country of emigrants and a country of immigrants. Drawing by Manfred Kiecol 1987 after the newspaper illustration "Welcome to the Country of Freedom" of 1887

Claus Leggewie

Germany as an Immigrant Country

Background: German Emigration and Immigration

Is Germany about to become an emigrant country again? The censuses taken in the last few years tend to suggest this. Following strong net immigration (more people immigrating than emigrating) in the 1990s, Germany now has a balanced migration pattern – with a downward trend; fewer foreigners are coming to Germany, while more Germans are moving abroad. This is a fairly dramatic change within a short space of time. Of course, in the longue durée, when long-term migration cycles are observed, this is not unusual: for a long time there were more people leaving this country on religious, political and economic grounds than there were foreigners arriving to settle here. Initially, the reasons for the departure and immigration were mostly of a religious nature – the result of religious wars and state intolerance. Persecuted Huguenots and Waldenses fled to Germany from France, whilst the faithful in Germany were leaving in droves for America. Then, during the 19th century, many thousands of emigrants left the German Reich for America on economic grounds. This exodus was only partially offset by immigrant workers from Poland and other eastern European territories.

In order to evaluate current trends more accurately, the history of immigration needs to be examined in more depth. This presents some surprising insights; it is for instance possible that Germany since reunification has reached the end of an immigration cycle before it has been recognized as such. Whatever the reason, despite all opinions to the contrary, between 1955 and 2005 Germany was a special kind of immigrant country. I say a "special kind," because Germany was never really an immigrant country of the classic type, like the former settlement colonies of Australia, Canada and the USA. Unlike its French neighbors (as early as the 19th century), the German Reich did not systematically bring in workers from the Mediterranean countries and North Africa to counteract pronounced demographic stagnation, nor did it absorb the colonial population from the Empire the way Britain did. What distinguishes Germany from the United States is that, in a standard immigrant country, the majority of immigrants turn their backs once and for all on their old home. They settle in the new environment and, despite all adversity, endeavour to assimilate with the host culture within the space of just a few generations, with the intention ultimately of assuming the new nationality. (Nowadays, the USA is increasingly moving away from this pattern and has recently introduced migrant worker programmes.)

The story of German immigration has three special features: firstly, it is characterized to a great degree by the compulsory recruitment of forced labor from all corners of National Socialist-occupied Europe during the Third Reich, leaving behind by 1945 a large number of so-called "displaced persons" – former forced laborers, prisoners from concentration camps and prisoners of war. The second peculiarity is the massive post-1945 tide of migration (ultimately involving around 12 million people) of ethnic German refugees from settlement areas that stretched from central and eastern Europe through to Central Asia. This forced and chaotic "Heim ins Reich" (literally, "Home to the Reich") program (which, in the case of the later settlers, mutatis mutandis, is still continuing into the present) took up a great deal of space in the collective memory of Germans and, as evidenced by broad popular interest in the theme of "flight and expulsion" in recent years, continues to overshadow recollections of the increasing "guest worker immigration" after 1955. Thirdly, this also applies to the great "intra-German migration" from the former Soviet Zone to west Germany between 1949 and 1961, which even the construction

Migration is a feature of man's existence. "Traveling folk" in Bremen-Blumenthal around 1900

Recklinghausen II Mine, around 1885. The proverbial "Ruhr Poles" were recruited as industrial workers for the rising German industry

of the Berlin Wall failed to halt completely and which increased again to a real exodus from 1988 to 1991. In that period, more than five million people left the German Democratic Republic for the West.

In other words, what is special about the history of German migration is that, to a considerable extent, it has been Germans immigrating into and returning to the former emigrant country, i.e. that immigration is intended to strengthen the domestic ethnic collective. This also affects collective identity. To put it bluntly, to this day Germany does not see itself as an immigrant country because (as elsewhere) the individual gains accruing to local employers are calculated to dovetail with those of foreign workers, but rather due to the fact that foreigners balance the German population figures and hence the hope is that they will be the saving the German welfare state. This strange tale will now be recounted briefly in four stages.

Guest Worker Immigration

The early Federal Republic was still characterized mainly by the historically unique mass-scale immigration of refugees of German origin from former eastern parts of the German Reich, when a second mass movement began. Initially, this new movement was not at all obvious and corresponded much more to the "classic" pattern of employee migration. But "guest worker immigration" was not intended as unequivocal immigration

with no ifs or buts, neither from the point of view of the declared recruiting country, the Federal Republic of Germany, nor from the point of view of the guest workers, who came from (southern) Italy and later from many other rural areas bordering the Mediterranean and for whom, at first, any kind of definitive settling in Germany was out of the question. The de facto immigration was, however, not only a deliberate move by west German employers and businesses, but one implemented by the state on an active and persistent basis, at all times on the illusory grounds of a requirement for a "rotating" supply of unqualified workers, mainly for the building, mining and processing industries and in the catering trade. The first recruitment agreement with Italy was concluded in December 1955. Agreements with Greece (1960), Spain (1960), Turkey (1961), Morocco (1963), Portugal, Tunisia (1965) and Yugoslavia (1968) followed in quick succession. At the time of the halt to recruitment in 1973 around four million foreigners were living in the Federal Republic. A short time later, the GDR followed suit as far as it was able to do so, that is, by concluding recruitment agreements with fellow socialist states and developing nations. In the West, the commonly accepted name for the working migrants was "Gastarbeiter" (guest workers); the politically correct term "foreign employees" corresponded with the factual perception: immigrants were perceived and categorized less according to their nationality and/or religion than simply as employees. As an exogenous underclass they made

possible the collective promotion mainstream German society within the continuous paternoster elevator of the social order, without the segmentation of the employment market disturbing the self-classification of the "level middle-class society."

The trade union understanding of the term "employee" assumes proletarian solidarity and an acceptance of ethnic differences, on the one hand among the immigrants themselves, who came variously from northern and southern Italy, from Croatia and Serbia, or who were Turks and Kurds (and therefore were the best of friends), and on the other hand with their German colleagues. This suggestion did not survive the crises in the employment market, which were exacerbated by the restrictive approach of the Federation of German Trade Unions (Deutscher Gewerkschaftsbund) vis-à-vis foreign wage competition and by subsequent "ethnicising" within the guest worker population, first attributed with national and, later, religious characteristics – most recently with the increase in numbers of the Turks recruited since 1961.

The state-controlled recruitment of guest workers was related to an economic consideration: the intention to prolong the economic miracle of the 1950s through labor-intensive methods. This relied on the combination

Women from eastern Europe in particular worked in the Bremen textile industry. Photo 1905

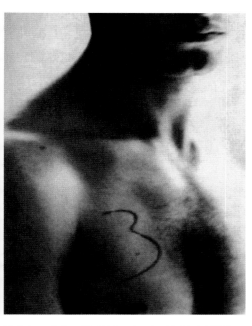

Medical examination of Turkish "guest workers" in Istanbul 1961

The one millionth "guest worker", a spectacular media event, 1964

What was the outcome of this phase of latent immigration? Today, there are up to 15 million people "with a migration background" living in the Federal Republic and, since these people came from the Mediterranean region in the broadest sense of the word, between 1955 and 1975 this development was in reality irreversible. It is difficult to make any kind of all-encompassing evaluation; the continually high number of people returning to their home country in itself illustrates the fact that not all "guest workers" have made it in Germany. On the other hand, the individual gamble has worked out for millions of people who have secured their family home in Germany and have, to some extent, been able to integrate into the domestic middle class.

Nowadays, the overall economic benefit of immigration for the west German welfare economy is undisputed. Nevertheless, problems of segregation and self-exclusion are becoming apparent with regard to the second and third generations and this will cause problems in the host country for some time to come. Germany's refusal for many decades to see itself as a country of immigrants has led to the marginalization of the guest worker population in the German system. International comparisons show that the Federal Republic did considerably more to include immigrants in the welfare state than it did to promote cultural and political integration. The guest workers became social citizens but, for the most part, they did not become members of German civil society and the cultural nation.

Refugee Migration

In theory, immigrants and refugees can be clearly distinguished. In line with a basic humanitarian principle, those who are subject to political persecution have a right to be taken in; those who wish to enter a country purely for personal economic gain, however, must balance their individual interests with those of the host country. These interests are by no means altruistically formulated, but strive rather to correct deficits in the employment market or demographic imbalances for the benefit of the state. In practice, this distinction can scarcely be maintained, as evidenced by the remarkably explosive phase of migration history in the 1980s. At that time,

of an inexpensive workforce with the highly-qualified (and well-organized) pool of German experts and thereby delayed the process of rationalisation and investment in automation. The global economic crisis, which started in 1973, and the advance of mass unemployment (which still prevails in the majority of the OECD states) could not be prevented, although their effects on the domestic workforce were lessened. Redundancies first affected the guest workers disproportionally because they had less protection under employment legislation and thus acted as buffers to the economic cycle.

From that point onward, however, employment market policy became more restrictive. Instead of recruiting for a limited period, the legislature and businesses began rewarding permanent returnees. This did not, however, lead to any overall reduction in the number of foreigners; on the contrary, despite marked emigration (around 300,000 returned to their country of origin in 1983 alone), the number of foreigners increased to 5 million by 1990, and to over 7 million by 1995. What we are dealing with here is obviously a lesson in the "unintended consequences of policy." In the absence of alternatives "at home', the halt on recruitment and the restrictions on returning led the men that had, until then, been living alone in Germany, to bring their families to join them, or indeed to start families in Germany, thus bringing them a step closer to definitive immigration.

those seeking employment became "asylum seekers" and, with an increasingly varied ethnic-cultural background, the criterion of "usefulness", which could easily stigmatize an asylum seeker (who was condemned, by law, to unemployment!) as a "sponger", replaced a social structural framework.

In any discussion of the heterogeneous group of asylum seekers, the multitude of reasons for fleeing a country must also be taken into account. In the latter days of the Cold War, with its ethnic proxy and civil wars, refugees relocated from Africa and Asia to Europe; the early phase of climate change, which, in the Sahel zone for example, destroyed millions of people's homes and set them on the move, should not be overlooked either. Migrants no longer came primarily from neighboring European regions, but from the Third World; furthermore, they rarely corresponded to the model political refugees of the 20th century – a small number of usually highly educated and politically active exiles, who were forced to flee the massive repression of Hitler's Germany or Soviet Russia, or the exodus of the Jews, the Roma and Sinti and others persecuted on grounds of their race. This divergence from the traditional refugee profile did not, of course, justify the underestimation of the grounds for having to flee and the collective denunciation of refugees as "pseudo-asylum seekers". This is, however, precisely what happened, despite the fact that

Above: Refugees from Nigeria around 1990
Below: Flyer advocating humane treatment of asylum seekers, 1989

an increasing percentage were not accepted as asylum seekers but merely "tolerated" in Germany. No doubt there were bold attempts to exploit the unguarded flank of German asylum legislation, and smugglers and traffickers also exploited the abject poverty of the refugees. But let's be clear here: the mindless and heartless asylum policy of the Federal government, which discredited the global refugee drama across the board as "immigration into the social systems" (ex-chancellor Helmut Kohl), itself provoked a large proportion of the societal uncertainty that arose during the 1980s in the face of sometimes dramatically increasing numbers of asylum applications.

Even before right-wing radicals and racists latched onto this, a collective stigma had been attached to the implementation of asylum policy. This was used to justify the weakening and erosion of Article 16 of the Grundgesetz,

which had established a unique individual right to asylum. This policy gained support among the population because the refugees had upset a cornerstone of the German societal contract by claiming services from the German welfare system into which they had never paid – indeed, how could they! Guest worker migration had been tolerated, and even unemployed migrants of this type were more often than not accepted, since they had "paid in" taxes and social security contributions during their working life, thereby validating their status as useful members of the welfare state. Apparently, migration caused by globalization was too much for German society to understand.

Some figures can help to illustrate the change in the 1990s. Between 1988 and 1997, more than 100,000 asylum seekers arrived annually. Only in rare cases were more than 5% of applications successful. A highpoint was reached in 1992 with 430,000 asylum seekers. Thereafter, the amendment of (procedural) asylum legislation, in particular the third-state provision (foreigners entering the country via a safe third state do not have a right to asylum), decreased the annual number to under 30,000, which is still the current annual number. Political debate in the 1990s upheld the blind spots and did not contribute to any relaxation of the situation. In their defense of the Asylum Laws the liberal left-wing camp tended to deny the misuse of them. At the same time, conservative politicians on the Right of the party spectrum encouraged racist resentment and misanthropic viewpoints

in competition for the national populist vote. At this time of all times, just as Germany was experiencing unprecedented migration from three sources (reuniting families, refugees and the most recent ethnic German emigrants), immigration legislation and policy seemed paralyzed and precious time was wasted on long-overdue politico-legal planning. It did not take much for this indolence in both the west and the east of unified Germany to shift to an atmosphere akin to that of a pogrom, which in some places developed into racially-motivated crime.

The most recent ethnic German immigrants were not immune to this either, although they did, as ethnic Germans, have a clear advantage over economic immigrants and asylum seekers. While the others often waited decades for politico-legal equality, the ethnic Germans enjoyed all citizenship rights within 24 hours, even if they spoke not a word of German. The asymmetry between foreigners of varying provenance was expressed in anachronistic legislation on foreigners, based on the ius sanguinis, which promoted the continuity over centuries of the community of origin and systematically negated the chances of a Republican community of acceptance. Nevertheless, German society saw the "new Germans" as Russians; the "Russians" then adopted standard migrant characteristics, in the same way as those "foreigners" who, allegedly or actually, set up parallel societies in Germany.

Sluggish Reforms, Unresolved Situations

By 1990, as the legacy of the waves of migration described above, around 5 million foreigners were living in Germany. The following years brought immigration into Germany to a high point. Asylum seekers, emigrants and migrant workers were arriving in Germany at the same time in numbers not seen before. The employment market, the social security system and the legal system were all unprepared for this influx, which furthermore hit the newly-reunited Germany at a time when it was experiencing a precarious phase in its collective search for identity, dealing with the teething problems of unification. The Federal government set clear ethnic priorities among the emigrants, viz. it encouraged the immediate immigration of "ethnic Germans". In

By giving the "guest workers" in the Federal Republic a more permanent status a bizarre situation arose: they lived as de facto immigrants in a country which did not see itself as an immigrant country. The migrants established their own religious institutions and fostered the cultural traditions of their old homeland. The Mevlana Mosque was opened in Bremen in 1987. Right: The Croatian Cultural Association in Bremen. Photo 1990

places, this policy was abused, while asylum legislation was tightened and the naturalization opportunities provided to foreigners living in Germany were restricted. At the peak referred to above, in 1992, 438,000 people applied for political asylum; 230,000 people came as immigrants and a further 300,000 as migrant workers with their family members. Even in absolute figures, this immigration, which was still not declared as such, reached American levels, already long surpassed in any case in relative terms (i.e. in proportion to the size of the population). Only slowly did the xenophobic pogroms mentioned earlier lead to political self-education in German society and even this did not lead to a political or legal change in status. This did not occur until the end of the decade, with the amendment of the laws on citizenship, and thereafter through (restrictive and half-hearted) immigration legislation.

One problem that had barely been recognized hitherto remained as the legacy of that period: the illegal immigration of non-registered persons. The number of such immigrants is today estimated at a minimum of 100,000 annually. The phenomenon of undocumented immigration seen in all rich countries is lessened by Germany's now advantageous central geographic location. The European single market rules, however, mean that, increasingly, illegal immigrants are also arriving in Germany. Dreadful scenes are played out on the shorelines of the EU states; in Germany, primarily in the eastern border regions and at airports, conditions are sometimes terrible, untenable under human rights legislation, but denounced only by the churches and some refugee organisations. According to many experts on migration, the regularisation policy practized in the western and southern European states, i.e. the granting of proper residency status and employment opportunities, would be advisable, not least because American attempts at sealing its borders, primarily against immigrants from Central America, have proved to be impracticable. The rich countries should not be able to use draconian segregation measures to deal with the fact that migration patterns have gone transcontinental due to the likes of genocidal civil wars, particularly in Africa, the growing poverty in even once-rich fast-developing countries in Latin America and global environmental disasters, which have triggered transnational migration over the last twenty years and which are likely to increase.

The Transnationalization and Culturalization of Migration

Transcontinental and provisional migration, again not intended as definitive resettlement, are side-effects of economic globalization, from which the EU states, and Germany in particular, have always profited. Efforts to prevent poverty-driven migration have been unsuccessful and the attempt in the 1990s to solve the serious shortage of highly-qualified workers in Germany with the help of the "Green Card" option also failed. The vast bulk of emigration, which has increased since that time, relates specifically to qualified workers, who find more attractive jobs in neighboring EU states and in Switzerland, as well as in the USA and emerging nations, than those on offer in the German employment market, which has become paralyzed at both the top and bottom ends. The hoped-for mass influx of Indian IT experts never materialized, nor did the exten-

The Schengen Agreement of 1985 brought greater freedom of movement across European borders. But what did this mean for refugees in the rest of the world? A plea for a liberal, tolerant, and humane immigration and refugee policy. Photo 1990

Guest workers? Immigrants? Turkish? German? Photo 1990

sive recruitment and repatriation of leading academics or the business elite.

Instead, throughout western Europe, fears of the apocryphal "Polish plumber" are rife. Incidentally, this cheap competition (viewed with scepticism by the host society) and sluggish elite immigration have something in common: both display only a low level of identification with the "new home". Here, a modified classic immigration model, as observed in all areas of the world, ideally involves permanent settlement, cultural assimilation and politico-legal naturalization. Transnational nomadic life, which also includes retired seasonal tourists in the south, is characterized by its impermanent nature. Transnational nomads take with them artefacts, metaphors and symbols, individual life stories and collective biographies; they live in two or more places on a permanent basis, are always comfortable in two or more languages, often have two or more passports and wander through improvized family homes, relationship networks, and spheres of communication in both directions. This is why in cultural sociology the routes of migration are more important than the roots of personal identity in the national collective. At the same time, the risks and conflicts inherent in transnational migration cause more obvious recourse to imagined identities of an ethnic and religious nature.

Thanks to modern transport and communications technologies, religious communities are also spreading across the globe,

less in the organisational and administrational manner of the major world religions than in the form of multi-faith civil societies. "Diaspora," once a catastrophic uprooting experience, is no longer an exception in the religious pluralism of our time; it has lost its horror because the protection of religious freedom has improved worldwide, leading to imported religious symbols becoming obvious in the public arena of secularized societies. Thus, since the end of the 1970s, the religious dimension has increasingly joined the ethnic strata in Germany, particularly in relation to the Muslims, who since then have appeared more openly in public as Muslims. "Foreign workers", a social-structural characteristic, became not only "Turks" (or "Kurds"); the vast majority of the immigrants from Turkey were now, irrespective of their actual piety and religious practice, identified as "Muslims". Islam is seen here as a particular troublemaker, fed by the politicization, radicalization and militancy originating since 1979 from Iran and the Palestinian Intifada. Since the attacks in the USA in 2001 and in Europe in 2003/04, immigration has been entirely overshadowed by issues of national security, and now "multiculturalism", which used to be a positive term, has turned into a derogatory word once and for all. The news magazine Spiegel announced the "failure of the multicultural society" years ago, alluding to the conflicts between Turks and Kurds and the formation of an ethnic subculture in the conurbations. This encoding can also be seen to have changed in the meantime; when a Spiegel headline in 2007 proclaimed "Mecca Deutschland", it was insinuating "Islamic infiltration'. The talk of "parallel societies" originating from the social sciences has become generalized, to which the voluntary and intentional segregation in some circles (not only Arabic/Turkish/Muslim) has contributed; this is countered with the talk of the so-called Leitkultur or core culture (translated literally as "leading culture'), which has a partially German-national and Christian-occidental, partly European-humanistic flavor to it. This idea either appeals to the homogeneous ideal circumstances which pre-dated globalization or it offers hybrid cultures a universalistic approach. In practice this means that justifiable group rights must always be balanced, by way of guarantees under human rights legislation and the constitution, against segregation

of the genders, Sharia law and restrictions on the freedom of speech and artistic freedom. The ongoing debate doesn't differentiate much between "Muslims and the rest" and is also disputed within the respective communities and in the courts. With regard to equal rights, gender equality and the protection of sexual orientations and alternative lifestyles in particular, the law and society in general are facing major challenges, which in the ideal scenario would translate monotonously declared "western values" into practiced principles – and transform dubious laissez faire into true tolerance. Thus, it is possible to assert and redefine a multiculturalism sobered by reality. People have the right to differences in lifestyle, but this makes certain demands on outdated ideas within the host society. In western societies, this is first and foremost an individual option anchored in the universal basic rights which may not be allowed to hold anyone hostage in the name of supposedly more important collective rights and which must guarantee one thing above all – the option of being able to leave an ethnic or religious community at any time, without having to state the reasons for doing so.

After 1945 west German society had to absorb and integrate more than 12 million expellees. Although they were German, these people suffered discrimination similar to that experienced by later immigrants. Work by grade 7 pupil Siegfried Geisler, 1954

Conclusion and Prospects for the Future

Naturally, following 60 years of "inhibited" and non-declared immigration, the results are mixed, since over 7 million foreigners and twice as many people with a "migration background" live in Germany. Overall, economically, migration has doubtless been worthwhile both for the immigrants and for the host society. Things look less rosy for some individual sectors and for the stability of the welfare state, and often the individual calculations of many immigrants did not work out, as evidenced by the consistently high number of returning migrants who failed to make their fortune in Germany. Anyway, it is not possible to make any kind of general report on the outcome. Immigrant communities differ greatly; almost seamless (and voluntary) Germanification and occasionally spectacular social careers stand in sharp contrast to sometimes forced, sometimes voluntary ghettoisation tendencies which indicate serious deficits in integration and are in places accompanied by a manifest disdain for German culture and society, especially among young second and third generation males. The German education system in particular has a responsibility to perform in this context. It has been less successful than other OECD countries in dealing with ethnic-cultural and religious heterogeneity and transforming this into an identity characterized by diversity. The half-heartedness of political integration has created a lasting dependency, namely the persistently preferential treatment of ethnic German immigrants and the subordination of individual migration intentions under illusory ambitions of conserving the German "social model" and rebuilding the population pyramid.

Why Germany, why not? Why should immigrants set out for Germany tomorrow and the day after; what will prevent them from doing so – and what is it that makes Germans turn their backs on Germany? Germany, as a homogeneous industrial society and a welfare state with a universal scope, was attractive for region-specific immigration, but did little to adapt its culture, policies and laws to accommodate this immigration. Nowadays, as a segregated service economy, the country is far less attractive for increasingly transnational immigration, not even within the framework of supranational EU freedom of movement, which

Some buildings exemplify a bizarre tradition: camp on Bahrsplate in Bremen Nord; originally a forced labor camp, later an outstation of the Neuengamme concentration camp and then a camp for expellees. Photo 1963
Family of a Turkish shipyard worker at AG Weser, Bremen, in the Halmerweg camp, a former forced labor camp. Photo 1990
Germany will have to come to terms with the fact that it is a country of immigrants and formulate relevant immigration and integration policies. Photo 1991

has been restricted on several occasions following pressure from Germany in the course of the expansion eastward. Migrants are a projection screen for such failures to modernize; at the same time, ethnic-religious stratification poses a serious threat to the coherence of a society of immigrants, which has oscillated between ethno-nationalism and xenophobia for too long and which the engine of time is threatening to leave behind.

Melilla, the border between Spain and Morocco: barbed wire, surveillance cameras, armed border guards. Two refugees bound together by the Spanish authorities, 2008

Aderanti Adepoju

Migration to, Within and From Africa: That's Where We Belong

The study of international migration in sub-Saharan Africa (SSA) is hampered by lack of data on both stock and flow of migrants. Only a few countries include questions on migration (nationality/citizenship; place of birth; residence status, etc.) in their censuses; even then analyses of such data have been severely restricted. Estimates of migration flows based on information provided by border control posts (the long borders without distinct barriers are un-policed) and registration centers and estimates of stock from field surveys, are generally inadequate. Consequently, information collected from those who cross recognised frontiers often combine all types of migrants: transients, immigrants, business travellers, etc. Besides, few countries regularly publish data collected at sea- and airports and border posts. These factors hinder

considerably the analysis of international migration in the region (Adepoju, 1988a).

The type, volume and direction of international migration are closely related to complex historical and political experiences and to economic structures in the region. Colonial rule, artificial boundaries that divide socially homogenous units into separate states and strong links with colonial countries have been reinforced by the politics of independence and the post-independence struggle for leadership, and ecological deterioration in most parts of the region, especially the Sahel, to generate economically motivated migrants and refugees. These, and the changing configurations of migration within, to and from SSA, are the key issues discussed in detail in this paper.

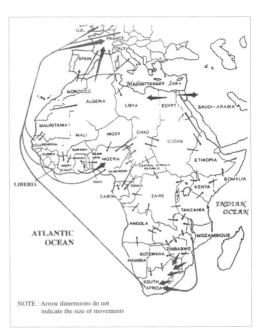

NOTE : Arrow dimensions do not indicate the size of movements

Intra-African migration. Map 2006 (Aderanti Adepoju)

Failed immigration attempt. Photo 2008

Migration Dynamics: Some Historical Antecedents

Migration in the region was initially associated with trade, slavery, evangelism, nomadism and internecine warfare. In most of the region, colonial rule altered both the causes and nature of such movement, institutionalised certain existing patterns and stimulated new waves of migration (Prothero, 1968). In particular, the strategy of economic development pursued by various colonial governments largely shaped the direction of inter-continental migration in both the colonial and post-colonial era. In the latter period, the post-independence political situation in the region, followed by deteriorating socio-economic situation, fuelled additional waves of migrants of especially

Peanut cultivation in Mali. These peasant farmers produce cash crops for the market in an attempt to make a living. As a result of globalization, however, they face stiff competition on world markets which has a considerable impact on their livelihood. Photo 1988

undocumented workers and refugees (Amin, 1974).

Flows from French-speaking west Africa to France, from English-speaking west and east Africa to the United Kingdom, the United States and Germany; from Zaire to Belgium and from the former Portuguese colonies to Portugal were almost uniformly directed to the metropolitan centres of the colonial governments. Indeed, various forms of migration also characterised the sub-regions. While labor migration is a feature common to all sub-regions, refugee flows were initially confined mainly to east Africa and especially countries of the Horn and the Sudan, and later, in the 1990s, it spread to the Mano River Union countries (Liberia, Sierra Leone, Guinea). Undocumented migration is a pervasive phenomenon in the region; however, strict labor recruitment laws in apartheid-era South Africa regulated such in-flow compared with the situation in west Africa where undocumented migration took place routinely. Seasonal labor migration also featured more prominently in west Africa than in other parts of the region (Adepoju, 1983; 2004).

West Africa

Migration within west Africa has been greatly influenced by political, economic, ecological, social and religious factors. The sub-region has a long history of population movement of individuals and groups in search of subsistence food, better shelter and greater security, especially during the period of internecine warfare of the 19th century (Addo, 1975). west Africans had migrated as explorers, laborers and warriors across frontiers far and near. Such movements were unsystematised and information is scanty (ECA, 1981). In the pre-colonial era, movements now regarded as international migration occurred over a wide area, restricted only by intertribal warfare and later, by fear of raids and slaving. Entire villages, tribes and clans are known to have moved to escape the ravages of internecine warfare and slave raids, or to avoid unfavourable agricultural and climatic conditions resulting in famine and drought (Zachariah and Conde, 1981). Commercial migration (Sudarkasa, 1974/1975) and movements connected with trade and evangelization (Addo, 1975) also featured during this period. Migrants had always

considered west Africa as an economic unit within which trade in goods and services flowed freely; the free movement of people was therefore an integral feature of prevailing economic interdependence among the nation states (Stapleton, 1959).

The colonial era ushered in a period of relative calm and security which also spurred additional waves of migration buttressed by the colonial administration's economic and related strategies. It also provided a new framework for large-scale migration, deriving from the labor requirements for plantations and later the administrative apparatus beyond the supply obtainable in neighbouring areas (Amin, 1974). A series of economic measures, especially the forced-labor system, was adopted to obtain labor in the required number and place. In the northern Ivory Coast, compulsory cropping system was designed largely to obtain the enormous labor-force needed for infrastructural work, especially roads and railways construction in the north and plantation agriculture in the south. Forced migration induced by taxes and compulsory cropping, sometimes colored with incentives, later became institutionalised into voluntary migration (Hinderink and Templeman,

Collecting fire wood in southern Ghana. Women spend half their working lives collecting wood. Photo 1988

1978). Forced recruitment also paved the way for free migration of individuals and families in search of better living conditions. This trend, and other streams of migration of unskilled labor from countries in the interior (Upper Volta, Mali, Niger and Chad) towards coastal countries, principally Ivory Coast and Gold Coast, became a dominant feature of international migration in west Africa. Similar movements were observed from Mali and the Guinean interior toward the Senegambian groundnut zone and the urban areas of Senegal (Zachariah and Conde, 1981).

Migration from the north to areas of prosperous agricultural activity in the coastal region was short-term and involved mainly males. Seasonal migrations from savannah areas in the north occurred especially during the long dry season when economic activity was at its lowest. It is to this extent that west Africa has been, as Prothero (1968) asserted, characterised by greater seasonal migration than elsewhere in tropical Africa.

Gold Coast (Ghana) and Ivory Coast (Côte d'Ivoire), and to a lesser extent Senegal, historically the major destination of immigrants in the region, was later joined by Nigeria. Migration to the Gold Coast began in the early 1920s (ECA, 1981). The introduction and/or expansion of mining and cocoa farming and the systematic orientation of the economy towards export products created a huge demand for labor which the indigenous people were unwilling or unable to satisfy. As a result laborers were recruited from Togo, Upper Volta and Nigeria. In 1969 Ghana expelled a large number of foreigners under the Aliens Compliance Order but by the late 70s, economic problems in the country forced many Ghanaians to emigrate to Nigeria and Côte d'Ivoire (Adamako-Sarfoh, 1974). Since the 1960s, Côte d'Ivoire has been replacing Ghana as the principal recipient of immigration in the sub-region.

Nigeria has became a country of immigration beginning in 1975 when the oil-led economic growth generated rapid expansion of road and building construction, infrastructure, education and allied sectors, and attracted workers, both skilled and unskilled, in droves from various west African countries. Most immigrants came from Ghana, Togo and Benin. They entered the country through both official and

A 3,000 year-old tree in the southern Sahara. Overgrazing, erosion and desertification increasingly reduce the area of arable land

unofficial routes, and by 1982, immigrants from west Africa living in Nigeria numbered about 2.5 million (Adepoju, 1988b). Senegal has also become a significant country of immigration; nearly half of the immigrants came from Guinea and Guinea-Bissau, the former consisting mostly of refugees who had fled their country for political reasons. Those from Gambia were mainly temporary migrants who moved back and forth between the two countries fairly frequently (Swindell, 1978).

The principal countries of emigration are Burkina Faso, Mali, Togo, and most recently Ghana. Since the beginning of the century workers from Burkina Faso have been attracted to the plantation and construction industries in Ivory Coast, and (during the 1950s and 1960s) to cocoa farms in Gold Coast. Indeed, by 1975 17 % of Burkinabes lived abroad. In Nigeria, substantial emigration was reported from the south-east to the plantations of Fernando Po and Spanish Guinea. These included contract laborers and others who migrated clandestinely (Zachariah and Conde, 1981).

A large part of the movement across frontiers has been facilitated by cultural affinity, especially where immigrants belong to the same tribes as the indigenous population of the host country, speak the same language, and share the same customs. Census data therefore probably

underestimate the number of migrants within the sub-region. In the cases of Ghana/Togo and Nigeria/Benin, frontier workers commute daily between their homes and their places of employment (Adepoju, 1983). Unlike other regions, most of what has been labelled labor migration in the literature can be more correctly regarded as commercial migration – by male and female traders; labor migration per se is essentially male-dominated (Sudarkasa, 1974/1975). The case of Nigerians in Ghana (prior to 1969) amply documents this phenomenon. What began as labor migration to the cocoa-growing and forestry areas of Ghana later became commercial migration in diamond mining, trading, and commerce (Addo, 1975).

Central Africa

In the pre-colonial period, Central Africa experienced a protracted mass population movement resulting from tribal expansionist expeditions – the Lub-Lunda in areas that now constitute Angola and Zaire; of the Magoni groups from the south into Zaire; and the Fang movements in Cameroon, Gabon and Equatorial Guinea in the late eighteenth and early 19th centuries. In the process, several villages were amalgamated and, in the case of the Fangs, over half a million were forced by Fulani raiders to move southwards from the savannah to the forest zone. They ultimately settled in the territory bordering Cameroon, Gabon and Equatorial Guinea (Halladay, 1972).

As in other sub-regions, populations were split along borders: the Fang between three countries – Gabon, Cameroon and Equatorial Guinea. In other cases, boundaries were drawn in defiance of ecological zones as in the case of Cameroon and Nigeria. Some of these boundaries actually divided village groups, and so movement between villages or homogenous ethnic groups became, statistically and legally, international migrations. The pygmies in the rain forest zone, especially in the northern Zaire, south-eastern Cameroon, north-eastern Congo and south-eastern Central African Republic are a special case. Subsisting on gathering, hunting and fishing, they freely roam across national boundaries, erecting semi-permanent houses along their

Temporary shanty dwellings of migrants and refugees who try to reach European countries. Photo 2008

routes, as do the Fulani nomads in north-west Cameroon.

The countries of Central Africa were ruled for a long period by several colonial powers: Cameroon by French and British, Equatorial Africa (Chad) by Spain; São Tomé and Príncipe and Angola by Portugal, and Zaire by Belgium. The pattern of immigration was therefore dominated by Europeans from these colonial countries as well as by Africans from countries under similar colonial administrations, and immigrant workers recruited under contract from other African countries. The earliest immigrants from Europe to Central Africa were mostly male explorers and colonists and workers in the labor-intensive activities of mining and plantation agriculture. This resulted in a high sex ratio among immigrants, especially in Gabon, Chad, Congo, Zaire and Cameroon. In small island states dominated by migrant workers, and in centres where immigrants were heavily concentrated, especially south-west Cameroon, Kinshasa and Shaba province in Zaire, the sex ratio was highly distorted.

Gabon and Zaire, both rich in mineral deposits, were the major centres of in-migration. The huge investments in Gabon and Zaire created jobs for both skilled and unskilled workers. The timber industries in Gabon and especially Equatorial Guinea, and the palm plantations in

Cameroon offered employment opportunities to immigrants, especially Nigerians. Immigrants from Senegal, Mali, Niger and Togo were mostly traders and domestic and service workers, in contrast to the Indian, Pakistani and Lebanese immigrants who dominated wholesale, retail trade and the skilled professions. European immigrants dominated the managerial and other skilled jobs, while African immigrants were mostly unskilled laborers, the exceptions being skilled personnel seconded from African countries to administrative positions in countries where few nationals occupied such posts.

The slave trade in Equatorial Africa, involving an estimated 3 million persons, mainly males, from Angola and about 1 million from Congo, was by far the most devastating mass population movement during this period. The affected areas still remain sparsely populated today (Duffy, 1962). During the colonial period, the establishment of European administrative networks was followed by contract and forced labor legislations, agreements and recruitment, whose implementation was greatly resented by Africans but nevertheless sparked large scale-legal and clandestine migration of unskilled adult males.

The colonial administrations also devised means of relocating skilled personnel from one colony to another, especially from Benin

and Cameroon to serve in the administration of French Equatorial Africa (Ballard, 1966). In the case of the Portuguese and Belgian colonies, such personnel were drawn from the metropolises to serve in the colonies. The situation was very different for unskilled labor. Angola is a typical example as source of labor supply for South Africa. In 1908, the Portuguese administrators in Angola signed labor agreements with South Africa and in 1926 a decree declared all unemployed males between age 18 and 55 liable to contract labor for up to six months within Angola, or six to twelve months outside the country. In 1959 about 180,000 licences were issued for legal recruitments to South Africa; this increased to 190,000 in 1962. The law provoked large-scale clandestine emigration to neighbouring countries in a bid to escape forced-labor recruitment and the abuses associated with its implementation. By 1962 when the decree was overhauled about a million Angolans had already emigrated illegally to Botswana, Zambia, Zaire and South Africa (Ritner, 1960).

Contract labor and forced-labor recruitment from Angola's hinterland to the cocoa, coffee and sugar plantations of São Tomé and Príncipe also took the form of disguised slavery. Later, immigrants were attracted — or recruited — from Liberia, Sierra Leone, and other parts of west and east Africa to supplement the labor requirements of the rapidly expanding plantations of São Tomé and Príncipe, thus increasing the proportion of foreigners there to 65% in 1921 up from 60% in 1900, thereafter it drastically dropped to 14% in 1970. The economic boom in cocoa and coffee production of the island of Fernando Po (Equatorial Guinea) also attracted migrants.

In 1934 Cameroon signed a convention with Fernando Po to permit emigration of up to 4,000 people for contract work for a maximum of six years. A co-operative agreement ratified in 1977 stipulated, among other things, that migrant workers could be recruited in Cameroon but that their contract of employment had to be visa'd in advance by the country's Ministry of Labor (ILO, 1980). Fishermen from Ghana and Nigeria maintain semi-permanent settlements along the riverine coast of Cameroon and Gabon, sometimes involving family groups. Migrant workers were also recruited on contract from

Above: The Fulani living in settlements adopted the Islamic faith at an early stage and were a driving force in its spread across west Africa. One tribal group, the Fulani-Bororo, are still living as semi-nomads rearing cattle. Photo 2001
Below: Slash and burn agriculture. This method of gaining arable land has a massive impact on the ecological balance and can contribute to further desertification. Photo Liberia 1992

the timber industry; others worked in coffee and cocoa plantations. In 1974 immigrants from Angola and Belgium predominated in the Kinshasa, lower Congo, Shaba and Kivu provinces of Zaire. Over 80% of Chad's immigrants resided in the south and occidental divisions.

The post-independence era witnessed the mass exodus of European settlers resulting from disturbances before or soon after political independence. This was the case of the Belgians in Zaire, the Portuguese in Angola, the Spaniards in Equatorial Guinea, São Tomé and Príncipe, and the French in Cameroon. Some later returned as temporary residents (especially in countries where expatriate military defence personnel were posted) or technical aid personnel and private investors. Thus Angola lost 90% of its European immigrants resulting from the exodus of more than 300,000 settlers to Portugal by March 1975. Within eleven years of independence in 1968, Equatorial Guinea also had lost almost half of its 400,000 population through emigration, and between 1974 and 1979, Sao Tome and Principe experienced a net loss of 80% of its immigrant population, including 90% of the Europeans (Adepoju, 1988a).

East Africa

The earliest population settlements in east Africa resulted from Bantu migrations from Congo and Zambezi rivers, westwards to the Indian Ocean in response to adverse environmental conditions and the outbreak of epidemics, and involved large groups of people, tribes and lineages. Later migrations was triggered mainly by internecine warfare and slavery. Colonization of new lands by Somali to the northern fringes of Kenya, and the Luo from the Nile Valley into Uganda and western Kenya also featured between the 15th and 19th centuries (Oliver, 1963). The movement of nomads in the pre-colonial era persisted into the colonial and post-colonial eras, especially pastoral movement between Somalia, Kenya and Tanganyika (Tanzania) in response to seasonal climate changes in various parts of the sub-region. These early migrations were aimed at restoring the balance between population and resources.

Slave trade routes provided the network for colonial and post-colonial labor

eastern Nigeria. By the time the contract agreement was terminated in 1964/65, over 7,000 migrant workers had been recruited yearly.

The migration of Africans was largely temporary: shuttling between mines, plantation and forest cash-crop areas and their rural homes, except for those who resettled in neighbouring locations to

escape forced-labor conscription. African immigrants, like Gabonese nationals, clustered in temporary unskilled jobs, especially in the construction industry. Immigrants in Equatorial Guinea were drawn mainly from Nigeria: 60% of the residents of the country were from that country and before they were repatriated in 1973, constituted 55% of the workforce in

migration. The west-east migration of slaves was replaced by movements of cheap labor from Zaire, Rwanda and Burundi to Uganda, Kenya and the eastern coastal estates and clove plantations of Tanzania. During the colonial period, the major streams of inter-continental migration were between east Africa, Europe and the Indian subcontinent. British immigrants formed the mainstreams to Uganda, Kenya, Tanganyika, Mauritius and Rhodesia and Nyasaland (Zambia and Malawi); the French-dominated streams to and from Madagascar; and the Belgians to and from Ruanda-Urundi (Burundi and Rwanda). Skilled and unskilled labor from the Indian subcontinent and China was recruited by colonial governments to work in industry, agriculture and commerce. Significant numbers of Europeans, especially British, formed isolated settle-ments in Kenya. Asian communities also followed their example (Oliver, 1963; Ohadike, 1974).

This pattern of historical movement shaped both the origin and the direction of migration during the post-colonial period. For instance, the slave trade route provided a network for colonial and post-colonial labor migration by replacing the west-east slave migration with unskilled labor from the Belgian Congo (Zaire), Ruanda-Urundi westward to Uganda and Kenya and to the eastern coastal estates of Tanganyika and the clove plantations of Zanzibar. These also necessitated periodic movements of contract labor between areas of "labor reserve" and area of colonial enterprises especially the mines and plantations of South Africa. Colonial economic activities accentu-ated regional inequalities both within and between countries of the region. The labor migrations were essentially short term, mostly young males recruited for specific contract periods to work in Uganda, Kenya and Tanganyika's estates and small older export crop product in mining areas, copper, tobacco farms (Mlay, 1983).

The main sources of labor migrants were locations of limited colonial invest-ments and hence employment. Kenya provided the largest number of emigrants to other east Africa countries, constituting 47% to Uganda, Kenya and Tanganyika (Tanzania) in the mid 50s. Uganda was the recipient of the largest number of immigrants, mainly from Ruanda-Urundi,

Rural scene in Zambia. In many African countries there is a sharp contrast between city and country. In rural areas, the infrastructure in regard to education, social services, access to clean drinking water, sewage disposal and hygiene, transportation systems, etc. is extremely underdeveloped. Photo 2008

which were densely populated and under-developed; these served as the major source of migrants in east Africa. The southern part of east Africa – the north-ern Rhodesian copper belt, farms and mining centres in southern Rhodesia and the industrial complexes in South Africa – formed a major destination of migrants (Monstead and Walji, 1978). Labor recruited under contract agreements from Malawi, Mozambique and Zambia for work in the mines, industry and plantations of Zimbabwe and South Africa for up to two years, and workers from Rwanda and Burundi for the rich agricultural areas of Uganda, the Republic of Tanzania, Zambia and Kenya, took the form of temporary and oscillatory migrations (Oucho, 1995).

In addition to labor migration, a substan-tial migration among the white population of east Africa, especially immediately prior to independence, was recorded towards Rhodesia and South Africa. Although this type of migration was motivated mainly by the fear of unrest, the attractive climatic and socio-economic conditions in Rhodesia and South Africa played a significant role. Even so, emigration and immigration between east Africa and Europe continued after independence, due mainly to continuing technical co-operation in various fields of socio-economic development between these countries and the former colonial powers.

Tanzania and Zambia enacted laws soon after independence prohibiting their

nationals from working in South Africa. That apart, the break-up of the Federation of Rhodesia and Nyasaland, and the indepen-dence by Rhodesia greatly reduced migra-tory movements.

The main centres of attraction for migrants were, in Kenya, the sugar and tea estates and the industrial centre of Nairobi; the cotton plantations in Uganda and the Sisal estate in Tanzania which employed both local and foreign laborers. Tanzania was both a labor-exporting and importing country, and attracted immigrants princi-pally from Burundi. Other sources include Mozambique, Rwanda, Kenya and Uganda.

Clandestine movement across interna-tional frontiers, especially by members of ethnic groups in adjacent counties, also prevailed and included the Kuria, Luo and Masai along the borders of Kenya and Tanzania, the Makonde between Tanzania and Mozambique, Rwandese and Rundi between Rwanda, Burundi and Tanzania, the Rwandese in both Rwanda and Uganda, the Kakwa and Nubi between Uganda, Sudan and Zaire, and Somali in Kenya, Somalia and Ethiopia. The boundar-ies separating these culturally homo-geneous groups split ethnic groups leading to unchecked boundary-crossing. Nomadic pastoralists also moved freely between Somalia, Kenya and Tanzania well after independence.

Refugees comprise the main type of international migration in east Africa.

Africa now contains about half the world's refugees, the majority of whom are in the Horn (Ethiopia, Somalia, Djibouti) and the Sudan. Refugee populations are created by political, ecological, and other unpredictable emergencies. The drought in Ethiopia, Somalia and the Sahel; internal strife in Ethiopia, Somalia and the Sahel; conflicts in Ethiopia, especially in the Eritrean region; and the war in the Ogaden, resulting from a boundary dispute between Ethiopia and Somalia generated refugees and displaced populations in droves (Adepoju, 1982).

Southern Africa

The economic development of countries in the southern Africa sub-region – Botswana, Lesotho, Namibia, South Africa and Swaziland – has been intricately interwoven with the movement of people across national boundaries as colonialists, refugees or migrant workers. The evolution of large-scale international migration in the sub-region can be traced to the "mineral revolution" of the 1860s in South Africa (Brythembach 1972; Cobbe, 1982). Gold-mining required a large labor force, production being based on the combination of a few skilled workers and a large number of unskilled African laborers.

Recruitment of African labor extended beyond the borders of South Africa; by the turn of the century, for instance, about 60 % of male workers in the gold-mines were from Mozambique and about 30,000 laborers from Basutoland (Lesotho) were employed in the mining and haulage industries. Because the supply of indigenous labor within South Africa was inadequate to meet the requirements of the rapidly expanding industry, the South African Chamber of Mines, set up principally as a central labor-recruitment body to prevent wage competition between individual mines, attracted additional laborers from the peripheral colonies. In time the movement of labor from these countries, especially from Botswana, Lesotho and Swaziland, became a dominant feature of labor migration in the sub-region (Stahl, 1982).

Apart from the "mineral revolution" in South Africa, the declining agricultural production in the labor-reserve countries of Botswana, Lesotho and Swaziland (referred to as BLS) was both cause and consequence of migration to the industrial sector of South

White mine workers wearing shoes and Blacks in bare feet. Tsumeb (Namibia) around 1890

Africa where higher wages could be earned. Several factors have been adduced for this situation, including the rapidly expanding population of peripheral states where the arable base had been exhausted, especially Lesotho; the anomalous geographical position of these countries sandwiched, within (Lesotho) or on the periphery (Swaziland, Botswana, Mozambique) of South Africa; alternatives which migration offered to indigenous people who wished to escape restrictive economic policies; the South African Government's preference for a temporary, oscillatory migrant system rather than a permanent indigenous labor force; and the mining employers' recruitment policy of establishing a labor reserve in order to minimize labor costs and welfare expenses (Cobbe, 1982; de Vetter, 1985; Bohning, 1981). The creation of a cheap labor reserve to meet South Africa's labor requirements influenced the volume, frequency and direction of migrant labor from peripheral countries. Immigrants also filled vacancies created on white farms by South Africa Blacks who migrated from the countryside to take up jobs in mining.

Some migrants are employed in agriculture and domestic services, and most of these entered South Africa clandestinely along the borders before the 1963

immigration control regulations came into force. Clandestine migration from peripheral countries to the mines, the white farms of the Orange Free State and Natal and the maize triangle in South Africa, was drastically curtailed rather than eliminated following the introduction of immigration controls in the mid-1960s (Breytenbach, 1972).

Prior to the introduction of immigration controls in the mid-1960s it was possible for entire families to migrate to, and settle in, South Africa. Laws introduced in June 1963 prohibited women or children from accompanying or joining male recruiters. As a result, the number of female immigrants from BLS declined sharply from 91,400 in 1960 to 43,400 in 1970 and to even smaller numbers thereafter. In 1960, 21 % of the African migrant population in South Africa were females; by 1970 it had declined to 11 % (de Vletter, 1985).

Circular migration in South Africa is facilitated by laws that do not allow migrants to remain for more than two years at a time or to bring their families. These laws greatly reduced the social costs normally sustained by receiving countries. Migrant workers were required to leave their families at home, work for the two years stipulated by laws of contract labor, and return to their families for as long

Country	Number of foreign-born stock
Australia	188.928
Austria	16.374
Belgium	107.716
Canada	271.095
Czech Republic	47.648
Denmark	25.355
Finland	7.930
Former CSFR	1.786
France	565.590
Germany	124.435
Great Britain	812.371
Greece	56.859
Hungary	2.170
Ireland	25.412
Japan	5.321
Luxembourg	4.558
Mexico	952
Netherlands	116.349
New Zealand	39.078
Norway	25.613
Poland	2.221
Portugal	348.263
Slovak Republic	354
Spain	79.263
Sweden	68.077
Turkey	11.059
USA	929.723
Total	3.884.500

Table 2 Migrants from sub-Saharan Africa in OECD countries (2002) (Aderanti Adepoju)

as was economically feasible. Because they were not prevented from entering into another contract, migration to South Africa was often termed "oscillatory". An average miner could make a dozen such contract trips to the mines during his working life (Stahl, 1982).

Until the end of the 1960s, Mozambique, Malawi and Lesotho were the major source of recruitment for South African mines. Recruitment of Mozambican mine labor was halted at independence in 1972. In 1973, a turbulent wave of strikes in the gold-mines led to the return of hundreds of contract workers to their countries of origin (AIM, 1984). In 1974 the Malawian Government ordered the cassation of recruitment of migrant laborers following an air crash that killed many of its nationals on their way to the South African mines.

During the 1970s, political and economic pressures induced the mining industry of South Africa to increase the proportion of workers recruited within the country. This led to a reduction in the number of foreign Africans employed from 80% of the black labor force in 1973 to 45% in 1978. Declines in the numbers of immigrants from Malawi and Mozambique were however compensated by an increase in the numbers recruited locally and from Lesotho. Although the numbers of migrants from Lesotho grew rapidly, total numbers from BLS remained stable, owing to a decline in recruitments from Botswana. In 1981 nearly 25% of the economically active population of Namibia

were migrants on short-term contracts, mainly to South Africa's mining sector. In 1981, 79% of all foreign workers were engaged in mining, compared with 5% in agriculture (Malan, 1983; Breytenbach, 1972).

The sub-region also had its own share of refugees, initially from South Africa, Namibia and, until 1980, Zimbabwe to Botswana, Lesotho and Swaziland. The war of liberation in the then Rhodesia (now Zimbabwe), Namibia and South Africa dramatically increased the flow of refugees from these countries to BLS, especially after the students' uprising in Soweto and other black townships, and the subsequent brutal crack-down by the apartheid regime in South Africa.

Recent Trends in International Migration

The people of sub-Saharan Africa are arguably the most mobile in the world. Internal, intra-regional and international migration takes place within diverse socio-ethnic, political and economic contexts. Emigration pressure is fuelled by unstable politics, ethno-religious conflicts, poverty and rapidly growing populations. Unlike in other world regions, these migrations – better

described as "circulations" – involving more than 7 million economically active persons and an unspecified number of undocumented migrants (ILO, 2004), are largely intra-regional. As Table 1 shows, each country accommodates varying numbers of nationals of other countries within their borders. These complex configurations are changing dynamically and are reflected in increasing female migration, diversification of migration destinations, transformation of labor flows into commercial migration, and emigration of skilled health and other professionals from sub-Saharan Africa (Adepoju, 2004). Others are trafficking in human beings and the changing map of refugee flows.

By accentuating inequalities within and between countries, previous colonial economic activities reinforced the foundation of present day stocks, flows and patterns of migration in the region, and spurred internal, intra-regional and international migrations in varying degrees. By enacting regulations to control immigration into their newly independent countries – to preserve scarce jobs for nationals – distinctions were introduced between internal, intra-regional and international migrations, movements which once involved free movement across wide space of the region. These new regulations

On their way to the "promised land" in Europe, migrants have to make many stopovers either in rural areas or in the slums of African metropolises. Privation forces them to look for food even on garbage dumps and to search for items which can be salvaged. Photo 2008

also imposed a distinction between "legal" and "illegal" immigration – making a requirement that immigrants must possess valid travel and entry documents into countries that crossed ethnic lines. Apart from South Africa, few sub-Saharan African countries have comprehensive immigration laws prescribing specific procedures for entry and for the employment of non-indigenous workers, and far fewer rigidly enforce such laws – which migrants in any case routinely flout (Adepoju, 2004).

In recent years, Botswana has become a major country of immigration. A prosperous, politically stable country, with a rapid and steady economic growth over the past decade, it has attracted highly skilled professionals, who are in short supply to the country's private sector, taking advantage of the relaxed laws on residence and entry introduced in the early 1990s. The new policy of localization of employment, especially in the education sector, however entails replacing expatriates at the university (Campbell, 2003).

Because of increasing disparities in income and living conditions between, on the one hand, South Africa, Botswana, Gabon, and – before on-going conflicts – Côte d'Ivoire, and, on the other, their respective neighbours and other parts of the region, intra-regional migration has taken root. Indeed, owing to the minuscule economy, geography and demography of countries such as Lesotho, Swaziland, Gambia, Guinea-Bissau, some migration that would elsewhere fall into the category of internal movement (based on spatial criteria) occurs across national frontiers.

Increasingly, the prospects of, and options for, internal migration are constrained by poverty, unemployment and socio-economic insecurity, transforming some of the migration that would otherwise take place internally into migration across borders to prosperous countries (Adepoju, 1998). In recent years, many who migrate are exploring a much wider set of destinations. A great number of west African French-speaking migrants who traditionally migrated to France are crossing the Atlantic to seek greener pastures as petty traders in the USA after they encountered an increasingly hostile reception in France, with a growing xenophobia, apprehension of foreigners, and anti-immigrant political mobilisations.

Migrants from Senegal and Mali are also moving to non-traditional OECD destinations – Italy, Portugal, Belgium, Germany and Spain – to which they have no linguistic, cultural or colonial ties. Initially, migrants moved to Zambia and, when its economy collapsed, shifted to Zimbabwe and then to South Africa following the demise of the apartheid regime (Adepoju, 2003).

There is also an overall trend of fewer labor migrants, and an increase in the commercial migration of entrepreneurs who are self-employed, especially in the informal sector. Migrants are also moving in stages, first from rural areas to cities, and then from cities to foreign destinations. From Côte d'Ivoire for instance, most emigrants moved to other west African countries, or to Europe and America, their place being taken by immigrants from neighbouring. Burkina Faso and Mali (Findley et al., 1995)

Sub-regional economic organisations have also become an important factor in intra-regional migration, more so that these are dominated by the economies of a single country, and movements of people have been directed to its core countries. Examples of these are Botswana and South Africa in southern Africa, Gabon in Central Africa, Kenya in eastern Africa, Côte d'Ivoire and Nigeria in west Africa.

The free movement of persons without visa within ECOWAS (Economic Community of west African States) has been

Table 1 Foreigners in the countries of sub-Saharan Africa in the 1970s and 1980s (Aderanti Adepoju)

Country	Reference date	Total population (thousands)	Foreign-born population (%)
Benin	1979	3,331	1.2
Botswana	1981	941	1.7
Burkina Faso	1975	5,638	2.0
Burundi	1979	4,028	2.1
Cameroon	1976	7,132	3.1
R C A	1975	1,781	2.5
Comoros	1980	335	4.1
Congo	1984	1,909	5.1
Cote d'Ivoire	1975	6,710	22.0
Egypt	1986	46,205	0.1
Gambia	1973	493	11.1
Ghana	1970	8,559	6.6
Guinea Bissau	1979	768	1.7
Kenya	1979	15,327	1.0
Liberia	1974	1,503	4.0
Libyan Arab Jam	1973	2,249	8.8
Malawi	1977	5,547	5.2
Mali	1976	6,395	2.3
Mauritania	1977	1,339	2.1
Mauritius	1972	851	1.2
Morocco	1982	20,450	0.3
Mozambique	1980	11,674	0.3
Reunion	1982	516	0.4
Rwanda	1978	4,832	0.9
Saint Helena	1976	5	0.8
Seychelles	1977	62	3.1
Sierra Leone	1974	2,735	2.9
South Africa	1985	23,386	8.0
Sudan	1973	14,114	1.6
Swaziland	1976	495	5.4
Togo	1970	1,951	7.4
Tunisia	1984	6,975	0.5
Tanzania	1978	17,513	2.4
Zambia	1980	5,662	4.1

Sub-region and country	Total number of expatriates	Percentage of expatriates who are highly skilled
West Africa		
Benin	13,669	43.8
Burkina Faso	6,237	38.4
Cape Verde	83,291	6.2
Cote d'Ivoire	58,843	27.5
Gambia	20,923	16.9
Ghana	150,665	34.0
Guinea	19,684	24.5
Guinea-Bissau	29,449	12.7
Liberia	41,756	33.0
Mali	45,034	12.6
Mauritania	14,813	18.5
Niger	4,948	38.0
Nigeria	247,497	55.1
Senegal	104,715	23.1
Sierra Leone	40,556	33.6
Togo	18,024	36.3
East Africa		
Burundi	10,095	38.6
Djibouti	5,359	29.7
Ethiopia	113,838	31.2
Kenya	197,445	37.4
Malawi	15,024	35.2
Mauritius	86,410	28.0
Mozambique	85,337	26.5
Rwanda	14,832	34.4
Tanzania	70,006	41.0
Uganda	82,232	39.2
Zambia	34,825	49.3
Zimbabwe	77,345	43.3
Central Africa		
Angola	195,674	19.6
Cameroon	57,050	42.3
Central Africa Republic	9,855	32.7
Chad	5,836	42.1
Congo	100,052	36.6
Equatorial Guinea	12,149	22.7
Dem. Republic of Congo	66,488	32.5
Southern Africa		
Botswana	4,298	37.4
Swaziland	2,103	41.7
South Africa	342,947	47.9
Lesotho	995	45.7
Namibia	3,390	45.3

Table 3 Migrants from sub-Saharan Africa in OECD countries (2000/01) and percentage of highly-qualified migrants according to sub-region and country

A poster proclaiming Namibia's independence, 1990. Henceforth March 21st is a national holiday, Independence Day

are to progressively replace national passports over a transitional period of ten years. The protocol on the free movement of persons in the Community of eastern and southern African States and the southern African Development Community's lacklustre attempts to facilitate intra-Community movement of nationals, have been marred by political wrangling

Emigration of Highly Skilled Professionals

The emigration of highly skilled professionals, including doctors, nurses, paramedical personnel, teachers, lecturers, engineers, scientists and technologists, labelled the "brain drain", had its antecedents in the 1960s when African countries engaged in unprecedented educational expansion. Emigration was later spurred by deteriorating economic, political and related factors, including lack of job satisfaction and a system in which efficient input was not recognised or rewarded. Uganda led the way in both volume and rapidity of exodus of its skilled manpower, as highly educated people were forced to migrate to Kenya, South Africa, Botswana, Europe and North America (Adepoju, 1991). For similar reasons, the vast majority of Somali, Ethiopian and Zambian graduates have been working overseas. The conditions which sparked off emigration from these countries later gripped Kenya. The bonding system where officials, trained at government expense were required to work for a specified number of years before they could opt out of the public service, and travel clearance demands imposed on Tanzanian, Ugandan and Kenyan professionals and civil

acclaimed as a pace-setter; the Protocol on Free Movement of Persons and the Right of Residence and Establishment, of May 1979, formalised the free movement of ECOWAS citizens within member countries (Adepoju, 2002). Abolishing the requirements for visas and entry permits has enabled Community citizens in possession of valid travel documentation to enter member states without a visa for up to ninety days. Political leaders decided in March 2000 to create a borderless sub-region; ECOWAS passports

servants to restrict their emigration, did little to stem the tide (Oucho, 1995).

Many professionals migrated to Canada, the USA, Britain, the Netherlands and Germany. These included students in various disciplines who stayed on at the end of their training, and others attracted by better working conditions and income in developed countries. France was and remains the dominant destination for both skilled professionals and unskilled emigrants from the former French colonies, especially Senegal, Togo, Côte d'Ivoire, Mali and Burkina Faso. Belgium, Canada, France, Germany, Ireland, Italy, the Netherlands, Portugal, Spain, the UK and the USA are the major recipients of sub-Saharan Africa's skilled professionals, due largely to the colonial legacy. Between 1960 and 1987, Africa lost 30% of its highly skilled nationals, mostly to Europe; between 1986 and 1990, an estimated 50,000 to 60,000 middle and high-level managers emigrated as local socio-economic and political conditions deteriorated. Since then, about 23,000 qualified academic staff emigrated each year in search of better working conditions (IOM, 2003).

Feminist women's magazine "sister" in English and Afrikaans, 1990

About 4 million Sub-Saharan Africans lived in rich OECD countries (Table 2). Many of these have tertiary education and consist of skilled professionals (Table 3). Highly skilled professionals constitute about a half of Nigerian and Zambian "expatriates". Two in every five nationals of Benin, Tanzania, Zimbabwe, Cameroon, Lesotho, Malawi and South Africa are highly skilled. Two in every five nationals of Benin, Tanzania, Zimbabwe, Cameroon, Lesotho, Malawi and South Africa working outside their home countries are highly skilled professionals. There are more Malawian doctors practising in Manchester, UK, than in Malawi itself, while 550 of the 600 Zambian doctors trained in medical school from 1978 to 1999 have emigrated abroad. More than half of nurses and doctors from Ethiopia have emigrated from Malawi, and another quarter of the remaining health workers are probably infected with HIV/AIDS. If statistics are to be trusted, Ghana has lost 50% of its doctors to Canada, Britain and the USA. Three-quarters of Zimbabwe's doctors emigrated since the early 1990s and half of social health workers have relocated abroad since 2001. In the last five years more that 16,000 nurses and about 12,500 doctors from the region are currently registered to work in Britain (UKNMC, 2005). However, African transnational communities rarely sever ties with home. They are active in political advocacy – especially in Nigeria and Ghana – and in charity and cultural exchange. Their associations help new arrivals adapt and insert themselves into labor markets, and they mobilise members' capital for investment and for community development projects "at home".

Both brain drain and brain circulation largely originate from the same group of countries which have invested heavily in human resources development: Ghana, Uganda, Nigeria and Kenya. During the past decade, skilled professionals migrating to southern Africa's relatively buoyant economies have been working in tertiary institutions and medical establishments, finding the booming economies of Gabon, Botswana, Namibia and South Africa to be convenient alternatives to Europe, the USA and the Middle East. Botswana has evolved from a migrant-sending to a migrant-receiving country, attracting skilled professionals – fuelled largely by political stability,

a fast-growing economy, prudent economic management and a small largely unskilled local labor force. The number of non-nationals legally resident in Botswana tripled from 10,860 in 1971 to 29,560 in 1991, and had reached 60,720 by 2001 (Lefko-Everett, 2004).

Increasing Female Migration

In SSA female international migrants increased substantially in number between 1960 and 2000 (IOM, 2003). west African women traders have, historically, been involved in cross-border migration, but women are now migrating independently of men, to fulfil their own economic needs within and across national borders. Anecdotal evidence reveals a striking increase in migration by women, who had traditionally remained at home, while men moved around in search of paid work. The improved access of females to education and training opportunities has enhanced their employability locally and across national borders.

Globalisation has introduced new labor market dynamics, including a demand for highly skilled health care workers. Professional women – nurses and doctors – have been recruited from Nigeria, Ghana, Kenya, Malawi, Zimbabwe, South Africa and Uganda to work in Britain's National Health Service and in private home care centres. Earlier on, women were recruited to work in Saudi Arabia and Kuwait, often leaving their spouses and children behind at home. Many professional women, especially nurses, who migrate from Nigeria, Ghana and Zimbabwe, leave their children to be looked after by their husbands. The remittances they send home are a lifeline for family sustenance. This relatively new phenomenon constitutes an important change in gender roles.

Once set in motion, the migration of skilled females has taken root. Statistics from the United Kingdom Nursing and Midwifery Council (UKNMC, 2005) show that, from a trickle of nurses and midwives recruited from Zimbabwe, Ghana, Zambia, Botswana and Malawi in 1998/99, the number had risen sharply, with a peak in 2001/2001, and continued to rise steadily till 2004/2005. South Africa topped the list for sub-Saharan Africa, with 2,114 nurses

An opencast pit in Namibia. Photo 2002

and midwives registered in 2001/2002. Nigeria followed with 432, rising to 511 in 2003/2004. Overall, the number of nurses and midwives from sub-Saharan Africa rose from 915 in 1998/99 to 3,789 in 2001/2002. It then declined erratically to 2,546 by 2004/2005. An unknown number were recruited by private agencies to work in care homes for the elderly.

Continuity and Changing Configurations of Migration in South Africa

Migration to South Africa was and remains a survival strategy by poor households from sending countries. Decades of conflict and poverty have made Mozambique a dominant source of emigrants to South Africa. Lesotho, a very poor country, is perhaps the most dependent on labor migration to South Africa; at its peak, about 50% of Basotho working in the mines and on the farms of South Africa, attracted 51% of the Gross Domestic Product through migrant remittances and deferred pay (Milazi, 1998). Skilled professionals drawn especially from Ghana and Uganda, and trickles from Nigeria, migrated clandestinely to the then Bantustans in South Africa (Prah, 1989). Their numbers were small and the immigrants remained hidden from the authorities, most having left their home countries illegally. They were mainly university professors, doctors and engineers – in contrast to the traditional immigrants who were mostly unskilled farm laborers and mine workers.

Majority rule in South Africa in 1994 was followed by a new wave of immigrants, from Africa and especially from eastern Europe. From west Africa came highly skilled Nigerian and Ghanaian professionals, joining the staff of universities and other professions; tradesmen from Senegal and Mali, including street vendors and small traders, who ingeniously invigorated the informal sector through their aggressive commercial acumen and also by engaging locals. These joined their counterparts from the then Zaire and Zimbabwe to swell the informal sector. Decades under the apartheid pass laws had left South Africa without an informal sector to generate employment for Blacks. Some immigrants from Mozambique apparently entered the country without proper documentation, and others – from Nigeria, Sierra Leone, Ethiopia and Zambia – overstayed their legal residency (Crush, 1999). Thousands of Mozambicans and Zimbabweans living illegally in South Africa were deported monthly.

Several political and economic factors have sustained, and in recent years dramatically altered, migration from and to South Africa. Before the demise of the apartheid regime, mechanisation of coal-mining, a more stable domestic labor force, rationalisation policies and localisation of specific employment opportunities drastically reduced the demand for mine-based foreign workers. Nationals of African countries previously barred from migrating to South Africa, including highly skilled professionals, now find South Africa a viable alternative to countries of the north and the Gulf States. These professionals have been, to some extent, replacing the skilled white engineers and doctors who emigrated to Australia, Canada, Britain and the USA. South Africa is thus concurrently a recipient and a sender, and perhaps also a transit country, exporting skilled migrants, especially doctors, nurses, and engineers to Europe, North America and Australia (Adepoju, 2003).

About 70,000 people, mostly skilled white South Africans and their families, emigrated between 1989 and 1992, and another 166,000 emigrated from 1998 to 2001, sceptical of the prospects of black majority rule and scared by the rising crime rate. Most emigrants are engineers, accountants and doctors – those with precisely the skills that South Africa needs for stimulating economic growth. Horowitz and Kaplan (2001) estimate that in spite of the high quality of their medical training, South African doctors earned one fifth of their counterparts in the USA. Jewish skilled emigrants – mostly young couples and professionals – to the USA, Israel, Britain, Canada and Australia totalled 21,000 between 1970 and 1979, and 18,000 in the period 1980–1991. Official statistics indicate that 16,000 highly-skilled South Africans emigrated between 1994 and 2001, but the real numbers may have been under-enumerated. Other sources indicate that between 70 and 100 doctors emigrate from South Africa every year, and about 10% of hospital doctors in Canada are South Africans (The Economist, 13 August 2005).

A highly exaggerated number of undocumented immigrants, of between two and ten million, has been flagged by the media and politicians. In reality, a plausible number of 1.5 million or less may have increased in recent years as the economy of neighbouring Zimbabwe has collapsed (Crush, 2000). The mining industry continues to employ foreigners, from Mozambique and Lesotho in particular, and farmers prefer to employ cross-border workers from Lesotho during the harvesting season to pick asparagus and do the jobs that most locals loathe – being paid low wages which locals spurn.

Internal, intra-regional and international migration in Africa takes place within diverse socio-ethnic, political and economic contexts. Distinctive forms of migration characterise the different sub-regions: labor migration from western and central Africa to other locations within the region, developed countries of the North and oil-rich countries of the Middle East; refugee flows within eastern, and increasingly in western, Africa; labor migration from eastern and southern African countries to South Africa, and cross-border clandestine migration of nomads in west and east Africa. However, unlike in other world regions, these migrations – better described as "circulations" are largely intra-regional. Hence, emotive public reactions based on "immigration myths" – that immigration from Africa is massive, with immigrants swarming into countries of Europe, and that immigrants are unskilled, mostly undocumented workers should be treated with caution as they are often not based on empirical data. Indeed, the preoccupation with the question of why people migrate tends to obscure the other side of the picture, which deals with the question of non-mobility, that is why most people do not migrate from the rural environment, or from their countries, in spite of the compelling pull and push factors at origin and potential destination areas.

The migration configuration in the region has become extremely complex. The traditional patterns of migration are feminising, migration destinations are diversifying, and the migration of entrepreneurs is replacing labor migration. In addition, brain circulation between countries within the region, is slowly replacing brain drain migration out of the region. Given favourable environment, many African emigrants would prefer to return to contribute to the development of their countries of origin; in the meantime, they maintain ties with home place in terms of remittances to family members left behind. But leaders must also address the conditions that prompted such emigration: poverty, mismanaged economies, corruption, conflicts, human rights abuse and so on. On their part, countries of destination should promote prospects for circular migration of workers and make residence rule flexible to allow professionals the opportunities to contribute to the development of their countries of origin without losing their residency rights.

References

Adamakoh-Sarfo J.L. 1974 "The Effects of the Expulsion of Migrant workers on Ghana's Economy, with Particular Reference to the Cocoa Industry". In: S. Amin (ed.), Modern Migrations in western Africa. London, Oxford University Press.

Addo. N.O. 1975 "Immigration and Socio-Demographic Change." in J.C. Caldwell et al. (ed.), Population Growth and Socio Economic Change in west Africa. New York, The Population Council.

Adepoju, A. 1982. "The Dimension of the Refugee Problem in Africa". African Affairs, No. 81

Adepoju, A. 1983. Undocumented Migration in Africa: Trends and Policies. International Migration, Vol. 12, No2

Adepoju, A. 1988 "International Migration in Africa South of the Sahara" in Appleyard, R. (ed.) International Migration Today Vol. 1: Trends and Prospects, UNESCO/ University of western Australia

Adepoju, A. 1988b, "Labor migration and employment of ECOWAS nationals in Nigeria", in T. Fashoyin (ed.) Labor and Development in Nigeria, Landmark Publications Ltd., Lagos.

Adepoju, A. 1991, "South-North Migration: The African Experience", International Migration, Vol. 29, No. 2.

Adepoju, A. 1995, "Emigration dynamics in Sub-Saharan Africa", International Migration, Vol. 33, Nos. 3 & 4.

Adepoju, A. 1998, "Links between internal and international migration: the African situation", Selected articles to commemorate 50th Anniversary of International Social Science Journal, UNESCO, Paris.

Adepoju, A. 2002, "Fostering free movements of persons in west Africa: Achievements, constraints and prospects for international migration", International Migration, Vol. 40, No. 2.

Adepoju, A. 2003, "Continuity and changing configurations of migration to and from the Republic of South Africa", International Migration, Vol. 41, No. 1.

Adepoju, A. 2004, "Trends in international migration in and from Africa", in D.S. Massey and J.E. Taylor (eds.) International Migration Prospects and Policies in a Global Market, Oxford University Press, Oxford.

Adepoju, A. 2006, "Internal and international migration within Africa", in P.D. Kok, J. Gelderblom, J. Oucho & J. van Zyl (eds.). Migration in South and southern Africa: Dynamics and determinants, Human Sciences Research Council, Cape Town.

Adepoju, A. and T. Hammar (eds.) 1996, International Migration in and from Africa: Dimension, Challenges and Prospects, PHRDA, Dakar; CEIFO, Stockholm.

Agency for Industrial Mission (AIM), 1984 That They Might Have Hope. Transvaal

Amin, S. 1974. "Introduction", in Amin, S. (ed.) 1974 Modern Migrations

The desert is extending in many areas along the southern margins of the Sahara. During the last decades numerous springs have dried up as the water table has sunk. Others have dwindled in importance and are slowly sanding over due to lack of maintenance. Photo 2001

Ho in the Volta region, southern Ghana. Ho, with approximately 60,000 inhabitants, is the capital of the Volta region. The main language is Ewe. Women from the surrounding areas sell their agricultural produce here in the regional market. Photo 1988

in western Africa. London, Oxford University Press.

Ballard, J. 1966. "Four Equatorial States". In: G.M Carter (ed.), National Unity and Regionalism in Eight African States. Ithaca, N.Y. Cornell University Press.

Boeder, R., 1973 "The effects of labor emigration on rural life in Malawi". Rural African, No. 20.

Böhning, W.R. 1981 Black Migration to South Africa: A Selection of Policy-oriented Research, International Labor Organization, Geneva.

Breytenback, W.J. 1972. Migratory labor agreements in southern Africa. Pretoria, African Institute.

Burke, B.M. 1981.The Outlook for Labor Growth and Employment in Lesotho 1980, 2000. Canadian Journal of African Studies, Vol. 12, No. 1.

Campbell, E.K. (2003), "Attitudes of Botswana citizens towards immigrants: Signs of xenophobia?", International Migration, Vol. 41, No. 4.

Chilivumbo, A. 1985, "Malawi's labor migration to the South: An historical review", in: United Nations Economic Commission for Africa, Migratory Labor in southern Africa, Addis Ababa.

Cobbe, J. 1982. Emigration and Development in southern Africa, with Special Reference to Lesotho. International Migration Review, Vol. 16, No. 4.

Cobbe, J. 1985. "Consequences for Lesotho of changing South Africa labor demand", African Affairs, 85.

Crush, J. 1999, "The discourse and dimensions of irregularity in post-apartheid South Africa", International Migration, Vol. 37, No. 1.

De Vletter, F. 1986, "Recent trends and prospects of black migration to South Africa", Journal of Modern African Studies, Vol. 23, No. 4.

De Vletter, F. (ed.) 1985. Recent Trends and Prospects of Black Migration to South Africa.

Development in southern Africa. Rome, FAO.

Duffy. J. 1962. Portugal in Africa. Princeton, N.J. Harvard University Press

Economic Commission for Africa (ECA) 1981, International migration trends and their implications. African Population Studies Series No. 4. Population Division, Addis Ababa.

Findley, S.E., S. Traore, D. Ouedraogo and S. Diarra 1995, "Emigration from the Sahel", International Migration, Vol. 33, Nos. 3 & 4.

Halladay, E. 1972. The Emergent Continent: Africa in the 19th Century. London, Ernest Benn

Hinderink, J.; Templeman, G. J. 1978. Rural Change and Types of Migration in northern Ivory Coast. In: W.M.J. Van Vinsbergen and H.A.Meilink (ed.), Migration and the Transformation of Modern African Society. Leiden, African Perspectives.

Horowitz, S. and D.E. Kaplan, 2001, "The Jewish Exodus from the new South Africa: realities and implications", International Migration, Vol. 39, No. 3.

Human Rights Watch 1998, Prohibited Persons: Abuse of Undocumented Migrants, Asylum Seekers, and Refugees in South Africa, Human Rights Watch, New York.

ILO 2004 Issues Paper: African Union Extraordinary Summit of Heads of State and Governments on Employment and Poverty Alleviation in Africa, Ouagadougou. International Labor Organization, September

IOM 2004, Migration for Development in Africa, General Strategy Paper, June 2004, International Organisation for Migration, Geneva.

Johns, D. 2001, "Health and development in South Africa: from principles to practice", Development, Vol. 44, No. 1.

Lefko-Everett, K. 2004, "Botswana's changing migration patterns", Migration Information Source. Washington DC: Migration Policy Institute,

Mabogunje A.L, 1972 Regional Mobility and Resource Development in west Africa. Montreal, McGill Queen's University Press.

Malan, T. 1985, "Migration labor in South Africa", Africa Insight, 15(2).

Milazi, D. 1998, "Migration within the context of poverty and landlessness in southern Africa", in R. Appleyard (ed.) Emigration Dynamics in Developing Countries, Vol. 1: Sub-Saharan Africa, Ashgate Publishing, Sydney.

Monstead, M.; Walji, P.A, 1978 Demographic Analysis of east Africa: A Sociological Interpretation. Uppsala, Scandinavian Institute of African Studies.

OECD 2005, Trends in International Migration: Annual Report 2004, Organisation for Economic Co-Operation and Development, Paris.

Ohadike, P.O. 1974 "Immigrants and development in Zambia". International Migration Review Vol. VIII.

Oliver, R. 1963 History of east Africa. Oxford, Clarendon Press.

Oucho, J.O. 1995, "Emigration Dynamics of eastern African countries", International Migration, Vol. 33, Nos. 3 & 4.

Oucho, J.O. 1998, "Regional integration and labor mobility in eastern and southern Africa", in R. Appleyard (ed.) Emigration Dynamics in Developing Countries, Vol. 1: Sub-Saharan Africa, Ashgate Publishing, Sydney.

Prah, K.K. 1989, "The Bantustan Brain Gain – A study into the nature and causes of brain drain from independent Africa to the South African Bantustans", southern African Studies Series No. 5. National University of Lesotho, Maseru.

Prothero, R.M. 1968.Migration in Tropical Africa. In J.C. Caldwell and C.O Okonjo (eds), The Population of Tropical Africa. London, Longmans.

Ricca, S. 1989, International Migration in Africa: Legal and Administrative Aspects, International Labor Organisation, Geneva.

Ritner, P. 1960 The Death of Africa. New York: Macmillan.

Stahl, C.W. 1982. Recent Changes in the Demand for Foreign African Labor in South Africa and Future Prospects. In: F de Vletter (ed.), Labor Migration and Agricultural Development in southern Africa. Rome, FAO.

Stapleton, G. 1959 Nigerians in Ghana. west African Magazine.

Swindell, K. 1978 Family Farms and Migrant Labor: The Strange Farmers in the Gambia. Canadian Journal of African Studies, Vol. 12 No. 1

Sudarkasa, N. 1974/75 Commercial Migration in west Africa with special reference to the Yoruba in Ghana. African Urban Notes, Series B, No. 1

United Nations 2003, "Reversing Africa's 'brain drain': New initiatives tap skills of African expatriates", Africa Recovery, Vol. 17, No. 2.

UKNMC 2005, Annual Statistics 2004-2005: Statistical Analysis of the Register, 1 April 2004–31 March 2005, United Kingdom Nursing and Midwifery Council, London.

Zachariah, K.C. and J. Conde, 1981, Migration in west Africa : Demographic Aspects Joint.

World Bank-OECD Study. London, Oxford University Press.

Above: At the Spanish-Moroccan border. Here, as in Lampedusa (Italy) and Chios (Greece), migrants and refugees are detained and interned. Photo 2008
Below: Fortress Europe. Photo 2008

Indians fight against the destruction of their homelands by an energy company. Rio Xingu, Brazil, 1989

Rainer Münz

Global Migration – The Past, the Present and the Future

History

From ancient times through the Middle Ages until the early modern era, migration was often synonymous with the conquering of land or the expansion of an existing culture's sphere of influence. This was true of the Celts, Greeks, Romans, Germanic tribes, the Huns, Arabs, Hungarians and Bulgarians. The same can also be said for the European conquerors and colonists settling overseas.

In the case of the former – from the advance of the Germanic tribes and Asian horseback nomads in ancient civilisations to the Arabs' expansion into the Mediterranean region and to Mesopotamia – all were a mixture of conquest and settlement migration. However, these migratory movements involved only few tens of thousands of people, at most.

The last migrants to Europe in the Middle Ages were the Ottoman Turks in the 14th century, whose ancestors were originally from central Asia. They extended their rule across a territory reaching from Anatolia to the Balkans. From there, they conquered Constantinople in 1453 to establish themselves as one of the great powers in Europe for the next 400 years.

Since the beginning of the modern era, migration patterns have been influenced by the overseas expansion of the European sea powers. In the early modern era this was primarily a mixture of the seizure of land and the expansion of political and economic power. Under the protection of the fleets of their native lands a small number of European pioneer-migrants built bridgeheads: trading bases, fixed harbours, garrisons and plantations. Many of them hoped to make a quick fortune and return to Europe. In the northeast of what is now the United States, however, settlement communities were established, as far back as in the early 17th century, by emigrants who wanted to live there on a

permanent basis as free citizens. They were truly pioneer migrants.

Only from the mid-18th century onwards did European expansion really become a massive settlement colonisation; rapidly altering the composition of the local population. Prior to this, however, the European colonial powers had already shipped Africans from West Africa to North and South America and to the Caribbean. They were brought as slaves to replace the rapidly dwindling numbers of indigenous workers. Some 11 to 12 million people were brought to America as slaves between the 17th century and the beginning of the 19th century. A further two million Africans were sold as slaves to Arab countries. Most Afro-American people living today between Brazil, the Caribbean and the USA are descendants of the slaves.

It was only after 1750 that Europe experienced a period of greater population growth. This formed the demographic prerequisite for the mass migration that began at that time. Greatly improved transport facilities – above all the establishment of efficient shipping routes and railways – were the other prerequisite. Moreover, the nature of migratory movements were influenced by the emergence of the Industrial Revolution. It was no longer agricultural settlers that were in demand, but workers for the factories that were being set up and, later, also for the service sector. Since 1750 a total of some 70 million Europeans migrated overseas, to Siberia and to central Asia. The number of internal migrants, however, was much greater still.

In contrast to the migration of tribes marking the transition from Late Antiquity to the early Middle Ages, European overseas migration did not involve entire populations, but rather, as a rule, individuals and families. Scores of Europeans emigrated on religious or political grounds. For the majority of emigrants, however, economic motives played a key role. For many Europeans, emigration

represented the only opportunity to escape poverty, the lack of land or the restrictions imposed by the professional guilds.

However, migration forced by intolerance and persecution also played a role in migration patterns within Europe. Since the beginning of the modern era, hundreds of thousands of people were persecuted for belonging to an ethnic or religious minority and finally fled overseas. In the 16th century for example, the Jews fled from Spain and Portugal to the Netherlands, North Africa and Turkey. In the 17th century, the Huguenots were banished from France and found exile in Prussia; in the 17th and even until the middle of the 18th century, Protestants were expelled from Salzburg and Tyrol as well as from other Habsburg territories. Further, in the 19th century, it was eastern European Jews fleeing from Tsarist Russia, particularly from the area that is now part of Ukraine, Poland and the Baltic States.

Caricature from 17th century France. Protestants saw themselves faced either with conversion to the Catholic faith or with the wheel, corporal punishment, the gallows, the galley, the prison tower, or exile

The industrial centers attracted workers from the agricultural peripheries. The Bremen jute spinning and weaving factory, for example, recruited workers in the east of the German Empire. Photo 1907

Regardless of the predominant motive, each of the movements examined here had considerable demographic effects. In North America, the Caribbean, in parts of South America and in Australia the indigenous peoples were either intentionally wiped out, killed by infectious diseases caught through contact with the colonists or ousted from their original habitat by European settlers. This is why today the terms "Native Americans" or "American Indians" are often associated with the inhabitants of inhospitable regions in the south-west of the USA or of hunter-gatherers in the Brazilian rainforest. The fact that there were once advanced American Indian civilizations (e.g. the Aztecs, Incas, Mayas and Olmecs) is less ingrained in western cultural memory.

In North and South America and in the Caribbean the descendants of European immigrants and African slaves today represent the demographic majority almost everywhere. In Australia and New Zealand, the majority of the population is also of European descent. The situation is similar in Siberia, the northern part of Kazakhstan and the northern areas of the Far East, where Russians and migrants from other parts of Europe have settled since the late 18th century. Some of the people who followed this route reached as far as Alaska, which Russia sold to the USA as recently as 1867.

European settlement colonisation also took place in southern Africa, the Maghreb

and, since the beginning of the 20th century, in Palestine. While European settlers and their descendents dominated the political and economic affairs in what was once Rhodesia (today Zambia and Zimbabwe) and in South Africa, Angola and Mozambique, in demographic terms they remained a small minority. Almost all French settlers and their descendents were forced to leave Algeria when it gained independence in 1961 at the end of a bloody colonial war.

In contrast to the Americas, Australia and southern Africa, European settlers did not play a significant role in other territories dominated by European colonial powers. In West and Central Africa, East Africa, southern Asia and south-east Asia as well as in the Pacific and in parts of the Caribbean, the colonial powers' presence was limited to soldiers, administrative officials and a small group of businessmen, plantation owners and adventurers.

From the Industrial Revolution to the Great Depression

Within Europe, industrialization brought modern forms of labor migration. Migrants found work in trade and manufacturing. Some sooner or later set up their own businesses.

A massive wave of intra-European migration to the new centres of the iron and steel

industries began in the 19th century. These areas included the British Midlands, the Lorraine region and the Ruhr area, as well as some industrial areas in Switzerland and Austria. In the case of France and Switzerland, a considerable proportion of labor migrants came from third countries. In contrast, the new residents of the Ruhr area were recruited from the Prussian part of Poland. They were internal migrants. The same applied to Irish migrants to the Midlands and to migrants from the Czech lands moving to other industrialized parts of the Habsburg monarchy. At the same time, mass migration, both international and internal, turned several European capitals – including London, Paris, Berlin, Vienna and Budapest – into cities with well over a million inhabitants within just a few decades. For many people, the opportunity to move to one of these economically and culturally prosperous cities was an alternative to overseas migration.

During and after the First World War, labor migration within Europe and immigration to the USA decreased on the whole. The reason for this was that most nation states, even traditional immigration countries such as the USA, had gradually begun to place restrictions on the immigration of foreign nationals at the beginning of the 20th century. In central Europe and in the Balkans the founding of new states also reduced the freedom of movement that had previously been possible within the German, the Austro-Hungarian and the Ottoman Empires. The successor states of these three "empires" were foreign countries to one another. Then, at the end of the 1920s, with the onset of the Great Depression, national labor markets in Europe and North America were completely closed off. At best, South America was a last option for Europeans wishing to emigrate. At the same time, extensive emigration and return migration from the USA to Europe was taking place. While there had been return migration from North America even before the 1930s, it had never before taken place on such a large scale.

Deportation, Flight and Ethnic Cleansing

Global migration reached a historical peak during the 20th century. A considerable proportion of these movements were involuntary, that is, flight, displacement or the state-enforced exchange of groups of people. Over

Public execution of Armenians in the Ottoman Empire 1915/16

the course of the 20th century in Europe, at least 60 million people were forced to leave their countries or regions of origin because of their ethnic descent or their religion. This was partially the result of deportation, "ethnic cleansing" or attempted genocide. Some triggers for mass exodus were, for example, the First World War (the Armenian massacre in Ottoman Turkey); the October Revolution of 1917 in Russia (1.5 million refugees) and the Turkish-Greek war of 1922. In the subsequent Treaty of Lausanne (1923) the Turkish victors and the defeated Greeks agreed on a two-way resettlement plan expelling 1.5 million Greek Orthodox Christians from Turkey and around 450,000 Muslims from Greece. Great Britain and France gave their blessing.

During National Socialist rule, Stalinism and the Second World War, forced migration and expulsion, collective relocation, deportation and forced labor were prevalent in Europe. Overall, the Nazi regime is likely to have forced some 12 million third country nationals to maintain agricultural and manufacturing activities. With the large majority of working-age German and Austrian men serving in the army, forced labor became the backbone of Nazi Germany's wartime economy. In some cases, deportation was coupled with genocide. This affected above all the Jews, the Sinti and Roma of central and eastern Europe (6 million genocide victims). Lastly, a great number of people fell victim to Stalinist deportation inside the Soviet Union. In the end, approximately 20 million Soviet citizens were internally displaced.

The political reorganisation of Europe after the end of World War II was partly based on continued displacement and ethnic cleansing. In Europe this affected first and foremost 12 million "ethnic Germans" living on former German territories or in neighboring central and south-eastern European countries (Czechoslovakia, Hungary, Poland, Romania, and Yugoslavia). 1.5 million Poles, together with hundreds of thousands of Ukrainians, Italians and Hungarians also became victims of state-sponsored forced resettlement. These measures were for the most part implemented with the consent of, or even under the orders of the victorious Allies.

Outside Europe, the establishment of India and Pakistan in 1947 led to large-scale involuntary migration. There were an estimated 11 million displaced Muslims, Hindus and Sikhs. Large scale involuntary migration also occurred when the state of Israel was established in 1948, which led to the flight and displacement of 0.8 million Palestinians.

After 1949/50 there was a mass exodus from countries under communist rule, in particular from the GDR, the People's Republic of China, Hungary, Cuba, Poland, Czechoslovakia and Vietnam. After Chiang Kai-Sheck and his army lost the Chinese civil war and fled to Taiwan, a large number of military officers and civilians followed. Later, Hong Kong and Macao were the destination for more than a million refugees from communist China. Since the early 1960s, hundreds of thousands of people who opposed the Castro regime, or were dissatisfied with the living conditions in general, fled Cuba. With its compulsory measures to assimilate ethnic Turks and other Muslims, Bulgaria twice launched a partly voluntary, partly forced mass migration to Turkey – around 1950 and again in the second half of the 1980s. In the 1970s and 1980s the Ceauşescu regime "sold" tens of thousands of German-speaking citizens to the Federal Republic of Germany. Following the collapse of the communist regimes in the Balkan states there was a new wave of mass emigration to the west: from Bulgaria (1989–1990), Romania (1990–1991) and from Albania (from 1990 onwards). During the Cold War, migrants arriving from communist countries had been recognised in the west as political refugees, despite the fact that, even then, for many of them economic motives were more important then political ones.

In the late 20th and early 21st centuries, civil wars and violent political conflicts in Afghanistan, Bosnia, Kosovo, Iraq, Rwanda, the Sudan, the Congo, Chechnya, Somalia and Zimbabwe resulted in large numbers of refugees.

Only a small minority of refugees and displaced persons of the 20th century were later able to return to their former homelands. The majority stayed abroad; many lived in refugee camps for years or in some cases for decades. The UN High Commissioner for Refugees in 2006 estimated some 9.2 million international refugees: the lowest number in a quarter of a century. The great majority of recognised refugees were taken in by poorer countries.

In recent years the most important refugee admitting countries, in addition to Germany, the USA and Canada, were above all the countries neighbouring the various crisis regions – that is, Iran, Pakistan, Jordan, Syria, Chad, several East African countries and the Republic of South Africa. In addition, there is the Palestinian refugee population, which has grown in the meantime to several million people and does not fall within the mandate of the UNHCR.

In western and central Europe a total of approximately 8 million asylum applications were submitted between 1989 and 2009. Since the end of the Cold War a clear tendency has however become apparent, whereby asylum seekers and the victims of civil war are no longer automatically recognised as political refugees, and are tolerated for a limited period, at best. The practice of refugee admission in the USA and Canada is also highly

Decolonization was accompanied not only by various political, religious and cultural conflicts but also by massive economic problems which can be witnessed to this day. In public spaces throughout India, as here along a river, along rail tracks or on empty sites, slums develop. Driven from their villages people leave their homes and hope to find better conditions for survival in the cities. The "ASW" (Action Group for World Solidarity) supports projects which improve the living conditions of people in the country and assists them in their struggle against dispossession, illegal seizure of their land, water shortage and destruction of their environment.
Calcutta slum. Photo 2006

selective. Due to their geographic distance from current crisis areas, there are currently hardly any spontaneous applications for asylum in these countries. Both countries take in a quota of refugees from abroad on humanitarian grounds. Unlike in Europe and North America, the number of refugees taken in by the poorer countries in Asia and Africa has increased significantly since the late 1980s. Thus, today it is the poorer countries bordering on crisis regions that bear the burden when dealing with refugee issues.

Involuntary migrants also include internally displaced persons, of whom there were around 26 million worldwide in 2008. Most were and continue to be the victims of prior or ongoing civil wars. In many cases these displaced persons belong to an ethnic or religious minority or sympathise with rebel factions; as a rule they are part of the civilian population terrorised by one or more of the warring parties.

Decolonization and Post-Colonial Migration

Until 1960, Europe was first and foremost an emigrant continent. Only from the late 1950s and 1960s onwards has there been any noteworthy immigration into Europe from other regions in the world. In countries like Great Britain, France, the Netherlands and later Portugal, this was due initially to the withdrawal of these countries from their colonies. When European colonial rule ended in Africa, the middle east, south and southeast Asia as well as in the Caribbean, several million civil servants and soldiers who had previously acted for the colonial administration, as well as settlers of European descent, returned to their respective homelands. In some cases the emigration of "white" settlers was an explicit or implicit part of the agreements between the former colonial powers and the newly emerging independent states. The Treaty of Évian between France and the Algerian liberation movement FLN provided for the complete expulsion and resettlement of around 1 million French citizens of Algeria – the so-called 'Pieds noirs'. The return migration to Russia of around 5 million ethnic Russians from central Asia, the Caucasus and the Baltic States, which took place during the 1990s, can also be interpreted as the result of the process of

Rue Dupuy in the French colonial district of Pondicherry. Painting 1940

decolonization following the disintegration of the Soviet Union.

The colonial return migrants, many of whom had never lived in their respective European "motherlands", were followed by large numbers of natives of the former colonies. It was mainly Indians, Pakistanis and Anglo-Caribbeans who came to Great Britain; mainly Algerians, Tunisians and Moroccans, as well as Vietnamese and west Africans who came to France. Both Christian and Muslim citizens of Indonesia, as well as people from Surinam and the Dutch Antilles, went to the Netherlands. Then, in the 1970s, inhabitants of Angola, Mozambique and the Cape Verde Islands migrated in large numbers to Portugal. All of these migrants came to Europe in search of jobs and better educational opportunities. Some also wanted to flee the various civil wars and political repression that had started in their countries of origin after decolonization. western Europe's increasing demand for cheap, less qualified workers additionally encouraged this migration.

In the beginning, post-colonial migration was made easier because most home countries had either granted citizenship to the inhabitants of their former overseas territories, or at least treated them as preferred immigrants. In addition, many of these immigrants already spoke English, French, Dutch or Portuguese. In the former "motherlands" this led to the creation of new minorities, which now shape urban societies in the large metropolitan

centers of western Europe. The economic and social integration of some of these immigrants and their children is still an unresolved problem. Today, migrants from former colonial territories and Third World countries, which have in the meantime gained independence, have formed new lower classes in many places in Europe. To some extent, however, new ethnic elites have also established themselves.

Labor Migration

The recruitment of workers already took place under the auspices of colonial rule. The slave trade between west Africa and America, which the British only prohibited in 1807, was the forerunner to this. Within the British Empire, Indians had been brought as workers to Mauritius, East Africa and South Africa, to

"Guest workers" from former Yugoslavia setting off for the Federal Republic of Germany. Photo around 1960

269

the Caribbean, Guyana and to the Fiji Islands since the 19th century. In south-east Asia, the British and Dutch brought in large numbers of Chinese workers to serve the rapidly growing plantation industry.

In North America there had been immigration since the beginning of the modern era. The targeted recruitment of migrant workers, however, only began in the second half of the 19th century, when settlers from the east of the continent were encouraged to "conquer" the "Wild West" and, on the other hand, Chinese migrants were brought in over the Pacific to the western USA and Canada. These workers were employed in the building of the transcontinental railways and as lumberjacks. Many immigrants of southern and eastern European descent found work (sometimes contrary to their original intentions) in factories. During the 1930s, temporary workers for US agriculture and manufacturing were mainly recruited from Latin America. Between 1942 and 1964, Mexicans were recruited on the basis of the so-called "Bracero Program". In contrast to regular US immigrants, the intention was that these workers would not stay permanently in the USA. After this recruitment program ended in 1964, however, large numbers of Latin American migrant workers continued to enter and settle illegally in the USA. Of these, more than 5 million were able to legalise their status between 1986 and 1989. According to a 2008 estimate, there were an additional 10–13 million illegal migrant workers living in the USA. These were mainly workers from Mexico and other Latin American countries, but also a growing number of Asians.

In Europe, France and Switzerland have a tradition of recruiting foreign workers that dates back to the 19th century. In the 1950s and in the 1960s, other west European countries – including Belgium, Germany and Austria – began recruiting unqualified labor migrants. The most important source countries were Italy, Spain, Portugal, Greece, Yugoslavia and Turkey, as well as Morocco and Tunisia. Furthermore, Sweden experienced considerable immigration from Finland, Great Britain from Ireland, Germany and Switzerland from Austria.

The majority of these migrant workers returned to their country of origin. A sizeable minority, however, stayed and established themselves as permanent residents. They and their children formed the core of new minority groups and diasporas within Europe, which

were the result of earlier labor migration. The trigger was the ban on new recruiting of foreign workers at the beginning of the 1970s. Switzerland was the first to enforce it in 1972. Germany, Austria and Sweden followed suit in 1973–1974. The richer countries of western Europe hoped that this would send a clear signal: "we no longer need you, please go home". However, many labor migrants understood it to mean quite the opposite: though the labor market had become less favorable, it was better not to go back home, as returning to Europe would prove difficult. The recruitment stop shifted the focus from labor migration to family reunion. Those who were determined to stay in western Europe now encouraged their spouses and children to join them. This was initially seen as a process that would soon be completed. The opposite was true, however. Younger immigrants often started families only in their destination countries – although usually with partners from their region of origin and from their extended family network. The same now applies to the children of these immigrants. They, too, often seek partners from their parents' home countries, ethnic groups, and family networks. Or, their parents arrange a marriage by choosing an "appropriate" partner from their community. As a consequence, family migration continues until today. In many European countries, this now is the most important means of legal entry for immigrants. It could also be said that many

use the option of marriage and family migration because they have no other legal options.

With the fall of the Iron Curtain and the end of communist rule in central and eastern Europe a new phase of intensive intra-European east-west migration began. Several million people from former communist parts of Europe moved to western and southern Europe both as legal and illegal migrant workers. Following the eastern enlargement of the EU in 2004 and 2007 this employment migration increased once again. The main destination countries of these new European migration flows were Great Britain and Ireland, Spain, Italy and Greece.

Since the late 1990s Russia has also become a prime destination for migrant workers. The majority of the immigrants originated from other successor states of the former Soviet Union as well as from China, Vietnam and Afghanistan.

Beyond Europe and North America, labor migration is taking place towards the Arab Gulf States. The majority of migrants to this prosperous region are either citizens of poorer North African and Middle eastern countries or citizens of south Asia and south-east Asian countries. At the same time, the number of Europeans and Americans living in the Gulf States is also growing. As a result of the massive inflows, today, the natives in all Gulf States – with the exception of Saudi Arabia – only represent a small part of the total resident

As a result of the construction of 200 dams along the holy Narmada river 200,000 people, in particular the Adivasi (aboriginal Indians), were driven from their homeland and tried to make a living in distant regions. Photo 2006

Refugees in Ethiopia. Photo around 1990

population. This is the main reason why foreign migrants living in the Gulf States are neither granted permanent residence status, nor the right to naturalize. The situation in Malaysia and Singapore is similar. There, the majority of migrants are citizens of neighboring south-east Asian countries, in particular Indonesia.

Significant labor migration is also taking place within west Africa, from neighboring states to the Republic of South Africa, and within South America from the poorer Andean countries into Brazil and Argentina.

Political Refugees and Ethnically Privileged Migrants

Between 1949 and 1990, a particular form of European east-west migration resulted from the ideological division of Europe and the Cold War. Citizens of Communist countries attempted to reach the west in considerable numbers. The largest flows took place between east and west Germany, until the GDR closed the last gap in the Iron Curtain by building the Berlin Wall. There was also spontaneous mass

emigration from other central and eastern European countries during periods of crisis affecting the local communist regimes: people fled in large numbers from Hungary in 1956, from Czechoslovakia in 1968, from Poland in 1980, and finally from the GDR again in 1989. Until 1990, those who emigrated from a country that was "behind" the Iron Curtain were generally recognised in western Europe as political refugees. The fact that economic motives also played a role was not an issue at that time.

It was only after the dismantling of the Iron Curtain that immigration and the inflow of asylum seekers became a controversial issue. This was because, instead of dwindling down, the number of east-west migrants and asylum seekers increased after the end of communism in Europe: the result of the removal of travel restrictions, hardship during economic transformation and the outbreak of violent ethnic conflicts after 1989. This was particularly true for Bosnia, Kosovo and Chechnya. Since 1992 the majority of asylum seekers in the EU were from Afghanistan, Iraq, Iran, Turkey, the Caucasus region, and more recently from several African countries.

western Europe's reaction to this development was to re-introduce visa requirements for a number of neighboring countries and to tighten national asylum laws. Moreover, closer cooperation on asylum, visa and border security issues ensued between the EU and Schengen member states. Those trying today to be recognised as political refugees in Europe find it much harder to plead their case.

Many states have special immigration rules, or at least preferential treatment programmes for members of their "own" ethnic or religious diasporas. The most commonly cited example is Israel, where all people of Jewish descent or Jewish faith enjoy the right to immigrate. Between 1948 and 2006, around 3.0 million people made use of this opportunity. In Europe, too, there are large numbers of migrants who had or still have the right to immigration and legal residence or citizenship because of their ethnicity. The largest of these groups is the ethnic Germans, who continued to live in Poland, Romania and the Soviet Union after 1945/48. Germany has taken in large numbers of them and their families, admitting some 4.7 million ethnic German immigrants between 1950 and 2009. Since the 1990s, however, Germany has been trying to slow this immigration.

Pontic Greeks from the Balkans and the Black Sea region were also granted privileged access to Greece; in Hungary this applied to ethnic Hungarians from Transylvania, Serbian Vojvodina and western Ukraine; in Poland for

Title page of the Pro Asyl magazine on the occasion of Refugee Day 2008: Stop the Dying! Observe human rights – Protect refugees!

ethnic Poles from Lithuania, the Ukraine and Belarus. In the Balkans similar privileges exist for ethnic Serbs in Serbia, for ethnic Croats in Croatia as well as for ethnic Turks and other Muslims in Turkey. Russia also accepted the immigration of citizens from other successor states of the USSR during the 1990s (1990–2000: around 5 million), most of which were ethnic Russians. The concept of citizenship based on ethnicity is less widespread outside central and eastern Europe. This means that the necessary ideological basis required for the concept of ethnically privileged immigration does not exist everywhere. Nevertheless, many countries grant some kind of "right of return" to former emigrants and their descendants.

Illegal and Newly Legalized Immigrants in Europe

Since the late 1980s illegal immigration to western Europe has grown. At that time, the most important countries of origin within Europe were Poland, Romania, Moldova, the Ukraine and Albania. Outside Europe the most important countries of origin were Morocco, Tunisia as well as some west African and Latin American states. The triggers for this immigration were the fall of the Iron Curtain, cheap transportation, and the emergence of the smuggling industry. In addition, the evolution and spread of informal labor markets in western Europe as well as the economic boom in southern Europe played a decisive role.

Illegal immigrants found and continue to find work first and foremost in agriculture, construction, as domestic helpers, informal care givers as well as in hotels and restaurants. The hourly rates paid in these sectors are no longer acceptable for local workers and in some cases there is a general lack of local labor. Several European countries (Belgium, Greece, Italy, Portugal and Spain in particular) reacted to this influx of workers with large-scale "amnesties" at intervals of several years. As part of such regularization programs, between 1995 and 2009, more than 3.5 million illegal immigrants were granted work and residency permits by EU member states and Switzerland.

At the same time, the eastern enlargement of the EU in 2004 and 2007 legalised the residence status of hundreds of thousands of central and eastern European citizens,

Favela in Rio de Janeiro, Brazil. Since the end of World War II impoverishment has been on the increase, a massive migration from the land rapidly leads to the growth of ever more slums in the cities

who had already found work or temporary residence in one of the "old" EU member states. Countries such as Great Britain, Ireland and Sweden immediately opened their labor markets to the new EU citizens; most other EU member states followed between 2006 and 2008. In contrast, the only exceptions are Germany and Austria, where immigrants from new EU member states now have a right to reside, but not to work legally; an arrangement which encourages illegal employment.

Migration of Elites and Retired Persons

In the past decades, economic globalization and the internationalization of educational systems have led to many more managers, specialists, researchers, and students moving from one country to another or being posted by their companies for job rotation and training purposes. The main destination for researchers and students was, and still is, the USA. At the same time, the number of foreign students at European universities is growing. In addition, the number of European, American and now also Asian companies that do business in more than one country has also increased, as has the number of staff

working in various countries in the course of their careers while staying within the same company. Many of these employees move with their spouses and children. Some "elite migrants" are tax evaders, who by preference settle in places where the tax rates are low or a proportion of their income or assets do not have to be declared.

Lastly, the migration of people over the age of 50, who wish to spend their retirement abroad, is growing in importance. To date, the main destinations in Europe have been the coastal areas of the western Mediterranean and the Iberian Peninsula. It is mainly the British, Dutch, Germans and Scandinavians who retire there. Thus far, the settlement of retired people to Greece has been far less significant. The number of retirees migrating to the southern coast of Turkey, in contrast, is on the rise. The extent of this kind of retirement migration has increased markedly. Older people of European and Japanese descent can also be found in Sri Lanka, Indonesia and the Philippines. In contrast, North American pensioners move primarily to the southern parts of the USA, with Florida and the southwest as prime destinations. However, unlike their European and Japanese counterparts, the mobile pensioners of the US are internal migrants moving within a far larger country.

For many retired people, old age brings with it a kind of seasonal migration, reminiscent of earlier movements of some groups of peoples between low-lying or urban winter residences and summer homes on higher or cooler ground, or between rainy and dry areas respectively. In other cases, people do not migrate for climatic reasons but because of their own migrant background. Some former migrant workers choose to return to their countries of origin. This applies to retired people as well as to a growing number of individuals who become professionally active in their country of origin or in their parents' former home countries.

Global Migration in the 20th and Early 21st Centuries

Colonial settlement migration, that is, the seizure of arable land in order to establish farms, villages, and cities, was typical historically in periods prior to the mid-19th century. At present, politically motivated and often coercive settlement colonization no longer

Small farmers lost their livelihood, because they were indebted to seed and pesticide merchants. Numerous native Adivasi are being robbed of their homeland through mining, damming and deforestation and hope to survive by transporting coal or firewood to prospective purchasers

plays a significant role. Some of the few exceptions, however, have been the seizure of land by Jewish settlers in the Golan Heights and the West Bank, the state-sponsored massive resettlement of Javanese inhabitants on other Indonesian islands, and the resettlement of Han Chinese in regions like Tibet and Xinjiang. Rather, since the mid-20th century, completely different types of migration have dominated: traditional labor migration, spouses and children joining a family member already working abroad, ethnically privileged and – to a lesser degree – post-colonial (return) migration, migration for the purposes of study and training, emergency migration due to poverty, political persecution or environmental disasters, and finally, forced migration triggered by civil wars, violence, "ethnic cleansing" or ecological disasters.

According to estimates made by the UN population division, in the early 1960s there were approximately 75 million international migrants worldwide. At that time, they represented 2.5 % of the world population. In the industrialised countries the share of immigrants at that time was 3.4 % of the population; in less developed countries this

share was 2.1 %. In absolute terms the majority of international migrants and refugees at that time lived in the Third World. For the most part these were people who had lost their homes as a result of decolonisation and the establishment of newly independent nation states in Asia and Africa. Worldwide, less than half of all migrants at that time lived in one of the richer industrial countries. This was due primarily to the fact that up until the 1960s, Europe was itself more of an emigrant region, while between 1921 and 1965 the USA, in contrast to the periods before and after, admitted only relatively few immigrants.

Until the mid-1970s, the global population grew faster than the number of immigrants and emigrants. In 1970 there were 82 million migrants worldwide. They accounted for a mere 2.2 % of the world population. By 1990, the number of migrants had increased to 120 million. Their share in the global population remained stable at 2.3 %. The target regions, however, differed dramatically. The share of the migrant population in richer countries and regions had increased to 4.3 % by 1990, while in developing countries and emerging markets this share had dropped to 1.8 %.

After 1990, the number of international migrants suddenly increased. There are two completely unrelated reasons for this: on the one hand, many more people have changed their country of residence during the last two decades – some voluntarily, others forced by prevailing circumstances. The latter had to do with ethno-political conflicts and civil wars (e.g. in Afghanistan, Bosnia, Kosovo, the Democratic Republic of the Congo, Rwanda, Somalia, Sudan and Chechnya), the former with the fall of the Iron Curtain and an increased demand for qualified and unqualified workers. The main destinations of international migration were western Europe, North America (USA and Canada), the Gulf States and Russia. In recent times, countries neighboring conflict zones, e.g. Chad, Iran, Jordan, Pakistan, and Syria, have grown in importance as destinations of international migration.

On the other hand, the increasing number of international migrants was a statistical artifact caused by the disintegration of the former Soviet Union, Yugoslavia and Czechoslovakia. By establishing new international borders, the 24 new nation states in Europe and central Asia defined many people as international migrants who had previously simply been internally mobile Soviet, Czechoslovak, or Yugoslav citizens. For some of them, this "statistical effect" had very tangible consequences. Overnight, many people were made stateless, because they belonged to the "wrong" ethnic group: these included hundreds of thousands of ethnic Russians, who had come to Estonia and Latvia at the time of Soviet rule as well as tens of thousands of Slovak Roma, who had already been living in the Czech part of the country for some time. They lost their civil and political rights. In many cases, the same applied to their children, who were already born in their country of residence. Other former internal migrants with the "wrong" ethnic background continued, on paper, to be citizens of the newly established nation states, but they became minorities in their own homeland and were often seen as "undesirable". This was coupled with a massive pressure to assimilate or to emigrate.

In 2005 there were around 191 million people worldwide who no longer lived in their country of birth. This accounted for just under 3 % of the global population. Of these, 116 million lived in the industrialised countries.

Here they accounted for, on average, nearly a tenth of the population (2005: 9.5 %). At least 75 million international migrants lived in developing countries and newly industrialised countries (share: 1.4 %), many of them being displaced persons and refugees.

More than a third of all international migrants live in Europe (34 %). Two poles of attraction can be identified on this continent: more than a fifth of all migrants (21 %) live in one of the 27 EU Member States or in a country associated with the EU,[1] in particular in the so-called "old" EU member states as well as in Norway and Switzerland. The second major centre of immigration in Europe is Russia, where around 8 % of all international migrants currently live. In the early 1990s it was mainly ethnic Russians from successor states of the former Soviet Union who came to Russia. Since 1999, labor migration from neighboring countries has become dominant.

More than a quarter of all international migrants (28 %) live in Asia, mostly in the Gulf States, India and the "Tiger States" of east and south-east Asia: i.e. South Korea, Hong Kong, Malaysia and Singapore. These are the most common destinations for migrant workers from poorer Asian countries. In Israel, Jewish immigrants dominate, although there is also temporary migration of workers from eastern Europe and south-east Asia. Lastly, the number of migrants in Pakistan, Iran and in Uzbekistan, where several million Afghan refugees are staying, is high. The same is true for Jordan and Syria, where several million Iraqis have found refuge. In contrast, migration to Japan is almost negligible.

Nearly a quarter of all international migrants (23 %) live in North America. Thus, the USA (20 %) is by far the most important destination in the world. Another relevant destination country is Canada (3 %). Australia and New Zealand, the Republic of South Africa, Libya and some west African states have been, and continue to be, attractive destinations for migrants. Lastly, civil war and ethnic cleansing brought large refugee

populations to several states in central and East Africa. According to ILO estimates, just over half of all international migrants are economically active.

Immigrants in "Traditional" Immigrant Countries

In the USA, Canada and Australia, censuses have regularly provided information on the immigrant population. Accordingly, changes in these countries can be traced over a period of more than 150 years.

USA

In the 19th and early 20th centuries, the USA was the main destination for European emigrants. Between 1820 and 1920 the total number of immigrants was 31 million. Due to a long period of restrictive migration policy the absolute size and share of the immigrant population declined during the first half of the 20th century. Return migration to Europe also played a role.

By 1950 there were only 10.1 million people born abroad living in the USA (6.9 % of the population), nearly all of which had come from Europe. By 1970 the number of immigrants had fallen further to 9.6 million, and their share had decreased to 4.7 %. After that time, fundamental changes in US immigration law started to show their long-term effects. The new immigration law enacted in 1965 made it much easier for citizens of non-European countries to acquire the so-called "Green Card." Since then, immigration to the USA has come mainly from Latin America and, increasingly, also from Asia. This has led to a significant rise in the number of immigrants. In 2008 there were already 40 million legal and illegal migrants living in the USA. This accounted for almost 13 % of the US population. In absolute terms, the immigrant population quadrupled between 1965 and 2008. These figures do not include those persons living in the USA on a temporary basis with a visa for employment or study purposes.

Canada

Between 1820 and the 1920s about 7 million people emigrated to Canada. In the second half of the 20th century the number of immigrants in Canada grew steadily: from 2.1 million in 1951 (14.7 % of the population) to 6.5 million

Year	World	Highly developed countries[1]	Proportion (in %)	Developing and newly industrialised countries	Proportion (in %)
1960	75	32	43	43	57
1970	81	38	47	43	53
1980	99	47	47	52	53
1990[2]	120	56	47	64	53
1995[2]	165	95	58	70	42
2000	177	105	59	72	41
2005	191	116	61	75	39

Source: United Nations/Population Division (2006): International Migration Data Base
1 Europe, North America, Australia, New Zealand, Japan, USSR/CIS.
2 Due to the disintegration of the Soviet Union, Yugoslavia and Czechoslovakia the number of international migrants increased after 1990, because this meant that internal migrants from the preceding period retrospectively became international migrants.

Number and distribution of international immigrants, 1960-2005

	Proportion of immigrants in population (in %)		
	In the world	In the highly developed countries[1]	In the developing and newly industrialised countries
1960	2.5	3.4	2.1
1970	2.2	3.6	1.6
1980	2.3	4.2	1.6
1990[2]	2.3	4.3	1.8
1995[2]	2.9	8.1	1.6
2000	2.9	8.8	1.5
2005	2.9	9.5	1.4

Source: United Nations/Population Division (2006): International Migration Data Base
1 Europe, North America, Australia, New Zealand, Japan, USSR/CIS.
2 Due to the disintegration of the Soviet Union, Yugoslavia and Czechoslovakia the number of international migrants increased after 1990, because this meant that internal migrants from the preceding period retrospectively became international migrants.

Proportion of international immigrants in overall population, 1960-2000

(20.0 %) in 2008. In absolute figures, the immigrant population tripled between 1951 and 2008. At the same time, the composition of the migrant population changed significantly. Here too, European immigrants were increasingly being replaced by migrants from Asia, North Africa and Latin America. In contrast to the USA, Canada recruits a number of its immigrants using a points system. The preferences are clear: younger, well-educated migrants with good language skills are the most desirable.

Australia

In Australia the proportion of immigrants in the 19th and early 20th centuries was substantial compared to the relatively small overall population. Between 1800 and the 1920s, some four million people came to Australia. Immigration dropped during the 1930s. At the end of World War II, the share of the immigrant population was at a low point, at around 9 % of the total population. Thereafter the number and share grew again, from 1.0 million (11.9 %) in 1951 to 4.0 million (23.6 %) in 1991. Since then, the immigrant population has remained stable overall in terms of numbers, while the proportion of

---

1 The EU has multilateral association agreements with the other EEA states (Iceland, Liechtenstein, Norway); and bilateral association agreements with Switzerland.

Region	Immigrants Absolut (millions)	Proportion of population (%)	Regional Distribution (%)
Africa	19	1,9	9
Asia	51	1,4	29
Europe	64	8,8	32
Latin America and Caribbean	7	1,2	3
North America	44	13,5	23
Australia	5	15,2	3
Total	191	2,9	100

Number, proportion, and regional distribution of international migrants, 2005

immigrants in the overall population has decreased, because of a growing total population (2007: 4.2 million; 20.7 %).

From the 18th century onwards, Australia was used by the British as a prison colony. Later, other immigrants came mainly from Great Britain and Ireland. Until the early 1970s, immigration into Australia was restricted, favoring almost exclusively persons of "European origin", in order to maintain a "white" population. Following the abolition of these restrictions, there was an increase in immigration from Asia. Australia also recruits a proportion of its immigrants by way of a points system. The criteria are similar to those applied in Canada.

in Europe – first in north-western Europe, then in southern Europe, and recently also in parts of central Europe. Since the 1990s Russia has also become an important destination for international migration, especially from successor states of the former Soviet Union and other neighboring countries.

Today there are more than 500 million people living in the 27 EU Member States. Of them 43 million are immigrants, that is, people born in another country; of these, 14 million have come from another EU country. The other 29 million were either born in Europe, although outside EU-27 or in a non-European country. These figures are based partly on estimates, since available population statistics of several European countries do not

differentiate between native-born and foreign-born residents, but between nationals and foreign citizens.

With a total of 43 million, in absolute terms there are more international immigrants living in western and central Europe than in the USA. However, if one disregards the migratory movements between the present 27 EU member states, the USA still comes first, with an immigrant population of 38 million, while the stock of immigrants in the EU who came from non-EU countries account for only 29 million. The difference can be attributed to migration between EU states, which would correspond to internal migration in the USA. Thus, there is one important difference: those moving from New York to California continue to be citizens of the same country. In contrast, those moving from Italy or Bulgaria to Germany or Austria, while they continue to be EU citizens in their destination country, are nevertheless foreigners with limited political rights. Those, however, entering the EU from a third country by all accounts have even fewer rights. This changes only if a migrant applies for citizenship, although it should be noted that access to citizenship is far more complicated in some European countries than in others. Over the last few decades, the Federal Republic of Germany has been the most important migrant destination in western and central Europe. At present there are some 10.1 million immigrants living there. This is – after the USA and Russia – the third largest

Europe: An Immigrant Continent

After the Second World War, refugees and displaced persons formed the largest group of international migrants. This was the main reason why there were only 3.8 million foreigners living in western Europe in 1950. The majority of these foreign nationals were migrant workers, most of them living in France and Switzerland. There were also a considerable number of stateless displaced persons. These figures do not, however, include the large number of foreign troops stationed in post-war Europe.

Only since the mid-1960s have there been more immigrants coming to western Europe than emigrants leaving this part of the world. Since then, the size and share of the foreign-born population has considerably increased

Courtyard of the housing for refugees at Frankfurt Airport. Photo 2008

immigrant population in the world. Other important destination countries in Europe are: France (6.5 million), Great Britain (5.6 million), Spain (4.8 million) and Italy (2.5 million). In a few other countries, the foreign-born population is also of a considerable size; in Switzerland (1.7 million), the Netherlands (1.6 million), Austria (1.3 million), Sweden (1.1 million) and in Greece (1.0 million).

The average share of immigrants in the 27 EU member states and the four associated countries is 8.5%. The share of immigrants is largest in small states like Luxembourg (37%) and Liechtenstein (34%). These countries are followed by Switzerland, where one in four residents is foreign-born (23%). Austria (15%), Ireland (14%), Sweden (12%), Germany (12%) and Spain (11%) are also above the European average.

The situation in the Baltic States is a particular one. Latvia (20%) and Estonia (15%) have a very high proportion of immigrants. The greatest proportion of these people, who were born in what are now foreign countries, came to Latvia and Estonia as internal migrants during the Soviet era. These people became international migrants (and thus, foreigners in their own homeland) only after the disintegration of the Soviet Union and the re-establishment of independent Baltic States. Only Lithuania granted all former Soviet citizens living on its territory Lithuanian citizenship. The same applies to many Slovaks in the Czech Republic and people of Bosnian, Croatian, Serbian or Kosovo-Albanian descent in Slovenia (total number of immigrants equal 9% of the population).

Europe, North America and Australia in Comparison

Today only the USA, Canada, Australia and New Zealand are "traditional immigrant countries". Historically, countries like Argentina, Chile or Brazil also belonged to this category. They differ from the European nation states in one fundamental point: since the 19th century, the overwhelming majority of their populations consisted of immigrants and their descendants. In all of these countries there is a national founding myth, which refers both to the pioneer migrants of the 17th, 18th and 19th centuries and to the emancipation from the European "motherlands". In the USA and in Latin America this emancipation from Great

Language instruction and occupational training in Australia. From a brochure of the Office of Multicultural Affairs 1990

Britain, Spain and Portugal plays a strong role in collective memories. In contrast, the majority of people living in Canada, Australia, New Zealand and the Anglophone countries of the Caribbean continue to see themselves as part of the British Commonwealth and continue to this day to consider the Queen of England as their head of state.

Even after having severed their ties with their historical motherlands, these traditional immigration countries saw themselves as communities of people of "superior" European origin; in the case of the USA, Canada (excluding Quebec), Australia and New Zealand, this concerned the dominant role of Protestants of north-western European descent. In Latin America, Catholics from southern Europe played a similar role. Only after 1965 did the USA and Canada, followed in 1973 by Australia and New Zealand, really open their doors to immigrants from Asia and Latin America, and later to those from Africa. Simultaneously, the claim that these countries were based on a superior culture based on Christian and Anglo-European roots was called into question and increasingly replaced by the concept of multicultural societies based on immigrants from various backgrounds. In New Zealand, Canada and a few of the Latin American states, the rights of indigenous peoples were also strengthened.

If one looks only at the share of residents born abroad, there is no big difference between Germany and the USA for instance. Germany's 10 million foreign-born residents account for about 12% of the population. Approximately 38 million immigrants in the

USA represent a similar percentage of the American population. In absolute numbers, Germany has significantly more immigrants than Canada or Australia. Indeed, compared to their total populations, European countries such as Switzerland (23%) and Austria (15%) have an even larger share of immigrants than the USA. It is, however, not primarily the number of immigrants that is decisive for a society's self perception, but rather the founding myth or the basic understanding of collective origins. The image of lasting roots plays a more important role for the identity of most Germans, Austrians and Swiss than citizens of the USA and Canada. In traditional immigration countries, most residents – even those born in the country – are aware that their ancestors came from Europe, Asia or Latin America and derive a part of their identity from this fact. Germany, Austria and many other European countries in contrast

Rio Bravo: border police have arrested a group of illegal immigrants. Those who cross the border illegally face many dangers. They are unscrupulously exploited by people smugglers

Through droughts or dispossession of their land many small farmers cannot survive in their villages. While the well-educated elite emigrate to the western industrial nations (brain drain) the poor living in the country seek opportunities to survive in and around the big cities of the so-called Third World, for instance as day laborers in road construction. Itinerant workers in tents on the outskirts of Pune, Maharashtra State, India. Photo 2006

see themselves primarily as rather homogenous nation states consisting of people whose ancestors were there "from the beginning".

It is obviously more difficult for immigrants to integrate into societies that see themselves as nations historically defined by common ethnicity or ancestry. It is somewhat easier to integrate into societies in which a greater degree of ethnic or religious difference is accepted or even part of the national identity. This is one of the reasons why in many European countries immigrants are more likely to be unemployed, have less attractive jobs, are paid less and have to settle for lower quality housing than the native-born majority. In many cases these differences persist through to the next generation. Children of immigrants less often attend higher education, abandon vocational training more often, have smaller chances of being promoted and have higher unemployment rates.

The clearest indication of the lack of integration is the fact that in Europe, 50 years after the initial recruitment of foreign workers during the post-war period, there are still significant numbers of immigrants who have still not been naturalised. In total, slightly more than half of all immigrants (approximately 24 million in total) are not citizens of their country of residence. Thus, although these migrants are subject to the laws of the country in which they live, as foreign nationals they are not represented in either the political or the law-making processes.

The result is that in Europe – depending on the country – between 3% and 30% of the population are excluded from political representation. In larger cities, the proportion of the adult population without voting rights is often considerably higher than the national average, as immigration from foreign countries focuses primarily on urban centres. Conversely, however, many states grant their nationals living abroad the right to participate in elections in their home country, even if these voters, for as long as they continue to live abroad, are only marginally affected by the outcome of the legislation in their country of origin.

The situation in the USA, Canada and Australia is different. There, the social permeability of society is greater. On average, immigrants are economically more successful than in Europe, are more likely to climb the social ladder and are after a certain time better integrated. In the USA, Canada and Australia immigrants can apply for citizenship after only 3 to 5 years of residence.

Without any doubt, the "traditional" immigration countries of North America and Oceania are a more attractive destination for many potential migrants than the richer countries of Europe. This is particularly true for highly-qualified, career-oriented and highly motivated migrants. This leaves the EU and its member states with a clear disadvantage in the global competition for qualified immigrants. A socio-economic analysis of migrant flows confirms this: in the USA, Canada, Australia and New Zealand, qualified people and their family members account for the majority of immigrants. In Europe, in contrast, those with fewer skills dominate.

As a consequence, Europe attracts fewer qualified migrants than the traditional immigration countries. This means that the preconditions for the subsequent socio-economic integration of these immigrants are less favorable, since in Europe immigrants, on average, bring less "human capital" with them than those coming to North America and Australia. As a result, many European societies are facing major social and political challenges linked to the lack of integration of immigrants and their children. Possible remedies include language training, teaching democratic values, improving the educational success of children with migrant backgrounds, encouraging naturalization and better integration into national labor markets. Several EU member states – including Austria, Denmark, Germany, and the Netherlands – have introduced obligatory language and integration courses for newly arriving immigrants coming from third countries. In contrast, the "traditional" immigration countries in North America and Oceania can rely on the fact that a considerable share of new immigrants, either because of the qualifications and language skills they bring along, or due to the less regulated and more permeable labor markets, will be able to integrate into their host society.

Refugee camp in Africa 1990

The 21st Century

Two demographic developments have become more apparent over the last few years. Firstly, in Europe and in east Asia, the number of countries in which the number of deaths exceeds the number of births is increasing. This means that the native-born population in these regions is shrinking. Whether the number of residents increases or decreases thus greatly depends on the size of net immigration flows. Secondly, the number of countries in the world that register more immigration than emigration is increasing. At the same time, the number of international immigrants is growing at a faster pace than the global population. Both developments are leading to a situation in which the populations of many countries are not only "greying" as a result of demographic aging, but, as a result of immigration are simultaneously becoming more "diverse" in ethnic, cultural and religious terms. This inevitably leads to new questions of identity and belonging. New lines of conflict also become apparent.

The developed societies of the future will consist of people with various ethnic backgrounds. From a legal perspective this is a matter of citizenship; in a narrow sense defining political rights and responsibilities. At the societal level, the main question is the following: which common values, rules, and perspectives will immigrants of completely different backgrounds be able to share with native-borns? The backdrop to this is the fundamental question: to what extent are separate identities in fact desirable and practical within one society? This question needs to be addressed at some point, since in the future both the traditional immigration countries and most western European countries will have immigrants with different religious backgrounds, including Muslims, Christian-Orthodox, Hindus and Buddhists. What does immigration mean for cultural identity in Europe and America and for both natives' and immigrants' sense of civic belonging? Unlike the USA and Canada, most European societies do not have national identities and national narratives that include both natives and immigrants. Rather, the "foreigners" who come to Europe are seen as challenging national identity, and integration is more narrowly defined in Europe than in North America. An immigrant can easily become an "American" during the course of his or her lifetime, but becoming a European is considerably more complicated. Moreover, the terrorist attacks by Muslim extremists in New York, London and Madrid and occasional calls for Jihad against all "non-believers" have further increased scepticism towards non-European immigrants.

Despite public opinion ranging from being sceptical to being outright dismissive, today most trends suggest that there will be more immigration in the coming decades, there are at least four particular reasons for this.

First: for the foreseeable future there will be huge differences in the worldwide distribution of income, resources and opportunities. As a result, migration from poorer countries to richer regions in the world will continue. In some cases there is in fact a direct link. In the EU and the USA, for example, there are strict restrictions on the import of agricultural products from other regions of the world, while the local agricultural sector is given a considerable competitive advantage through high subsidies. The over-fishing of the world's oceans by high-tech, subsidised western fishing fleets, has similar effects. Such factors considerably reduce the economic opportunities of rural populations in other parts of the world. In combination with the deterioration of livelihoods this transforms emigration from a welfare enhancing possibility into a strategy necessary for survival.

Second: the local populations in some regions, particularly in Europe, are ageing. In several countries – including Germany, Russia and the Balkan states – demographic shrinking is already underway. Other countries will follow. The EU as a whole provides a good example of this: without immigration, the overall number of people between the ages of 15 and 65 in the EU would fall by 88 million by 2050, while the number of people aged 65 and above will grow by at least 62 million. Falling birth rates mean that, in the future, fewer young people with fresh skills will join the labor market. Thus, sooner or later, there will be a lack of younger, well-qualified workers. In some sectors of the economy this is already apparent. At the same time, the demand for qualified workers and personal services – especially for older people – will automatically grow. In other words, demographically ageing and shrinking, but rich European societies are, to a certain extent, dependent on future immigration. As a result, it is very likely that countries in western and central Europe will switch from a restrictive to a proactive migration policy sooner rather than later.

Third: there are still regions with youthful and rapidly growing populations directly in the neighborhood of rich regions of the world. For the USA, this is true for Mexico and central America. Europe's demographically growing neighbors are North Africa and the Middle East. There, the number of people aged 15 to 65, at present totaling 195 million, will have almost doubled to 365 million by 2050. Similar growth is to be expected in the countries of sub-Saharan Africa. It is highly unlikely that Europe will be able to counter the desire of people to emigrate from these regions toward a supposedly better life simply by upgrading the technical facilities and placing more staff at its borders.

Fourth: in the future, in addition to political refugees and displaced persons, there will be a growing number of "environmental refugees". Global warming will result in rising sea levels, dislodging people from coastal zones are likely to be most affected. Climate change will also lead to an expansion of deserts as well as to the salinization of formerly fertile and arable land. Without any doubt, ecological degradation and the flooding of habitats will lead to higher numbers of internally displaced people and international migrants. To date, there is no appropriate legal framework for dealing with persons whose habitats have been destroyed by environmental degradation or rising sea levels.

Itinerant workers have erected their tents amongst the houses of the well-to-do. They try to earn a living by working as servants, porters, construction workers, etc. Photo Pune, India, 2006

Acknowledgements

This book is essentially based on Dirk Hoerder/Diethelm Knauf (eds.) "Fame, Fortune and Sweet Liberty: The Great European Emigration," which was also published in 1992 by Edition Temmen. The present book, however, has been enlarged, completely revised, and redesigned. It has been extended by a completely new section dealing with migration from the First World War to the present day, and it also contains many more illustrations, some of them previously unpublished.
Selection and contextualization of the illustrations, with the exception of the chapters by Walther Kamphoefner, Brian Lambkin (Mellon Family), James Bade (Tonga), Helga Rathjen, Manfred Wichmann und Henriette Holleuffer, are by Diethelm Knauf.

The publishers wish to thank Prof. Dirk Hoerder.

The following institutes have supported this publication:
National Park Service/Ellis Island Museum; Deutsches Auswandererhaus Bremerhaven and the Freundeskreis des Deutschen Auswandererhauses; Auswanderermuseum BallinStadt Hamburg; National Archives Washington; Amnesty International; Pro Asyl; Aktion Solidarische Welt – Indien (Detlef Stüber); Südost-Medienagentur Bremen (Christoph Sodemann); Bremen Overseas Research and Development Association (Borda); Staatsarchiv Bremen, and Staatsarchiv Hamburg.

Translation into English by Hildegard Pesch-Skevington, Translation into German by Dr. Horst Rössler

Layout and design by Ramona Breyer

The editors warmly thank all contributors!

Diethelm Knauf/Barry Moreno

Picture Credits

Also available from EDITION TEMMEN …

Diethelm Knauf
Destination America / Aufbruch in die Fremde
This DVD has no region code and can be played worldwide
Illustrated booklet – German / English
DVD, 150 min.
ISBN 978-3-86108-499-0
19.90 €

Arno Hartog
Bremerhavens Tor zur Welt
80 Jahre Columbuskaje
140 S.; 128 Abb.
ISBN 978-3-86108-590-4
19.90 €

Jörn Bullerdiek,
Daniel Tilgner (Hrsg.)
»Was fernern vorkömmmt werde ich prompt berichten«
Der Auswanderer-Kapitän Heinrich Wieting – Briefe 1847 bis 1856
304 S.; 182 Abb.
ISBN 978-3-86108-885-1
24.90 €

Andrea Brinckmann,
Peter Gabrielsson (Hrsg.)
»Seht, wie sie übers große Weltmeer ziehn!«
Die Geschichte der Auswanderung über Hamburg
256 S.; 237 Abb.
ISBN 978-3-86108-888-2
24.90 €